DRESSED IN BLACK

The Shangri-Las in 1965: Betty Weiss, Mary Ann Ganser, Marge Ganser and Mary Weiss (*Pictorial Press Ltd / Alamy*)

DRESSED IN BLACK
The Shangri-Las
& their recorded legacy

Lisa MacKinney

VERSE CHORUS PRESS

If the world is so wrong
You can break them all
With one song.
—Hole, "Awful" (1999)

Published by Verse Chorus Press
Portland, Oregon
info@versechorus.com

Front cover photograph © David Dalton. Reproduced with permission
Design and layout by Steve Connell Book Design | *steveconnell.net*

Author and publisher wish to thank all those who supplied photographs and gave permission to reproduce copyright material in this book. Every effort has been made to contact all copyright holders; the publisher welcomes communication from any copyright owners from whom permission was inadvertently not obtained. In such cases, we will gladly obtain appropriate permission and provide suitable acknowledgment in future editions.

Some of the images reproduced here are of less-than-perfect quality; this is an inevitable consequence of the imperfect preservation of contemporary newsprint sources.

The above-quoted lyric from "Awful" by Hole, is copyright Auf der Maur/Erlandson/Love/Schemel (Mother May I Music, BMI).

Country of manufacture as stated on the last page of this book

Library of Congress Cataloging-in-Publication Data

Names: MacKinney, Lisa (Historian), author.
Title: Dressed in black : the Shangri-Las & their recorded legacy / Lisa MacKinney.
Description: Portland, Oregon : Verse Chorus Press, 2025. | Includes bibliographical references and index. | Summary: "The first full-length history of 1960s pop group the Shangri-Las, which radically rewrites the accepted narrative of their place in rock history, foregrounding their considerable musical abilities and establishing the centrality of their performance of their songs to the group's underappreciated artistic achievement"– Provided by publisher.
Identifiers: LCCN 2024049885 (print) | LCCN 2024049886 (ebook) | ISBN 9781959163077 (trade paperback) | ISBN 9781959163084 (epub)
Subjects: LCSH: Shangri-Las (Musical group) | Girl groups (Musical groups)—United States—History—20th century. | Popular music—United States—1961-1970—History and criticism.
Classification: LCC ML421.S482 M33 2025 (print) | LCC ML421.S482 (ebook) | DDC 782.42164092/2—dc23/eng/20241028
LC record available at https://lccn.loc.gov/2024049885
LC ebook record available at https://lccn.loc.gov/2024049886

Contents

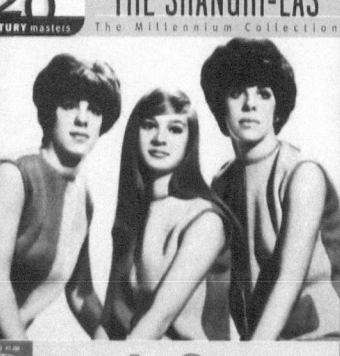

Preface

This is the first ever full-length study of the Shangri-Las, a female teenage pop group from Cambria Heights in Queens, New York. Sisters Mary and Betty Weiss, together with twins Mary Ann and Marguerite Ganser, formed the group while attending school together in the early 1960s, and are most famous for their single "Leader of the Pack." They enjoy an enduring following among rock fans and musicians, yet the Shangri-Las have been trivialised in a variety of important and lastingly influential ways by mainstream rock criticism, the context in which the bulk of commentary on the group has been published. The reasons for this and the ways in which it has been expressed are complex, interconnected, and not always immediately obvious. As young women and minors, the Shangri-Las had relatively little agency within a male-dominated recording industry that perceived teenagers as fodder for manipulation and exploitation. Typically, this has been used as an excuse to devalue the musical input of the group members and marginalise their recordings within the canon of what is regarded as 'authentic' rock music. I argue here for a substantial reassessment of the Shangri-Las' considerable abilities, talent and musicality, and for the centrality of their performances to the group's largely unacknowledged artistic achievement.

The first chapter examines the critical reception of the Shangri-Las, which has been dominated by their rigid inclusion within an anachronistic 'genre' known as 'girl groups.' I unpack the origins of this terminology and show that it was not in use in its current sense, as a term denoting a specific genre, until the early 1970s, when it gained currency among rock journalists in conjunction with highly problematic understandings of the place of girls and women in rock music. This has had significant implications for the young performers who were categorised in this gendered way, and particularly for the Shangri-Las.

The next three chapters constitute a history of the group as a functioning entity. In chapter 2, I look at the post-WWII development of Queens, and particularly Cambria Heights, the neighbourhood in which the Weiss and Ganser sisters grew up and formed the Shangri-Las. Chapter 3 examines the circumstances and personalities associated with the founding of the Red Bird record label and the events leading up to the signing of the Shangri-Las. The early months of the Shangri-Las as a famous, touring group in 1964 are then detailed in the context of exploitative and largely unregulated music industry practices, sometimes involving Mafia figures. These ultimately led to the collapse of Red Bird, an event from which the Shangri-Las never recovered. It resulted in an ill-fated move to the Mercury label, and the demise of the group in 1968, for reasons largely beyond their control, is discussed in chapter 4.

Some key events in the subsequent lives of the four women, including the tragic death of Mary Ann Ganser in 1970 and an abandoned reformation of the Shangri-Las as a three-piece in 1977, are considered in chapter 5.

The rest of the book is devoted to a thematic and musicological analysis of key recordings by the Shangri-Las. In chapter 6 I look at "Leader of the Pack" in the context of motorcycle culture, its ties to various forms of juvenile delinquency, and the manner in which social norms are reflected and subverted in the song. "Remember (Walkin' in the Sand)" and "Past, Present and Future" have strong ties to the nineteenth-century European Romantic tradition; both are examined in detail in chapter 7. Chapter 8 discusses the Shangri-Las' final recordings—two singles generally perceived to be failures but which offer telling insights into the professional decline of the group. This final chapter also contributes to a re-reading of the notion of 'the Sixties' as an era characterised by unanimous youth protest, particularly against US involvement in the Vietnam War.

By locating the Shangri-Las and their recordings within a wider and more informed historical, artistic and musical context than that in which the group is routinely considered, I have made it possible to grasp more completely the significance of the Shangri-Las and their recordings, and justified a thorough reconsideration of their musical and artistic achievements and their place in the history of popular music.

Introduction

When interviewing Shangri-Las lead singer Mary Weiss in 2007 for her BBC radio show 'Heroes of Rock 'n' Roll,' Suzi Quatro said, of the Shangri-Las' 1965 hit "I Can Never Go Home Anymore":

> Oh! It made me cry. Seriously, it made me cry. I felt that like a knife in the heart, that song . . . I have never felt anything so real or poignant in a pop record in my life.[1]

Born in 1950, one year after Weiss, Quatro had experienced this song in 1965 as a member of its target audience of fellow teenagers. I didn't hear it until the early 1990s when I was about 22, but my reaction was identical. For many years, I could not listen to "I Can Never Go Home Anymore" and remain dry-eyed. In fact, the emotional impact of the (by today's standards) handful of recordings made by these teenaged girls between 1964 and 1967 is so powerful that it ultimately impelled me to write this book.

The Shangri-Las were a rock vocal group that formed in Queens, New York, while the four members—sisters Mary and Elizabeth (Betty, Liz) Weiss,* and twins Mary Ann and Marguerite (Margie, Marge) Ganser—were still in high school.[2] They had a string of hits between 1964 and 1967, the most famous of which was "Leader of the Pack," released late in 1964.[3] It reached #1 on the *Billboard Hot 100*, achieved substantial notoriety, and was banned from BBC radio in England for

---

* Elizabeth Weiss seemed generally to be known as Betty while the group was operational in the 1960s, but later preferred Liz. Both names are used throughout this book, depending on source material and context. Given that Mary and Betty's mother's name was also Elizabeth Weiss, I have tried to be as specific as possible to avoid confusion.

lyrics that concerned dating bikers 'from the wrong side of town' and death.[4] The group achieved considerable fame: they performed at the Paramount Theatre in New York City with the Beatles in 1964 and toured extensively on bills with James Brown, Stevie Wonder, Del Shannon, Herman's Hermits and the Beach Boys, among many others.[5] As 'happening' teenagers, they also did endorsements for Revlon's *Natural Wonder* make-up and in 1965 promoted a national Revlon-sponsored contest called 'Swingstakes'—first prize was a trip to England to meet the Dave Clark Five.[6] By 1965 the Shangri-Las were a hugely popular group, and the Weiss and Ganser sisters famous pop stars, before any of them were out of their teens.[7] By 1968 it was all over, the group in tatters and its members burnt out amid a morass of collapsed labels, lawsuits and circumstances that remain murky to this day.

Despite a relatively small body of recorded work (around 30 songs over 5 years), the Shangri-Las have enjoyed an enduring and passionately devoted following among baby boomers who grew up listening to them, as well as rock fans and musicians of many of ages and persuasions. The New York Dolls' singer David Johansen poutily began their song "Looking for a Kiss" with the spoken introduction 'When I say I'm in love, you best believe I'm in love L-U-V,' quoting from the Shangri-Las' 1964 hit, "Give Him a Great Big Kiss."[8] Johansen explained, 'We saw the Shangri-Las many, many times. I used to see them every chance I had, they were our local band, on local TV a lot. Really, they're my favourite band from the sixties.'[9]

"Looking for a Kiss" also borrows its opening chords from "Give Him a Great Big Kiss." It appears on the New York Dolls' self-titled first album, released in 1973. Their second album, *Too Much Too Soon*, was produced by George 'Shadow' Morton, who is most famous for the body of work he made together with the Shangri-Las.

Blondie covered a Shangri-Las song, "Out in the Streets," on their first EP, recorded in 1975 and produced by Alan Betrock.[10] When the Shangri-Las reformed briefly in 1977, for 'one magical performance before the leather-jacketed elite of Lower Manhattan,' it was at legendary rock club CBGBs, the bar on the Bowery where the New York punk scene coalesced.[11] Television, Richard Hell and the Voidoids, the Ramones, Blondie and Patti Smith played there regularly. On the night the Shangri-Las performed, their backing group included sound engineer Andy Paley as well as guitarist Lenny Kaye and drummer Jay Dee

Daugherty from the Patti Smith Group.[12] Artists as diverse as Aero-smith, Bette Midler, and Australian guitarist Rowland S. Howard have released versions of songs by the Shangri-Las.[13] In an extraordinary concert film of the Go-Go's performing at a Los Angeles high school in 1981, the group closed their set with a riotous version of "Remember (Walkin' in the Sand)."[14] The influence of the Shangri-Las on Kim Gordon is clearly evident in her work with Sonic Youth; Amy Winehouse and Bat for Lashes, too, have incorporated aspects of the Shangri-Las' style and knowing nods to the group in their songs.* In 2020, "Remember (Walkin' in the Sand)" found a new life and context on Tik Tok via a sampled, sped-up, chipmunk-style version of the song's 'Oh no' section, which has been used there as backing music for countless social media video disasters. Although subsequently appropriated by others, this version, as a song entitled "Oh No," seems to have originated with rappers (and fellow Queens natives) Capone-N-Noreaga in 2004.[15]

I include myself among the rock fans and musicians for whom the Shangri-Las have been of lasting importance. I have been playing guitar and organ in various contexts for over thirty years and worked in record stores for almost as long.[16] I first heard the Shangri-Las in my early twenties and was immediately hooked; I identified strongly with their intense emotionalism and themes of heartbreak and parental conflict, which mirrored my own experiences closely. While working in a book and record store in around 2002 and in charge of ordering for the music book section, I realised, during a lengthy conversation with a co-worker, that there had never been a book, popular or academic, published about the Shangri-Las. I was incredulous; it seemed astonishing to me that a group as significant and influential as the Shangri-Las had not been the subject of a dedicated study or biography.[17] Although bringing it to fruition would be a long, complicated and circuitous process encom-

---

* "Little Trouble Girl" from Sonic Youth's 1995 album *Washing Machine* is a dark, teen-themed song that quotes from "Give Him a Great Big Kiss," touches on themes in "I Can Never Go Home Anymore," and is almost entirely spoken, a style for which the Shangri-Las are famous. In live performances of her 2006 hit "Back to Black," Amy Winehouse would often segue into "Remember (Walkin' in the Sand)." Winehouse regularly cited the Shangri-Las as a significant influence and her album *Back to Black* is replete with doo-wop and vocal group stylings. The name of Bat for Lashes 2007 single, "What's A Girl to Do" closely recalls "What's a Girl Supposed to Do," from the album *Shangri-Las 65!*, and incorporates a breathy, Mary Weiss–style spoken-word delivery of teen-themed boy/girl breakup subject matter.

passing two decades and a PhD dissertation, this book project began at that moment.[18]

After years of research and writing, two trips to New York City and a stint living there, I now understand very well why it has taken so long for a book on the Shangri-Las to appear. The reasons are complex and interconnected, and go to the heart of many of the issues explored in the following pages. They were teenagers and they were girls—two groups that have been consistently neglected historically. Furthermore, despite the following the group enjoys, the Shangri-Las have been underrated in significant and lastingly influential ways by mainstream rock criticism, the context in which the group has received the most coverage.[19] Central to this are widely accepted understandings of 'girl group' as a genre, the origins and development of this term within a specific framework of rock journalism, and the effect on the Shangri-Las of persistently being categorised in this way. Deeply embedded in this nomenclature are assumptions about age, gender, authenticity and race that have remained largely unquestioned in rock mythology, to the point where they are virtually invisible.[20]

Furthermore, the credibility and musical reputation of the Shangri-Las (and other vocal groups from this era) has suffered terribly because the fact that many neither wrote their own material nor played instruments in the groups for which they are famous is now viewed negatively. It is an unquestioned assumption today that the composition and performance of musical material constitutes the artistic expression of any 'serious' musical artist; performers who are singers without being songwriters and/or instrumentalists are simply not accorded the same critical regard.[21] It routinely goes unnoticed that only during the early 1960s did the roles of 'songwriter' and 'singer' *begin* to be inextricably conflated, most notably and spectacularly with the Beatles, although the Beach Boys, for example, were also writing their own material at that time. Before then, it was *not* the norm for singers, especially pop singers, to write their own material—they sang songs written by professional songwriters. Inherent in the assumption that an 'authentic artist' must write their own material is the notion that this has always been the yardstick by which authenticity is measured, and those who did not write their own material (or play instruments) in their groups were incapable of doing so.[22] This was not the case. The Shangri-Las need to be located within an earlier era in which singers were totally credible without being songwriters, and their music should be reassessed within its historical context and on its own terms.

This is not to say that the Shangri-Las' *recordings* are not respected and or enjoyed, more that the members of the group are not perceived as having any great input into them.[23] The principal reason why there has been no full-length study of the Shangri-Las is because we have been repeatedly informed by respected rock journalists that, since they were a 'girl group' whose material was written by professional songwriters and strongly shaped by a producer, the *group itself* is unworthy of sustained examination. Until recently, academic writing on popular music of the late-1950s and early 1960s had largely accepted this schema, but a growing body of contemporary work is providing much-needed revision, for example by reclaiming 'the girl' from a devalued, trivial, pejoratively viewed status.[24] Of particular importance here is the work of Jacqueline Warwick, whose *Girl Groups, Girl Culture: Popular Music and Identity in the 1960s* is a ground-breaking reassessment of these consistently marginalised teenaged singers.

The other reason there has not been a full-length study of the Shangri-Las lies with the group members themselves. There is a wall of silence around the Shangri-Las, and the staunch gatekeeper was their former lead singer Mary Weiss, who died early in 2024 from chronic obstructive pulmonary disease, as this book was nearing completion for publication.[25] Mary's sister Betty—who has remained largely out of the public eye since the demise of the group in the late 1960s, and of whom Mary was reportedly extremely protective—is now the only surviving member. Mary Ann Ganser died in 1970 of complications resulting from an overdose, probably of barbiturates, and her twin sister Marguerite (Marge) died of breast cancer in 1996.* Despite my attempts, both directly and via others with closer access, Mary Weiss steadfastly refused to be interviewed for this project, to meet with me, or be involved in any way.† As a researcher and musician committed to reassessing the Shangri-Las' undervalued role in the history of popular music, I found Weiss's position tremendously disappointing, of course. But I also understood and respected it, recognising that it was

---

* These events are discussed in more detail in chapter 5.

† It goes without saying that I did not have access to archival material in the Weiss sisters' personal collections, including photos, fan club material and fan mail.

deeply rooted in her experiences as a teenage performer contracted to an industry notorious for consuming its young.

Mary Weiss also made clear her disapproval of what she saw as 'unauthorised biographies,' so her opposition to my work placed me in a complicated position ethically. I have attempted to balance requirements of historical accuracy with considerations for the privacy of the Weiss sisters, all the while remaining acutely aware of Mary's repeated complaint that 'there's lots of BS written about our group,' a statement with which I certainly concur.[26]

Mary's opposition naturally, if unfortunately, made others who might have been willing to share their own insights reluctant to participate in this project. Still others had their own reasons for keeping silent, possibly involving ongoing litigation.[27] Happily, several people did agree to talk to me about the Shangri-Las—producer George 'Shadow' Morton and engineers Rod McBrien and Brooks Arthur* (all three now deceased).

The fact that I live in Australia exacerbated these difficulties; generous funding from my university enabled me to travel twice to New York City and spend a few months there each time, but I was not able to communicate with those who did not want to be contacted, nor put sustained effort, in person, into gaining the trust of those who had been burned to varying degrees by the events of fifty years ago.

Source material has also been a complex issue, but my training as a medieval historian has been of unexpected value for this project.[28] The historian of the Middle Ages regularly encounters a paucity of documentary material, enormous gaps in records, as well as damaged and fragmentary materials. One is required to do a lot with a little. The absence of serious critical attention to the Shangri-Las in the decades following the demise of the group has resulted in a marked lack of press material, newspaper coverage and interviews in magazines. The teen magazines in which the Shangri-Las received coverage while they were a functioning group are only represented in extremely piecemeal fashion in library collections, having by and large not been regarded as worthy of preservation.[29] By the time a journalism was developing that endeavoured to cover rock and popular music seriously, in 1966–67,

---

*After some initial scepticism, the co-operation and enthusiasm of all three resulted in voluntary promises to try to persuade Mary Weiss to rethink her position, all of which were unsuccessful.

the landscape of popular music was changing so rapidly that the focus of attention was on counter-cultural rock groups and singer-songwriters rather than vocal groups like the Shangri-Las, who appeared passé and outdated from this perspective, their concerns trivial by comparison.

Given these circumstances, it was a happy coincidence that Mary Weiss recorded and released her first solo record in 2007. To promote the release on Brooklyn's Norton Records, label owners Billy Miller and Miriam Linna conducted a long interview with Weiss that was posted on the label's website, along with rare photos from her collection.[30] This was Mary Weiss's first interview in decades, and certainly the most detailed and lengthy she has ever given. The release of the album *Dangerous Game* (2007) generated substantial press coverage, including several long radio and television interviews, and feature articles in various newspapers and magazines. Although Weiss made it clear on several occasions that certain topics were off-limits, she nevertheless spoke in more detail than ever before about the Shangri-Las and her experiences as a teen star in the mid-1960s.

These interviews were of immeasurable assistance as I tried to piece together details concerning the Ganser and Weiss families, the formation of the Shangri-Las, and the manner in which the group's fortunes played out. This combination of circumstances has also meant that the available evidence has shaped the resulting narrative in quite particular ways. Ironically, given her lack of personal involvement, Mary Weiss is the member of the Shangri-Las most comprehensively represented. By the time I embarked on this project, both Mary Ann and Marguerite Ganser had been dead for many years, and their mother Rita died in 2004. However, Phil Milstein, a meticulous popular music researcher and writer based in Massachusetts, had interviewed Rita Ganser and her son Robert (brother of Mary Ann and Marguerite) in 2001 for a piece about the Shangri-Las' 1977 reunion;[31] he generously supplied me with recordings of his interviews, and allowed me access to all the material he had accumulated in the process of researching his article, which was absolutely invaluable in affording me some glimpses into the personalities and lives of Mary Ann and Marguerite Ganser.

Although there have always been books by and about female musicians, in the last decade or so there has been a renewed interest in the stories of women in the music industry. The gender landscape has also been changed by the #metoo movement (and associated high-profile court cases): in galvanising significant numbers of women and drawing attention to the endemic nature of sexual assault and harassment, the act of listening to and acknowledging these stories has become normalised and expected. Not unconnected with this is the close attention being paid to diversity and inclusion in the context of musical performance, and the body of literature that has developed around this in both academic and mainstream contexts. Today, venue bookers, musicians putting shows together, and festival organisers are generally far more aware of a community expectation that gender inclusivity be reflected in their line-ups.[32]

This cultural shift is reflected in a plethora of material focusing on the experiences and artistic development of female musicians navigating their way through the music industry. These include autobiographies by Cherie Currie (Runaways), Viv Albertine (Slits), Kim Gordon (Sonic Youth), Carrie Brownstein (Sleater-Kinney), Laura Jane Grace (Against Me!), Kathy Valentine (Go-Go's), Cosey Fanni Tutti (Throbbing Gristle, Chris & Cosey) and Sinéad O'Connor, to name a few.[33] Kathleen Hanna (Bikini Kill), Amy Winehouse, Janis Joplin, Nina Simone, Suzi Quatro, the Go-Go's, Fanny, Mary J Blige, Britney Spears and more, including back-up singers, have been the subjects of major documentaries.[34] A biopic based on Ronnie Spector's extraordinary autobiography *Be My Baby*, first published over thirty years ago, is now in production, with Zendaya playing Spector. Before her death in January 2022, Spector personally selected Zendaya for the role, and was an executive producer on the film.[35] Tracey Thorn (Everything But the Girl) was so furious at the treatment meted out to her friend, Lindy Morrison, and at Morrison's devaluation in the received history of the Go-Betweens (the band in which Morrison was the long-time drummer) that she decided to rewrite the story herself.[36] London-based academic Jennifer Otter Bickerdike, author of a recent study of Britney Spears, has also published a new biography of Nico that provides a much-needed rehabilitation of a difficult, maligned and misunderstood musician. In fact, reading Bickerdike's introduction, it struck me that much of what she observed about Nico applies equally to the Shangri-Las:

> Almost every aspect of Nico's life has been haphazardly recorded, if accurately chronicled at all. The repetition of the same anecdotes

has somehow mutated random incidents specific to contextualized moments into grand brushstrokes of overarching truisms. The more I tried to find out who the 'real' Nico was, the greater the rupture became between the oft-repeated myths, the few documented facts and the personal memories of those who knew her best.[37]

A reappraisal of the Shangri-Las' small but tremendously significant and influential body of work is long overdue. Repeatedly marginalised in traditional rock narratives, the Shangri-Las deserve to be examined in more informed historical contexts and on their own terms, right now and not later. The impact of the Shangri-Las was not only due to the 'genius' of George 'Shadow' Morton or technological innovations in recording techniques. These are important factors, of course, but they also feed the narrative of conventional US historiography and national mythologies—that it is male genius and capitalist technological innovation which lead to greatness. Traditionally absent from this story are women and workers. This book removes the 'girls' in the Shangri-Las from rock literature's overwhelmingly sexist condescension and emphasises their considerable abilities as musicians, workers and performers whose musicality and emotional honesty elicited a massive popular response. Despite their talent, ability, and hard work, however, they remained structurally weak in the face of the recorded music industry, which quickly disposed of them, and its intellectual apparatus—rock journalism—was equally happy to relegate them to a 'girl group' footnote. This examination of the Shangri-Las and their recordings analyses a wealth of evidence in order to arrive at a radically different assessment of their place in popular music history, and in doing so celebrates their spectacular artistic achievement.

"THE SHANGRI-LAS"

Red Bird RECORDS
1619 B'WAY., N. Y. C.   LT 1-3420

Red Bird publicity photo, 1964. (*Pictorial Press Ltd/Alamy*)

CHAPTER ONE

Genre and Gender:
the Shangri-Las and 'Girl Group' Mythology

> Totally manufactured as they were—the singers
> mere pawns of the industry—the girl-group records
> preserve a form of charm as potent as any other.
> —Greg Shaw[1]

> Never get caught up in categories. It's individuals
> who make the difference.
> —Duke Ellington[2]

In 1966, Columbia University journalism graduate Richard Goldstein
wrote an article about the Shangri-Las for 'Pop Eye,' his music column
in New York's *Village Voice*.[3] He took the intense emotionalism of their
music seriously:

> The Shangri-Las, three white girls from Queens, have soul. Their
> look and their sound is New York.[4]

Revising this piece in 1970 for publication in book form, Goldstein put
it slightly differently:

> Their look and sound are the city. And if soul means evoking hyper-
> reality, the Shangri-Las have it, blue eyes, glottal stops, and all.[5]

He observed the continuity of the 'anti-hero' delinquent male in their
songs, and how this allowed for the treatment of conflict between 'pas-

sion and filial obligation' that characterised much of their material. He described the Shangri-Las as 'mythic' and 'eternal,' likening the function of the backing vocals in "I Can Never Go Home Anymore" to that of the chorus in Greek tragedy—'Sophocles on Second Avenue'— and observing that the use of Beethoven's 'Moonlight' Sonata in "Past, Present and Future" was symbolic of 'weltschmerz,' or world-weariness.[6] Goldstein noted the significant role of George 'Shadow' Morton in their success, but not in terms that negated the importance of the group members, whose individual personalities and performative abilities he made a considerable effort to convey. At no point in his original article, nor in his 1970 revision, did Goldstein refer to the Shangri-Las as a 'girl group,' or indicate a perception of the group or their recordings as belonging to a genre.[7]

If more music critics had noted Goldstein's work and taken their lead from his astute observations, the body of writing on the Shangri-Las and their recorded legacy might well be very different.[8] As it stands, such writing has been characterised by the inclusion of the Shangri-Las within a category of popular music, understood to be a genre, known as 'girl groups.' In the tradition of rock criticism, 'girl group' is not a catch-all term that refers to female bands; rather it denotes US female vocal groups who recorded and performed between approximately 1958 and 1966, and shared certain stylistic and production values. The women were young, often teenaged, and many were Black. The songs they performed were usually written by professional songwriters, generally about boys, love, dating and related concerns of particular importance to teenagers. In most cases, the young women did not play instruments on their recordings, and the recording, production and release of the material was overseen by producers whose input and control over the end result was considerable.

This 'girl group' appellation, which was applied retrospectively by male music journalists, has had far-reaching ramifications for the evaluation of the groups in question, but particularly for the Shangri-Las; it has played a major role in preventing a more sophisticated understanding of their musical and artistic accomplishments. I should emphasise that in making this observation I am in no way disparaging the singing groups with which the Shangri-Las are routinely compared and categorised. My issue is with the label and the consequences of its blanket application, not with those who have been so labelled. There are indeed many valid comparisons to be made between the various female singing groups that became known after the fact as 'girl groups,' and perfectly sensible reasons for why they are generally discussed together. As musicologist Jacqueline Warwick has demonstrated, there are clear thematic, musical and stylistic continuities that argue for a collective analysis of 'girl groups,' which opens new windows into the study of girlhood in the USA in the 1950s and 60s.[9] Warwick's work differs from previous writing about 'girl groups' most notably in her rehabilitation of girls, particularly girls' voices, from the pejorative interpretations they have acquired in the context of traditional notions of rock authenticity. In doing so, Warwick has made visible and at the same time dismantled many of the core rock assumptions on which these interpretations rest; her work is part of a growing body of scholarship that explores these themes.

However, there are larger issues here that need to be addressed, too. These can be traced to the *origins* of the term 'girl group' and the development of its usage within a particular framework of popular music criticism that viewed the late 50s and early 60s as a low point in rock music's development. As critic/producer Robert Palmer noted in 1995, the era of the late 50s and early 60s is 'often dismissed as a dull interregnum between the original fifties rock explosion and the arrival of the "modern pop band" in the person of the Beach Boys and the Beatles.'[10] A typical rendering of the standard narrative is this example by Timothy E. Scheurer from 1996:

> The market was changing because of the controversies and upheavals that rocked the industry in the late 1950s. Elvis's induction into the army, Little Richard's retreat into the ministry, Jerry Lee Lewis's marital controversy, Buddy Holly's death, and the payola scandal were among the most serious blows dealt to the early vitality of the rock revolution. Into the *vacuum* stepped the forces of Tin Pan Alley (as well as rockers like the Beach Boys). Using their own talents (as in the case of Neil Sedaka, Neil Diamond, Paul Anka), or that of *malleable teen-oriented groups and teen idols* (including the Chiffons, the Shirelles, Bobby Vee, and Rick Nelson), *the songwriters and producers allied* to produce a musical product that blended the feel of early rock with the craftsmanship of the songwriters of the Tin Pan Alley era.[11]

According to this widely accepted mythology, 'authentic' rock and roll was forced underground, leaving a 'vacuum' which 'songwriters and producers' filled with their 'malleable teen-oriented groups and teen idols.'[12] Other enduring assumptions are also present here. All four supposed torch-bearers of the 'rock revolution' were male singer-instrumentalists and, with the exception of Little Richard, all were white. This account also privileged Presley et al. over those who were singers only, although this hierarchy was not part of how rock 'n' roll was perceived in the late 50s and early 60s. Furthermore, it implied an opposition between the work of these performers and 'Tin Pan Alley,' when Presley's hit 'Blue Moon' was in fact a Rodgers and Hart standard, and 'Hound Dog,' later recorded by Presley, was written for Willie Mae 'Big Mama' Thornton by two professional 'Tin Pan Alley' songwriters, Jerry Leiber and Mike Stoller. Leiber and Stoller also wrote 'Jailhouse Rock' for Presley, as well as '(You're So Square) Baby, I Don't Care,' which was later recorded by Buddy Holly.[13] Nevertheless, the white, male singer/instrumentalist is characterised here as the 'authentic' rock performer, even though this belief did not gain currency until the late 60s, some ten years *after* the period under discussion.

The roots of this widely accepted perception of the late 50s and early 60s can be traced to the development of 'serious' rock journalism in the mid-60s, as Lisa Rhodes has detailed comprehensively in *Electric Ladyland: Women and Rock Culture*.[14] Before this, media coverage of popular music was largely confined to record industry journals, like *Billboard* and *Cash Box*, which advised record sellers on trends, promotions, and what was 'hot' in terms of sales; and to teen magazines, which featured pin-ups, pop-star gossip, fan-club information and the like.[15] In response to the lack of substantial coverage of pop and rock music by its peers, Boston College student Paul Williams founded *Crawdaddy* magazine in 1966. Along with Richard Goldstein's 'Pop Eye' column in the *Village Voice*, *Crawdaddy* is widely credited with initiating rock journalism by publishing writing on pop and rock music that engaged with it as an art form.[16] Significantly, Williams had to publish and finance *Crawdaddy* himself, because 'no publisher could be convinced of a future for a serious rock 'n' roll magazine.'[17] The next year, *Rolling Stone* was founded in San Francisco by Jann Wenner and Ralph Gleason. These publications were established with the conscious aim of reporting on the music of the counterculture, as their editors saw it, which defined itself *against* what preceded it, namely those 'malleable teen-oriented groups and teen idols' which included male doo-wop groups and the female singers commonly referred to as 'girl groups.'[18]

The journalism that subsequently developed to report on the important developments in late 1960s rock did so within a perniciously masculine framework that did not take women, let alone teenage girls, seriously.[19] To read Goldstein's "Pop Eye" column, as Lisa Rhodes points out, 'is to glimpse the possibilities of the field of rock journalism before *Rolling Stone* laid its misogynist hands on it,'[20] while Brenda Johnson-Grau has observed,

> In the late 1960s, as the first generation of rockers saw their children reach the age of consent, "rock 'n' roll" was redefined as "rock" to accommodate a new generation's need to trash the past and define itself. In the process, many successful and influential female artists were derided and marginalized as "girl groups" or simply expunged from the record.[21]

This negative understanding of 'girls' in relation to rock is exemplified in a 1973 *Billboard* review of the album 'Mother's Pride,' by the all-female rock group Fanny:

> The excellence of the set should hopefully make people think of music rather than 'that all-girl group' when they think of Fanny . . . All members are highly competent instrumentalists. Fine production from Todd Rundgren.[22]

The writer of this review acknowledged quite openly that the term 'all-girl group' had a pejorative connotation. Furthermore, the writer felt the need to point out that not only did the members of Fanny play instruments (unlike, by implication, those other 'girl groups' who did not), they were actually good at it, too. And just in case the reader had any lingering doubts, the album was overseen by producer extraordinaire Todd Rundgren, thereby lending it his stamp of approval. These few lines encapsulate much of what is problematic about the term 'girl group,' and why it is necessary to rethink this categorisation.

By 1975, these assumptions were so well-entrenched as to be part of rock lore. The members of teenage all-female band the Runaways experienced the consequences of this repeatedly, as their singer Cherie Currie has related:

> The people who did the interviews didn't have a clue what to make of us. Most of the time they were these long-haired, jaded guys who didn't think for a minute that we played our own instruments. In fact, they'd ask us outright to confess to the 'lies,' and demand that we tell them that this whole thing was some kind of scam concocted by [producer] Kim Fowley. They'd ask Joan [Jett] dumb questions like, 'So, uh, what makes you *think* you can play the guitar?'[23]

As late as 1981, the Go-Go's had immense difficulty securing a US record deal, despite having toured the UK, released a single on London's Stiff Records, and built a massive following for their live shows in LA. Belinda Carlisle recalled:

> Every label said they couldn't sign us because there hadn't been a band with a proven track record that looked like us. We were told 'We love you and we can see that everybody loves you but there's never been a successful all-female band.' The Runaways were so great and had some success on a cult level but nobody wanted to be cult. They wanted to be a success.[24]

The group was finally signed by independent label I.R.S. Records and their debut album *Beauty and the Beat* issued in July 1981. This ideology regarding girls was also internalised by women. Patti Smith, whose debut album *Horses* was released in 1975, famously took her inspiration from Jim Morrison, Keith Richards and Mick Jagger in part because, as she put it, 'I was always under the impression that girls were silly when I was younger.'[25] In an era characterised by glam rock's gender fluidity, Smith immersed herself in New York City's 'downtown post-glam scene' which 'was a mix of Warholian drag queens and glitter boys slumming as women.'[26] Smith deliberately distanced herself from the feminine,* cultivating an androgynous persona that was, from her perspective, integral to her development as an artist in the early 1970s.[27]

---

* This observation is not intended as a swipe at Patti Smith (of whom I'm a great fan), but to demonstrate how pejoratively girls were regarded in rock lore and perceived to be antithetical to 'genuine' rock artistry.

The narratives identified here are tied up with notions of artistic authenticity and the development of the singer/songwriter, both as a solo artist and within groups, in the second half of the 60s. In the post–Beatles/Bob Dylan/Joni Mitchell/Neil Young singer-songwriter era, it is an unquestioned belief that writing and performing one's musical material is essential to being a 'serious' musical artist. As Jacqueline Warwick points out,

> The necessity of performing self-penned material became central to rock ideology in the mid-60s and after. Music that stemmed from other practices came to be seen as inferior to the supposedly unmediated expressions of pure feeling emanating from the new bands. Ironically, mastery of an instrument became a badge of musical truth, while bringing music out from within the body itself was dismissed as facile and "inauthentic."[28]

It is rarely acknowledged that only in the early 60s did the roles of 'songwriter' and 'singer' begin to be inextricably linked. Before the mid-60s it was *not* the norm for singers, particularly pop singers, to write their own material—their material was primarily written by professional songwriters.[29] This was true of the great singers in many genres—Frank Sinatra, Patsy Cline, Elvis Presley, and Ella Fitzgerald, to name a few*—while the entire repertoire of Western classical music involves the performance of material written by professional composers. Few would argue that the authenticity of Maria Callas was somehow compromised because she did not sing material she wrote herself. Blues, country and folk musicians also drew on an established repertoire of songs transmitted through an oral tradition over generations, although a strong current in 'countercultural' rock music of the mid/late-60s nevertheless looked to blues, folk and R&B traditions as 'authentic' expressions of feeling and oppression.[30]

This shift established a blueprint for rock that has remained largely intact: the album became the serious artistic statement, as opposed to the single releases of individual songs that characterised the 50s and early 60s. In addition to artistic considerations, albums were more

---

* Although Fitzgerald wrote or co-wrote some of her own material, including the 1938 hit "A-Tisket, A-Tasket," she is most famous for her recordings of Broadway standards by Cole Porter, George Gershwin, Harold Arlen and others.

costly to purchase than singles, which meant a larger margin of profit both for shops and for the 'rack-jobbers' who supplied record retailers with stock.[31] Albums were larger and thicker, and therefore less fragile than singles; furthermore, the cost of distribution was only marginally greater. Concurrent developments in FM radio fidelity and its adoption as the preferred rock medium, and the use of these new stereo recording techniques by rock producers, all contributed to making the long-player (LP) the dominant format for the sale of recorded music.[32]

By the late 60s, this state of affairs was established as the industry standard, and it is from this later standpoint that the Shangri-Las and their vocal group contemporaries have largely been examined and judged, i.e., according to a set of criteria that only evolved *after* the group was active. The credibility and musical reputation of *singing* groups has suffered greatly in retrospect because the fact that they did not write their own material or play instruments is now viewed pejoratively, when in fact they were the product of an earlier era, one in which singers were regarded as completely credible performers *without* being songwriters.

Much of the academic work on this earlier era also relies on the criteria established later by rock journalists, as we shall see.[33] Academics were slow to embrace the study of popular music: *Popular Music and Society*, one of the earliest academic journals devoted to popular music, was established in 1971. The International Association for the Study of Popular Music (IASPM), an organisation formed specifically to forge academic networks between scholars working in this area of study, was set up in 1981.[34] Despite these developments, rock/popular music and musicology remained deeply suspicious of one another. Many rock journalists and musicians are for the most part still very sceptical about the value of academic work on rock and popular music,* while the academic discipline of musicology traditionally defined popular music as 'the enemy.' Indeed, the criteria for analysing Western classical music are largely irrelevant in the study of pop music, which placed scholars of popular music in something of a 'methodological vacuum.'[35] It is therefore not surprising that scholarly writing about rock and pop is increasingly cross-disciplinary—the work of sociologists, scholars of literature, cultural analysts, historians, as well as musicologists—and this

---

*This has certainly been my experience, and, since I have a foot in each camp, I am (still!) regularly regarded with suspicion by both.

has manifested itself in an explosion of academic writing about various aspects and permutations of popular music.[36]

Academic coverage of the Shangri-Las has mostly been piecemeal, as a sidebar to the main theme or subject being discussed. Important details have often been obscured, and blatant factual inaccuracies perpetrated, in the interests of a grand narrative or argument being advanced by the author. An article by Jon Stratton offers a particularly glaring example:

> As Jews, and whites, became disillusioned with suburban life, so the Brill Building sound lost its popularity. I argue that the songs recorded by the Shangri-Las, *a Jewish girl group* singing songs of familial death and destruction mostly written by Brill Building writers, are an expression of this disillusionment.[37]

The Shangri-Las were not Jewish. The Ganser family were Catholics of Austrian descent; Mary Ann and Marguerite attended Sacred Heart School in Cambria Heights until the eighth grade, graduating in 1962.[38] When Mary Ann Ganser died in 1970, her funeral was held at the Sacred Heart Roman Catholic Church, adjacent to the school she had attended as a child.[39] Henry Petroski, who moved with his family to Cambria Heights in 1954, noted that the suburb 'was now home to so many Catholic families with children that the [Sacred Heart] school was unable to accommodate all the new kids that were moving into the neighbourhood.'[40] The Weiss family was also Catholic. Mary Weiss attended a Catholic grammar school, and a lengthy interview on the Norton Records website contains two photos from her private collection showing Weiss dressed up for her confirmation.[41]

In addition to this false claim, Stratton also asserted that

> Suburbia was thought of as an American Shangri-La . . . By calling themselves the Shangri-Las, the Weiss and Ganser sisters from Queens signalled this reference in their disillusioned regret for a lost American utopia.[42]

This is pure presumption on Stratton's part. The group members evidently had no such thought in mind. According to Mary Weiss, who was about 14 at the time, the group was about to make its first record and did not yet have a name:

We said, "We better get a name—fast!" We were driving on Long
Island and saw a restaurant called the Shangri-La. That's where we
got the name.[43]

There was plenty of 'disillusioned regret' to come for the Shangri-
Las, but not at the time they named their group, and certainly not for
anything as abstract as a lost suburban utopia.[44] Stratton, impervious to
evidence (tellingly, none is cited to support his claims), characterises the
Shangri-Las as Jewish in order to advance his overall argument about
Brill Building songwriters, many of whom, unlike the Shangri-Las, *were*
Jewish. His article is a particularly unfortunate example of the tendency
to treat the Shangri-Las as a blank slate upon which to inscribe already
formulated arguments; flagrantly inaccurate assertions then follow.[45]

Furthermore, when scholars of popular music like Stratton have written about the Shangri-Las, they refer to them almost without exception
as a 'girl group' and discuss them only within this restrictive category.
They simply follow the schema established by rock journalists and
music critics, who are responsible for the bulk of writing about the
Shangri-Las.

As Jacqueline Warwick has pointed out, the early 60s 'marked the
first instance in U.S. history of a music centred around adolescent girls
and their experiences of coming of age.'[46] The Shirelles, the Ronettes,
the Crystals, the Marvelettes, the Supremes and the Shangri-Las, to
name a few, jostled for top ten spots with the Beach Boys and, as the
decade progressed, the Beatles and the Rolling Stones. By the late 60s,
however, popular music had undergone such a transformation in style,
content and methods of construction that many vocal groups from the
early 60s appeared hopelessly outdated and their 'teen' concerns trivial
by comparison.

No-one is quite sure who coined the term 'girl group' or exactly
when, but it seems that over time it metamorphosed from being one of a
number of terms used to describe groups of female performers into one
that was understood to refer to a very specific era and type of music. Few
writers have questioned either the appropriateness or the consequences
of this nomenclature, so little attempt has been made to investigate the
origins of the term.[47] The organisation of events and time periods into
named categories is standard practice among historians as a means of
enabling analysis. The term 'girl group' is one example of this practice

among many, but its largely unquestioned usage needs to be investigated, particularly since it seems that at the time, at least in relation to the Shangri-Las, the term was not in general use or was not felt to be applicable to them. According to Mary Weiss:

'We never thought of ourselves as a "girl group." We were rock and rollers, same as the guys. True rock and roll has no sex—it's rock and roll.' [48]

If Weiss is using the term 'true rock and roll' as it was originally understood in the 50s and early 60s, my research certainly supports her claim. When Frankie Laine introduced Frankie Lymon and the Teenagers during their first television appearance on his show in 1956, he described them as an example of 'what is now the most popular style of music in this country: rock and roll.' [49] Similarly, eight years later when the Shangri-Las performed "Leader of the Pack" on *I've Got a Secret*, on 16 November 1964, it was announced as 'the country's top rock and roll hit,' and the words 'the Number 1 rock 'n roll song hit' were shown onscreen. [50] In February 1965, *Billboard* described the Shangri-Las' newly released first album as

A socko album debut for the younger set by one of the most popular of the new rock vocal teams. Two of the gals' hits are represented: "Walking in the Sand" and "Leader of the Pack." [51]

As late as 1965, then, the Shangri-Las were not a 'girl group'—they were one of the 'new rock vocal teams.' In the late 50s and well into the mid-60s, no one spoke of 'doo-wop' and 'girl groups,' because these terms had not yet been applied to the music being discussed. It was all rock and roll. This underscores a point that goes to the heart of this study— that artificial genre distinctions imposed later have had serious ramifications for how teen-oriented vocal group music has since been perceived, whether it is doo-wop or what is now referred to as 'girl group' music.

In a 1964 article about the Shangri-Las in British music magazine *New Musical Express*, journalist Richard Green began,

The way the chart-topping Supremes wave their arms about when singing captivated thousands of British fans on their recent visit here.

But not many people know that another *girl team* climbing the charts adopt a similar technique on stage.[52]

The 'girl team' in question was the Shangri-Las. And in June 1965, *Ebony* magazine ran an eight-page feature article on the Supremes that used a variety of titles and subtitles. Its cover heralded the article as 'The Supremes: Girl singers top rock 'n' roll field'; the table of contents listed it as 'The Supremes Make It Big: New rulers of rock 'n' roll boast three consecutive million seller[s].'[53] The feature itself was entitled 'The Supremes: Sweet-sounding Detroiters push to top as new rulers of "rock."' Within the piece, a variety of terms were used to describe the group, including 'world's hottest female vocal group,' 'girl vocal trio,' 'vocal group,' 'female group,' and 'girl vocal group'—but not 'girl group.'[54] Further on, the writer tried to convey the Supremes' sonic qualities in a little more depth:

> The Supremes feature what the record industry calls that "Detroit Sound," a mixture of blues, gospel, rock 'n' roll, and pop music. "It's less wild than most of the big beat music you hear today," says Diana, "but it still has feeling to it. We call it sweet music." [55]

The Supremes, it seems, did not think of themselves as a 'girl group' either, and nor did the author of this article, for whom they were in the first instance exemplars of 'that "Detroit Sound."' In that same year, in the summer edition of *16 Magazine Spectacular*, the results of '16's Fourth Annual Geegee Gold Star Awards' were published. This was a poll of the teen readers of *16 Magazine*, and the voting categories were significant. The 'Best American Female Group' award went to the Supremes, 'Most Promising American Female Group' to the Shangri-Las, and 'Best LP American Female Group' to the Dixie Cups for *Iko Iko*.[56] These three groups are now considered prime examples of the 'girl group' genre, but here, in 1965, there was no mention of the term.

In 1966 *Ebony* ran a special on the Ronettes that was styled similarly to the earlier Supremes feature.[57] The headline of the article was 'The Ronettes: Rock 'n' roll girls trio teams up with the Beatles on a whirlwind, 14-city, U.S. entertainment tour.' In the body of the article they were described as 'a trio of rock 'n' roll singers,' after which the writer observed that they had been named 'The Best Girl Group in England'

16's
FOURTH ANNUAL
GEEGEE
GOLD STAR
AWARDS

**Given for Highest Achievement by Young Stars
in the Fields of Motion Pictures, Television and Records**

ONCE AGAIN 16 raises the curtain on its annual GeeGee Awards for outstanding achievements by young stars in motion pictures, television and records.

As always, the winners of this year's GeeGee Awards, for extraordinary performances during the past twelve months, were chosen by 16's readers. They were chosen by you in the ballots and letters you mailed to us day after day, in which you told us who were your favorite young stars. We tabulated each and every vote, and the stars you see on the next three pages are the stars you voted tops in their field. (Divisions were made for performers in some of the categories for obvious reasons.)

To the winners of this year's GeeGee Awards, 16 speaks for every 16 reader in saying, "Congratulations and all good wishes for a long and successful career."

Best American Male Group

The Beach Boys

Best American Female Group

The Supremes

Most Promising American Male Group

Gary Lewis and Playboys

Most Promising American Female Group

The Shangri-Las

Best British Group

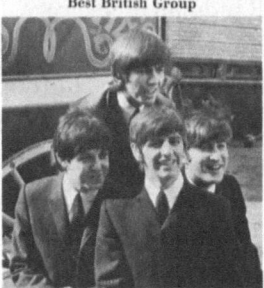

The Beatles

Most Promising British Group

Herman & His Hermits

Extracts from *16 Magazine*'s 'Fourth Annual Geegee Gold Star Awards,' Summer 1965.

following the success there of 'Be My Baby,' and then, a year later, 'voted the third top singing group in England,' after the Beatles and the Rolling Stones.[58] This indicates that in the mid-60s, 'girl group' was no more than one of a number of terms used to describe a group of young women who performed together. Earlier in 1966, *Jet* magazine ran a very similar article by Bobbee Barbee called 'Rocking Ronettes Rocket Toward Fame: Two Sisters and a First Cousin,' on which the writer of the *Ebony* feature had likely drawn. Barbee referred to the Ronettes as 'a singing group' and as an 'impressive, intelligent and individualistic trio.'[59] Furthermore, the fact that the Ronettes were included in a poll with the Beatles and the Rolling Stones gives further weight to Weiss's assertion that, at least in the minds of the (presumably) teen voters, the Ronettes too 'were rock and rollers, same as the guys.'

Songwriter Ellie Greenwich, who wrote for both the Ronettes and the Shangri-Las, is on record as saying, 'we didn't think in terms of "girl groups." We never put a label on it.'[60] Two advertisements that appeared in an April 1967 issue of *Billboard*, in the 'Help Wanted' section, cast further intriguing light on this question. The first ran:

GIRL GROUPS, VOCAL OR INSTRUMENTAL. Must be young, pretty. Real Pros Only. Apply week of April 17, 1967, 3pm. Leo Stone, 1639 Broadway.

And just below:

WANTED QUALIFIED GIRL ROCK AND ROLL Lead Guitar or Organ Player for one of country's leading girl groups, with prestige playing credits, pending record contract and strong teen following. Seeking compatible experienced girl to join up.
   If qualified, write for audition, giving age, present occupation, music group you belong to, whether union member, etc., to:
   BOX B309, 188 W. Randolph St, Chicago, Ill.[61]

Both these advertisements used 'girl group' descriptively, rather than to refer to a particular genre. And both made clear reference to playing instruments, which was unheard of in the later, still current understanding of the term, according to which the 'girl groups' were singing groups, not bands, who recorded with studio musicians and played live with (male) backing bands.

It seems clear that in the early and mid-60s, and as late as 1967, the term 'girl group' was not used generally to refer to a *type* of music. By the early 1970s, however, the term was widely understood in such a specific way that Greg Shaw could write:

> For the uninitiated, Charlie Feathers was to rockabilly what Charlie Patton was to the blues, what the Ronettes were to girl groups, what the Small Faces were to the English Invasion . . .

and expect that his readers would interpret the term as referring to a style of music, a genre.[62] In his 1974 article 'How the Other Half Lives: The Best of Girl Group Rock,' Greil Marcus enunciated a definition of 'girl group' as a genre in terms that have remained largely unquestioned since:

> The girls were usually black, always urban, and the groups featured one completely distinctive lead singer and more or less replaceable back-ups (they met in high school, posed in their prom dresses). If they weren't teenage, they sang as if they were. They neither wrote songs nor played instruments; *all needed a producer for the identifiable, striking sound that was the first necessity of any girl group record.* The music wasn't R&B or soul—it was straight rock, simple but embellished and ornamented, aimed right at Top 40, not the black charts.[63]

Leaving aside for the moment Marcus's characterisation of the music as 'simple but embellished and ornamented,' the very real similarities he lists between the groups are largely responsible for their categorisation into a genre, 'girl groups.' The fact that many of the same song-writing, recording and production personnel were involved with multiple groups has served to emphasise their similarities. For instance, Ellie Greenwich wrote material for the Shangri-Las, the Dixie Cups, the Ronettes, and the Crystals, among others. In New York City, the centre of operations was the Brill Building at 1619 Broadway, in which professional songwriters including Greenwich, her husband Jeff Barry, Neil Sedaka, Gerry Goffin and Carol King, worked, writing for singers and vocal groups signed to labels whose offices were likely to be in the same building, or nearby at 1650 Broadway.[64] In Detroit, the staff songwriters for Motown Records included Smokey Robinson, Eddie Holland,

Lamont Dozier, and Brian Holland, who wrote songs for the male and female vocal groups to record in conjunction with the 'house' band of staff musicians. As a consequence, the Motown groups had a more obvious 'signature sound' than the New York City-based groups. [65]

The codification of the term 'girl group' was cemented with the publication of Alan Betrock's *Girl Groups: The Story of a Sound* in 1982.[66] Betrock reiterated Marcus's characterisation of 'girl groups' as being

> so called because they were, for the most part, both groups and girls. Their story is not one of *females* in rock 'n' roll (for there were hundreds of female stars who had nothing to do with the girl-group sound), but of a musical setting, lyrical direction and business organization that added up to the creation of a unique genre.[67]

Betrock had great affection for the 'girl groups'; his research was thorough; and he wrote with care, enormous enthusiasm, and a keen eye for their musical significance. He clearly believed that the artistic achievement of the groups in question was worthy of detailed, book-length coverage: in this alone, his work was groundbreaking. Betrock's book contains a 12-page chapter on the Shangri-Las, which was without doubt the most in-depth survey of the group until the publication of John Grecco's lengthy online article, *Out in the Streets: The Story of the Shangri-Las* in 2002, and more recently Ada Wolin's volume in the 33⅓ album series, *Golden Hits of the Shangri-Las*.[68] Betrock was a native of Queens, New York, and an obsessive record and ephemera collector, as well as a music producer.[69] He therefore wrote to some extent as an insider, and, while this was undoubtedly advantageous in many ways, he clearly accepted without question what Jacqueline Warwick has described as a 'hierarchy that places producers and songwriters at the head of the musical enterprise,'[70] writing that

> The girl-group sound was primarily based in and around New York, because as a *writer/producer medium*, most of the well-connected writers, arrangers, producers, musicians, and studios were to be found there.[71]

Of course, recordings of pop music could not get made without producers—or songwriters, for that matter. Conspicuously absent from his list, however, is any mention of actual groups of singers, which is surely telling in a discussion of a genre called 'girl groups.'* It may not have been deliberate, but the implication is that singers can be found anywhere; they are so peripheral to the exercise that they did not even rate a mention in Betrock's list. This hierarchy plays an important role in constantly undermining the artistic achievement of the groups that Betrock so painstakingly chronicled throughout his book; the tension between these conflicting positions is never resolved.† In his contemporary review of *Girl Groups*, Barney Hoskyns noted that had Betrock 'been a little more alert to the sexual codes that determined the genre we know as "girl groups,"' he might have produced 'a book which rather more radically challenged our assumptions' about the groups and their recordings. Betrock, however, was 'always content to sit this side of popular myth.'[72]

Greil Marcus follows the same line in the *Rolling Stone Illustrated History of Rock and Roll*:

> Girl group rock was producers' music; the songs came out of the Brill Building, written by contract songwriters. The 'artists' had no 'creative freedom.'[73]

Just as Phil Spector is perceived to be largely responsible for the recorded output of, for example, the Ronettes, so are the Shangri-Las predominantly seen as the brainchild of George 'Shadow' Morton. Spector and Morton were, in their different ways, spectacularly innovative and creative producers; they broke down established conventions and irrevocably changed the way records were made and heard.[74] However, this absolutely relentless emphasis on the producer (followed closely by the songwriters) in almost all discussions of 'girl groups' has resulted in a radical undervaluation of the performers themselves. As Jacqueline Warwick has put it,

> The music of the girl groups in the early 1960s is typically . . . dismissed as the inane chirpings of mindless puppets controlled by some behind-the-scenes Svengali.[75]

---

*I am quite sure that Betrock was not including singing groups when he referred to 'musicians.'

† This is not an issue unique to Betrock, as will be discussed shortly.

Their 'image,' including matching outfits, as well as their age and sex, were also cited to support such an assessment. Charlotte Greig challenged this view as early as 1989 in her book *Will You Still Love Me Tomorrow? Girl Groups from the 50s On . . .* , offering a trenchant response to Betrock's placement of the teenage singers at the bottom of his hierarchical schema.[76] Jacqueline Warwick has shown how systematically pervasive this idea was, and provided an overdue dismantling of this fundamental tenet of 'girl group' lore, repositioning 'vocalists as the central musicians.'[77]

In the case of the Shangri-Las, however, there is another layer of complexity that might not unreasonably be termed the 'Spector factor.' In 'girl group' mythology, Phil Spector is the undisputed king, *the* maverick auteur producer, and 'Be My Baby' by the Ronettes the jewel in his crown. And not without some justification, for Spector was driven, eccentric, intense and revolutionary.* He applied Wagnerian Romantic agony, and *his* version of a 'wall of sound,' to music written for and aimed at teenagers, famously creating 'little symphonies for kids.'[78] Craig Schuftan summarises this well:

> Spector had realised that in high school, every time a boy *looks* at you, let alone asks you on a date or dumps you just before the dance, it feels like *Tristan und Isolde*. So Spector decided to treat these teen tragedies with the dignity their protagonists instinctively felt they deserved. He would tell the teens of America that their emotions were every bit as important as they imagined.[79]

Conceptually, this was brilliant, and it clearly influenced George 'Shadow' Morton, who took similar notions into new terrains of sonic emptiness that were quite different but every bit as innovative as Spector's.†

---

* These aspects of Spector's personality also manifested themselves in increasingly unhinged, controlling and psychopathic behaviour over the course of his life, culminating in his 2009 conviction and incarceration for the brutal murder of Lana Clarkson.

† Schuftan's comments are equally applicable to Morton, if not more so. Morton's use of emptiness, space, echo, and reverb is discussed in detail in chapter 7, where the Shangri-Las' own version of Romantic agony is examined.

Rarely are Morton's innovations seen on their own terms, however.[80] In his lengthy 1974 interview with Morton, Lenny Kaye stated a widespread view:

If the Ronettes were the royalty of sixties girl groups, the Crystals their unwilling ladies-in-waiting, the Shangri-Las were the handmaidens that made good, rising from virtual kitchen scullions to the rank of pop cinderellas.[81]

Morton is generally presented as something of a second-rate Spector, and the Shangri-Las, as his 'vehicle,' suffer accordingly. In Paul Gripp's estimation, for example, the Ronettes 'represent the high water mark of the Girl Group music' and 'the Shangri-Las represent its ebb tide. In their work, the form plays itself out—there is no place left for the music to go after this group exposes the limitations of the Girl Group ideology.'[82] For Gripp, writing in 1999, 'girl group' is not merely a genre but an 'ideology.' What exactly he means by this is unclear, but it indicates how entrenched such a terminology, categorisation and conception of these female vocal groups had become. More importantly, it assumes that the groups were consciously adhering to some codified philosophical framework in the creation of their records under the 'girl group' banner, which, as we have already seen, was not the case. As recently as 2019, Ada Wolin expressed a similar take on the Shangri-Las:

They weren't necessarily the most talented vocalists, but they were certainly the most bizarre and by far the most theatrical. Their death discs are the *death rattle of the girl-group sound*, and this is why they stand apart as such a deeply misunderstood group. They are transitional, one foot in the "sound" and one foot in the outer reaches of dirty, rebellious rock 'n' roll.[83]

The effect of generalisations about 'girl groups' and various manifestations of the cult of the producer on the Shangri-Las' reputation is even more starkly revealed in this discussion by James M. Curtis:

When the girl group sound broke, it broke big. 'Leader of the Pack,' 'He's a Rebel,' 'Da Doo Ron Ron,' 'My Boyfriend's Back,' 'Chapel of Love' and 'Be My Baby' all went to #1 in the early sixties. So we need to ask why this happened at this particular time. I think that we cannot explain the appeal of the girl groups by simply listening to the records or praising Phil's genius. Rather, we need to turn to television, the ground against which rock and roll was the figure.[84]

Only three of the six songs Curtis lists were Phil Spector productions. 'Leader of the Pack,' was of course by the Shangri-Las, produced and co-written by Morton. It went to #1 in November 1964, not exactly 'the early sixties.' But *all six songs* are presented as though they somehow coexisted in one happy conglomerate under the guiding hand of his chum 'Phil's genius.' In one of the more spectacularly misogynist explanations for the popularity of 'girl groups,' Curtis goes on to argue,

> There was one television star in the early sixties who outshone all the others and who mesmerized the American people . . . I believe that President Kennedy was so much the man of the hour and we were so infatuated with the way he was obsolescing the distinction between politics and showbiz that we were not interested in other male heroes. But we were very receptive to young, nubile girls who sang about male heroes. So it makes sense to say that the girl groups enjoyed great success because they were properly positioned (to use a marketing term) between Phil Spector on the one hand and President Kennedy on the other.[85]

This patronising and reductive assessment, deeply sexist and laden with innuendo, was constructed within an established set of parameters that treated 'girl groups' as interchangeable components of a genre, the male producer as Svengali, and the late 50s and early 60s as a low point in rock history between Elvis and the Beatles. Curtis was likely following the lead of Greil Marcus here, who stated in 1975 that:

> Girl group records were based in the relationship of a young girl and an older man (white, until Berry Gordy) who put her on a pedestal and held her in thrall; out of that relationship came some of the most urgent and intense rock and roll ever made.[86]

Jacqueline Warwick's observation that the 'conventional girl' is a powerful cultural emblem is also relevant to this discussion:

She has served and continues to serve as a token of nostalgia for some idealized past; an icon for a bright future; an embodiment of innocence to be protected at all costs; a symbol of hope and inspiration; a helpless and tragic manifestation of pathos; an unspoiled object of lust; and a model of pouting selfishness and egocentrism.[87]

Most of these are evident in Curtis's argument, in which young female performers are reduced to 'nubile girls who sang about male heroes,' and nostalgically linked to a societal 'infatuation' with John F. Kennedy.[88]

The dangers of projecting pre-formed conclusions and unexamined assumptions onto the historical evidence are exemplified in a 2003 article on the image of 'girl groups,' in which Cynthia Cyrus discusses the importance of matching costumes to their 'image,' and argues that

> even when nominally off-stage, the members of a particular girl group frequently dressed alike. Take, for example, recording sessions. Because the focus was on the sound and not the visual image, the studio session demanded less pageantry than did the public performance. The girl groups, however, responded not with mutual independence, but rather with a different kind of costume. The look might be informal, merely a shirt paired with comfortable pants, but all members of the group would be carefully dressed alike.[89]

Cyrus cites as evidence for her claim two photographs—one of the Cookies, the other of Martha and the Vandellas. She provides no references, but her descriptions strongly suggest two images that appear in Alan Betrock's *Girl Groups*.[90] The shot of the Vandellas with Marvin Gaye reproduced there is clearly staged; it was evidently taken in the studio but there is no equipment visible, nor anything to suggest the group is in the *process* of recording. Betrock's caption reads, 'Martha and the Vandellas at their earliest recording session where they backed Marvin Gaye,' so possibly this photo was taken before or after a recording session, in which case the Vandellas were dressed alike because it was a publicity photo, not because they were so wedded to their supposed 'girl group' identity that they were unable to respond 'with mutual independence' while engaged in the recording process. This conclusion is supported by another photo on the opposite page, clearly from the same session and without Marvin Gaye, that is captioned 'The first Martha and The Vandellas group photo.'[91] The photo of the Cookies, although taken in a recording studio, is also obviously staged—the group is profession-ally lit and carefully placed around the microphone, arms arranged in harmonious lines, the two tallest members at either side. Tellingly, the two Cookies on the left are squashed against each other, positioned not to allow the unencumbered breathing required for singing, but simply so that all members fit in the shot.[92] Genuine *in situ* recording shots—like the one of the Cookies on engineer Brooks Arthur's website—are characterised by ambient lighting, and show singers concentrating on their craft, with space around each other, not dressed identically, and with notes and music stands in evidence.[93] This example demonstrates the pitfalls of an uncritical approach to source material without even the most basic visual analytical skills, or an appreciation of the practicalities of the recording process, and is a serious flaw in an article which pur-ports to shed light on the 'image' of 'girl groups.'* More importantly, it reveals how evidence assembled around unquestioned notions of a 'girl group' genre serves to inaccurately perpetuate an understanding of that genre that is far from unproblematic.

Little wonder that lead singer Mary Weiss bristled at the term 'girl group' being applied to the Shangri-Las. In the 2006 interview con-ducted by Miriam Linna (ML) and Billy Miller (BM) in conjunction with the recording and release of Weiss's solo album *Dangerous Game,* Weiss (MW) made her antipathy clear:

BM: When you gals . . .

MW: You gals?! At least you didn't say Girl Groups.

BM: Sorry Mary. No, I know better than to mention Girl Groups.

MW: Oh, kill me now! Thank you. How do you take an entire sex and dump them into one category? Girl Groups, I mean, please! What if we all had penises?

BM: Uh, that would have seriously affected the crush I had on you as a kid.

---

*I am not aware of these arguments being made about male groups performing in matching outfits—in 1963/4 these included the Beatles, the Rolling Stones, the Ani-mals, the Beach Boys and the Kingsmen, among others. Vocal groups the Tempta-tions and the Miracles were performing in matching outfits as late as 1969.

ML: People tend to categorize . . .

MW: Count me out. If Girl Groups were products, what were Boy Groups?[94]

Weiss raised two significant and related issues here—the lumping together of the groups into one category, and the name given to that category, with its pejorative 'product' implications. The first of these, the dumping of an entire sex in one category, as Weiss put it, has implications beyond 'girl groups,' too. As Brenda Johnson-Grau has shown, the persistent discussion of 'women in rock' and the equally persistent characterisation of rock as 'a male domain' and 'inhospitable to women' since at least the late 1960s has ensured that female musicians are routinely compared to one another on the basis of gender and presented as anomalies in the 'male dominated' sphere of rock:

> These stories, seemingly magnanimous (and inevitably self-congratulatory) in their tributes to female rock 'n' rollers, rob women of their historical presence in rock 'n' roll. Each female musician, in effect, must start from scratch. Each generation (girls and boys) believes that women in rock are somehow 'new.' As a hegemonizing action, it works well. Women artists get defined more by their gender and less by their music. Therefore they (as well as their music and their ideas) are continually marginalized.[95]

The 'girl group' category is a micro version of this macro tendency.

The second, closely related issue Weiss raises has to do with the term 'girl group' itself.[96] Returning for a moment to Greil Marcus's characterisation:

> Girl group rock flourished between 1958 and 1965, and though, with the passing of the Brill Building and the coming of the sophistication of the soul beat, the tradition thinned out, it's still around . . .
>
> 'Group' is merely a convention; the crucial word is 'girl.' Tina Turner's 'River Deep–Mountain High' doesn't fit, because that is a *woman* singing. Raitt and Midler sing as women too, not girls, but it seems to me they look for some of that crazy, blind innocence and simple joy when they take on the classic girl-group songs.[97]

It is noteworthy that Marcus posits the '*sophistication* of the soul beat' against the decline of the Brill Building 'hit factory' style of record making, as if one was a replacement of sorts for the other. Implicitly, soul music is seen as worthier, more authentic, performed by adults; Brian Ward has observed a similar phenomenon with regard to black pop music, which is widely perceived as less 'authentic' and 'legitimate' than 'undiluted' 1950s R&B, and later 1960s soul music.[98] This value judgment is reinforced by Marcus's characterisation of 'that crazy, blind *innocence* and *simple* joy' of '*classic girl-group* songs' (italics mine), which betrays a similar 'nostalgic-fetishistic bent' to that detected by Barney Hoskyns in Betrock's writing about 'girl groups.'[99] There are also echoes here of Theodor Adorno's famous excoriation of 'inauthentic' mass-produced popular music and, as Norma Coates has pointed out, of the Modernist conception (as identified by Andreas Huyssen) of a 'mass culture as feminine/high culture as masculine binary' that informed the work of early rock critics.[100]

This characterisation of the songs performed by 'girl groups' as 'simple' and 'innocent' is a pervasive and recurrent one.[101] Marcus, as we have seen, described them in 1974 as 'simple but embellished and ornamented.' Greg Shaw began his 1982 piece as follows:

> Of all the musical *fads* that came and went in the early Sixties, the *girl-group phenomenon* has succeeded best in retaining its appeal.
>
> For while most of the male teen singers of the period were being groomed for the Vegas route, becoming tame and predictable 'all-round entertainers,' girl groups continued to aim directly at the teenage market. *The singers, for the most part, had little original talent themselves*—the songs were written by contract songwriters and brought to life by producers—but the raw emotion often expressed in their tales of teen anguish captured the hearts and imagination of teenagers everywhere.[102]

Shaw then lauded the merits of the Chantels and the Marvelettes, while failing to mention that both songs on the Chantels' first single, 'He's Gone' b/w 'The Plea'* were written by Arlene Smith, the group's lead

---

*I use here (and throughout) the standard abbreviation used by trade journals including *Billboard*, of "b/w" ("backed with") to indicate and distinguish between the A and B-sides of 7" singles. The A-side was expected to receive airplay and/or chart; often less care was taken with the B-side which was regarded as somewhat

singer, who was fifteen at the time.[103] The copyright on both songs was registered to Arlene Smith and George Goldner, although the presence of his name in no way denotes co-authorship (much more on this later).[104] In fairness to Shaw, mention should also be made here of Greil Marcus's eyewateringly patronising discussion of Arlene Smith, from 1975:

> Goldner drove Arlene mercilessly. She would *sing the songs he gave her* and he would curse; she would sing again and he would scream and order her out of the studio. He kept at it until the tears were coming, until she was ready to do anything to get away from this terrible man, and then Goldner, fully aware that he had before him the greatest voice in rock 'n' roll, would turn his back, shrug his shoulders, and let her sing it one last time. And that was the take he was reaching for. *Arlene, just a little girl really, scared, agonized, would sing for her life.*[105]

Smith and the other members of the Chantels sang together in the choir at their high school, St Anthony of Padua in the Bronx, where they received extensive musical training that included playing instruments and sight reading. Fellow Chantel Lois Harris remembered:

> That was basically where we got the harmony and learned how to sing a cappella. Because a lot of what we sang in church was a cappella. Gregorian Chants, three part and four part Liturgical Music, sung in Latin for the most part.[106]

Greg Shaw also neglected to mention that 'Please Mr Postman,' the Marvelettes' first and most famous single (and Motown's first *Billboard* #1) was co-written by Georgia Dobbins, one of the original members of the group.* It was covered by the Beatles on their 1963 album *With the Beatles*.[107] Shaw went on to praise the 'urgent, *unsophisticated*' voice of Shirley Alston, lead singer of the Shirelles. On this point, Russell A. Potter has observed that the early blues folklorists 'treated its performers as necessarily naive and untutored practitioners of an oral tradition.'[108]

---

throwaway. A double A-sided single was indicated by the use of "c/w," which stands for "coupled with." See Cecil Adams, 'In the record business, what do "b/w" and "c/w" mean?' (online).

* Dobbins was forced to leave the Marvelettes before the song was recorded because her father refused to sign her recording contract, which she, as a minor like the rest of the Marvelettes, could not sign herself.

The two paragraphs Shaw devotes to the Shangri-Las celebrate their 'unforgettable gems of teen melodrama,' but entirely in terms of 'Shadow' Morton and the Brill songwriters. In conclusion, he decided,

> The Girl Groups had made the most honest music of their time. The singers had rarely pretended to be anything more than *naïve teenagers* willing to go along with whatever ideas their producers might have. And the producers for their part never cared about sounding slick— they were after raw emotion which, by and large, they succeeded admirably in capturing. Totally *manufactured* as they were—the singers mere *pawns of the industry*—the girl-group records preserve *a form of charm* as potent as any other.[109]

Shaw managed to praise this music while totally trivialising it as a 'fad,' a 'phenomenon' performed by 'naive teenagers' with 'little original talent.'* In the case of the Marvelettes, the Chantels, and the Shangri-Las, significant input by the performers was omitted by Shaw in favour of a grand 'girl group' narrative that posited the performers as talentless putty, ripe for moulding by genius producers.[110]

The not-so-subtle undercurrent here is that liking this music is a kind of kitsch indulgence, a guilty pleasure that needs to be explained and apologised for. In addition, Greil Marcus and Greg Shaw are (or were— Shaw died in 2004) highly respected music writers; each contributed multiple chapters to the *Rolling Stone Illustrated History of Rock and Roll*, first published in 1976 and in updated editions in 1980 and 1992. That their work has been extremely influential is not open to question.[111] As Norma Coates has argued,

> Early *Rolling Stone* writers, especially Greil Marcus, became creators and keepers of rock mythology, heavily inflected with a masculine accent, thus inscribing spiritual and musical significance into rock music and culture.[112]

---

*Norma Coates has identified a similar set of contradictions at work with regard to the Monkees: 'The critical strategy used in hindsight to evaluate the Monkees is to accept and even celebrate their music as great pop, but to continue to disparage both their origins as a network television band-for-hire who did not write and perform its own music and the audience who catapulted sales of their records and related merchandise to Beatle-esque heights in the mid-1960s.' Coates, 72.

Interviewed as an expert commentator in a 2001 documentary about the Brill Building songwriters, Shaw described the Shangri-Las as 'the tough sluts ... who would go out with "Leader of the Pack" kind of guys.'[113] The degree to which such ideas about all-female groups have remained prevalent among rock critics is exemplified in a 2010 review of the self-titled album by Beaches, a critically acclaimed five-piece gui-tar-based rock group from Melbourne, Australia, who toured the US in 2011.[114] The reviewer called them 'the Australian equivalent of Vivian Girls ... fuzzy and shimmeringly hip gal-rock,' and went on to note that they 'stomp on the wah pedal with enough masculine force' to, among other things, 'make Kim Gordon proud.'[115] After referring to the band as 'some Australian birds,' the reviewer concludes,

> I can't deny liking this a bit (and I'd have liked it even a bit more in 1994) just as I can't deny past ownership of some Velocity Girl records. Could be a massive college radio hit, if college radio meant something anymore.[116]

A superficially positive assessment functions here, as we have seen before, to simultaneously undermine and trivialise its female subjects. Beaches are approached as women first and musicians second; the reviewer compares them only to other females, then apologises to his readers for being unable to 'deny liking this a bit.' The implication is that the reviewer, as a member of the rock cognoscenti, *knows* that music made by women is fundamentally second-rate and inauthentic, but is unable to make the tough decisions and banish it altogether. He has completely absorbed an ideology concerning female musicians—and particularly all-female groups—that can be traced back to the patron-ising and reductive assessments of 'girl groups' that became codified in rock journalism in the 1970s.

Recognising the way in which this gendered categorisation functions is fundamental to understanding why there has been so little serious discus-sion of the Shangri-Las and their body of recorded work. For the Shangri-Las were not 'innocent,' nor was their music 'simple and straightforward.' Their recordings are passionately performed, subtle, intricately arranged, replete with layers of meaning. The subject matter of their songs, as well as the intense emotionality of their performances, engages in a highly sophisticated manner with much earlier currents in the Western artistic tradition. Yet the group has been relegated to a subordinate, gendered category to which sweeping generalisations about naivety, innocence, industry pawns, simplicity and an array of other reductive epithets are routinely applied. In the case of the Shangri-Las, this has meant that the complexities inherent in their music are regularly overlooked. David Quantick, writing in 1983, did a better job than most at offering a sensitive appraisal of their legacy, but of "I Can Never Go Home Anymore," commented,

> It's pro-family propaganda, it's ideologically appalling, but it's a sparkling record. And when the despairing cry of "*Mama!*" rends the air, followed by the whirling violins . . . pardon the cliché, but *this is pop*.[117]

As I will demonstrate in chapter 6, this complex song is far from straightforward 'pro-family propaganda.' For all his enthusiasm, Quantick was swept away on a wave of 'girl group'/producer-oriented/glories of Brill Building gushing and completely missed the point.

Worse still, Greil Marcus concludes his 1974 'girl group' article by running through a checklist of those he lacked the space and/or inclination to discuss in depth, and proclaiming,

> There's the Shangri-Las, great but overrated by critics because their concepts are so perfect for criticism.[118]

It is difficult to imagine anyone dismissing, say, Bob Dylan for having 'concepts . . . so perfect for criticism.' In this one revealing sentence, Marcus acknowledges the quality of the Shangri-Las work but dismisses it as unworthy of in-depth analysis. In his schema, the output of 'girl groups' was 'music of celebration—of simple joy, of innocence, of sex, of life itself, at times.'[119] Rather than questioning the applicability of the 'girl group' moniker, and reflecting on the ramifications of genre, Marcus excoriated the Shangri-Las because they did not fit his criteria for a 'genre' that did not even *exist* when they made their records.

It does seem that Marcus has rethought his position somewhat in the intervening years. In an article about Mary Weiss's return to music in 2007, for which he was interviewed as a critical expert, Marcus claimed that the Shangri-Las were often categorised as a 'girl-group' for 'lack of imagination' (!). He praised their 'storytelling,' their 'characters' and the 'cinematic sense to the songs' that 'left wounds in their listeners.'[120]

Nevertheless, it remains the case that, as Brenda Johnson-Grau has observed, 'the parameters of rock are frequently redefined—after the fact—to exclude the achievements of women musicians.'[121]

There are other significant differences between the Shangri-Las and the groups with which they are routinely categorised. Not the least of these is race—the four members of the Shangri-Las were white, but are considered to be part of a genre whose practitioners were predominantly African-American.[122] I am not suggesting that no one noticed this—although Mary Weiss has related that

> right after *Remember* came out, James Brown hired us to do a Coliseum show in Texas. . . When we did the afternoon sound check, James Brown's mouth fell open! He turned around and looked at me—here's this little blonde girl. He thought we were black. All the other performers were black and we were very nervous because we didn't know how the audience was going to respond.*

Brown's assumption is revealing. Other prominent, chart-topping female vocal groups from New York City who performed songs by Brill Building songwriters were African-American, and it is likely that the Shangri-Las sounded to him like a Black group that had 'crossed over.'[123] The renowned songwriting team of Leiber and Stoller, co-owners of the Red Bird label to which the Shangri-Las were signed, had encountered a similar confusion. Jerry Leiber recounted that when they took some new material to R&B singer Wynonie Harris, Harris said,

> 'If you don't mind boys, I must admit, I didn't know you were white.' We'd run into this a number of times. James Brown thought we were black, too.[124]

The lived experience of racial segregation that characterised US society and extended into the record industry was surely largely responsible for the racial assumptions made by Harris and Brown. US record com-

---

* In the same interview, Weiss related another revealing anecdote: 'They had signs put up COLORED GIRLS' and WHITE GIRLS' bathrooms and I got in a huge fight with a cop because I used the black women's bathroom and he drew his gun on me. I was absolutely amazed. This is backstage in a Coliseum and the white bathroom is on the entire other side of the floor. I really had to go and then get onstage!' Linna, *Mary Weiss of the Shangri-Las*, part 4

panies RCA, Paramount and Columbia set up subsidiary 'race' labels in the 1920s in order to market 'Black' music to a Black audience.[125] By the 1950s, 'race' music had become 'rhythm and blues' (shortened to R&B), and white teenagers were listening to the 'Black' music that would become known as rock and roll on the radio.[126] But what is particularly significant about the Shangri-Las' whiteness is that in the racially charged atmosphere of the USA in the mid-60s it gave them greater freedom to present an image of rebelliousness, both visually, and musically.[127] This is discussed in more detail in chapter 4.

By now it should be clear that 'girl group' is far from being a neutral term, and that deeply embedded in it are historically determined ideas of what a 'girl' is, and, more specifically, of the place of girls and women in rock and popular music. Throughout history, teenagers—particularly teenage girls—have been considered of marginal importance in society, and their roles and interests have consequently been neglected as an object of study. As Jacqueline Warwick has pointed out, 'Girls have little social power, and their interests and concerns are often regarded with derision (if they are noticed at all).'[128]

More recently, however, a growing body of work has succeeded in resituating children and teenagers in historical narratives.[129] Of particular importance in this context are studies that free the concept of 'the girl' from entrenched negative connotations and reconfigure our understanding of girlhood and the experiences of young women and teenagers, especially in relation to popular music. In their essay 'Beatlemania: Girls Just Want to Have Fun,' Barbara Ehrenreich, Elizabeth Hess and Gloria Jacobs argued that 'Beatlemania' was an intense expression of empowerment for young women, and that a crucial part of this was the direction of fervent sexual desire at the Beatles. The authors show that the responses of these young women were not irrational hysteria, which is how they had usually been stereotyped, but something far more complex, and that through them these women were able to envisage a more exciting set of life options than the suburban future expected of them, as the former Beatlemaniacs they interviewed testify.[130] Their study has implications for an understanding of the overt emotionality that characterises the Shangri-Las' recordings, which, as we shall see, even recent writing on the group seems to have trouble taking seriously.

Susan Douglas's *Where the Girls Are: Growing Up Female with the Mass Media* also acknowledges the empowering qualities the Beatles offered to young women, including Douglas herself. In addition, she examines the significance of the Shirelles' enunciation of specifically female adolescent sexual dilemmas on commercial radio in the early 1960s; in doing so she was one of the first scholars to discuss the female teenage singers known as 'girl groups' in an academic/non–rock critic context. She drew attention to the manner in which traditional rock writing 'either ignored . . . or trashed' these performers and their recordings, which, as she makes clear, were narratives of considerable complexity that 'helped cultivate inside us a desire to rebel.'[131] Douglas's discussion of working women also has applications for an understanding of the relationship of the Shangri-Las, and other young women, to the music industry in the mid-60s (see chapter 3).

Lisa Rhodes's analysis of early US rock journalism and her close readings of primary source material in *Electric Ladyland* have informed my own analysis of the origins of the term 'girl group' and the context in which it came into use. As we have seen, it began to gain currency among rock journalists in the early 1970s, and ever since has been integral to negative perceptions of women and girls in relation to rock and popular music. In 'Teenyboppers, Groupies and Other Grotesques,' Norma Coates has explicated the profoundly disparaging characterisations of young girls who followed in the footsteps of the Beatlemaniacs and became known as teenyboppers. The manner in which the 'inauthentic' fan was typified as young, female, and unable to distinguish 'real' from 'superficial' music is central to understanding how the Shangri-Las and many of their vocal group contemporaries came to be relegated to the footnotes of rock narratives.[132]

These themes were developed further in *She's So Fine: Reflections on Whiteness, Femininity, Adolescence and Class in 1960s Music*, edited by Laurie Stras with contributions from Stras herself, Warwick, Coates, and Annie J. Randall, author of an incisive study of Dusty Springfield that illuminates the complexities inherent in her life and work.[133] Stras's essay in this collection examines the vocal technique of young female singers in the 60s; she observed of the Shangri-Las that their nasal Queens accents added to their 'apparent vocal honesty,' which allowed them to connect in a very real way with their teen audience 'as if they were speaking (or whining, or shrieking, or sobbing, or yelling).'[134] Stras argued that this, along with her use of a spoken style of address, gave Mary Weiss a unique and recognisable vocal identity. This is obviously relevant to understanding the emotional conviction conveyed by the Shangri-Las, which quickly became their trademark, and throughout this book I argue that this emotionality is central to a greater recognition of their tremendous abilities as performers.

The work of these scholars has contributed immeasurably to a greater understanding of teenage girls, women, and popular music, especially in the 60s. However, few of them, with the exception of Jacqueline Warwick, devote more than a page or two specifically to the Shangri-Las. And for all the strengths of Warwick's work, which are considerable, an informed understanding of the collaborative process that took place between George 'Shadow' Morton and the Shangri-Las is not enhanced by discussing the Shangri-Las within the 'girl group' genre. Warwick in fact downplays Morton's role with the group, no doubt in response to the chronic overemphasis on the role of the producer which characterises so much writing on 'girl groups' and is central to the perception of 'girl groups' as interchangeable, talentless puppets, as both Warwick and I have demonstrated.[135] In all Warwick's discussions of the Shangri-Las, Morton is only ever referred to as the producer of 'most Shangri-Las recordings'—which he was, of course, but he also *wrote* approximately one third of the songs the group recorded for Red Bird.[136] In a discussion of the roles of Carole King and Ellie Greenwich at the Brill Building, Warwick notes that 'by the time they wrote "Leader of the Pack" in 1964, Jeff Barry and [Ellie] Greenwich had married and decided to collaborate professionally only with one another.'[137]

This implies that Barry and Greenwich were the sole writers of "Leader of the Pack," when in fact Morton is credited as a co-writer. Morton has also claimed that he wrote the song himself, and, despite his considerable truth-obscuring abilities, there is some evidence beyond his own statements to support this claim (see chapter 6). I am not attempting to make a case either way about the authorship of "Leader of the Pack"; I am simply making informed assessments based on the available evidence, with an emphasis on primary source material, about the collaborative process between Morton and the Shangri-Las. Morton's role, while far from unproblematic, *was* central to the unique aesthetics of the Shangri-Las' recordings; it is not necessary to elide his involvement in that process in order to 'rehabilitate' the Shangri-Las.

Warwick's playing down of Morton's role may also be connected to her treatment of the emotionality of the Shangri-Las; it is the material penned by Morton that is the most overtly anguished in their repertoire, particularly "Remember (Walkin' in the Sand)," "Past, Present and Future," and "I Can Never Go Home Anymore." If this material is located within the context of other 'girl groups,' it *is*, by comparison, completely off the emotional scale. This leads Warwick to comment that 'melodrama is undoubtedly the most apt term I could use to describe the oeuvre of the Shangri-Las.' After noting that the 'stormy emotions' enunciated by the protagonist of "Remember (Walkin' in the Sand)" were 'heightened by the sound of waves crashing on the beach and a veritable army of seagulls crying overhead,' she remarks,

> "Past, Present and Future" . . . consists solely of a portentous spoken monologue about suffering in love and trepidation about future romances over a piano part borrowing heavily from the well-known first movement of Beethoven's "Moonlight" Sonata.[138]

Although in musicological terms a 'melodrama' is indeed 'a dramatic work, or a part of one, in which the dialogue is spoken over a musical accompaniment,' the term undeniably carries with it pejorative overtones of emotional sensationalism that is contrived and not to be taken too seriously, especially given Warwick's somewhat distant and irony-tinged tone here.[139] Ada Wolin's lengthy written battle to take this song seriously is even more damning; she asserts that 'Weiss was able to find genuineness in a song that was never meant to be genuine' and that its 'chart aspirations' were 'ludicrous':

> What's off-putting about "Past, Present and Future" is that it's a loose seam in the otherwise neatly sewn world of the Shangri-las, where melancholy is beautiful, jangly and cathartic.[140]

It is two decades since I began writing about the Shangri-Las, and in that time I have found no evidence that the group members, nor anyone else involved in their recordings, regarded their performances as 'melodramatic' and 'portentous,' or perceived "Past, Present and Future" as 'a song that was never meant to be genuine.' Mary Weiss has said she 'always thought "Past, Present and Future" was a unique-sounding record,' and in an interview with Suzi Quatro, in which Quatro described "Past, Present and Future" as 'the Shangri-Las' greatest moment,' Mary reflected,

> I had no conception of what love was at the time. But I really, I had to have almost every light in the studio out on that one, and I was crying my brains out.[141]

The emotion with which the Shangri-Las imbued their performances was unremittingly sincere and central to their artistic accomplishment, their relationship with Morton, and the enduring power of their recordings.[142] My reading of the songs locates "Past, Present and Future" and "Remember (Walkin' in the Sand)" within the heightened emotionalism of 19th-century Romanticism—which is self-suggested by the Beethoven 'sampling' in the song (see chapter 7). This approach offers fresh insights into both songs, demonstrating that the 'girl group' category is only one context through which to examine the Shangri-Las; other frameworks have much to offer, and suggest a very different understanding of the Shangri-Las' and their recordings.

We have established that the term 'girl group' was not in use during the late 50s and early 60s, and as late as 1967, except as one of several descriptive terms; it did not refer to a genre. The young female singers did not think of or describe themselves 'as 'girl groups,' nor did the songwriters they worked with, nor the contemporary music trade or teen press. 'Girl group' was an appellation applied retrospectively by male rock journalists within a largely misogynist critical framework. Both the term itself *and* its use to categorise certain performers on the basis of sex, age, and a variety of recording production values have played a major role in trivialising and marginalising these teenage groups. A 2006 book on the New York Dolls contains the following characterisation, immediately following the passage in which lead singer David Johansen is cited lauding the Shangri-Las as his favourite '60s band:

> There were a lot of girl groups, mainly puppets in the hands of avaricious producers who used them to realise their own musical vision (and make pots of money in the process). The subject matter of their songs had a narrow constituency, being rooted in pure teenage angst,

lust and love . . . handclaps, glamour and sass gave otherwise vapid post rock 'n' roll pop an injection of sexy street smarts. Records like 'He's So Fine' by the Chiffons were simple perfection and struck a potent chord with young lovers everywhere.[143]

"He's So Fine" stayed at #1 on the *Billboard Hot 100* for four weeks in 1963, which hardly indicates that the 'subject matter' of the record 'had a narrow constituency.'[144] Moreover, it was a crossover hit in 1971 for Jody Miller (#5 on the *Billboard* country singles chart, #53 on the *Billboard Hot 100*, #2 on the Easy Listening chart).[145] It is clear that the term 'girl group' has survived into the 21st century with its complex set of deeply rooted negative associations largely intact. The implications of this for the other singing groups who are invariably characterised as 'girl groups' are beyond the scope of this study, but at the very least the term needs to be critiqued and its usage rethought.[146]

When asked by an interviewer about competition between the Shangri-Las and other 'female groups of the sixties,' Mary Weiss answered,

> "Everybody asks me that. I never felt that. I don't feel that the Shangri-Las fit with the other girl bands. We were just . . . us."[147]

Weiss's oft-repeated refusal to allow the Shangri-Las to be catego-rised as a 'girl group' needs to be respected and examined. Despite their persistent categorisation within this 'genre,' it has been widely acknowl-edged that the Shangri-Las were unusual, remarkable and compelling, and that their recordings possess unique qualities that set them apart in certain ways from other 'girl groups.'[148] Ada Wolin, in a discussion that purports to challenge received perceptions of the Shangri-Las and 'girl groups,' doggedly insists,

> This is our challenge while approaching the Shangri-Las—we must consider them as different, innovative, but remain wary of pitting them against their own genre or defining them against some of its essential qualities in order to praise them. The Shangri-Las are a girl-group, so let's talk about girl-groups.[149]

I venture to suggest that if we stop insisting that the Shangri-Las must be labelled a 'girl group,' much less ink will be spilled on redundant astonishment about how different they are from other 'girl groups' and more time can be devoted to their actual artistic achievements. As Laurie Stras has observed: 'Until very recently, few academic articles and even fewer books have discussed girls' contributions to pop music as integral parts of popular culture and social history *on their own terms.*'[150]

It is time to focus on the group and their recordings in a wider historical setting, to look closely at the group members and their place within the music industry in mid-60s New York City. The members of the Shangri-Las grew up very near one another in Cambria Heights, Queens, and it is to this pocket of New York City that we must now travel.

CHAPTER TWO

Queens, Doo-Wop, and Two Pairs of Sisters

> There was a lot of street corner singing.
> I grew up hearing a lot of doo-wop.
> —Mary Weiss

QUEENS

Sisters Mary and Betty Weiss and twins Marguerite (Marge) and Mary Ann Ganser grew up within blocks of each other in Cambria Heights, Queens, New York. Their neighbourhood was in many ways a typical product of the post-WWII housing boom: modest homes for working-class families who aspired to something a little better. The borough of Queens was marketed to young white families as a suburban paradise, with plenty of space, grass, and clean air, and—most importantly—affordable.

Queens was created in 1683 as a county of the province of New York.[1] It had a predominantly agricultural economy until late in the 19th century, when industries, particularly heavily polluting ones, began to relocate there from Manhattan.[2] The opening of the Long Island Railroad (LIRR) in 1861 led to the establishment of suburbs along its route, including Queens Village, Richmond Hill and Flushing, from which it was an easy commute (by rail and ferry) to the business districts of New York City.[3] The western part of Queens County became the borough of Queens when New York City was reconfigured into five boroughs in 1898. In the early decades of the twentieth century, urban expansion of Queens took place at a rapid rate; the opening in 1909 of the Queensboro Bridge, which provided a direct link between Queens and Manhattan, further hastened this development. By 1929 the population of Queens exceeded one million.[4] Many new suburban developments were established; some, like Jackson Heights and Sunnyside Gardens, were planned as middle-class white-collar suburbs,[5] but most were for working families of modest means, like those built in Astoria, Sunnyside and Woodside by the Metropolitan Life Insurance Company in 1922, whose aim was to 'build healthy homes for working class families and realize a profit at the same time.'[6]

The expansion of Queens continued apace during the inter-war period.[7] As demand for affordable housing increased, particularly after World War II, Queens enjoyed a reputation for affordable, family-oriented housing in a 'pastoral environment.'[8] Journalist Carol Taylor wrote in October 1948:

> Ten miles as the crow flies from the Manhattan maze of vertical dwellings . . . is a street named Utopia. It is a street of pretty, one-family houses, of backyard tomato patches and front yard flower gardens, of television sets in the living room and automobiles in the garages.
>
> This is Utopia Parkway, in Bayside, Queens, the borough of homes. Less than two decades ago, the section was farmland. It is still reminiscent of open fields ablaze with black-eyed Susans; of crickets chirping at dusk and woodpeckers a-pecking in the morning.[9]

Taylor deliberately contrasted Manhattan's 'maze of vertical dwellings' with (horizontal) 'backyard tomato patches' and land 'reminiscent of open fields,' portraying an ideal, verdant paradise for families.[10] For many, keen to escape overcrowded neighbourhoods in Brooklyn and Manhattan, the opportunities afforded by a house in Queens were irresistible, as well as economically viable. Henry Petroski moved from Park Slope, Brooklyn to Cambria Heights, Queens, in 1954, when he was twelve. In his memoir *Paperboy*, Petroski, later a distinguished engineer and academic, relates,

> We traded a world of curbs, sidewalks and stoops for one of driveways, lawns and porches . . . On the drive from the old to the new house, my father repeated what he had been saying for weeks: that we were moving up in the world. We were leaving behind an icebox for a refrigerator, a bathtub for a shower, a party line for a private phone, the subway and trolleys for buses and a car.[11]

For Petroski's father, a piece of the spacious suburban idyll that was Queens also meant the acquisition of a middle-class identity, 'moving up in the world.' Some of the more upmarket suburbs in Queens, like Kew Gardens, advertised this a little more forthrightly:

a most charming community both as to architecture and personnel . . . completely safeguarded by beneficial restrictions and by its physical surroundings. These protect it permanently from any possible future contact with undesirable neighbourhoods.[12]

The advertisement proclaimed that this suburb was, and would remain, homogeneous. In other words, Kew Gardens was a white suburb, like many others in Queens. In her study of community politics in postwar Queens, Sylvie Murray noted that, for many grassroots neighbourhood activists, 'the defence of a segregated home was central to forging a middle-class identity.'[13] Suburbs throughout the USA were consciously constructed quite literally along racial lines by means of restrictive covenants,[14] as George Lipsitz explains,

Between 1924 and 1950 realtors throughout the United States subscribed to a national code that bound them to the view that "a realtor should never be instrumental in introducing to a neighbourhood a character of property or occupancy, members of any race or nationality, or any individual whose presence will clearly be detrimental to property values in the neighbourhood."[15]

Within Queens, parts of Flushing and Jamaica were home to growing Black communities, where active NAACP members and community organisations promoted brotherhood and inter-cultural understanding.[16] St. Albans, which bordered Cambria Heights, had been a predominantly middle-class Black suburb since the 1940s, and its prestigious Addisleigh Park enclave was home to many musicians, including Fats Waller and James Brown.[17] These were exceptions, however, and "as late as 1957, New York City's special census of population revealed that, of all the boroughs of New York City, Queens had the largest proportion of all-white census tracts (61 percent, as compared to Manhattan, which had the lowest proportion with 8 percent)."[18] Throughout the 1950s, Queens remained a predominantly white borough.

In his 1947 study of restrictive covenants in the New York area, John Dean found that 'the race clause is becoming customary among restrictive covenants,' and the larger the housing development, the greater the likelihood that a racially restrictive covenant would be applied.[19] Furthermore, as he continued his research,

> the influence of the Federal Housing Administration on race restrictions began to stand out with embarrassing clarity. Covenants with those special building and occupancy restrictions associated with the FHA house almost invariably included a race clause.[20]

In New York, such clauses aimed to restrict both ownership *and* occupancy, and were aimed 'primarily at Negroes.'[21] The following wording was typical:

> 'Said [premises] shall be maintained for the use and occupancy of persons of the Caucasian race, and no race or nationality other than those for whom the premises are intended shall use or occupy any building or lot.'

Exceptions were allowed in the case of domestics and servants.[22]

Further out past Queens, the first Levittown development at Hicksville, Long Island, employed racially restrictive policies even more blatantly, with its founder, William Levitt, famously refusing to sell to Blacks. This was, Levitt argued, 'not a matter of prejudice, but one of business . . . if we sell one house to a Negro family, then 90 to 95 percent of our white customers will not buy into the community.'[23]

Sylvie Murray found that, for many members of the community groups she examined, protecting the value of their investment was of paramount importance, and that maintaining a racially homogeneous neighbourhood was perceived to be integral to this.[24] Such groups could and did exert considerable pressure on tenants. As Stephen Grant Meyer has observed, racially restrictive housing covenants

> reflected a popular unwillingness on the part of whites to have African Americans living in their midst. Before the states and cities enacted restrictive zoning statutes and real estate boards and government agencies developed policies to maintain residential segre-

gation, white homeowners used violence and intimidation to scare blacks out of white neighborhoods.[25]

William Durham was the first Black to move into Cambria Heights in 1960. He recalled rocks thrown at his windows, and crosses burnt on his lawn by white neighbours protesting the presence of him and his family in the suburb.[26] This was despite the Supreme Court declaring restrictive covenants unconstitutional in 1948, an indication that community sentiment often lagged well behind the law.[27]

THE GANSER AND WEISS FAMILIES OF CAMBRIA HEIGHTS

The early inhabitants of Cambria Heights were mainly of Italian, German and Irish descent; many moved there from overcrowded neighbourhoods in Manhattan and Brooklyn.[28] In 1950, 16 percent of the white residents of Queens had been born in another country, and of these the highest percentage (23.8) was German.[29] Herman Ganser was born on 2 May 1909[30] in Gmünd, a small town in the Waldviertel (literally 'forest quarter') region of northeastern Austria, close to what is now the Czech border.[31] Herman's parents, Anna (Mlinarik or Milnaschk) and Alfred Ganser, are buried in the local cemetery; it seems they spent most of their lives in that area as several of their children are buried with them.[32] Not their third son, Herman, though; at the age of 20, he made his way to the French port of Le Havre and on 19 April 1930 boarded the *Calgaric*, a steamship on the White Star-Dominion Line bound for Canada.[33] Herman arrived at the port of Montreal nine days later on 28 April 1930. According to the passenger list, Herman was single, born in Gmünd, Austria, spoke and read German and was travelling to Canada to work as a farm labourer. He answered 'yes' to the question of whether he intended to reside permanently in Canada, and listed his father, Alfred Ganser, also of Gmünd, as his next of kin.[34]

Herman Ganser's immediate destination, as recorded in the shipping ledger, was the CNR (Canadian National Railways) Colonization Department in Winnipeg, where newly arrived immigrants were processed.[35] This is significant because Herman's impetus for travel was likely the aggressive recruitment in Europe of immigrant labour for Canada.[36] As historian Jonathan Wagner explains, failure to attract sufficient numbers of the British immigrants they preferred, despite incentives including resettlement subsidies and assistance with farming equipment, meant that 'Ottawa was forced to increase its recruiting efforts beyond Great Britain . . . by facilitating and encouraging the two main Canadian railways . . . to step up their recruitment efforts on the Continent. The so-called Railways Agreements . . . provided the railways with freedom to recruit "bona fide" farmers and agricultural workers at will in southern and eastern Europe.'[37]

It is clear from even a cursory glance at the log for the *Calgaric* voyage which brought Herman Ganser to Canada that a significant number of the 635 passengers had a similar goal.[38] They came from multiple locations including England, Ireland, Austria, Croatia, Romania, Hungary, Poland, Ukraine and Czechoslovakia. Some women had travelled to work as domestics in Canada; others stated that they were joining their husbands there and were accompanied by children.[39]

It seems likely that Herman worked as a labourer for a time, rather than purchasing land as many others (mainly families) did. However, as the effects of the Great Depression began to really bite in the early 1930s, immigration was drastically scaled back, dropping from 88,000 in 1931 to 11,000 in 1936, and any immigrants who found themselves out of work, unable to work, or in debt, faced the prospect of being deported.[40] This change may well have been a contributing factor in Herman Ganser's decision to cross the border into the USA; perhaps he was able to secure better, more agreeable or stable work there. Whatever the reason, by 1936 he had settled in New York and, at the age of 27, married 20-year-old Rita Conrad in Manhattan on June 14, 1936.[41]

Rita's parents, Mary Walsh (b. 1880) and Peter Conrad (b. 1877), had married in New Jersey in 1915.[42] This was not Peter's first marriage; on 1 May 1898, he had married an Irish woman named Johanna Clancy (b. 1877) in Manhattan.[43] The couple was living in rented accommodation at 624 Greenwich St, New York when the United States Federal census of 1900 was taken on 4 June, with Peter listing his occupation as 'driver.'[44] Their first child Margaret was born on 10 July 1899 but had died on 4 May 1900, so no children were listed.[45] By the time of the 1910 census, they had moved at least three times within a few blocks in the Greenwich/West Village area of Manhattan, and were resident about eight blocks north at 751 Washington Street.[46] On 19 April, Peter and Johanna told the census data collector that they had been married for twelve years and had had seven children of whom five were still living;

of these Irene (9), Harold (4) and Raymond (3) were at home with them on census day.[47]

By the time of the 1915 census, the family's circumstances had changed dramatically. Johanna had been admitted to Bellevue Hospital in Manhattan, baptised on 14 September 1912, and then died shortly afterward of unknown causes at the age of 35.[48] Her funeral was held on 16 September 1912.[49] Bellevue Hospital later became infamous for its psychiatric practices but at that time it was a public hospital where, famously, no one was turned away, irrespective of social standing or ability to pay.

When Peter Conrad remarried in 1915, his new wife Mary (Walsh) inherited Peter's now motherless children. The family had moved again, and were now at 449 West 19th Street in Manhattan.[50] It was into this somewhat chaotic situation that Rita Marie Conrad was born on 18 November 1915, and her brother Gerard Thomas Conrad on 30 October 1918.[51] At the time of the 1920 census, taken on 5 January, the family had been living at 449 West 19th Street since at least 1915, and seven children were living there with Peter and Mary: Irene (18), Peter (15), Harold (12), Raymond (12), Agnes (10), Rita (4) and Gerard (2). Peter was still working as a teamster/driver in the trucking business; his draft card from 1918 lists his employer as W.C. Deyo & Bro., a fruit produce company located at 859 Washington Street, Manhattan.[52]

A month after the 1920 census was taken, Mary Conrad died, on 4 February 1920. The notice for her funeral read:

> CONRAD—February 4. Mary Walsh, beloved wife of Peter M. Conrad and daughter of the late James and Mary Walsh. Funeral from her late residence, 449 West Nineteenth St., Saturday, February 7, at 2 p.m. Interment Calvary.[53]

That the funeral was held at the Conrad home suggests that Mary died there; other notices on the page indicate that home funerals were not uncommon. Given the mid-winter date, it is very possible Mary succumbed to what was then called Spanish Flu, the fourth wave of which hit New York City from December 1919 to April 1920 and disproportionately affected 20- to 40-year-olds.[54] The suddenness of Mary's death, as well as other death notices on the same page that made reference to pneumonia and/or influenza, points to this as the likely cause.[55]

On 2 June 1922, Peter Conrad married a Russian woman named Ludmilla Helen Mascotte.[56] In the New York State census of 1925, Peter and Ludmilla were listed as living at 201 West 145th St in Harlem with Harold (19), Raymond (18), Agnes (16), Rita (9) and Gerard (6). By 1930 the Conrads had moved to Queens and were living in Jackson Heights at 3760 94th Street, near the corner of Roosevelt Avenue. Only Peter, Ludmilla and Gerard (11) were listed as being at home when the census collector visited.[57] Interestingly, given Rita's absence from the Conrad household, there was a Rita Conrad listed in the 1930 census as residing with John and Anna Martin and their three daughters at 409 Beach 130th Street in Far Rockaway, Queens. This Rita was 14 years old and her relationship to the head of the household was recorded as 'nurse,' with the word 'servant' squeezed in at the top.[58] It is entirely possible, given the size of the Conrad family, that the children went out to work as soon as they were able, but whether this Rita was in fact Peter and Mary Conrad's daughter remains unconfirmed. By 1940, Peter and Ludmilla had moved again, and were living at 405 57th Street near the corner of 4th Avenue in the Sunset Park area of Brooklyn. Rita's younger brother Gerard, now 21, was the only one of the children recorded as still living with them.[59]

What we do know, though, is that Peter and Mary Conrad's daughter Rita married Herman Ganser in 1936. The 1940 Federal census records Herman (30), his wife Rita (24) and their three-year-old son Robert as resident at 368 63rd Street in the Sunset Park area of Brooklyn. This address is a five-minute walk from where Peter and Ludmilla were living in 1940; conceivably this has some bearing on how Rita and Herman met—perhaps the Conrads and Herman had been living in the same neighbourhood for some years.[60] This address was home to five other families, so it is likely that this three-storey building was divided into apartments (apartment numbers are not recorded in the 1940 census). All six families indicated that they rented their homes at prices ranging between $35 and $42 per month; the Gansers paid $40 per month for theirs.[61] Rita told the census collector that both she and Herman had been living in New York in 1935, and that Herman worked full-time as a machinist, earning an annual wage of $1400.[62]

Rita and Herman eventually settled in Queens, at 116-19 219th Street in Cambria Heights. Given that the Gansers were still living at this address in 1970, it is probable that they had purchased this as their family home, like many other young families.[63] Rita and Herman Ganser had five children—two boys, Robert and Fred, and three girls: Gail and twins Mary Ann and Marguerite, born in nearby Laurelton on February 4, 1948.[64] The twins attended Sacred Heart Catholic School on nearby 221st Street, from which they graduated after completing eighth grade in 1962.[65] They then attended Andrew Jackson High School in Cambria Heights.

Mary Ann and Marguerite both displayed musical talent early, and had piano lessons (for seven years, according to John Grecco) as well as some training in theory and composition.[66] According to their brother Robert, both twins had a natural, innate musicality and 'ear,' which he attributed to their mother Rita.[67] Rita Ganser was a pianist, and when she was younger had been a sometime nightclub singer who would 'work around in small lounges,' as she put it.[68] She recalled that 'in those days they didn't have . . . microphones,' and commented,

> now if I had had a mic, I would have probably done a little better, but of course I didn't . . . I had to sing a couple of times with a megaphone, believe it or not![69]

Rita particularly praised her daughter Mary Ann's musical talent, noting that she was an accomplished guitarist in addition to her considerable abilities as a singer. Marguerite (Marge) had also written some songs, and the twins sang and harmonised together.[70]

Marge and Mary Ann Ganser knew of sisters Mary and Betty Weiss, who lived a couple of blocks away.[71] Their parents, Harry Weiss (b. 1909) and Elizabeth Ann Treubig (b. 1913), had married on 31 July 1939 in Queens and were recorded in the 1940 Federal census as living at 118-46 220th St in Cambria Heights.[72] Elizabeth worked as a secretary at the Personal Finance Company of New York, which in 1940 had seven branches in Queens and six more elsewhere in New York City.[73] Harry worked as a splicer's helper with the New York Telephone Company, the Long Island Headquarters of which was located at 97-105 Willoughby St, Brooklyn.[74] Cable splicers are listed under 'Telephone Installation and Maintenance Craftsmen' in the US Department of Labor's *Occupational Outlook Handbook* for 1951; their job being to 'splice and maintain aerial and underground cable.' As for splicer's helpers, the *Handbook* noted, 'Cable splicers get their training on the job

Top: a typical street in Sunset Park, Brooklyn, where Rita and Herman Ganser were living in the early 1940s; *below left*: the Ganser family home at 116-19 219th Street in Cambria Heights, Queens, where Marge and Mary Ann grew up; *below right*: a recent photo of the nearby Weiss family home at 118-46 220th Street.

and it usually takes about 4 years to become fully qualified. Workers usually begin as helpers and then are promoted to be assistant or junior splicers. In these jobs they are gradually assigned more difficult tasks as their knowledge of the work increases.'[75]

Harry and Elizabeth Weiss had three children: George, born February 1942,[76] Elizabeth (Betty/Liz) in November 1946,[77] and Mary, born at Jamaica Hospital in Jamaica, Queens, in December 1948.[78]

The Cambria Heights neighbourhood they shared with the Gansers was, as Mary later put it, 'middle to low-middle class' with 'a lot of kids.'[79] According to Henry Petroski, 'Cambria Heights in 1954 was a community of upwardly mobile, or at least upwardly striving, families, most of whom did not require or expect their children to work to earn money.'[80]

If this was the case, the Weiss family was poorer than the average family in their neighbourhood. Mary described their childhood and upbringing as 'difficult':

My father died six weeks after I was born . . . He worked for the phone company and they found him dangling from a pole. People who die young never believe in insurance. We had to raise my mother.[81]

In 1940 Harry Weiss had been a splicer's helper, but by 14 February, 1949, when this horrific accident occurred, he had likely progressed to being a qualified splicer and was perhaps working alone. Cable splicing was clearly a dangerous occupation; in June 1940 *The New York Times* ran a report about Furn Underwood, a splicer's helper rewarded with a Vail Award for 'noteworthy public service' that saved a colleague's life:

While Underwood was assisting in the repair of a telephone cable at Newport Beach, Calif., on Sept. 25, 1939, during a severe storm of wind and rain, he was informed by a passing motorist that there were two men on a pole three blocks away from which there were calls for help.

He found that a power company man, apparently unconscious, was being supported and held free of the power lines by a fellow worker. The man had already come in contact with high voltage power circuits and had received a severe shock and burns.

Disregarding the danger of grave personal injury, Underwood climbed to the top of the fifty-foot pole in the wind and rain. The victim's fellow-worker was at the point of exhaustion when Underwood succeeded in relieving him of the injured man's weight.

Carefully protecting the unconscious man from the dangerous high tension wires, Underwood lowered him to the ground with the help of others who had gathered at the scene. The man later fully recovered.[82]

Harry Weiss was not so fortunate; given his daughter's account, it was likely an accident of this nature that claimed his life.

Her father's death only weeks after Mary was born meant that she 'never knew him':

This actually bothered me more than anyone knows. My father did not believe in insurance, intense poverty ensued for years to come. To men out there that think they are in charge of only supporting your children you are just so wrong. My father was a self-taught person, an excellent photographer, and an exceptional builder.[83]

When the census was taken in 1950, Elizabeth Weiss, aged 36, widowed, was now listed as 'head' of a household of three young children: George (8), Elizabeth (3) and Mary (1).[84] Their mother 'had periodic jobs on occasion, but nothing really substantial.'[85] The family was 'pretty poor' and struggled to make ends meet, a situation Mary later described as 'a hell of a way to grow up.'[86]

For a while, Marge and Mary Ann Ganser and Mary and Betty Weiss all attended Andrew Jackson High School, located close by on 116th Avenue in Cambria Heights.[87] Henry Petroski remembered the school and its environs as having 'a questionable reputation':

It would have been very convenient for me to walk to the school or even to ride my bike and then go to the [Long Island] Press office [where he had a paper route] after school. According to my mother, however, Jackson was a school where there were a lot of gangs and where a lot of gang fighting went on. I had heard about and on occa-

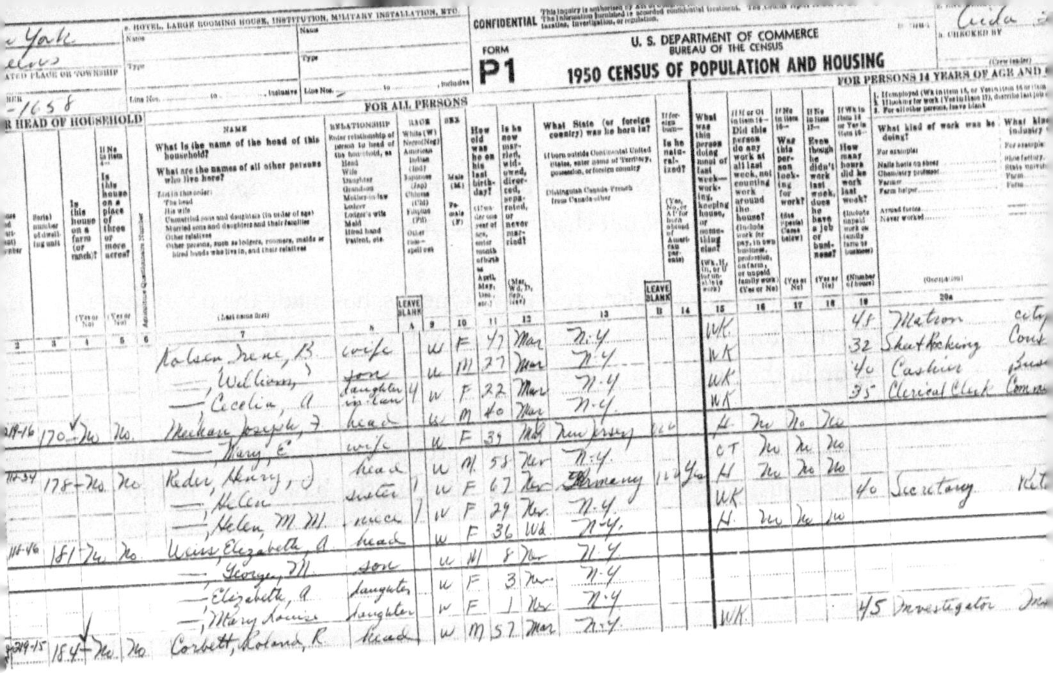

CONFIDENTIAL

FORM P1

U.S. DEPARTMENT OF COMMERCE
BUREAU OF THE CENSUS

1950 CENSUS OF POPULATION AND HOUSING

Census entry (handwritten, best reading):

Name	Relationship	Race	Sex	Age	Marital	Birthplace		Work
Nolsen, Irene B	wife	W	F	47	Mar	N.Y.		48 Matron — city
— Williams	son	W	M	27	Mar	N.Y.		32 Shoe Hocking — Cons
— Cecelia A	daughter-in-law	W	F	22	Mar	N.Y.		40 Cashier — Bus
Meehan, Joseph J	head	W	M	40	Mar	New Jersey		35 Clerical Clerk — Com
— Mary E	wife	W	F	39	Mar	New Jersey		
Rader, Henry J	head	W	M	58	Mar	Germany		
— Helen	sister	W	F	67	Mar	N.Y.		40 Secretary — Ret
— Helen M.M.	niece	W	F	29	Wd	N.Y.		
Weiss, Elizabeth A	head	W	F	36	Wd	N.Y.		
— George M	son	W	M	8	Mar	N.Y.		
— Elizabeth A	daughter	W	F	3	Mar	N.Y.		
— Mary Louise	daughter	W	F	1	Mar	N.Y.		45 Investigator — In
Corbett, Roland R	head	W	M	57	Mar	N.Y.		

Top: 1950 Census entry for the Weiss family; *left*: Linden Blvd. at 218th Street, Cambria Heights, in 1955; *below*: Andrew Jackson High School, where the Weiss and Ganser sisters were students.

sion seen at the *Press* office brass knuckles, chains, zip guns, and switch blade knives, but I had never seen any of them used in a fight.[88]

John Grecco, who also grew up in Queens, has made the point that a degree of toughness and street-wisdom was necessary if you were growing up in the neighbourhood:

> It was not uncommon to have small groups of kids, some gangs and some just neighborhood kids, dividing up the blocks into territories ... nothing as drastic by today's standards, but still enough that you would want to stand up and call anyone's bluff.[89]

Henry Petroski did not attend Andrew Jackson—his parents chose to send him to Holy Cross High School, which was still under construction but taking enrolments for its first classes in the fall of 1955:

> Jackson was also attended by many black kids from St. Albans, and we were not used to going to school with them. Just as they did not deliver the *Press* out of our circulation office, so blacks did not attend Sacred Heart with us. Though we cheered for Jackie Robinson and other blacks who followed him into baseball, dark-skinned people were virtually unknown to us on a personal level.[90]

This observation seems perfectly in keeping with the deliberately constructed homogeneous white neighbourhood ideology that characterised Cambria Heights and much of Queens. It is no coincidence that Petroski's mother associated Andrew Jackson High School with gangs and violence; these were regarded by many as a product of 'lower class' culture and 'undesirable' neighbourhoods, a perception that was inextricably linked to race.[91] Andrew Jackson High was located very close to the border of Cambria Heights with St. Albans, one of the few neighbourhoods in Queens with a predominantly Black population.

The prestigious Addisleigh Park enclave of St. Albans featured stately, freestanding, neo-Tudor–style houses on large allotments, and the suburb had been marketed as an elegant 'English'-style development in the 1920s and 30s.[92] It was bound by racially restrictive covenants until Henry Neely and his wife, despite court action against them, sold their house to a Black family in 1942.[93] This set in motion an uneasy process of white flight which would see Addisleigh Park, after another major court case in 1947, transformed into a suburban haven for Blacks who could afford to buy their way out of the overcrowded neighbourhoods, particularly in Harlem and Brooklyn, to which Blacks were mostly confined.[94] Departing white families seized the chance to inflate their profits by demanding higher prices, knowing their prospective buyers were subject to severely restricted buying options and would have little choice but to pay.[95] Those who could afford to do so included Count Basie, who relocated to Addisleigh Park from Harlem in 1946. Cab Calloway recommended the neighbourhood to Lena Horne, who moved there in 1946.[96] Others included Fats Waller, whose home contained a built-in Hammond organ, double bassist Milt Hinton, John Coltrane, and James Brown.[97] This vibrant musical neighbourhood was only a mile or two away from where the Ganser and Weiss sisters lived. In fact, Mary later recalled,

> We worked with James [Brown] a few times. I was at his house once. He lived in St. Albans, the next town over from Cambria Heights. He had 'JB' on the gate. We were just BS'ing there, basically. I liked him.[98]

Mary also remembered that she had 'often visited gospel tents in St. Albans.'[99] These were large tents erected to function as portable churches and accommodate the revival meetings of travelling evangelists. Music was an integral component of the services. In 1951, a case involving a gospel tent in West Harlem was reported in the *New York Times* due to noise complaints from nearby residents. They described

> gospel meetings [which] were the source of "singing, screaming, organ playing, screeching, and hand-clapping in unison, all interspersed with blood-curdling screams that pierce the air."[100]

The complainant was evidently describing this music in pejorative terms in order to emphasise its alleged disturbance; it was likely that this was also a conflict between an older established family and more recent Southern arrivals.[101] Nevertheless, it is clear from this complaint that the music emanating from the gospel tent was intensely devotional, loud, and passionate.

As noted earlier, Black families began moving into Cambria Heights in 1960, beginning with William Durham. An anonymous poster on the *Gotham Center for New York City History* discussion board remembered moving into Cambria Heights:

> I lived at 118-45 204th Street, between 118th & 119th Avenues. When my family moved there in 1963, we were the first black family on the block. Our next door neighbors were named Lucas. They owned a dry cleaning shop on Farmers Blvd. In less than 10 years after we moved in it seemed like all of the white people were gone . . . except the Lucas[es]. They loved their home and were determined to stay regardless of who else moved into the neighborhood. Mr Lucas had a train set up on a platform that filled his entire basement. He used to always have the neighborhood kids over to see all of his different trains. By 1960s standards that was very cool.[102]

By the time the Weiss and Ganser sisters were approaching high-school age, their neighbourhood was becoming increasingly, if tensely, integrated. By 1969, its demographic had transformed to such an extent that Andrew Jackson High School was described in the *New York Times* as 'in the predominantly Negro Cambria Heights area' and 'rocked by clashes between white and Negro students.'[103]

For Mary Weiss, music was both a refuge and outlet. She recalled,

> 'I always kind of supported myself—it was a question of survival. And I always sang, I sang since I could talk.'[104]

As a child, the harmonising vocal quartet the Ink Spots was a favourite; more on them shortly. A little later, via older brother George's record collection, Mary was exposed to Elvis Presley, Neil Sedaka and the Everly Brothers, who she has regularly cited as a formative influence.[105] While in grammar school, Mary went on a school excursion to Freedomland, a US history–themed fun park in the Bronx. Freedomland was the creation and brainchild of Cornelius Vanderbilt Wood, who had worked closely with Walt Disney on Disneyland until the pair had a dispute that resulted in Wood's dismissal from the company. Freedomland opened in 1960 and in 1962, in an attempt to bolster falling visitor numbers, began featuring performances by celebrity artists in the newly built 'Moon Bowl,' which had '4000 seats and a 15,000-square foot dance floor.' In a season that ran from 27 May through September 9, 1962, 'big names' including Paul Anka, Xavier Cugat, Stan Kenton, Bobby Rydel, Benny Goodman, and the Everly Brothers were booked to play at Freedomland.[106] The Everly Brothers played there on 20 August 1962; it seems that a young Mary Weiss was in the audience.[107] She remembered being

> very influenced by the Everly Brothers ... I think a lot of people were, more so than they've gotten credit for actually, because it's all there, just in those two parts, everything is there, if you're into harmony. I remember the first concert I ever saw was the Everly Brothers. I was in grammar school and I went to Freedomland and I saw them live, it was great.[108]

Taking inspiration from a variety of influences and drawn together by a love of music-making and singing, the Ganser and Weiss sisters 'climbed trees together and harmonized,' and were singing together in earnest by the time Mary was twelve.[109] According to Mary, song parts came together easily and naturally 'because we were all very much into harmony, so it kind of just fell into place by itself.'[110]

DOO-WOP

The repeated emphasis on harmony evident in Mary Weiss's discussions of her musical practice is significant. She noted, when discussing her early musical influences,

> 'When I was about 13 or 14 we hung out at a place called Ed's,' she recalled. 'There was a lot of street corner singing. I grew up hearing a lot of doo-wop.'[111]

Mary recalled that she, Betty and the Gansers sang together at each other's houses, in the playground, and in the street:

> The neighbourhood I grew up in, there were maybe 300 kids around the same age or in the same age bracket, and we used to sing on the street corner, all of us, so that's how we really got started.[112]

A cappella vocal harmonising—doo-wop, as it came to be known—was *the* teen music of New York City and Long Island in the late 1950s and early 1960s. The *Oxford English Dictionary* entry for 'Doo Wop' lists the earliest occurrence of the term in a review of "Kiss Me Again and Again" by the De Villes, in *Billboard*, 5 May 1958. The B-side of this single was called "Do Wop," of which the reviewer noted: 'Male lead shouts a fair chorus with "do wop" rhythm backing by the group.'[113] This is descriptive: the reviewer is describing a literal backing of singers singing the non-narrative harmonic/percussive syllables 'do wop do wop,' so the term is not being used to refer to a genre. Like 'girl group,' 'doo-wop' was applied retrospectively as a stylistic descriptor; according to Anthony Gribin and Matthew Schiff, it seems to be largely untraceable before 1969. Gribin and Schiff also note that doo-wop

> didn't have a name until its popularity had already waned. It was never considered as a separate entity in its heyday, being subsumed under the general categories of rock 'n' roll, rhythm and blues, '50s music or oldies (after 1960).[114]

The Mills Brothers, who formed in Ohio in the 1920s, were the first Black vocal group to achieve widespread commercial success with both black and white audiences and were noteworthy forerunners of doo-wop. Significantly, when the group first began having hits in 1931, the members were teenagers, ranging in age from sixteen to twenty.[115] The Ink Spots followed in their footsteps; they formed a few years later and had their first hit in 1939. With their emphasis on vocal harmonising and smooth ballads, they also achieved significant mainstream success, performing with Glenn Miller's Orchestra, appearing in movies and regularly breaking attendance records.[116] The Ink Spots were an important antecedent of the teenage vocal groups that formed in the late 40s and 50s, singing in a style that would later be known as doo-wop. Their popularity was such that a young Mary Weiss heard enough of their harmonising to cite them as an influence. And for young Black teenagers, the influence of the Ink Spots was not merely stylistic—it demonstrated that a Black group in the USA could make it big and be a commercial success. For poor adolescents looking at bleak and severely racially restricted futures, this possibility was an alluring one.[117]

Such adolescents were extremely vulnerable to exploitation by unscrupulous music industry operators, and there are countless tales of the manipulation and abuse of teenagers and young people in the music industry that extend well beyond the 50s and 60s. Grace Palladino writes in her history of teenagers:

> Rock 'n' roll offered teenagers opportunities, but it did not provide protection or guarantee success. As countless would-be stars learned the hard way, desire and ambition counted for very little unless teenagers had the discipline to work hard and learn the industry's ropes, something they were rarely willing to do when visions of easy money and celebrity danced in their heads.[118]

Implicit in this is the notion that 'work[ing] hard' and learning the 'industry's ropes' could somehow enable high school kids to transcend the machinations of ruthless industry professionals who had a vested interest in making sure they did not. Moreover, the exploitation of artists was enshrined legally in standard music industry contracts, which were specifically constructed to direct revenue away from the artist.[119] The experiences of groups like the Frankie Lymon and the Teenagers have ensured that it is now common knowledge that artists should not sign contracts without legal advice, but this was not the case in 1956. In addition, prevailing racial codes make the presumption patently ludicrous that music attorneys would be accessible, financially or otherwise, to impoverished Black adolescents in Harlem. Even in cases where attorneys might be accessible, this was not automatically advantageous; Katherine Anderson of the Marvelettes recalled,

> My mother did have a copy of the contract and she had gotten together with a couple of the other parents and did try to find an attorney that could help them in regards to the contract, but no one [in Inkster] was aware of entertainment and entertainment law . . . there was no such thing as an entertainment lawyer.[120]

The activities of unscrupulous operators in a largely unregulated industry were allowed to remain unchecked, and the financial rewards were enjoyed by label owners and managers at the expense of their vulnerable teenaged performers.

Doo-wop had its roots in the Black ghettos that were a product of the great postwar northern migration of Blacks to industrial centres including Chicago, New York, Pittsburgh and Philadelphia.[121] Restrictive covenants, like those effective in Queens, were in place across the USA; they confined Blacks to specific areas of cities and contributed greatly to overcrowding and poverty.[122] Many impoverished teenagers, still in school, some with training in the gospel vocal traditions of harmonising and call-and-response, as well as exposure to rhythm and blues, sang. Typically, this took place in the street, outside their overcrowded tenement apartments and away from their parents.[123] This was common in New York, especially in Black and Puerto Rican neighbourhoods:

> Street-corner talent-spotting became the normal way for a group to obtain a record contract. An audition from the guy who crossed the road to listen might mean gifts for all the folks and a shiny Cadillac. As groups proliferated, the age at which they turned professional took a nosedive. They called themselves the Classmates, the Juniors, the Sixteens, establishing a solidarity between themselves and their audience.[124]

Doo-wop groups generally consisted of four or five members with 'wide ranging voices' singing in group harmony. Usually this was some configuration of lead, first tenor (sometimes falsetto), second tenor, baritone and bass. No expensive instruments were required; voices cost nothing. Rhythm came from handclaps, finger snaps, or punctuating bass singing (bom bom bom BOM, for example).[125]

In the main, doo-wop was sung by teenagers for teenagers; it was often written by them too. Lyrics tended to be uncomplicated and repetitive, and focused almost solely on teenage concerns—the confusion and longing of love and its various entanglements. In the view of doo-wop commentators Gribin and Schiff,

> Taken together, the lyrics and melodies of doo-wop songs reach the hormones and emotions but do not offer much in the way of intellectual stimulation.[126]

Doo-wop almost always employed nonsense syllables, like ooo-wah, shoo-wop, mmm-bop and similar variations, which provided a vehicle for the harmonic vocalising accompaniments of the other members around the lead singer.[127] In 1954, two significant doo-wop releases, "Gee" by the Crows, and "Sh-Boom" by the Chords, were 'crossover' hits on the pop as well as R&B charts.[128] In early 1955, reviewing the previous year in music, *Billboard* ran several articles in a section entitled 'Spotlight on Rhythm and Blues: Talent, Tunes and Records.' It was noted that 'the most important story in the r.&b. field last year was its new-found sales versatility, with r.&b. disks breaking into the pop market with amazing regularity thruout 1954,' and that 'the demand for the platters in the pop field was mainly sparked by teen-agers.'[129] In addition to the spending power of teenagers, this also acknowledged that white teens (the 'pop' market) were buying records by Black ('r.&b.') artists. The power of radio was central to these developments, as Susan Douglas points out:

> whites themselves—the DJs, the performers, and their fans— embraced a hybridity that confounded and defied the existing racial order. And it was precisely because of radio's invisibility that such hybridizations could flourish.[130]

In many ways, George Goldner's approach to releasing records epitomised this idea of hybridity.

GEORGE GOLDNER, FRANKIE LYMON AND ARTIE RIPP

Teenage rock and roll/rhythm and blues singing, later known as doo-wop, was put firmly on the national map with a record released early in 1956 by a group of Harlem high school students. When *Billboard* reviewed "Why Do Fools Fall in Love" by Frankie Lymon and the Teenagers in February 1956, the writer noted that it was 'a hot new disk' that 'could easily break pop.'[131] It did, reaching #1 on the R&B charts and #6 on the pop charts; it was also a #1 hit in the UK.[132] It was released on the Gee label, which was founded, owned, and managed by George Goldner. Born in New York City in 1918, Goldner worked briefly in the garment industry before opening a chain of dance halls. He became increasingly fascinated with Latin music, partly due to the influence of his Puerto Rican wife, Gracie.[133] Goldner established Tico Records in 1948 as a means to release music in the United States by Latin stars Tito Puente and Machito, among others. In 1953 he began releasing rhythm and blues records on his newly created Rama label.[134] One of the most significant signings to Rama was very popular doo-wop group the Valentines, whose singer Richard Barrett brought Goldner Lymon and the Teenagers. In addition to working closely with them alongside Goldner, Barrett would also discover the Chantels, forming a similar relationship that would result in their signing to another of Goldner's labels.[135] Also released on Rama was "Gee" by the Crows, one of the first doo-wop songs to be a crossover hit on the pop charts. Goldner named his next label Gee, after the Crows hit, and the second release on Gee was "Why Do Fools Fall in Love."

"Why Do Fools Fall in Love" was an immediate and enormous hit; significantly, Frankie Lymon, who was 13 at the time, and George Goldner were credited as the authors.[136] Newspaper articles, concert bookings and television appearances speedily ensued. Fellow Teenager Jimmy Merchant recalled that the first few months of 1956 were a whirlwind of performances, television appearances, record hops, photo-shoots, newspaper and magazine interviews:

> They took us out of public school and by February we were in a private school, Quintano's School for Young Professionals, located in mid-town. When we were in town, we attended Quintano's. When we were out of town, we did correspondence and had a private tutor.[137]

As the Teenagers' popularity increased, so did demand for their public appearances. In a scenario that will become increasingly familiar, the Teenagers were 'pulled out on the road for strings of thirty, forty and even sixty one-night shows.'[138] These tours were gruelling, chaotic, physically and emotionally dislocating, and largely unsupervised. In mid-1957, while on tour in London, the group imploded amid mounting frustration that Lymon was being marketed with increasing prominence and the other members marginalised. Matters came to a head when the rest of the group found out that Lymon was in the process of recording a solo album, *Live at the London Palladium*. Their new manager, notorious music industry figure Morris Levy, apparently decided that the best way to solve the dissension was for Lymon to leave the group and pursue a solo career.[139]

How Morris Levy came to be managing Frankie Lymon and the Teenagers can be traced to his relationship with George Goldner. As noted earlier, Goldner had established a series of pioneering Latin and rhythm and blues labels, including Gee, to which Lymon and the Teenagers were signed. In 1956, he also co-founded the Roulette label with Levy. However, early in 1957, *Billboard* announced,

> George Goldner has sold his interests in the Roulette, Rama, Gee and Tico labels outright to the Morris Levy combine and has resigned from his artist and repertoire duties with Rama, Gee and Tico.[140]

In addition to owning a record label, Levy owned the famous Manhattan jazz club Birdland. His ties to the Mob and close involvement with the Genovese crime family were an open secret; Levy regularly engaged in extortion and employed Mafia figures as brutal enforcers.[141] Decades later, in 1986, Levy and Gaetano Vastola (a mobster from the DeCavelcante family who had financial interests in the Roulette label) would be indicted by a federal grand jury for extortion.[142] What the 1956 *Billboard* article neglected to mention, unsurprisingly, was that Goldner was a chronic gambler and had been in the habit of borrowing funds from Levy to cover his often crippling debts from betting on horse races. The mass label sell-off by Goldner was one of Levy's methods of debt recovery.[143] Another was the false attribution of songwriting credits, as we shall see shortly. If the song was in question was a hit, songwriting royalties could be incredibly lucrative; they were far more substantial than the performance royalties received by the artists.[144]

Frankie Lymon and the rest of the Teenagers, through no fault of their own, were caught in the middle of Levy and Goldner's machinations. Levy acquired Lymon as part of his buyout of Goldner's Gee label, which took place in April 1957, while the group was in London. Levy already had Lymon working on *Live at the London Palladium*, which was issued on his Roulette label later in 1957. Since Lymon was clearly a phenomenal talent, and was credited as the writer of "Why Do Fools Fall in Love," he was Levy's primary concern. It is likely that the impetus for Lymon's departure from the Teenagers came from Levy; Lymon recalled in 1967, 'At that time, it was felt that we could make twice as much money with two separate and independent acts as we could with one.'[145]

The Teenagers kept recording for Goldner without Lymon. After selling his labels to Levy, Goldner then established two new ones, End and Gone, and the Teenagers released two singles on End in 1960.[146]

The first album produced and released by Goldner on End, in October 1958, was by the Chantels, whose hit "Maybe" was later covered by the Shangri-Las.

As separate entities, neither Lymon nor the Teenagers could repeat the triumphs they had achieved together, and after some brief success Lymon's career foundered. With the benefit of hindsight, it is not difficult to comprehend that Lymon's impoverished childhood left him, barely into his teens, completely ill-equipped to handle the pressures that came with having a nationwide hit, and vulnerable in the extreme. He said later,

> In the neighbourhood where I lived, there was no time to be a child. There were five children in my family, and my folks had to scuffle to make ends meet. My father was a truck driver and my mother was a domestic in white folks' homes. While most kids my age were playing stick ball and marbles, I was working in the corner grocery store carrying orders to help pay the rent.[147]

Lymon added,

> 'I've known all about women as long as I can remember. When I was ten, I made a good living hustling prostitutes for the white men who would come up to Harlem looking for Negro girls. I knew every prostitute in our neighbourhood and I'd get a commission for every customer I brought them. I was a fresh young kid and some of them thought I was cute. Sometimes, they'd pay me off with something extra . . . the kids in my neighbourhood grew up fast. Smoking 'pot' (marijuana) was so commonplace that kids 11 and 12 years old puffed reefers on the street corners. I had been smoking marijuana when I was in grade school. But I didn't start using the real stuff (heroin) until I got into show business.'[148]

While partying with other musicians, in all likelihood after a show and/or on tour, he was introduced to heroin in 1958 at the age of 15, and quickly developed a chronic addiction. Lymon spent the next ten years making various abortive attempts to record again and overcome his addiction, as well as lengthy periods as a down-and-out street addict and a stint in the army. In 1967 he was hospitalised; after treatment he emerged with new management and hopes of making a comeback, but he died of an overdose in the Harlem apartment where he had grown up in February 1968. He was 26.[149]

While all this was going on, Levy and Goldner were engaging in unscrupulous manoeuvring with the writing credits for "Why Do Fools Fall in Love." Richard Perez-Pena, covering the 1992 federal court case over the song for the *New York Times*, described what had taken place as a 'tangled history of music-business chicanery' in which 'Mr. Lymon and Mr. Goldner, not [fellow Teenagers] Mr. Merchant and Mr. Santiago, were named in the copyright as authors':

> "We were ignorant," Mr. Merchant said. "We did not understand contracts. We didn't know what publishing was. We didn't know about percentages. They said, 'We'll take care of you; the money will be there when you turn 21' and we believed them."[150]

Perez-Pena reported further,

> Most of the royalties went to Mr. Goldner and Morris Levy, who was an important promoter and music company owner in the early days of rock-and-roll, and the music companies they owned. In 1964, Mr. Goldner mysteriously signed over the copyright to "Why Do Fools Fall in Love" and other works to Mr. Levy, asserting that he had mistakenly taken songwriting credit that belonged to his colleague.[151]

Attempts by Merchant and Santiago to redress this situation were received with threats and intimidation, and Santiago testified that 'a record company executive told him in 1969 that his life would be in danger if he pursued his claim.' In its coverage of the trial, *Billboard* reported,

> the jury found that Goldner and Levy had 'deliberately' concealed the accrual of royalties for the song from Merchant and Santiago, both of whom were fifteen when the song was written . . .

Jurors also found that Levy had threatened Merchant and Santiago with 'physical force' which partly explained why the lawsuit had not been brought sooner.[152]

The jury ultimately ruled that 'Frankie Lymon might have had some role,' but that Teenagers Jimmy Merchant and Herman Santiago 'were the true and rightful authors' of the song. Their legal team estimated that they stood to receive something in the order of $4 million each in royalties. Lymon *had* been receiving royalties, but as Merchant explained, 'In the beginning, I was angry at Frankie, but through the years, I began to realize that he was completely manipulated by these people.'[153]

The jury's findings were entirely consistent with other reports of Levy's behaviour.[154] Tommy James, who with his group the Shondells had a nationwide hit with "Hanky Panky," signed with Roulette in 1966. He remembered the first time he visited Morris Levy in his office:

> Morris excused himself and walked out into the hallway. Even though they were trying to be quiet, I could hear every word clearly. Evidently they had just beaten up some guy in New Jersey with baseball bats who they believed was bootlegging their records. They were giving Morris the details. Everybody in the room was trying to pretend they could not hear.[155]

In a decision that Merchant and Santiago must have found devastating, the jury's findings from the 1992 case were overturned on appeal in 1996, largely, it was argued, because legal proceedings should have commenced earlier.[156] To this day, the performance rights organization BMI lists 349 songs for which Morris Levy, who never wrote a song in his life, is credited as writer or co-writer. These include "Why Do Fools Fall in Love," and "Gee," the Crows hit that George Goldner had named his label after.[157]

As the appalling circumstances surrounding "Why Do Fools Fall in Love" show, no amount of hard work and learning the ropes on the part of Frankie Lymon or the Teenagers could have given them any control over the behind-the-scenes skulduggery engaged in by Goldner and Levy, particularly the latter's mob-connected enforcements, which rendered him victorious even from the grave (Levy died in 1990). The actions of unscrupulous operators in a largely unregulated industry were allowed to remain completely unchecked and, unfortunately, provided inspiration for at least one other young industry hustler determined to grab a share of the financial rewards such opportunities presented.

In 1956, at the age of about 16, Arthur Marcus "Artie" Ripp had been part of a white Queens-based doo-wop group called the Four Temptations. (It should be noted at this point that, although the roots of doo-wop were Black, by the mid-1950s there was also a considerable number of white doo-wop groups.[158]) Ripp's group recorded a single that was released in 1958 on ABC-Paramount, a major label formed in 1955 in New York City. Unlike other major labels at the time—Decca, RCA, Columbia—that were not particularly interested in marketing music to teenagers, ABC-Paramount saw their market potential and would often license recordings from independent producers.[159] It is likely that this is how ABC-Paramount came to release the Four Temptations single, "Cathy" b/w "Rock n Roll Baby," on which Artie Ripp was credited as co-writer of both songs.[160] The single was reviewed favourably in *Billboard*:

> **Cathy** Rocka-rhumba has a fair sound from male group and combo. Bears watching.
> **Rock and Roll Baby** Driving rocker is nicely handled by lead and group, with guitar solo work. Can do some business.[161]

The single's moderate success led to two more, for which the group dropped the 'Four' and used the name the Temptations—"Barbara" b/w "Someday," and "Letter of Devotion" b/w "Fickle Little Girl." Ripp was credited as co-writer on all four sides.[162] Both singles were released in 1960 on the Goldisc label, and "Barbara" received four stars in *Billboard*, with the reviewer noting that it 'features an appealing vocal by the lead with an okay group assist' and 'can sell.' The B-side, "Someday" had a 'pleading vocal by the lead on the pounding rockaballad . . . nicely backed by the group.'[163] A few weeks later, an advertisement taken out in *Billboard* proclaimed, 'First release on Goldisc an overnight hit! "BARBARA" The Temptations GOLDISC #3001.'[164]

The Goldisc label was established, owned, and run by George Goldner. Ripp would later explain that 'I saw George Goldner and bugged him about a job and taking the song ["Barbara"].'[165]

Artie Ripp, once described as someone who could 'hardly hit the right keys' and possessing 'a voice like a hinge,' was by his own admission insufficiently adept at singing and songwriting to make a career out of either.[166] He explained that in the early 1960s,

George Goldner and the members of the Teenagers on the cover of *Cash Box*, April 14, 1956. *Left to right*: Teenagers Herman Santiago, Sherman Garnes, Joe Negroni, and Jimmy Merchant, Goldner, 13-year-old lead singer Frankie Lyman, and Joe Kolsky, Goldner's partner in Gee Records.

Morris Levy, president of Roulette Records, pictured in *Billboard* (July 20, 1959) as part of a "series of industry personality statements."

Kama-Sutra principals Hy Mizrahi, Artie Ripp, and Phil Steinberg, with MGM Records Lenny Scheer (left) and president Mort Nasatir (seated) as they signed a distribution deal with MGM in 1965. (*Billboard*)

I started walking around Broadway and I'd see these kids who were making records and not getting paid. They could have a Number 1 record on the charts and end up owing the record company half a million dollars.

I thought, "This business has some system."

Every party was charged to the artist. "I've got a hundred hookers. Charge them to the artist."

Here I was, out of high school, no diploma, not going anywhere. The music business seemed terrific, so I decided I needed to learn absolutely everything I could about it—A&R, promotion, sales, publishing.[167]

Having written (or at least, acquired the credit for writing) and performed on a few records, Ripp had grasped clearly and quickly that the substantial financial rewards in the recording industry were not made by the artists. He saw teenage performers who recorded hits going unremunerated, while those involved in the production, manufacture and distribution of the records seemed to be reaping substantial profits. Since this 'seemed terrific,' Ripp set about learning how to get part of the action:

I looked to find that one guy who owned his own company, who produced his own records, someone who was a creative, entrepreneurial kind of hustler. And that's how I got to George Goldner, owner of Rama and Gee Records...

I said, "Mr. Goldner, you're the greatest. I have to work for you. I want to be the next George Goldner. I need twenty dollars a week. I'll come in from Queens. I'll work seven days a week, twenty-four hours a day, whatever you want." He must have had pity for me. He gave me fifty dollars a week.

A year later, I had a car and I was the third-highest-paid person in the company. And learning. All the time learning.[168]

George Goldner was twice Ripp's age, with a track record of high-quality productions and hit releases on his labels. Despite his less than honourable business practices, he was reputed to possess an infallible ear for a hit, while also being a tyrant in the studio. There is little evidence to suggest Ripp possessed any such qualities, but by 1960 he had inveigled his way into a job as Goldner's assistant at Gone and End Records. Its offices were at 1650 Broadway, in a building that was wall-to-wall record labels and music publishers, and adjacent to the Brill Building at 1619 Broadway.[169] When the Gone and End labels went the way of Gee and Rama, again sold to Morris Levy to pay off Goldner's gambling debts, Ripp stayed in the building and got a job promoting songs at the publisher Aldon Music.[170] Ripp then struck out on his own in 1963, forming Kama Sutra Productions with Phil Steinberg and Hy (Herman) Mizrahi.[171]

THE SHANGRI-LAS

In 1962 or early 1963, Ripp saw a young and as yet unnamed quartet of female singers performing in Queens. The Weiss and Ganser sisters had practiced their harmonising and dance moves, and progressed to performing at 'little hops and dances and things like that,' since they were 'too young to be in a bar' or to perform at clubs.[172] Mary and Betty's older brother George had been accompanying them as a kind of quasi manager/chaperone.[173] Probably at some point in 1963, Artie Ripp signed the quartet to 'an exclusive contract' with Kama Sutra Productions. According to John Grecco,

> At this point, Kama Sutra Productions was still trying to get a foothold in the industry and would sign acts, record them and then sometimes shop the master tapes around to different labels.[174]

By this time, the group had acquired a manager, Tony Giannattasio, better known as Tony Michaels.[175] Although he was not a 'president' of, or officially involved with Kama Sutra, it seems he must have had at least a working relationship with Ripp and Kama Sutra, if not more, since Michaels is listed as co-writer with Hy Mizrahi on at least two songs, "Girl to Girl" and "Seven Strong."[176] Michaels and Ripp were both involved in the recording of the quartet's first single, which, according to Mary Weiss, provided the impetus for the naming of the group.[177] About to make a record and without a name, they went past a restaurant on Long Island called the Shangri-La, and decided to call themselves after it.[178]

The Shangri-Las' first single was "Simon Says" b/w "Simon Speaks," released late in 1963 on the Smash label.[179] Smash had been launched in

1961 as a subsidiary of Mercury Records, because, as Shelby Singleton explained,

> if you had more than five or six records in the radio station's Top 40 chart on the Mercury label, a disc jockey would say to me, "Now look, I know the record's great, but I can't put it on because you got too many records on the play list." So we just started another label, Smash. Columbia did the same thing when they started Epic . . . we all did the same thing to stop getting the disc jockey in trouble.[180]

The A and B sides of the Shangri-Las' Smash single were essentially the same song; "Simon Speaks" is a predominantly instrumental version (lead vocal replaced with saxophone) of "Simon Says," which is an infectiously catchy, blues-based dance song ('Simon says a-well shake your hips') with a Bo Diddley beat. According to Mary, her older sister Liz sang the lead on this track.[181] A spoken introduction, 'the Four Season(s) proudly present the dynamic Shangri-Las!' and crowd cheering imply that this is a live recording, but this could just as easily be a studio conceit.[182]

According to John Grecco, this record was not released until around a year after it was recorded.[183] The writing credits are instructive—Tony Michaels received sole credit for the A side, 'Simon Says,' while the mainly instrumental version of the same song on the B-side is credited to Hy Mizrahi and Phil Steinberg, Artie Ripp's two partners in Kama Sutra Productions. It is likely that Tony Michaels wrote the song (as he would later co-write some of the group's strongest material), and Mizrahi and Steinberg received a writing credit as part of Kama Sutra's cut. Later events will bear this out, and, as we have seen, songwriting credits were not necessarily an indication of authorship.

"Simon Says" appeared in the 'Four-Star Singles' list, in *Billboard*'s last issue for 1963. This rating, noted *Billboard*, 'is awarded to new singles with sufficient commercial potential in their respective categories to merit being stocked by dealers, one-stops and rack jobbers handling that category.'[184] Even better, *Cash Box* reviewed "Simon Says" and included it in its 'Best Bets' singles section, noting that:

Songsters and musicians have a happy-rock-time-of-it here, and their zest could get strong teen acceptance. A wild, party-time date that should be eyed closely.[185]

The B-side, "Simon Speaks", heralded 'further rock joy', according to the Cash Box reviewer. The arrival of the Shangri-Las on the recorded music landscape did not go unnoticed, and it appears that there may have been something of a buzz about the group, even at this very early stage.

The second Shangri-Las single was released in April 1964 on the Spokane label—"Wishing Well" b/w "Hate to Say I Told You So."[186] "Wishing Well" is credited to Tony Michaels and Joe Monaco, who, with his brother Marty, had the small Dynamic Recording Studio in the basement of a house in Hicksville, Long Island.[187] It is likely that the single was recorded there, especially since, as we shall see, Monaco and Michaels had been collaborating and using the studio for other projects since the late 1950s. Betty sang lead again on both these tracks; Mary has indicated that Betty was originally the group's lead singer. [188] The record was a moderate success locally, and both sides feature short reverb-laden spoken-word intros. This is noteworthy, as the Shangri-Las would eventually become famous for spoken-word sections in their songs. George 'Shadow' Morton is generally assumed to be responsible for this aspect of their work, but he apparently had no involvement with the group at this point. It may well have been a technique of their own for which they have never received acknowledgement or credit. The Shangri-Las' version of "He Cried" (1966), originally recorded as "She Cried" by Jay and the Americans in 1962, also features a spoken intro, one that is found neither in the Jay and the Americans version nor in other roughly contemporary versions by Del Shannon and Billy Fury.[189]

Around this time, according to Mary Weiss, their manager Michaels arranged a meeting for them with popular and influential WABC radio DJ Bob 'Babalu' Lewis. Weiss has recalled that when she and her sister were growing up, they listened to 'Babalu, and Cousin Brucie on WABC' and would ring up and vote for their favourite new releases.[190] Celebrity disk jockeys wielded considerable power, and their relationships with their teenage audience could mean massive sales for the record companies that received airplay.[191] 'Cousin Brucie' Morrow has stated emphatically, 'The mid-fifties doo wop boom was due to the burgeon-

Above and right: the Shangri-Las
(misspelt Shangra-Las!) first single
"Simon Says" on Smash (1963);
below: their second single "Wishing
Well" b/w "Hate to Say I Told
You So", originally released on the
Spokane label in April 1964; this
is the Scepter reissue from January
1965 (*both from author's collection*).

ing relationship of radio and the record industry. Symbiosis between the two was yielding unprecedented success for both.'[192]

An audience with Lewis, then, was an important coup for the group. Mary related,

> Tony Michaels . . . wanted Bob Lewis to hear us singing so he had made an appointment and we went up to his apartment, just to hear us, and we got up and sang for him a cappella. George was there, Shadow, sitting there. And that's when I met him.[193]

Again, a cappella, vocal harmony. The Shangri-Las emerged as a late, pop expression of this particular tradition of vocal harmonising, not from the band tradition which later became the norm—the singers categorised as 'girl groups' are to a large extent female doo-wop groups. They were singers, and, like the groups that influenced them, their musical interests revolved around harmonising. Most of the record industry figures who were involved with the Shangri-Las, especially before the group became famous, also had strong connections to the doo-wop tradition. This is just as true of George Morton, whose collaboration with the Shangri-Las as a songwriter and producer would generate the body of work on which their reputation rests, and (along with a large amount of self-mythologising) cement his fame as a maverick auteur producer.

CHAPTER THREE

The Shangri-Las, George 'Shadow' Morton, and Red Bird Records

> Give me more PURPLE!
> —George 'Shadow' Morton

GEORGE MORTON AND 'SHADOW'

Most people who have heard anything at all about George 'Shadow' Morton will have the impression that he had no music industry experience prior to making "Remember (Walkin' in the Sand)" with the Shangri-Las. According to legend, it was at this point, by accident and as the result of a joke, that his genius burst forth fully formed and Morton proceeded to launch a series of incursions on the *Billboard Hot 100*, cementing his reputation as a brilliant, maverick producer. Early on, his habit of disappearing without notice earned him the nickname 'Shadow,' and Morton played up to this, actively cultivating an elusive, mysterious persona.

A lengthy 1991 interview with Morton conducted by Richard Arfin in *Goldmine* magazine opened by noting that he was 'born on September 3, 1944' in either Richmond, Virginia, or Brooklyn, New York—because Morton was apparently not sure. The year of his birth has been variously listed elsewhere as 1940, 1942, 1944 and 1947.[1] Morton's first known recordings and writing credits are in fact from 1958, so 1947 is clearly incorrect. Given that Ellie Greenwich (on whom more shortly) was born in 1940 and Morton's group 'used to sing back-up for her' while they were *all* in high school (Greenwich at Levittown Memorial High, Morton at nearby Bethpage), a birth date of 1940 or 1942 for Morton seems likely.[2] I include all this to illustrate how difficult it was, pre-internet and digitised genealogy databases, to pin down Morton's vitals. It is also an indication of Morton's cultivation of elusiveness, since many aspects of Morton's life and career have been similarly difficult to clarify.

George Francis Morton was born on 3 September 1941 in Kings County (Brooklyn), New York.[3] His parents, George Francis Morton Sr and Irene Regina Kelly, had married on 22 August 1936 in Brooklyn.[4] The 1940 Federal census, taken on 10 April, records George Sr (aged 26) and Irene (aged 24) as living in rented accommodation at 219 13th St, which is in the Park Slope area of Brooklyn.[5] Then as now, this five-storey building contained multiple separate dwellings; in 1940 it housed over twenty families of various sizes. These included George Morton Sr's parents, Francis Louis (Frank) and Martha Morton, both born in New York of Irish descent. In 1940 they were still renting at 219 13th St, as they had been in 1930 with their then 16-year-old son George, according to that year's Federal census.[6] So when son George (Sr), at the age of 22, married Irene Kelly in 1936, it seems the newly-weds moved into an apartment/rooms that had become vacant in the same building George had lived in with his parents for a good portion of his life. In 1940, George Sr was working as an assistant compositor (typesetter) in the printing industry, Irene as a 'counter girl' in a bakery.[7] George Morton's Sr's draft card, from later in 1940, lists his employer as W.W. Fitzhugh, of 145 49th St, Brooklyn, a manufacturer of labels and folding cartons.[8]

When George Francis Morton was born in 1941, his parents were in all likelihood still living in their Park Slope rental, since young George would later attend the St Thomas Aquinas Parochial School,* located a five-minute walk away on Fourth Avenue between 7th and 8th Streets.[9] As he recounted in 1991,

> In one of my new songs, there's a line "I got my education in the alley of St. Tom's . . ." That was my school, St. Thomas Aquinas. I got more education in the streets than I did from the sisters.[10]

In the first of several extraordinary coincidences, this was the same school attended by Henry Petroski, the future engineer who, as a teenager, moved to Cambria Heights from Park Slope, Brooklyn with his

---

* Since 2013, this building has been home to P.S. 118, The Maurice Sendak Community School, named for the author of the famous children's book *Where the Wild Things Are*; see P.S. 118 homepage.

family in 1954.[11] He remembers Thomas Aquinas being 'barely fifty yards from our old house,' which was at 228 8th St, virtually next door to the Holy Family St Thomas Aquinas Church adjacent to the school.[12] I include these details because in his meticulously researched liner notes to the significant Ace Records collection *Sophisticated Boom Boom: The Shadow Morton Story*, Mick Patrick states that Morton was born in Richmond, Virginia, and raised in the Bedford-Stuyvesant area of Brooklyn, neither of which is correct.[13] This confusion may have arisen because there are two St Thomas parishes in Brooklyn—in Park Slope and Flatlands—but neither have any connection to or are very near Bedford-Stuyvesant.[14] Nevertheless, it is one more indication of how consistently difficult it has been to be accurate about Morton.

Before George Morton Jr had turned ten, the Morton household underwent significant upheaval. When the census was taken in April, 1950, George Morton Sr was back living with his parents (still at 219 13th St, Brooklyn) and his marital status was listed as divorced.[15] His marriage to Irene had evidently ended several years earlier; Irene Morton had married a man named Santo Grimaldi on 16 July, 1948 in Richmond, Virginia.[16] It is unclear why the couple were not married in Brooklyn when both had been living there for least a decade, but Irene (Kelly) Morton was born and raised in Richmond, Virginia, and provided a Virginia address for the marriage certificate. This is the source of the Richmond connection that often arises in reference to George 'Shadow' Morton, and his maternal lineage was also the source of his songwriting alias Billy Kell(e)y, about which we will learn more shortly. Like his family, who appear to have dropped the 'e' in later years, Morton used 'Kelley' and 'Kelly' interchangeably.

Irene's parents, Christina Smith and Robert Lee Kelley, married on 10 October, 1901 in Richmond, Virginia.[17] In 1910 they were living at 215 Linden Ave in Richmond, and told the census collector that they had had five children, of whom four were still living.[18] In the next few years they had at least two more: Robert West was born on October 29, 1912 and Irene on 8 July, 1914.[19] Tragedy struck in 1918: on 16 October, Christina died at 38 of 'pneumonia following influenza,' which was almost certainly the 'Spanish Flu' pandemic that was sweeping the world at this time. Her condition was further complicated by a miscarriage.[20] In the US census for 1920, an Irene Kelley, aged about seven, was listed as resident at St Joseph's Institute, also known as St Joseph's

Academy and Orphan Asylum, then located at 4th and Marshall Streets in downtown Richmond, Virginia.[21] It was established in 1834 to care for orphaned and impoverished children in Richmond, and originally took in only girls.[22] This seems to have still been the case in 1920, as Irene Kelley was one of approximately 100 girls living at the orphanage on census day.[23]

With the death of Christina Kelley in 1918, it seems probable that Irene, likely the youngest of the Kelley children, was temporarily placed with St Joseph's because her remaining family was not able to care for her at this time. This was a very common occurrence, the likelihood of which is strengthened by the apparent relocation of Irene's father, Robert Lee Kelley, into the home of his widowed mother Annie and unmarried brother Joseph at 221 Linden Ave, Richmond, according to the 1920 census.[24] Annie and Joseph had been living there since at least 1910, a few doors up from where Robert and Christina Kelley had also lived with their children in 1910, and presumably until her death.[25] It is not clear where the rest of their children were in 1920, and Robert died from pancreatic cancer in 1927.[26]

As we have seen, by 1936 Irene Kell(e)y had married George Morton Sr and in 1940 they were living at 219 13th St, Brooklyn, New York. At this time, Santo Grimaldi, Irene's future second husband, was living mere metres away (a three-minute walk) at 165 13th St. He was twenty years old and one of six children ranging in age from 10 to 27 living with their parents, Alfonso and Frances Grimaldi, who had emigrated to the US from Italy.[27] How the relationship developed between Santo and Irene is unclear (as is their navigation of divorce in a Catholic context) but they married in July 1948 and a daughter, Geraldine, was born on 12 July, 1949.[28] In the US census of 1950, the new family was living at 196 8th St Brooklyn, in the top left apartment. The occupants were Santo Grimaldi, head (of household), 30 years old, from New York, working as a truck driver with the Sanitation Department; Irene Grimaldi, wife, 34, from Virginia, not working; Geraldine Grimaldi, 1 year old, daughter, and George Morton, 9, stepson.[29] Incredibly, this is metres from where Henry Petroski, 8 years old and fellow St Thomas Aquinas student, was living with his family at 228 8th St, Brooklyn in 1950, making his recollections all the more pertinent in this context.[30]

When George Morton Jr was about fourteen, so in the mid-1950s, he moved with his mother (and presumably, step-father and younger

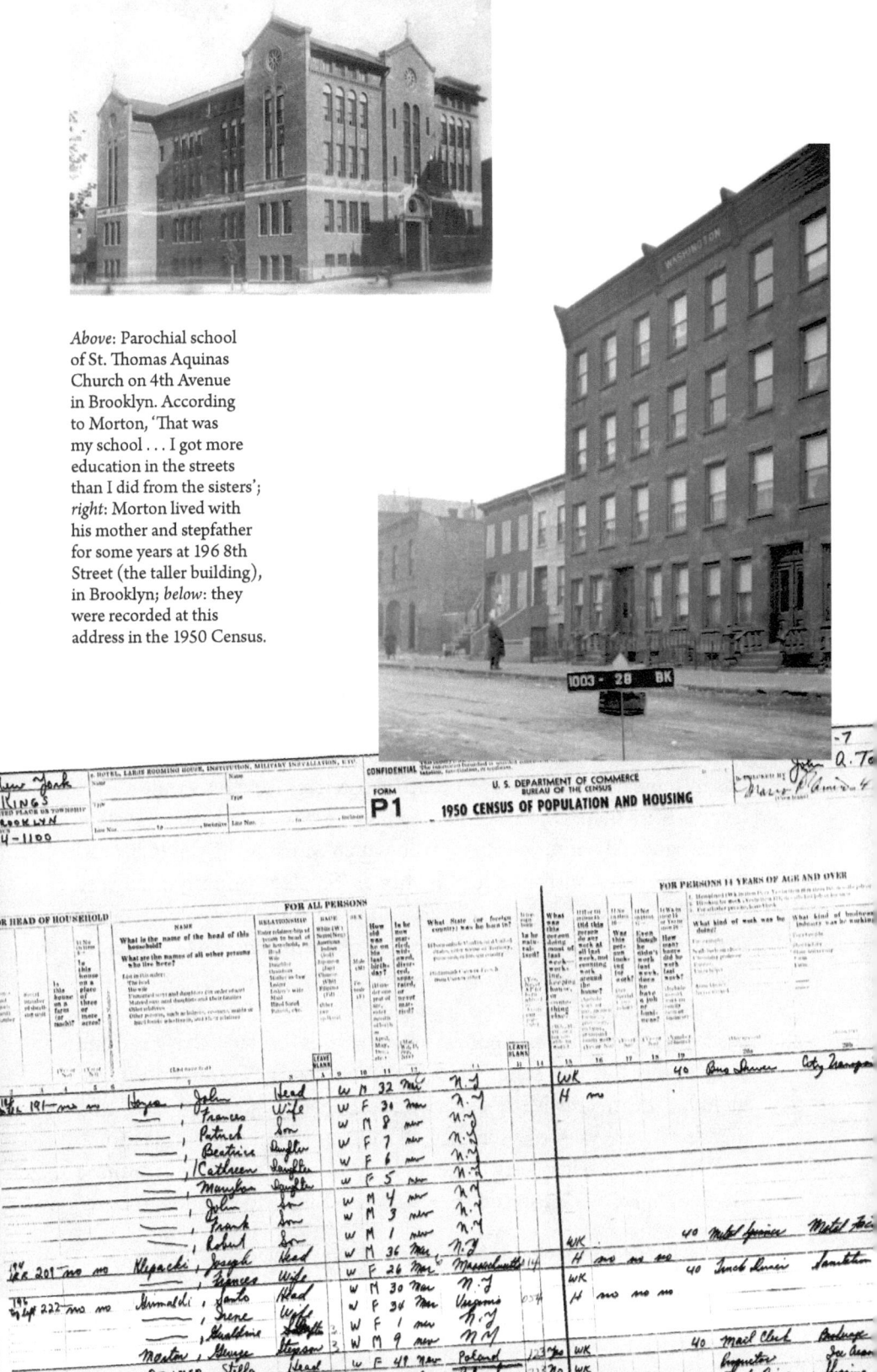

Above: Parochial school of St. Thomas Aquinas Church on 4th Avenue in Brooklyn. According to Morton, 'That was my school . . . I got more education in the streets than I did from the sisters'; *right*: Morton lived with his mother and stepfather for some years at 196 8th Street (the taller building), in Brooklyn; *below*: they were recorded at this address in the 1950 Census.

step-sister) to Hicksville, Long Island.[31] According to Morton's later
recollections, this was at least in part motivated by the desire to remove
young George from Brooklyn, where it appears he was becoming
increasingly involved with gang culture.* George Francis Morton Jr
subsequently attended Bethpage High School in Nassau County, and
in their 1956 yearbook he can be seen grinning cheekily on the end of
the front row in the photo of class 9-2, aged around 15.[32] He is the only
person in the entire school wearing a motorcycle jacket, which may or
may not be significant.

It was while attending Bethpage High that Morton formed his first
group; one of its other members, Anthony Giannattasio, aka Tony
Michaels, was in the same year as Morton, in class 9-3.[33] Morton's first
known recordings date from 1958, when he would have been around
seventeen; they were with a doo-wop outfit called the Markeys† and
mark the starting point of a long history of involvement in making
records. This is significant because Morton has persistently played down
his earliest work and presented himself as having been an untutored
music industry novice when he came to work with the Shangri-Las. In
fact, these early recordings illuminate his later work with the Shangri-
Las, revealing a continuity not only of theme and technique but even of
personnel. Some of his fellow Markeys were involved with the Shangri-
Las in the early stages of the group's existence; Morton would call in
favours from them when he recorded the demo of "Remember (Walkin'
in the Sand)." In addition, the way in which Morton has elided his earlier experience, cultivated his identity as 'Shadow,' and mythologised
himself and his work, is of relevance in understanding the persistence
of the biker/anti-hero figure in the songs of the Shangri-Las—I argue in
chapter 6 that this is based on Morton's fantasy of himself.

George Morton sang the lead part with the Markeys, which he
described as his 'high school group' —'we got on stage, five guys, and
sang.'[34] Morton has stated that 'Tony Michaels [Giannattasio] was
included in it,' and Mick Patrick's research indicates that the other
members were Victor Eusepi, Sal DiTroia and Martin (Marty) Monaco.[35] The group released two singles in 1958 as 'The Markeys featuring
George Morton'—"Hot Rod" b/w "Yakkity Yak," and "A Time to Love"

---

* The implications of this for "Leader of the Pack" are examined in chapter 6.
† Morton's group is not to be confused with (and has no connection to) Stax session
band the Mar-Keys.

Above: George Morton's 9th-grade class photo at Bethpage High; he's on the far right in the front row—the only one in a leather jacket; *below left*: his bandmate in the Markeys, Anthony Giannattasio (aka Tony Michaels), who would later write songs for and manage the Shangri-Las, was in a different 9th-grade class at Bethpage; he's in the middle in the second row from the top; *below right*: Eleanor (Ellie) Greenwich, pictured on the left in the second row from the top in her 1955 class photo, attended nearby Levittown Memorial High; Morton's group 'used to sing back-up for her' while they were all still in high school.

b/w "Make A Record, Man." The copyright for the first Markeys single, "Hot Rod" was registered on 16 June 1958, credited to Joseph Monaco (words) and George Morton (music); this marks Morton's earliest appearance as a songwriter.[36] He would continue to collaborate with Joseph (Joe) Monaco (brother of group member Marty); they also co-wrote both sides of the second Markeys single.[37] According to Mick Patrick, Joe Monaco had a small recording studio in the Hicksville area:

> Marty Monaco's mother had a basic recording studio in her basement in nearby Levittown where the guys wrote, rehearsed and taped demos of their songs.[38]

Given that they were all in high school at this point, a small-scale recording set-up in the basement of the Monaco family home makes sense; this is the one referred to elsewhere as Dynamic Recording Studio. Morton later made reference to

> this studio, where my high school group, The Marquees [sic], had hung out and done all this singing. It was in Bethpage, off Bloomingdale Road down from Ray's Diner . . . and this guy, Joe Mondria,* had set up a small studio in his basement because of us singing down there—he still had my old tape machine there.[39]

Joe Monaco would later co-write the Shangri-Las second single "Wishing Well," released in April 1964.[40] The other writer of "Wishing Well" was Tony Michaels (Giannattasio), who had been a member of the Markeys with Morton, had written the Shangri-Las very first single, "Simon Says," released in December 1963, and at some point around then had begun managing the Shangri-Las.[41]

The two Markeys singles were released, not on a small independent label, as one might expect, but on RCA Victor, which is in itself noteworthy. And they were released both in the US and internationally (I own a copy of the Australian release of "Hot Rod"). Mick Patrick notes that this came about because 'the owner of a local record store took a liking to the young quintet and helped arrange for them to audition for RCA.'[42]

---

*All other references to 'the basement studio' indicate that it was Joe Monaco's. 'Mondria' is likely a misprint or mistranscription from a recorded interview.

In December 1958, *Billboard* reviewed the second Markeys single and gave the A-side, "A Time to Love," three stars:

George Morton gives a quavering teen-age type lead to this slow ballad. Organ leads the backing with the Markeys giving it their all. This could make itself felt with the teen market.

The B-side, "Make a Record, Man," got two stars:

This is an upbeat blues which employs various pop song titles to sell its message. Has a good bit of life and could get action.[43]

The reviewer noted Morton's 'quavering teenage-type' vocalising, and other reviewers would also comment on Morton's singing style. It is also noteworthy that Morton made records as a teenager for a teen audience. Furthermore, the use of pop song titles in "Make a Record, Man" is a technique that Morton would utilise again a few years later.

Morton was also the lead singer in a group called the Lonely Ones, which may in fact have simply been the Markeys recording under a different name.[44] The Lonely Ones recorded a single on the Sir label in 1959, "My Wish" b/w "I Want My Girl."[45] It too was reviewed in *Billboard* and described as a 'tender rockaballad . . . wrapped up in meaningful interpretation by lead singer.'[46] Again, Morton's vocal abilities were noted, and Rod McBrien, an engineer with whom Morton worked in the early 60s at Ultra-Sonic studios in Hempstead, Long Island, concurred that Morton was 'a good singer' with a great sense of drama.[47] Tony Giannattasio/Michaels and Morton were credited as co-writers for the A-side, and Morton and Monaco for the B-side.

"Some of These Days" b/w "My Mammy" was released under the name Georgie Morton on the Swirl label in April 1961.[48] "Some of These Days" is a well-covered standard most closely associated with Sophie Tucker, whose 1926 version sold over a million copies, but Brenda Lee, Bobby Darin and Big Maybelle had all released versions in 1959.[49] Similarly, "My Mammy" is best known from 1920s recordings by the Peerless Quartet and Al Jolson, but in 1961 Bobby Rydell and the Everly Brothers also released versions, as did Dion in 1963.[50] Although Morton's recording career was only a few years old, this material is a clear departure from singing his own compositions; the other contem-

Left: The Markeys: Tony Giannattasio (aka Tony Michaels), Victor Eusepi, Sal DiTroia (*standing*); Marty Monaco and George Morton (*from Mick Patrick, liner notes to* Sophisticated Boom Boom: The Shadow Morton Story, *Ace Records*).

Below: The two singles recorded by the Markeys for RCA in 1958 (including the Australian pressing of "Hot Rod"); "Some of These Days" b/w "My Mammy" recorded by Morton in 1961 (*all from author's collection*).

porary recordings of these songs suggest that Morton was watching current trends closely and perhaps trying his hand in different genres to see what stuck. And he *was* getting noticed. When *Billboard* reviewed this single in the 'Special Merit Spotlights' with 'STRONG SALES POTENTIAL' section, the writer gave both sides four stars, calling "Some of These Days"

> a wildly exciting performance of the fine oldie by young singer, Georgie Morton, that is loaded with spirit and enthusiasm. The arrangement is solid and the chanter hands it a zingy reading. Watch this one.

The reviewer was similarly effusive about "My Mammy":

> The tune, associated with Al Jolson, is handed a very impressive reading here by Georgie Morton who sings it in semi-rockaballad fashion over a haunting arrangement. Interesting side with a chance.[51]

In addition to very positive commentary on both of Morton's vocal performances, both reviews mention the arrangements; in the case of "My Mammy," they are described as 'haunting.' This is significant, because both sides of the single read 'Arranged by Billy Kelly,' which is one of several aliases Morton used during this period. As noted earlier, Morton's mother's name was Irene Kelly and this side of his family lineage seems the likely impetus for the Kelly moniker. This single may be the first time he used it, as well as marking Morton's first credit as an arranger—an important step on the way to becoming a producer. The musicians were credited as the 'Sal Detroia [*sic*] Orch.'—Sal DiTroia, who had sung in the Markeys with Morton, was by now leading ensembles of musicians on recordings; he would later become a renowned session guitarist.[52]

"The Stretch" b/w "Come On In" was released under the name Morton George on the Amy label in 1962. The authorship of both songs was credited to Billy Kelley (i.e., Morton, this time with an additional *e*) and Arthur Hilliard.[53] The singles reviewer for *Billboard* thought "The Stretch" was really something, giving it four stars:

> Another new dance, with a blues and Twist format and with an additional south-of-the-border touch. Hand-clapping rhythm and a lot of excitement in the vocal here. Watch it.[54]

Cash Box reviewed "The Stretch" in their 'Best Bets' section, giving it a B+ (the highest rating):

> Yet another teen-step is explained—with lots of teen-beat author-ity—by the songster and his combo-chorus backdrop. Worth nov-elty dance programming.

"Come On In" got a B:

> An off-beat affair about a shy fella who's asked to join a party, and when he does, he has a ball.[55]

"Come On In" was a blueprint for Morton's 1965 composition, "Sophisticated Boom Boom," in which lyrical phrases, the storyline and the 'feel' of the earlier song were replicated.[56] It was recorded first by another Long Island group called the Goodies, then later by the Shangri-Las, under circumstances that will be discussed shortly.

Morton used the pseudonym Lance Martin for "I Feel Majestic," which he also wrote and performed; it was released on the Mala label in 1963.[57] *Cash Box* was again enthusiastic:

> Martin does a striking, unhurried job on the strong teen-romantic. Part of his full ork-chorus backdrop is attention-getting drum rolls, which get the deck off to a very interesting start. Enough exposure can mean a chart ride.[58]

Again, the reviewer noted the arrangements—but this outing of Morton's was 'arranged and conducted by Teacho Wilshire,' a New York-based pianist, arranger and orchestra leader who worked on countless recordings from the early 1950s onwards. These include Dion's 1961 hit "Runaround Sue," "Tell Him" by the Exciters (1962), and soul classics by Wilson Pickett, Solomon Burke, and many other lesser-known artists.[59] In a 1979 interview with Ralph Newman, Morton mentioned this song dismissively as one of his early records, incorrectly stating that it was by the Markeys (although they may have been uncredited backing singers).[60] Morton also used the 'Billy Kelly' writing alias for a one-off single released on New York label Jubilee in late February 1964. "Only Seven-teen" b/w "Now We're Together" was performed by an all-female group called the Beattle-ettes, and is a catchy, guitar-driven rocker that used the titles of Beatles' songs as lyrics.[61] *Billboard* said of "Only Seventeen":

> The gals do a creditable take-off on the four haircuts duplicating the sound and the snappy beat. A good teen-pegged lyric ad[d]s to the fun. Flip is "Now We're Together."[62]

"Only Seventeen" was co-written with Joe Monaco and may have been recorded at his Dynamic studio or, equally possibly, at Ultra-Sonic in Hempstead. Significantly the label on the record reads, 'Produced by George Morton.'[63] To this day, the group of young women who sang (it's not clear whether they also played instruments on the record) "Only Seventeen" has not been conclusively identified, and for many years rumours were rife that it was the Shangri-Las—to the point where this single is listed in some Shangri-Las discographies. Mary Weiss has consistently and vehemently denied this.[64] Certainly, the five young white women captioned as the Beattle-ettes in *Billboard* with Hal Jackson at Palisades Amusement Park in New Jersey look nothing like the Shangri-Las.[65]

To make things even more confusing, there was also a Black vocal group called the Beatlettes (also spelled Beatlette's and Beatle-ettes) as opposed to the white, Morton-connected one, which was spelled Beattle-ettes. The one-t Beatle-ettes were Helen Hutchinson, Lucille Dunbar and Vera Carey and were more commonly known as the Persian-

WWRL (New York) program director and deejay Hal Jackson are surrounded by the Beatle-ettes during the gal's perform-ance on Hal's Friday evening show at Palisades Amusement Park in New Jersey.

ONLY SEVENTEEN
(B. Kelly-J. Monaco)
THE BEATTLE-ETTES
Produced by George Morton

Left: the Beattle-ettes (*Billboard*, May 9, 1964); *right*: A-side of the Beattle-ettes first single, "produced by George Morton" and co-written by him under his "B[illy]. K[elly]." alias.

ettes.[66] They formed in Camden, New Jersey, and also worked as backing singers for fellow New Jersey soul singer Timmy Carr.[67] As the Beatlettes, they recorded two singles. The first, as the Beatlette's, was "Dance Beatle Dance" b/w "We Were Meant to be Married," released in January 1964 on the Philadelphia label Jamie.[68] Both sides were written by Bob Finiz, aka Robert Finizio, a songwriter and producer whose work appears on many other Jamie releases and Philadelphia-area soul tracks, including by Timothy/Timmy Carr.[69] Jamie Records was recently the subject of renewed interest for supplying key gems from its vaults for the soundtrack of the Oscar-winning movie *Green Book* (2018).[70] Amazingly, on the very comprehensive Jamie (and affiliated label) Guyden Records website, even though the group are described as a trio, the accompanying photo is of a quintet of young white women wearing matching Beatles' suits and wigs.[71] Equally amazingly, this photo is actually of yet another group, the French-Canadian Les Beatlettes from Montreal, an instrument-playing band rather than a singing group that released two singles and was one of the opening acts for the Dave Clark Five when they played in Montreal on 29 October 1964.[72]

The Persianettes-Beatlettes other single was "Yes!!! You Can Hold My Hand Part One" b/w "Yes!!! You Can Hold My Hand Part Two" released in February 1964 on the Assault label, this time as the Beatlettes.[73] The single's label lists Assault's address as 1741 Broadway, about six blocks north of the Brill Building in New York City. It was reviewed positively in *Cash Box* in a week in which the Beatles had the #1 single and album with "I Want to Hold Your Hand" and *Meet the Beatles* respectively.[74] The timing of this is more significant than it may at first appear. The Beatles had taken the UK and Europe by storm throughout 1963, with the term 'Beatlemania' having been coined in October of that year with reference to British audiences. In early December 1963, however, the Beatles were still without an available US release, having only had a couple of singles licensed by independent labels Vee-Jay and Swan.[75]

After refusing four times on the grounds that the group wouldn't sell in the USA, Capitol Records (the affiliate of their British Parlophone/EMI label) had finally agreed to sign the Beatles following intense pressure from their manager, Brian Epstein. Capitol's pressing schedule had copies landing in stores in mid-January 1964 until the actions of 15-year-old Marsha Albert of Silver Spring, Maryland, set in motion an extraordinary chain of events that culminated in Capitol rush-releasing

"I Want to Hold Your Hand" over Christmas in 1963. By mid-January it had sold a million copies and was #1 on the *Cash Box* singles chart.[76]

Despite regular confusion and conflation of the Beattle-ettes with the Beatle-ettes/Beatlettes/Beatlette's and Les Beatlettes, available evidence points to the three groups being separate and unconnected entities. "Only Seventeen" does not appear on the Persianettes discography and Morton seems not to have any connection with the Persianettes, nor do the songs released on Jamie and Assault appear in his BMI listing.[77] Given that "Dance Beatle Dance" was released in January 1964 by the group whose name correctly spelled Beatle, it does seem plausible that Morton was at the very least aware enough of the existence of the Beatle-ettes/Beatlettes/Persianettes group to spell the name of *his* group differently. It is possible he had time to lift the idea from the first group; on the other hand, at least two other sets of people had the same idea.[78] Given the well-established popularity of 'answer' records and a group (English, funny haircuts, catchy songs) that would have been an obvious choice for such treatment, it's quite conceivable that none of these groups and their writers/producers were copying anyone except the Beatles.[79]

As noted earlier, Morton has repeatedly downplayed all his early writing and recording experience, either by denying it outright or only discussing it dismissively. On the rare occasions when he *has* gone into more detail, he has named his groups wrongly and denied it all elsewhere anyway. I'll cite a few of many examples here.

In a lengthy interview in 1979, when Ralph Newman pressed Morton for more details about his early doo-wop recordings, Morton claimed,

> We did a show at the high school, and a couple of guys saw us. A guy named Parsons said he wanted to manage us. He called some people who came and saw us. And the next thing you know, RCA signed us up. It was nothing.[80]

In 1982, Alan Betrock quoted Morton as saying, 'I had never really written songs—it was a complete lie,' and in a lengthy 1991 interview with *Goldmine* magazine, Morton declared that he 'got into this business as a joke,' in order to prove a point to someone (Jeff Barry) who had rubbed him up the wrong way.[81] This version of events has rarely been seriously questioned; on the contrary, as a mythic construction it has proved remarkably resilient. In 1989, Charlotte Greig, describing the success of "Remember (Walkin' in the Sand)," commented,

> This was a triumph for Morton; he had no experience in the business, was unable even to play an instrument, and (he claims) had written the song in twenty minutes.[82]

In the Shangri-Las entry for the *All Music Guide*, Richie Unterberger remarks,

> The quality of Morton's work with the Shangri-Las on Red Bird (with assistance from Jeff Barry and Artie Butler) was remarkable considering that he had virtually no prior experience in the music business.[83]

Billy Joel's biographer Bill Smith, recalling the "Remember" session, writes,

> Shadow had never written or produced anything before this, but had talked his way into this recording studio promising a hit song. A little nervous now that he had the studio rented and the musicians waiting to record but no song, Shadow was on his way to the studio, still unsure of how he was going to pull this off, when it came to him as he crossed the railroad tracks. Pulling his car over he jotted down some lyrics to a melody that was in his head, and continued on to the studio. Once there this genius of improvising took the two pairs of sisters . . . aside and taught them the lyrics.[84]

When Suzi Quatro interviewed Mary Weiss for the BBC in 2007 she reiterated the standard understanding of Morton, stating that 'he was kinda green . . . he wasn't like a professional music business guy.'[85] And after Morton died, on Valentine's Day in 2013, his obituary in the *New York Times* included the following:

> By all accounts possessed of a brazen, naïve genius—he played no instrument, could not read music and wrote his songs in his head— Mr. Morton was almost single-handedly responsible for the wild success of the Shangri-Las, the Queens girl group he introduced and propelled to international stardom.

The group had its first hit in 1964 with "Remember," recorded more or less on a dare in a session frantically pulled together by Mr. Morton, who had never written a song before.[86]

The most important rebuttal of such accounts of Morton's pre-Shangri-Las career came in Mick Patrick's liner notes to *Sophisticated Boom Boom: The Shadow Morton Story*, a compilation CD released by Ace Records in 2013.[87] This was released after Morton's death (although Patrick had already been working on the release and had hoped to interview Morton), and after my own research on Morton that is included in my PhD dissertation of 2012, the first version of the present book.[88] Three of Morton's pre-Shangri-Las recordings that I discuss here are included on *Sophisticated Boom Boom*, and Patrick's liner notes list, discuss and assemble substantial evidence for the existence of a solid 'indie' body of writing, performance and production work by Morton before he struck gold with the Shangri-Las. Nevertheless, despite the availability of this material, Ada Wolin manages to write in her 2019 discussion of *Golden Hits of the Shangri-Las*,

> True to his tough adolescence and the moniker he would later receive, "Shadow," "Remember" was a case of sheer entrepreneurial bluff. Sure, many of the top songwriters at the Brill Building were young, but *Morton had never even written a song before 1964.*[89]

This claim of Morton's is also repeated without qualification in Laura Flam and Emily Sieu Liebowitz's 2023 book, *But Will You Love Me Tomorrow: An Oral History of the '60s Girl Groups.*[90]

One important result of this persistent mythology, as the remarks of Joel's biographer attest, has been to present Morton as an extraordinary and untutored talent, the possessor of a natural, untrammelled genius. For reasons that will become clearer in the next chapter, it is quite possible that when he dismissed and denied this entire period of his early work, Morton was engaged in more than myth-making—he was also consciously trying to distance himself, at least publicly, from anyone who had been involved with the Shangri-Las before they signed to the Red Bird label, particularly Artie Ripp and Kama Sutra Productions.

Be that as it may, it is quite clear that George Morton had a long history of involvement in making records. By the time he came into contact with the Shangri-Las, probably early in 1964, he had been writing, performing on, and later producing records for at least six years. He was well-connected, had regular writing partners, and had at least one studio at his disposal, owned and managed by people he worked with on a regular basis. Furthermore, a number of his early recordings hint at innovations that would be more fully realised in his work with the Shangri-Las—emotion, teen drama, sound effects, and death (see the discussion of "Hot Rod" in chapter 6). The Beattle-ettes record is particularly revealing in this regard. It is a fully realised, well-performed and well-produced song, raw and rocking, but in no way amateurish. Not only that, the whole idea of making a Beatle-connected record when, as Mick Patrick put it, 'most people in the American industry were still trying to unravel during those first few weeks of Beatlemania' what on earth all the fuss was about, indicates that Morton was concerned to keep his finger on the pulse, to stay abreast of, indeed ahead of, trends in the teen music market.[91]

The teenagers who sent the Beatles to #1 in January 1964—*before* their now legendary appearance on the Ed Sullivan show on 9 February 1964—knew exactly what was going on, and Morton was attempting to exploit this mounting tidal wave of adulation.[92] Morton's involvement in the record business was not an accident, nor the result of a dare or joke; on the contrary, he had been steadily working at establishing a profile, and his producer credit on the Beattle-ettes record is a clear indication of the direction he intended to move in. His pre-Shangri-Las work was perfect training for the records he would shortly be making at Red Bird, and significant enough to garner regular and positive reviews in *Billboard*, the biggest music trade journal in the country. So when the big league presented an opportunity, Morton knew precisely what to do to capitalise on it.

THE BIRTH OF THE PRODUCER

Today, a record producer is generally understood to be a kind of project manager, someone who supervises or directs a number of processes involved in the recording of a piece of music or sonic art. Most producers have a particular sound or style and are hired (often at great cost) for their ability to 'stamp' this onto the artists they work with, or 'produce.' A good contemporary example is Rick Rubin, whose production credits include albums by Slayer, Danzig, Public Enemy, the Beastie Boys and the final five albums recorded by Johnny Cash. Rubin's reputation, cachet and power as a producer are such that he is largely credited with resurrecting Cash's career in the early 1990s. Rubin's distinctive and recognisable 'minimalist' style is tight and punchy, characterised by crisp, compressed guitar sounds with a lot of space and presence around the vocals.[93]

Producers are also assumed to possess a kind of omnipotent critical distance that is unavailable to the artist (who is too intimately involved), which allows them to conceptualise the project as a whole, and so are 'generally considered the final arbiter of aesthetic judgements through-out the recording process.'[94] It is now standard practice, and has been for some decades, to place credits on an album sleeve (and singles, as we have seen) for the producer, the engineer, and other roles that contrib-ute to the recording process. In the context of the history of recorded sound, however, this is a relatively recent phenomenon. The earliest sound recordings allowed little scope for aesthetic input into the record-ing process beyond the placement of artists in the studio, room (or field, for that matter) in relation to a single piece of recording apparatus. Such recordings were essentially documents of performances.[95] The develop-ment of magnetic tape and multi-tracking made the recording process more complicated, allowing for the different instrumentalists and sing-ers— of a band, for example—to be recorded on different 'tracks,' so that their levels relative to one another could be adjusted and altered separately.[96] Importantly, this introduced the means for aesthetic and creative decisions to be made by the person doing the recording, ena-bling the creation of a certain effect or mood.[97] As Virgil Moorefield has noted, 'For rock and pop, the interest generally lies not in virtuosity or harmonic complexity, but in a mood, an atmosphere, an unusual combi-nation of sounds; these are greatly enhanced by good production.'[98] The rise of what is commonly known as the 'auteur producer' is to a large extent a result of this technological development; certainly, it would have been both unnecessary and impossible without it.

Jerry Leiber and Mike Stoller were a consummate songwriting team, responsible for "Hound Dog," "Kansas City," "Love Potion #9" and "Yakety Yak," among many other hits. They were songwriters who became 'producers' at a time when this role had not yet been codified into what it means today, or indeed into the meaning it had attained by the early 60s. In the late 50s, when Leiber and Stoller were working for

Atlantic Records, they fought to have themselves credited as producers, as Jerry Leiber has explained:

> 'We were doing it, but we were not receiving more than the song-writer's royalty, so we were doing two jobs and thought we should be given credit for it and also given a royalty. *This was unheard of at the time*, but I think we were probably the first to break the ice, creating the situation where a [production] credit was given and a royalty established.'[99]

This is significant because Leiber and Stoller trained one of rock's earliest and famously eccentric auteur producers, Phil Spector, who moved from Los Angeles to New York in the early 60s and was apprenticed to Leiber and Stoller 'for about a year and a half.'[100] Dissatisfied with constantly getting short-changed on royalties, Leiber and Stoller had made a couple of abortive attempts to set up a record label of their own, Tiger and Daisy. Early in 1964, they established the Red Bird label with George Goldner, both parties recognising that their union could be mutually advantageous. Leiber and Stoller were highly respected hit-making songwriters, but apparently lacked competence when it came to marketing their material; Goldner, on the other hand, was '"the best salesman ever."'[101] Red Bird Records and its subsidiary, Blue Cat, were located in the Brill Building at 1619 Broadway, and around the middle of 1964, Leiber and Stoller found themselves training another aspiring young producer, George Morton.

In order to gain an informed understanding of Morton's methods, and of his input and contribution to the Shangri-Las' material, it is important first to grasp Leiber and Stoller's then-novel method of working. They became producers 'in self-defence,' as they put it, because they envisaged their material 'as records rather than as a song that exists on a piece of paper . . . When we took our songs to an A & R man [they] never came back in the way that we had imagined them.'[102]

The 'A & R' [Artist & Repertoire] figure was the forerunner of the producer, responsible 'for matching the artist with the material (repertoire) and ensuring that all came together in the studio at the right time.'[103] The role was not an artistic or aesthetic one; in most cases it was more an organisational one, although talent-spotting and an ear for sellable artists and/or material were essential.[104] Leiber and Stoller worked quite differently, however, and it is significant that they conceived of their songs as recordings, rather than scores. Mike Stoller described how they would

> tailor the material to the individual singers . . . As time went on, we knew exactly what they could do and couldn't do, and we would create the material that way in the first place . . . It was like a play, a radio play.[105]

Stoller was here speaking specifically about the Coasters, an African-American vocal group that began life as doo-wop group the Robins. Their close relationship with Leiber and Stoller resulted in a string of hits, including "Yakety Yak" and "Searchin." In Leiber's view,

> they were like mini-rhythm and blues operas, those songs, three-minute operas . . . and the Coasters were to some extent selected because of their existing personalities . . . they were almost like characters out of a comic strip, and they always played the same role.[106]

Leiber and Stoller had clearly conceptualised ideas for their songs, for the performers, and for how they wanted the end result to *sound*, and they possessed the experience and technical knowledge to convey this to the musicians and singers they worked with. Their methods had a major impact on George Morton, who Leiber described as having 'a tremendous amount of raw talent,' while also noting that he 'was inexperienced, didn't know the spectrum of the orchestra nor what it would do':

> Shadow would come in with pieces of an idea, and I spent many hours showing him how to structure and shape his bizarre little radio dramas, although they were somewhat different from ours. His were soap operas and melodramas, ours were comedies. He had seagulls clacking in the background and surf washing up—they were kind of romantic, teenage romances.[107]

What is clear from this account is that Morton, like Leiber and Stoller, had a 'vision' for his material, a concept, feel, mood, aesthetic for his 'radio dramas.' He had less technical ability than his far more experienced supervisors (although, as we have seen, he was not the novice he would later pretend to have been), but in the same way that Leiber and Stoller tailored their material for and wrote to the strengths of the Coasters, so would Morton with the Shangri-Las.

The combination of Morton's ideas and musical aesthetics with the Shangri-Las' talent, personalities and ability to interpret and convey his ideas, as well as their willingness to immerse themselves in this collaborative process, produced the body of material for which the Shangri-Las—and Morton—would become famous. The song Leiber referred to, with 'seagulls clacking in the background and surf washing up,' is the Shangri-Las' first single for Red Bird, "Remember (Walkin' in the Sand)." It was penned by Morton, and the circumstances of its creation and the signing of the Shangri-Las to Leiber, Stoller and Goldner's Red Bird label are inextricably intertwined.

THE CREATION OF "REMEMBER (WALKIN' IN THE SAND)"

When asked by Suzi Quatro in 2007 to describe George 'Shadow' Morton, Mary Weiss replied, 'He was a maniac.'[108] In a long interview with *Goldmine* in 1991, Morton recounted at length what has become the standard narrative of his entry into the music industry, and his involvement with the Shangri-Las. Morton related that, before getting involved in the production of music, he had no real idea what he wanted to be, 'everything from a priest to owning restaurants.'[109] However, he had

> done some things with a group out on Long Island . . . Tony Michaels was included in it . . . We did rock 'n' roll stuff, all kinds of stuff . . . we got on stage—five guys—and sang. Doo-wop, black, rock 'n' roll—big time . . . The name of the group was the Marquees [i.e., Markeys]. RCA was interested. They signed the group for a couple of records . . . We sang in the basement, we sang at the high schools. That's how I met Ellie Greenwich. She was an accordion player at Levittown High or maybe East Meadow . . . down Wantagh Avenue, just before Southern State Parkway.[110]

Like almost everyone involved with the Shangri-Las, Morton's musical background was, as we have seen, in vocal harmonising, doo-wop. According to Morton, his friend Jerry Love happened to mention one night that their mutual acquaintance from Levittown, the aforementioned Ellie Greenwich, was working as a songwriter in the Brill Building. Disc jockey Murray 'the K' Kaufman referred to Jerry Love as 'the Jolly Green Giant,' and 'the biggest (in height) record promotion man in town,' so if Love and Morton were friends, then even at this early stage Morton had solid music industry connections.[111] Ellie Greenwich had already co-written several hit singles including "Be My Baby" (the Ronettes) and "Da Doo Ron Ron" (the Crystals), and was now signed to Leiber and Stoller's publishing company, Trio, which released records on their newly formed Red Bird label; she had a thriving songwriting partnership with her husband, Jeff Barry.[112] Morton apparently called Greenwich and arranged to visit her at her workplace, and, after some verbal sparring with Barry, during which Morton declared that he, like Barry, wrote 'hit songs' for a living, left with a loose arrangement to return to their Brill Building office with one.[113]

Morton has told the story of this encounter multiple times, presenting his composition and recording of "Remember" as 'just a joke,' or something he did 'just for the hell of it, just for the sheer craziness of it.' He was apparently riled by Barry's behaviour:

> I didn't like his attitude. I mean, I'm originally from Brooklyn and you don't take that attitude with me very long. But he was just being himself. When he turned to me, because he kept his back to me while he was tinkling on the piano and I didn't like that . . . he turned to me, and I guess to jam me, said, 'And what do you do for a living?' To jam him back, I said, 'Same thing you do—I write songs.' And he said, 'What kind of songs?' And I said, 'Hit songs!' And he said, 'Bring 'em to me.' I exited the room, I remember waiting about ten seconds, and then I knocked on the door. When he leaned over to open the door, I guess he figured I was going to apologize or come up with some excuse because he put a smile on his face and said, 'Yeah . . . go ahead.' And I said, 'We forgot to discuss something. Do you want a fast hit or a slow hit?' He laughed and said, 'Kid, bring me a slow hit.' [114]

Morton claims he 'went back to Long Island and called a friend, Joe Monaco, who had a studio in his basement'—Dynamic, where Morton had recorded many times before. He hastily assembled some musicians and got in touch with 'some girls who were singing in Cambria Heights, Queens.'[115] These 'girls' were, of course, the Shangri-Las, and Joe Monaco was Morton's old songwriting partner from the Markeys. Presumably, the meeting at which Mary Weiss described their first encounter at Bob 'Babalu' Lewis's apartment had already taken place, and Morton got in touch with the Shangri-Las about singing on a demo via his old friend, their manager Tony Michaels [Giannattasio]. According to Morton, the Shangri-Las, the musicians, and Morton himself were on their way to Dynamic in Bethpage for the recording session when Morton realised he did not have a song; he then pulled the car over and wrote "Remember (Walkin' in the Sand)" on 'the side of South Oyster Bay Road' in twenty minutes.[116]

Morton's version of these events is far more colourful than indicated here. John Grecco relates in his comprehensive liner notes for a Shangri-Las vinyl compilation in 2021,

> I knew Shadow for about twenty years and over those years he told me many stories . . . but he never deviated from the tale of the day the session took place for "Remember (Walkin in the Sand)."[117]

According to Morton,

> I walked into the studio that day. I didn't know how arrangements went 'cause it was all in my head. I don't play an instrument or anything. So I said to the piano player, 'You play bom, bom, bom. Do this, don't do that . . .'[118]

That piano player was Billy Joel, who was about 15 at the time and played in a Long Island band called the Echoes. In a 1987 interview with Tom Hibbert, he recalled being approached at a gig by Morton about playing on a recording:

> So I go down to this little studio in a guy's basement in Levittown, Dynamic Studios, and they've got this sheet music down there. There's two songs, one's called 'Leader of the Pack' and the other is called 'Remember (Walkin' in the Sand)' and this is pretty easy stuff to play and then Shadow comes in.[119]

Joel's recollections are noteworthy, given Morton's apparent and oft-professed *lack* of familiarity with such things as sheet music and notation. It also calls into question Morton's now legendary story of hastily penning "Remember" on the way to the studio, if there was already sheet music there. On the other hand, it is unlikely that Morton would have worked using sheet music; his description of telling Joel to 'play bom bom bom' and having it 'all in my head' is consistent with Jerry Leiber's recollections of working with Morton shortly *after* this session took place. In Grecco's telling of the story,

> Shadow proceeded to hand out the lyrics to the girls, but he had no lead sheets for the musicians. He told each one, "I want you to play this, I want you to play that" and so on, mimicking the sounds he wanted each musician to play.[120]

So the 'sheets' Joel recalled may have actually been lyric sheets, not music. The other possibility is that Morton had hired an arranger, which he would certainly have had access to later, after signing with Red Bird, as Ellie Greenwich has explained:

> Very often arrangers are used for their ideas, to some degree, but very much to notate what's to be played. Sometimes a songwriter hears an entire record in his head, but doesn't want to take the time, and is probably not that well equipped, to write down all these parts. So they'll hire an arranger, pay him whatever, and have him arrange a session.[121]

Moreover, in contrast to Joel's recollection, the generally accepted version of the story has "Leader of the Pack" being written *after* the success of "Remember."

Joel continued,

> He's a pretty strange guy, Shadow. He's wearing this big cape and dark glasses and he played the producer role to the hilt. I think he had a thing about Phil Spector. He wanted to be the Phil Spector of the East Coast. And he talked in these wild, dramatic, theatrical terms— he wanted more 'thunder' and he wanted more 'purple' in the record. He's waving his arms in the air saying 'give me more PURPLE.' And I'm sitting there kinda nervous—this is my first time ever in a recording studio—and I'm hissing to the other musicians, What does that

mean? How do I play "purple"? And the guitar player leans over and says, Oh, just play louder, kid.[122]

Theatrics aside, this anecdote is significant because it demonstrates that what was uppermost in Morton's mind was not note-for-note technical perfection, but infusing this recording with intensity and drama, which he articulated as 'thunder' and 'purple.' He also, as far as Joel was concerned, very definitely envisaged himself as a wild, eccentric producer, a role he played 'to the hilt' even at this point. Interestingly, this sense of dramatic tension is not as evident on Morton's earlier records—there are certainly hints of it, but nothing as fully realised as this. Perhaps the distinctive qualities of Mary Weiss's voice and its inherent emotional intensity suggested to Morton at this early stage that angst-ridden teen drama would be the appropriate material for the group. In any case, it was clear to the first people who heard "Remember" that the collaboration between Morton and the Shangri-Las was exceptional and compelling.

The original demo version of "Remember" on which Joel played apparently ran for about seven minutes; Morton took this recording to Jeff Barry and Ellie Greenwich at Red Bird. Greenwich recalls,

'Well, he came back and played us this weird little record. It was like seven minutes long with this long narration by George in the beginning. I knew there was no way we could put out anything like that, but I thought, "Gee, that girl's voice is so strange, and the song is so interesting." So we played it for Leiber and Stoller and they said, "Go cut it." [123]

Greenwich was immediately taken with the combination of the voice(s) *and* the song, the performers *and* the material, but it was Morton who was signed up first—like Greenwich and Barry, to Trio Music. In Morton's account,

The door opens up and a guy with one blue eye and one brown eye sticks his head in—Jerry Leiber—and asks me, "Did you write this?" I said, "Yeah." "Did you produce this?" I said, "What does that mean?" "Did you tell everybody what to play and how to play it? Did you tell them how to sing?" I said, "Yeah." He must have opened the

biggest new label success story of 1964 is, of course, the Red Bird story. Under the
re of three veterans, label president George Goldner and creative execs Jerry Leiber
Mike Stoller (on left) the infant label has come up with a chain of top ten hits that has
truly fantastic. Greatly responsible for the label's strong debut are the people on the
At the piano are Jeff Barry and his wife Ellie Greenwich, the hot writing-producing
who played a role in the success of "Chapel Of Love" by the Dixie Cups who are seen in
roto with them, their follow-up "People Say," and the Jelly Beans' top tenner "I Wanna
Him So Bad." The label is also burning-up the charts with other singles including the
by the Shangri-Las, "Remember (Walking In The Sand)." Red Bird is obviously a
label with unlimited potential

Cover of the August 29, 1964, issue of *Cash Box,* devoted to Red Bird as "the biggest new label success story of 1964." The cover text continues: "Under the guidance of three veterans, label president George Goldner and creative execs Jerry Leiber and Mike Stoller (on left) the infant label has come up with a chain of top ten hits that has been truly fantastic. Greatly responsible for the label's strong debut are the people on the right. At the piano are Jeff Barry and his wife Ellie Greenwich, the hot writing-producing team who played a role in the success of "Chapel of Love" by the Dixie Cups, who are seen in the photo with them, their follow-up "People Say," and the Jelly Beans top tenner "I Wanna Love Him So Bad." The label is also burning-up the charts with other singles including the new issue by the Shangri-Las, "Remember (Walking in the Sand).'"

door and asked me if I wrote it and produced it about three times. I took it to mean that he didn't believe me. He opens the door again and says, "Well, how would you like to work here?" I said, "What do I have to do?" "Do exactly what you did here! Make songs! Make some records!" So I did . . . and the money was good.[124]

Morton's supposed lack of understanding of what it meant to produce a recording is patently ludicrous; as we have seen, Morton was credited as producer on the record label of "Only Seventeen" by the Beattle-ettes, released earlier in 1964, and already 'played the producer role to the hilt,' as Billy Joel put it.

According to Morton, Jerry Leiber said that 'we're going to have re-record a bunch of this' because the recording quality was inadequate, since it was fundamentally a demo.[125] It would have been entirely standard practice to sign Morton for the *song* (and others he would subsequently write) but select one of the singers or groups already on Red Bird's roster to record the song. Multiple artists on a label's roster would, at management's discretion, record versions of songs owned by the label's publishing company. In some cases, as Greenwich pointed out, the notion of an artist was dispensed with altogether:

[We] would make demonstration records of the songs we wrote . . . A case like that was a group called the Raindrops, but there really wasn't a group, it was just myself and Jeff doing all the voices. We did this demo for a [doo-wop] group called the Sensations, who'd had a hit with "Let Me In," [*sings*] 'Let me in, wee-oo, oop wee-oo.' We wrote a song called "What a Guy" that we thought would be a great follow-up for them. We went in and made the demo. The publishers heard it and thought it could be a record. But there was no group. Back then, a lot of labels put out what they called dummy groups. We'd throw a few people together, go out and lip-synch the records, but there really wasn't a group called the Raindrops.[126]

This demonstrates the great extent to which singers were perceived primarily as vehicles to sell *the song*:

The artist is real powerful nowadays. Back then they weren't. If a *songwriter* had three or four things in a row that made it, they had some power. The artist might have been on the bottom rung in the 60s, but not today.[127]

In the case of the Shangri-Las however, as Greenwich also noted (above), the combination of artist and song was sufficiently persuasive and compelling to warrant the signing of both the songwriter and the performers. The Shangri-Las signed 'an exclusive five-year contract with Red Bird in April of 1964'; since they were all minors, their parents had to sign for them.[128] Then they ran into a problem, says Ellie Greenwich,

George signed on with Trio and we started getting together with the girls and working on arrangements and vocals and just when we were getting ready to go into the studio, all of a sudden everything came to a halt, because in walked Artie Ripp and the Kama Sutra people, and *they had contracts with the girls* and there was nothing we could do about it.'[129]

There is some question as to whether contracts had actually been signed with Kama Sutra. According to Morton,

Tony Michaels had the deal with—well I didn't know he had a deal—I knew he was *talking* to people, but I didn't know he had a *deal* with Artie Ripp. Believe me that has caused *legal* complications over the years . . . When Ripp and his people heard 'Remember' and found out it was the Shangri-Las . . . Ripp had used the girls on four demos—*demos*! There was no contract. But with that organisation, shall we say, a demo means we own you. And they came through the doors saying, '*We* own the Shangri-Las.'[130]

The 'demos' recorded by the Shangri-Las were "Simon Says" and "Wishing Well," both of which had "Kama Sutra Productions" on their record labels. As Mary pointed out a few years ago, '"Wishing Well" was actually our demo and they played around with it and released it.'[131] As Greenwich's earlier comments indicate, this was not an uncommon occurrence.

However, Morton suggested darkly that Ripp's claim on the Shangri-Las had rather more sinister backing than a contract:

You know how they say the pen is more powerful than the sword? Well, the bullet is more powerful than the pen. Artie Ripp said he owned it . . . and the people who worked in his company owned his company . . . they didn't have a contract either, they just owned the company. So. They ended up getting part of the publishing and part of the production, me and the girls got screwed big time on that one. But we didn't know, we were kids like everyone else. They said, 'This is for your own good, sign here,' we'd sign here.[132]

Morton is alluding here to the source of Kama Sutra's initial company funding, some of which came from mobster John 'Sonny' Franzese, apparently a frequent visitor to Kama Sutra's offices.[133] Franzese was a capo in the Colombo family, one of the five *Cosa Nostra* families of New York City; his reputation for enforcement using brutality was formidable.[134] The involvement of Mafia figures will become far more problematic later in the story; for the moment though, the point is that, contract or no contract, Ripp's demands were met, with the power of Kama Sutra's Mafia backing a likely factor. An arrangement was reached between Red Bird and Kama Sutra whereby the latter would receive 'some credit, some publishing and some royalties,' and the recording proceeded.'[135] One consequence of this was a change to the record's credits. Ellie Greenwich again:

All of a sudden George [Morton] and I are off the label as producers, and Jeff and Artie Ripp share production credits. And you know, Artie Ripp *wasn't even there* . . .[136]

This is borne out by a full-page advertisement in *Cash Box* in which 'Kama Sutra Productions thanks the music business for these hits and salutes the music operators of America.' The records listed below include:

Red Bird Records
"REMEMBER"
(Walkin' in the Sand)
THE SHANGRI-LAS
Produced by
Artie Ripp and Jeff Barry
Tender Tunes Music Co.[137]

Artie Ripp recently recounted a scandalously revisionist version of this story to Laura Flam and Emily Sieu Liebowitz, asserting that he picked the original seven-minute demo of "Remember" out of the filing cabinet at Kama Sutra, then 'went into the studio and produced a shorter version' which he then presented 'to George Goldner, who was now in partnership with Leiber and Stoller at Red Bird Records.' Ripp also stated that the Shangri-Las were 'starting, at that time, at Mercury Records and [had] put out a record called "Simon Says" that didn't go anyplace.'[138] Smash, the label on which "Simon Says" was released in 1963, was a subsidiary of Mercury Records, so technically this is correct, if not completely accurate.[139] More significantly, Ripp omitted the rather important details that it was *his* company, Kama Sutra Productions, that was responsible for this one-off Smash release, and that his partners in Kama Sutra, Hy Mizrahi and Phil Steinberg, were credited as writers of the B-side of this single. In a 1968 *Cash Box* feature on Kama Sutra, Ripp stated:

> Within 90 days after the formation of Kama Sutra Productions in 1964 we had two records in the top ten: "Remember Walkin' In the Sand" by The Shangri-Las, and "Come A Little Bit Closer" by Jay & The Americans.[140]

The company clearly existed much earlier than this, however, as "Kama Sutra Productions" appears on the Smash record label for "Simon Says" (on which the group's name was also misspelt as 'Shangra-Las'), released late in 1963; "Remember" entered the Top Ten (at #9) on 12 September 1964 and "Come A Little Bit Closer" (at #7) on 7 November 1964. Ripp has consistently attempted to rewrite the history of his association with the group, eliding his earlier activities and presenting himself as closely involved with the production of "Remember," rather than receiving a bogus credit because he had signed the Shangri-Las to an earlier exploitative contract with Kama Sutra.

It became something of a running joke in the record business that the term 'rip off' was coined in reference to Artie Ripp; a few years later, he signed a young Billy Joel to a contract 'so severe' that it seemed 'almost to deprive Joel of the right to earn a living' and from which it took Joel years and considerable expense to extricate himself.[141] Worse still, Joel's first album *Cold Spring Harbor* (1971), a product of this arrangement and for which Ripp received multiple credits including mixing, engineering and producing, was mastered at the wrong speed, which Joel described furiously as making him sound like Alvin and the Chipmunks.[142]

WORKERS

"Remember (Walkin' in the Sand)" was released in July 1964, and on 1 August it was reviewed in *Billboard's* 'Hot Pop Spotlights':

> For those who like a different sound, try this haunting delivery. Sea gulls in the background will no doubt help this side fly away. Quite a switch. Flip: "It's Easier to Cry."[143]

"Remember" entered the Hot 100 at #78 on 22 August and peaked at #5 on 26 September 1964. Miriam Linna asked Mary Weiss about the success of "Remember" in 2006:

> ML: When *Remember* hit, you started playing right away . . .
> MW: Right away, yes. The Brooklyn Fox Theater. I was travelling all the time. When I wasn't doing that I was in the studio. When I wasn't doing that I was rehearsing.[144]

Although the group had been performing already at dances and hops around Queens, a record in the *Billboard Hot 100* brought fame on a totally different level. As with Frankie Lymon and the Teenagers almost ten years earlier, concert performances, television appearances and tours began immediately. Mary Weiss later commented to Suzi Quatro, 'When you put out your first record and it hits, you have to. So we were ill-prepared for it . . . we kind of fudged our way through it!'[145]

The Marvelettes, another set of teen female singers, were similarly unprepared when their first single "Please Mr. Postman" was a #1 hit for Motown in 1961. As Marvelettes member Katherine Anderson remembered, with some anger,

> 'When we went on stage, we were 16 and 17 years old and there wasn't a *damn* person at Motown who could give us any real advice on *how* we should be doing it . . . We got a lot of our performing experience from doing record hops. You go and you do your one little record—and you pantomime that—and then you're supposed

to be able to get out there and perform live on stage with a band? It's a totally different ballgame . . . when we had "Please Mr. Postman," no one was prepared for what was going to happen. And I beg to differ [with] anyone who says they were prepared. That's a damn lie . . . Motown was *not* ready when it happened.'[146]

In fact, it was the Marvelettes' perceived lack of 'polish' that was partly responsible for the establishment of the Motown Artist Development Department, which 'involved lessons with vocal coach Maurice King, rehearsals with choreographer Charles 'Cholly' Atkins, and "finishing school" with Maxine Powell.' Motown groups that followed in the Marvelettes' footsteps, most notably the Supremes and Martha and the Vandellas, would benefit greatly from this.[147]

Red Bird was not prepared either; it seems that, like the Marvelettes, the Shangri-Las were thrust into the turbulent world of showbusiness with little choice but to learn as they went, and fast. Their first TV appearance, performing "Remember," was 'on the Clark Race Show in Pittsburgh.'[148] Race was a popular disk jockey on radio KDKA-AM Pittsburgh, having relocated from Hudson, New York, in 1959. In 1963, KDKA-TV launched "Dance Party," a weekly Saturday show which featured local teen dancers and live performances by current artists with hits.[149] Mary Weiss described their performance:

'We didn't know anything about TV. We wore skirts and white shell blouses. We didn't have any makeup on. And we shone like a bunch of headlights. You know the kids in the audience can tell if you're professional or amateur. Boy did we come on amateur. They held their breaths for us. Then afterward, this 14-year-old kid came up and said, "Don't worry kid, you'll make it."'[150]

Nevertheless, the Shangri-Las' performing ability and stage presence quickly began to attract attention. In an interview with *New Musical Express* (*NME*) from November 1964, Chris Curtis of British group the Searchers spoke of performing with the Shangri-Las in the USA a couple of months earlier. Both groups had been part of 'a six-day run at Brooklyn Fox Theatre' in one of Murray 'the K' Kaufman's famous revues.[151] Murray the K was an extremely influential and popular radio host on New York City's WINS. He befriended the Beatles on their first

Right: full-page advertisement in *Cash Box* (August 15, 1964), with Artie Ripp listed as co-producer with Jeff Barry; *below left*: *Cash Box*'s "Bios for Deejays" column in their September 12, 1964 edition featured the Shangri-Las; *below right*: manager Larry Martire's booking advertisement (*Cash Box*, January 2, 1965)

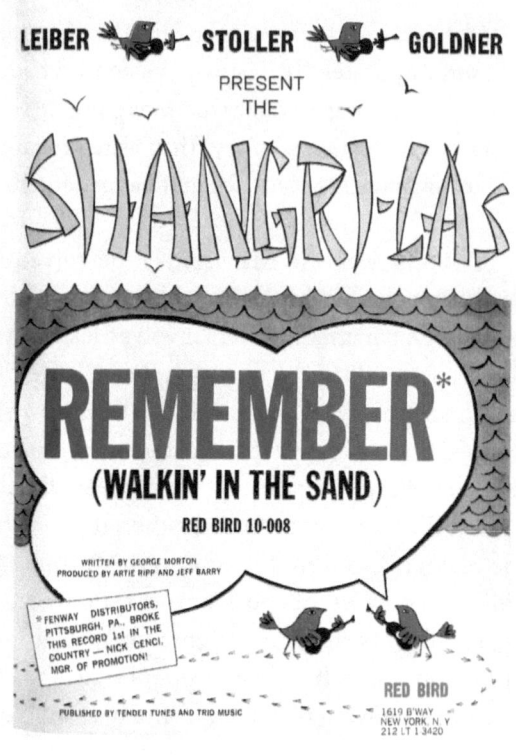

BIOS FOR DEEJAYS

Shangri-las

The Shangri-las (Mary Ann, Marge, Betty and Mary) started singing together while they were attending Andrew Jackson High School in Queens, New York. They had been singing together for about eight months when they were asked to audition for George Goldner, head of Red Bird Records. They were immediately signed to a long term contract and their very first deck, "Remember (Walkin' In The Sand)," became a smash hit. The single is currently holding down the No. 13 spot on this week's Top 100.

Unlike many recording stars who have risen to prominence with a single record, the Shangri-las are firm believers in top-drawer showmanship which means, as they see it, a versatile, well-paced act which gives all four maximum opportunity to show off their best sides.

HOTTEST ACT
ON THE MARKET! ! !

THE

SHANGRI-LAS

RED BIRD RECORDS

FOR ALL BOOKINGS

CONTACT:

LARRY MARTIRE

1619 BROADWAY
NEW YORK CITY
(212) LT 1-3420

visit to New York in February 1964, largely because the Beatles knew of him from US groups that had toured Britain. He marketed himself as 'the fifth Beatle,' and, not surprisingly, was hugely popular with teenage audiences. His shows at the Brooklyn Fox were famously multi-racial, the performers and the audience, and were aimed at teenagers whose summer vacations were just coming to an end.[152]

One of these shows, probably the first of the 'six-day run' Curtis referred to, took place on Friday 4 September 1964. On the same day, another big teen show opened for a ten-day run at the Paramount Theatre on Times Square in Manhattan, with the Animals as the headlining act. Howard Thompson, writing in *The New York Times*, reported that 'Teen-agers Howl for the Animals,' and called them '5 Beatle-like Britons' who 'ambled on stage almost diffidently, to a symphony of squeals.' Thompson also mentioned that 'another stage jamboree also opened yesterday at the Brooklyn Fox.'[153]

Both the Fox and Paramount shows received detailed coverage in *Hit Parader*, a magazine aimed at a teen audience that attempted to cover pop music more meaningfully than most teen-oriented music publications. It is unusual to have such a lengthy and detailed description of one of these shows, and significantly, the perspective was not an imperious and condescending adult viewpoint like the *New York Times* coverage of the Animals show at the Paramount, which was a show organised according to a similar 'revue' format. This account constitutes a fascinating and revealing snapshot of a couple of hours at the Brooklyn Fox in mid-1964, and I will cite it at length to indicate how such shows operated, and the way in which they reflected musical and cultural trends that are completely at odds with later (and still deeply entrenched) notions of performance and authenticity.

Under the heading 'A Rock 'n' Roll Doubleheader,' the author noted,

The two theatres were only 20 minutes apart by subway. Many ambitious devotees sat through two shows in one theatre then hopped on a train and caught two more across the river.[154]

At the Brooklyn Fox Theatre on Flatbush Avenue, Chris Curtis recalled that, in addition to his own group and the Shangri-Las, others on the bill included Motown artists Martha and the Vandellas and Marvin Gaye.[155] *Hit Parader* noted that Jamaican singer Millie Small opened proceedings, performing her heavily ska-inflected hit "My Boy Lollipop."[156] Small was followed by the Dovells, a male doo-wop group from Philadelphia, who performed their 1961 hit "The Bristol Stomp," which had been released on the Cameo-Parkway label.[157] That a doo-wop group singing a hit from 1961 was included on a bill aimed specifically at teenagers in 1964 demonstrates that doo-wop was still very much relevant in the culture and musical climate of 1964.[158] After the Dovells came the Shangri-Las. They performed just one song, their hit "Remember (Walkin' in the Sand)," which had yet to reach its chart peak of #5. As the *Hit Parader* reviewer reported,

> The mood becomes plaintive as four attractive young ladies step up to the mike and sing their lament for a lost summer love, "Remember (Walkin' in the Sand)."[159]

Their performance made quite an impression on Chris Curtis, as he told Richard Green in *NME*:

> 'It's quite a weird presentation they've got . . . the lead singer stands right over on one side of the stage, and the three others stand in the middle, instead of the other way round. It's because when they sing 'remember' and she goes 'walkin' in the sand,' she turns her head away and looks down all dispassionately, and they wave their arms about. They do a lot of weird actions, it's like choreography with arms, if you can have such a thing. One girl's hand goes down, then the next, then the next. I've never seen anything like it before.' [160]

Earlier in the article, Green had noted,

> The way the chart-topping Supremes wave their arms about when singing captivated thousands of British fans on their recent visit here. But not many people know that another girl team climbing the charts adopt a similar technique on stage.'[161]

It is noteworthy that the Supremes were trained by a professional choreographer, Charles 'Cholly' Atkins. Atkins had had a distinguished career as a singer as well as a jazz and tap dancer, performing with big band stars Duke Ellington, Cab Calloway and Count Basie. In the mid-to late 1950s he began 'choreographing singers,' developing a 'language of sophisticated movements' through which singers '*perform* their music, not by retelling a song's storyline in predictable pantomime, but by punctuating it with rhythmical dance steps, turns and gestures drawn from the rich bedrock of American vernacular dance.'[162]

George Goldner and Richard Barrett had earlier hired Atkins to work with Frankie Lymon and the Teenagers; Mary Wilson of the Supremes met Atkins the Apollo Theatre in 1962, and he later accepted a full-time position as choreographer at Motown.[163] It seems that the Shangri-Las were strongly influenced by this style of performative choreography; certainly, Richard Green noted the similarities in his piece. Given that they were largely left to fend for themselves during their first television appearance, it is not clear whether the Shangri-Las would have had professional choreographers at their disposal to help them develop their routines, or that their label would have seen fit, especially at this early stage, to invest in one.[164]

At the Brooklyn Fox, the Shangri-Las were followed by Motown group the Temptations: 'five dapper, swinging, very talented young men' whose 'footwork is brisk and dazzling, their harmony . . . smooth and groovy.'[165] Then came Motown's biggest group at that time, the Supremes, who proceeded to 'build a soulful, hand-clapping mood that fills the theatre.' Next up were Jay and the Americans, another group whose roots were firmly in Long Island doo-wop; they were signed with Leiber and Stoller and also involved with Artie Ripp. They performed two songs, "Only in America" and "Come a Bit Closer." (Two years later, the Shangri-Las would record their 1962 hit, "She Cried"). Next on the bill were the Contours, a Motown male vocal group, then the Ronettes, 'popular with their bump and grind choreography,' followed by the Searchers, 'direct from England, who perform their great hits, "Needles and Pins," "Don't Throw Your Love Away" and "Someday We're Gonna Love Again."'[166] Martha and the Vandellas then delivered their hits "Heatwave" and "Dancing in the Street," followed by doo-wop group Little Anthony and the Imperials, who recorded a large quantity of material on George Goldner's End label; the reviewer was of the opinion that they 'are returning to the heights of popularity they enjoyed in the 50s, and rightfully so.' Then came another British import, Dusty Springfield,' who sang "Wishin' and Hopin'." The last two acts on the bill were

The Miracles . . . demonstrating the superb showmanship that's made them a top group over the years. When they finish their act with "Mickey's Monkey," their ties and jackets cast aside in the spirited workout, the audience goes ape.

Wrapping up the show is Marvin Gaye, the epitome of cool soul. With his smooth, easy-going style, he shakes up the house singing his many hits, including "Try It Baby" and "Baby Don't You Do It."

All the performers join Murray and Marvin onstage for the big finale, as the curtain closes.[167]

The first thing to note here is the enormous number of performers on the bill—fifteen in total. Each performer was limited to a few songs—those higher up the bill had a correspondingly greater allocation. On this occasion, Marvin Gaye had top billing, and performed, as the author put it, 'his many hits.' Richard Green, the *NME* reporter who interviewed Chris Curtis about the Shangri-Las, wrote, 'Chris told me that the girls used to only sing the one number in their act. The Searchers were kept down to three.'[168]

This differs completely from what is now taken for granted at a live concert—an approximately hour-long performance by a single singer or group, with maybe one or two support acts also on the bill. To a large extent this is because from the mid- to late 1960s onward, the primary format for the musical artistic statement and the consumption of same was an *album* of around forty minutes in length (two approximately twenty-minute sides of an LP), which expanded to an hour or more with the advent of the compact disc in the mid-80s. In 1964 the dominant format for the consumption of popular music was the 7-inch 45 rpm single, with one song on each side. Generally speaking, the 'A-side' was the song expected to chart; the 'B-side' was often throwaway material. This was a deliberate strategy; if the buyer could get two hit songs on one record instead of having to purchase each separately, sales would be halved.[169]

Teenagers generally experienced these singles either by playing their own copies on a turntable or, far more commonly, by hearing them played on the radio by disk jockeys that at this time included Murray the K, Bob 'Babalu' Lewis, or Cousin Brucie. The concert performance and experience reflected this—Murray the K's revue was almost like a radio show performed live. Annie J. Randall, in her study of Dusty Springfield, who performed at the same Brooklyn Fox shows, noted: 'In a single show, the screaming and dancing-in-the-aisles teens could hear the current hit songs of their favourite performers.'[170]

A 'house' band of professional musicians would provide the backing music for all the groups. This ensured minimal changeover time was required between the different acts as it was simply a matter of one set of singers walking off stage and another coming on. The musical component of the show would run for 60 to 90 minutes in total, with a film usually screened before the musical performances.[171]

One important factor that made a concert like this possible to stage at all, then, was that most of the performers—almost all of them, in fact—were vocal groups: *singing groups*, not bands. The Searchers were the major exception on this bill. After all, these shows were enormously popular, and hundreds of teenagers would not flock to the Brooklyn Fox to see concerts in some kind of old-fashioned, outdated format. Ronnie Spector of the Ronettes, who were particular favourites of Murray the K and regular performers at the Brooklyn Fox, recalled,

> Going to one of Murray the K's rock and roll revues at the Brooklyn Fox was the highlight of any New York kid's week in the early sixties. For two dollars and fifty cents you got to see at least a dozen acts, and these were the top names in rock and roll—from Little Stevie Wonder to Bobby Vee to the Temptations, everybody played these shows.[172]

Singers and singing groups had been—and remained—a dominant presence in popular music. Beatlemania had just hit, but established forms did not change or disappear overnight. The vocal groups were heavily steeped in the harmonising traditions of doo-wop, which was the dominant form of teen music in New York City, but particularly in Brooklyn and Queens (and over the Hudson in New Jersey too, for that matter) from the mid-50s until well into the 60s. This was reflected in the choice of artists on this bill—the Dovells and Little Anthony and the Imperials were functioning doo-wop groups, and Jay and the Americans had begun as a doo-wop group and still performed in a heavily doo-wop–inflected style.

As we have seen, those who performed were limited to a very small number of songs, so at first glance it seems extraordinary that artists like the Searchers and Dusty Springfield would come all the way from

England for such appearances. However, the Murray the K revues ran all day—the entire show was performed six or seven times over, and the artists were at the venue, the Brooklyn Fox, for twelve hours at a time. In Ronnie Spector's recollection,

> We all knew we'd be stuck back in the theatre for like twelve hours straight. So everyone tried to make the best of it. The dressing rooms were all next to each other on this long hall, so the acts couldn't help but mingle. Diana Ross would come in to borrow our lipstick.[173]

Mary Weiss described these shows as '*real* brutal':

> You would come downstairs, and everyone would do an opening. You'd go upstairs—the elevator never worked in this building—and the rooms were on like six, seven and eight . . . then you'd come down and do your set. Then you'd go back up. Then you'd come back down for the finale. And you'd do that seven times.[174]

There was little time for socialising. Chris Curtis lamented, 'We didn't have any time to meet them [the Shangri-Las] socially . . . we did a lot of shows and then in between, we tried to eat, rest, and do thousands of other things in five minutes.'[175] For Weiss, these 'other things' included even more work:

> My manager, I'd go in the dressing room and he'd have somebody sitting in the corner, and I'm going, 'Who are you?' and he goes, 'I'm here to teach you "Remember" in French!' And I'm like looking . . . in between what I'm doing . . . 'you are out of your mind!'

The purpose of teaching Mary to sing "Remember" in French would have been to release a version in Europe with French vocals, thereby expanding their market and selling more records. Weiss commented ruefully, 'that's the pace that everything was at, my entire life was like that.'[176]

Another notable feature of the *Hit Parader* review was the overall equality with which the groups were treated. The writer did not trivialise the female groups; they were generally treated respectfully and praised for their musicality.[177] Their appearance was commented on, but so was that of the male groups. What's more, at no point did the reviewer use the term 'girl group.' Annie Randall has drawn attention to one more aspect of these shows:

> Those who attended the concerts describe the atmosphere as barely controlled pandemonium among the mixed audience of black and white teens, although with little of the racial tension that was a common feature of daily life outside the theater. The pandemonium was not confined to the theatre but spilled out onto the sidewalk in front, where Murray the K and various fan clubs fuelled the flames of teen enthusiasm and increased ticket sales by staging events for the singers, complete with fans wielding "WELCOME!" banners.[178]

This ease of racial intermingling reflected developments in radio, where, as Susan Douglas has pointed out, DJs 'who embraced black music and slang' encouraged 'identification with the music and talk as a form of generational and racial rebellion against the status quo.'[179]

Murray the K cultivated a close relationship with his teenage listeners by addressing them directly, as 'baby,' in the way dating teenagers might address each other. He also used 'slangy rhymed couplets' that gave the impression of up-with-the-latest hipness.[180] This kind of personal connection was at least in part responsible for the adulation Murray the K received as the convenor of the Brooklyn Fox pandemonium:

> I threw a kiss and looked towards the balcony. In the front row my eye caught two girls, about fifteen years old, crying hysterically, and over on the left side, three redheads—laughing and standing on their seats—screaming at me! I stood alone on the stage of the Fox Theater in Brooklyn, listening to this fantastic, unbelievable demonstration from the 4,500 groovy kids who were there that Saturday morning.[181]

That enthusiasm was shared by the performers, as Ronnie Spector indicated: 'Thank god for the Brooklyn Fox! Hit or no hit, that audience made us feel like stars.'[182] This spectacle of thousands of screaming young fans is of course reminiscent of the greatest object of US teenage pandemonium in 1964, the Beatles, and makes it clear that they were not the only artists to elicit wild responses.

Above: on 20 September 1964, the Shangri-Las were on the bill of a charity benefit for United Cerebral Palsy of New York City, Inc. and Retarded Infants Services Inc., at the Paramount Theatre on Times Square in Manhattan, headlined by the Beatles; *below*: a more mundane appearance at a Stay-in-School Rally in December 1964 (*Cash Box*, 19 December 1964).

STAY IN SCHOOL RALLY: WABC in New York held a Stay-in-School Rally last week at Eastern District High School in Brooklyn. WABC jocks were there as were top record names like the Shangri-La's above. Others on the bill were Candy and the Kisses, Randy and the Rainbows, Bernadette Carol, Frankie Callan, the Tee-Mates, the Tymes, and the You-Know-Who's.

A couple of weeks later, on 20 September 1964, the Shangri-Las performed at a charity benefit for United Cerebral Palsy of New York City, Inc. and Retarded Infants Services Inc., at the Paramount Theatre on Times Square.[183] The headlining act was the Beatles. Tickets ranged in price from $5 to $100, and all artists, including the Beatles, donated their services. Besides the Shangri-Las, the other performers were Steve Lawrence and Eydie Gorme, Leslie Uggams, the Tokens, Bobby Goldsboro, the Brothers Four, Jackie De Shannon and Nancy Ames. Gay Talese reported in the *The New York Times*,

> Coolly elegant women in mink coats and pearls, together with men in black tie and in no need of a haircut, found themselves in the Paramount Theater last night sitting amid 3,600 hysterical teen-agers.

Talese commented further that it was it was 'an incongruous sight . . . that brought together the chic and the shriek sets.'[184] In what was by now typical at their shows,

> The Beatles, when they finally got on stage, shortly after 10 P.M., sang for 25 minutes strumming out tunes that nobody could hear. They sang ten numbers, but as they did, teenagers rose to their feet and jumped and twisted in the aisles; others tossed jelly beans, slices of bread or toilet tissue toward the stage.[185]

The Shangri-Las went from being virtual unknowns to performing on the same bill as the Beatles in front of 3,600 people in the space of a few months. Mary Weiss remembered that, in terms of backstage arrangements before the show,

> They put the Beatles on one floor and everybody else on another floor . . . Margie . . . went up to a high floor and started sticking her fingers through the blinds to make the crowds go nuts in the streets, they did, it was bizarre.[186]

This show had a similar format to the Brooklyn Fox shows; with nine performers, each would have performed a handful of songs; the Shangri-Las, as relative newcomers, may have been limited to their one hit song, "Remember."

To perform with the Beatles must have been a great thrill for the Shangri-Las. One teenaged Beatles fan recalled that just being a *fan* of the Beatles was

> about wanting freedom. I didn't want to grow up and be a wife and it seemed to me the Beatles had the kind of freedom I wanted ... I didn't want to sleep with Paul McCartney, I was too young. But I wanted to be like them, something larger than life.[187]

For other teenagers, actually being *in* a pop group and making records was the ticket to 'something larger than life.' As Richard Goldstein observed in 1966, the Shangri-Las 'are in pop because Rock and Roll is to the middle class teenager what boxing is to the underprivileged: a key to wealth, power and status.'[188] However, as Grace Palladino has pointed out, 'teenage stars were more likely to gain celebrity than riches from their early efforts, especially since they tended to confuse the two.'[189] This is borne out by Ronnie Spector's recollection of performing at the Brooklyn Fox:

> our pay was two hundred dollars apiece for a ten-day run, which we thought was a fortune. Of course, every time we needed a new outfit or a few cans of hairspray, we'd hit Murray up for a fifty dollar advance, and those added up. By the time we got our paychecks, we'd usually have about a hundred dollars each left. But money was never the big thing anyway. We would've done those shows for free, if only for the chance to be around all those stars.[190]

Although such events were undeniably thrilling for these teenaged performers, their youthful enthusiasm, excitement and fame was capitalised on by those who exploited it for financial gain.

The frantic pace continued for the Shangri-Las. On October 12, 1964, they performed at the New York World's Fair, held at Flushing Meadows, Queens. The Fair was an enormous undertaking on a massive scale—the federal government spent $17 million on the United States Pavilion alone, and General Motors, General Electric, the Chrysler Corporation and many other companies invested heavily in displays and exhibitions to display their futuristic wares to the public. The artistic

The daily World's Fair calendar printed in the *New York Times* on 12 October 1964 announced: '5PM.—The Shangri-Las sing current hits at the A.M.F. Monorail.' That day was named 'Shangri-Las Day' at the Fair, and the front car of the monorail was adorned with the group's name. (*Photos by Bob Golby, courtesy Queens Museum Special Collections and Archives*)

aql:1138 1987.110.526aWF64 QMOA

Fair Calendar

Oct. 12, 1964

9:30 A.M.—Gates open.

10 A.M.—Official opening of the Gaslight Patio, Festival of Gas Pavilion.

10 A.M.—Trick or treat day; Mrs. Sybil Leek, one of Britain's 80 professional witches, will cast a good witch spell, judge & window-painting contest and distribute candy and gifts.

Noon—New York State Pavilion presents the Celestial Choral Ensemble of the Blind to open its program of continuous entertainment for the day.

Noon—"The Boy Friend," hour version of the hit musical; presented by Fides House (Washington). Again at 4 P.M. United States Pavilion.

1 P.M.—The Puppetry Guild of Greater New York offers puppet and marionette entertainment throughout the afternoon. Beginning and ending the series of puppeteers, the Manteo Sicilian Marionettes, about 4 feet high and up to 100 pounds. New York State Pavilion.

1 P.M.—Glee clubs from Rhode Island colleges and universities. Again at 2:30, 4 and 5:30 P.M. New England States Exhibition.

2 P.M.—Fides House variety show —ancient and contemporary song and dance. Again at 6 P.M. United States Pavilion.

2 P.M.—Steinway's Concert in Miniature; Luis and Marta Garcia-Renart, R.C.A. Pavilion.

5 P.M.—The Shangri-Las sing current hits at the A.M.F. Monorail.

6 P.M.—Brown University male

aql:1145 1987.110.533aWF64 QMOA

and cultural elements of the Fair were also significant. Many nations had their own pavilions in which Fair goers could experience aspects of the arts and culture of the many countries represented; in a quite extraordinary coup, the Vatican pavilion even managed to arrange for the loan of Michelangelo's *Pietà* for its display. The Fair attracted 51 million people between 21 April 1964 and 21 October 1965, and made an indelible impression on those who attended.[191] It has attracted correspondingly widespread coverage in books, online, and was also the subject of major exhibitions at the Queens Museum of Art in 1989, 2002 and 2004.[192]

Music was an important component of the Fair. In the *New York Times*, Gay Talese reported on the 'Swirl of Sounds' at the Fair:

> There is Calypso rhythm, followed by jazz a few feet away, and further on there is pop, then Gregorian chants and Bach . . . The Royal Burundi dancers and Drummers, sent here with the compliments of King Mwami Mwambusta IV, made a successful debut at the Africa pavilion . . . the thumping of the drums could be heard a mile away.[193]

Many pop and rock groups performed at the Fair, including the Satellites and the Galaxies IV from New Jersey, New York surf band the Malibooz, as well as Candy Johnson and the Exciters.[194] Ska group Byron Lee and the Dragonaires received sponsorship from the Jamaican government to play their first performance outside Jamaica.[195] The daily World's Fair calendar printed in the *New York Times* on 12 October 1964 announced: '5PM The Shangri-Las sing current hits at the A.M.F. Monorail.'[196] October 12 was named 'Shangri-Las Day' at the Fair, and the front car of the monorail was adorned with the group's name.[197]

Later that month, the Shangri-Las visited England briefly for a promotional tour.[198] *New Musical Express* reported,

> The Shangri-Las, who make their debut in the NME chart this week with "Remember," pay a brief visit to London next weekend.
>
> The American quartet arrives on Thursday, travels direct to Manchester to appear on Granada-TV's "Scene at 6.30," and then back to London to be interviewed on BBC Light's "Top Gear" on the same night.
>
> The following day (Friday), the Shangri-Las guest on Rediffusion-TV's "Ready Steady Go!" On the Sunday they telerecord an

appearance for the October 31 edition of ABC-TV's "Thank Your Lucky Stars," and fly back to America the next day.[199]

Mary remembered partying with Dusty Springfield while in London; they appeared on one of the television shows together and had been on the bill together at the Brooklyn Fox:

> Dusty was having a very large party in her flat. It all started out very civilized, nice French doors and antique desks, but she liked to start food fights. And she started one and I'm hiding under this lovely French desk with her manager and food and fish are flying by! . . . So Mary Ann goes to put her boots on and they were full of fish! But, Mary Ann got even with Dusty. She waited and waited and the next time we were there with Dusty at the Brooklyn Fox, Mary Ann put fish in Dusty's shoes.[200]

Only three members of the group made the trip to England, however. Chris Curtis, who had witnessed their performances as a four-piece, commented on this:

> We were with them . . . for a six-day run at Brooklyn Fox Theatre last time we were in America . . . I was very choked to find out the prettiest one didn't come over with them, though.[201]

It was around this time that the group started appearing at shows and in photographs as a three-piece, with Mary Weiss flanked by the Ganser twins. The reasons for this have either been obfuscated, explained away as Betty not liking travelling, or not explained at all. Alan Betrock writes that 'after their initial hit, Betty had left the group, and the Shangri-Las became a trio,'[202] and Charlotte Greig claims that 'Betty had left the group early on.'[203] Yet by the latter part of 1965, the group was appearing on teen music shows *Shindig!* and *Shivaree* as a quartet again—with Betty.[204] Richie Unterberger, writing on the *All Music* website, remarks,

> Their constant personnel changes baffle historians; sometimes they are pictured as a trio, and sometimes one of the members in the photos is clearly not one of the Weiss *or* Ganser sisters.[205]

The Shangri-Las as a trio (without Betty) in London, October 1964. (*Pictorial Press Ltd / Alamy*)

THE SHANGRI-LAS—motor-bike noises, plenty of screaming and a death type lyric which put it on the list of "restricted" discs by the BBC. Could it follow Twinkle's "Terry" into the best sellers?

In fact, around the time "Remember" was in the chart and the group were looking to record a follow-up single, it became apparent that Betty Weiss had become pregnant. To be 17, unmarried, pregnant and in a pop group in 1964 was a completely untenable situation. It was unthinkable that Betty's pregnancy should become public knowledge when the group had such a predominantly teen (and younger) audience, and—from a practical point of view—the punishing concert and recording schedules that were about to get underway would have been difficult for her, if not impossible. Of far greater concern to Red Bird management, of course, was that sexual mores in mid-60s USA simply did not accommodate unwed teenage mothers.[206] In her beautiful memoir *Just Kids*, Patti Smith, who fell pregnant aged 19 in 1966, has related:

> I was raised at a time when sex and marriage were absolutely synonymous. There was no available birth control and at nineteen I was still naïve about sex . . .
>   Judgemental neighbours made it impossible for my family, treating them as if they were harbouring a criminal. I found a surrogate family, also called Smith, farther south by the sea. A painter and his wife, a potter, kindly took me in.[207]

Smith's description of going into labour and her treatment in a New Jersey hospital is a moving reminder of the hostility young women at this time in history faced:

> Due to my unwed status, the nurses were very cruel and uncaring, and left me on a table for several hours before informing the doctor that I had gone into labor. They ridiculed me for my beatnik appearance and immoral behavior, calling me "Dracula's daughter" and threatening to cut my long black hair. When my doctor arrived, he was very angry. I could hear him yelling at the nurses that I was having a breech birth and I should not have been left alone. Through an open window, while I lay in labor, I could hear boys singing a cappella songs through the night. Four part harmony on the street corners of Camden, New Jersey. As the anesthesia took effect, the last thing I remember was the doctor's concerned face and the whispers of attendants.[208]

It is to be hoped that Betty escaped such horrible treatment when she married her child's father on 27 July 1964,[209] but it is inconceivable that she did not encounter prejudice and experience some degree of trauma from the whole situation. Betty was quietly 'disappeared' from the group she had co-founded and was the original lead vocalist for, obliged to marry and watch from the wings while the Shangri-Las performed and were photographed as a trio (with Mary assuming Betty's lead role), travelled to England, and had a succession of hits. Betty's daughter, Tracy, was born in the early months of 1965, and from approximately mid-1965 onwards, Betty returned to recording with the group, appeared in television performances, and participated in at least some touring.[210]

From the outset, the Shangri-Las were shrouded in anguish and mystery, even if this was, by necessity, not immediately apparent to their teenage audience. As time passed, though, it became increasingly obvious. Four group members, then three, then four again—with no consistent explanation for why. Betty's pregnancy plunged the group (and its management) into a conspiracy of silence, an absolutely unavoidable cover-up. The fact that this occurred in mid-1964, just as "Remember" was climbing the charts, meant that from the very beginning of their success, the group members were custodians of a huge secret—so huge, in fact, that to this day no one will talk about it. Betty's early absence from the group is a topic that was always absolutely off-limits in interviews with Mary Weiss and was doubtless one of the factors in her refusal to participate in this book.

One unfortunate consequence of this situation has been that the pressure and strain exerted on *all* the group members to maintain this secrecy has gone unacknowledged for decades. For the Weiss sisters particularly, living in impoverished circumstances in a one-parent household shattered by the accidental death of their father in 1949, this new and complicated situation must have been particularly difficult. The bulk of responsibility for keeping the show on the road, so to speak, landed on the shoulders of Mary Weiss, who was 15 at the time. Little wonder that Mary has indicated, on multiple occasions, that she 'had enough pain in me at the time to pull off anything and get into it and sound believable.'[211] For the Shangri-Las, emotional intensity was not an act; the darkness was real.

For the remaining members, life as the Shangri-Las continued at a frantic pace. The success of Remember" demanded a quick follow-up single to capitalise on the group's popularity. "Leader of the Pack" was probably recorded in September 1964, as it had already been released in the US while the group were in England on their promotional tour. According to Morton, the song was planned for another group initially:

> It was written for another Long Island group called the Goodies. They never had a lot of success—I have no answer as to why?—Four girls . . . good singers. I found this group during the time "Remember . . ." was out. It just seemed natural to me. I liked them. They liked me. They sang good. I simply wanted to make a record with them. And when the company came to me and said, "No dice! You give everything you've got to one group." Of course, nowadays that's all changed. But not then—I got shot down. That was it for me . . . I was ready to quit.[212]

In all likelihood, the management at Red Bird did not want anything interfering with the Morton/Shangri-Las formula, and certainly the relationship between Morton and the Shangri-Las would solidify increasingly from this point on. But the process through which the Shangri-Las came to record "Leader of the Pack" indicates just how disposable young teenaged artists were perceived to be by record companies.

The original line-up of the Goodies was Maryann Gesmundo, Diane Reilling, Maureen Reilling and Sue Gelber.[213] Like the Shangri-Las, they all went to the same high school, where they heard each other sing at their school variety show and formed a group to sing together.[214] Ron Schubert, manager of Long Island doo-wop group Nick and the Nacks, decided to represent the Goodies, and at some point introduced them to George Morton.[215] They performed for Morton at Ultrasonic, the studio in Hempstead, Long Island, that he used sometimes. Morton took the group into the Red Bird offices, and they 'were immediately asked to sign'—which they did, to the affiliated Blue Cat label. Mary Ann from the Goodies recalls, 'there was some scepticism . . . but we convinced our parents that this was the way that we thought we should go, and they actually supported us in the end, and we were under age so they signed contracts for us.'[216] Dianne continues,

So we started going to the Brill Building a lot and rehearsing different songs ... we would meet with George and songwriters and rehearse various songs, and one of the first songs that we rehearsed was "Leader of the Pack" ... we made a demo of it, and we had actually expected that it would be our first record—that was our understanding.[217]

Unbeknown to the Goodies, however, the 'company,' as Morton put it, had decided the song would be recorded by the Shangri-Las, since they needed a follow-up for "Remember"; it would almost certainly have been the Goodies demo that Mary was referring to when she said of "Leader of the Pack":

I took it home and listened to it for a very long time before I agreed to do it ... even at the time, it was pretty much out there.[218]

The Goodies 'had no idea' about this change of plan, and only found out about the Shangri-Las' version of the song when they heard it on the radio. Incredulous, they phoned Morton and the label management, who 'explained' that the Shangri-Las needed a follow-up song, quickly, and assured the members of the Goodies that 'we've got another great song, it's going to be a hit, you'll record this next song...'[219]

Disappointed but undaunted, the Goodies began work on the next song they were given and made another demo. The song was "Give Him a Great Big Kiss." *Again* it was given to the Shangri-Las; it became their third single. Dianne from the Goodies relates,

A friend of my called on the phone and said, I just heard you on the radio! I just heard your song! I said, well it couldn't be us, because we hadn't cut the master, we just had done the demo. She said, No, no, they just played your song! "Give Him a Great Big Kiss"! I said, Oh no! Not **AGAIN**! [220]

The degree of deceit engaged in by Red Bird's management is remark-able, but it was very likely motivated by striking while the iron was hot with the Shangri-Las so as not to lose revenue-generating momentum, rather than intentional abuse of the Goodies. Nevertheless, it absolutely involved exploiting the kind of enthusiasm and excitement that had made Ronnie Spector declare that the Ronettes would have played the

Brooklyn Fox shows for nothing. The members of the Goodies hold no grudge toward the Shangri-Las and feel strongly that the Shangri-Las were not aware all this was going on at the time, and would not have had any control over it even if they had been. Eventually the Goodies did record their own single, "Dum Dum Ditty" b/w "Sophisticated Boom Boom."[221] The single sold moderately well (according to the Goodies, it peaked at #38). However, as they remembered,

> Because we were so young, we didn't really have great representation, so we didn't have somebody who was in our corner, and we didn't understand the business, so we didn't really know, there was no way for us to know whether our record was being promoted or not promoted.[222]

In a final irony, both songs were later also recorded by the Shangri-Las, and it is fair to say that the Goodies' versions of the songs, although earlier, were eclipsed by those of their more famous counterparts.[223] In retrospect, it seems likely that the Goodies, despite what they were being told by Red Bird management, were being used to 'demo' the material, not necessarily with a view to cutting the songs as single releases themselves. The Goodies had a similar sound to the Shangri-Las, and from a practical perspective, it made sense to work on arrangements and iron out all the kinks in the early stages, which is something that could be undertaken with another group. To do this would save studio time and money later, when cutting the master. An additional advantage was that the Shangri-Las could be out performing shows and promoting their records while the other group rehearsed and solidified the arrangements for their next song.[224]

This is what happened, it seems, as the Shangri-Las began a punishing tour schedule. In October they appeared on some dates with the Rolling Stones on their second tour of North America, with other acts including Joey Paige, Marvin Gaye, Gerry and the Pacemakers, Chuck Berry, James Brown and the Supremes.[225] The Shangri-Las also did at least three shows in November 1964 with the Beach Boys, on 27 November at the Cleveland Arena (Cleveland, Ohio), 28 November (Olympia, Detroit, Michigan), and 29 November (Cincinnati Gardens, Cincinnati, Ohio). Jay and the Americans were also on the bill for all the Beach Boys shows.[226] On 16 November 1964, the Shangri-Las appeared on TV quiz show *I've Got a Secret* and performed "Leader of the Pack" to the delight of the teens in the audience and the bemused bewilderment of the adult contestants.[227] By 28 November, "Leader of the Pack" had reached #1 on the *Billboard* singles chart, but it is likely that they were on the road with the Beach Boys when this happened, and had little time to savour the moment. 1964 closed with the simultaneous release of two more singles, the aforementioned "Give Him a Great Big Kiss" b/w "Twist and Shout," and "Maybe" b/w "Shout."[228] The Shangri-Las were named "#1 New Vocal Group" for 1964 in *Cash Box* on 26 December 1964.[229]

This concluded an extraordinary year for the Shangri-Las—two hit singles, a promotional tour to the UK, sharing a bill with the Beatles, concert performances, television appearances, and transnational fame—all in the space of about six months. Their working partnership with George 'Shadow' Morton was central to the success of both Morton and the group, and although Morton has repeatedly presented himself as someone who 'accidently' found himself in the business of making records, it is clear from his experience prior to working with the Shangri-Las that he had very definite ideas about becoming a producer and was consciously working toward realising this goal. The immediate sensation caused by his first collaboration with the Shangri-Las, "Remember (Walkin' in the Sand)," thrust the group into a non-stop performing and recording schedule for which they had very little practical preparation. Singing groups were regarded primarily as a vehicle for the performance and dissemination of material written by professional songwriters, as the events that befell the Goodies attest. Nevertheless, within this context of structural disempowerment the Shangri-Las possessed tremendous cultural and aesthetic power, as reflected in their popularity, sales of their records, and their artistic achievement. The manner in which all this was destroyed by factors beyond the group's control is explored in the next chapter.

Cash Box

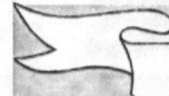

The red-hot Red Bird label recently gave birth to a new teen-beat sensation, a femme threesome called The Shangri-Las. In quick succession, the gals have come-up with three smash sides, "Remember (Walkin' In The Sand)," "Leader Of The Pack," followed by a novelty answer hit, and currently "Give Him A Great Big Kiss," it's a certainty that the teen market can't wait to get its hands on the team's first LP, named after them, just marketed by the label. Within the next week or so, a new single is also due. Gals will also receive hefty TV exposure in the near future via guest appearances on "Hullabaloo" and the "Lloyd Thaxton" program.

INTERNATIONAL SECTION BEGINS PAGE 53

Cash Box
SAN REMO WINNERS
"SE PIANGI, SE RIDI"
BOBBY SOLO
NEW CHRISTY MINSTRELS
1965

Cover of *Cash Box*, 13 February, 1965

CHAPTER FOUR

Red Bird's Demise, the Mob, and Mercury Records

You want royalties? Then go to England!

—Morris Levy[1]

I've got a hundred hookers. Charge them to the artist.

—Artie Ripp

LEADER OF THE PACK

The Shangri-Las self-titled first album, sometimes referred to as *Leader of the Pack*, was released in February 1965.[2] Hastily assembled to capitalise on the group's popularity, it contained both sides of all four of their Red Bird singles, in addition to a Leiber and Stoller composition called "Bull Dog" that would surface later in 1965 as the B-side of another single. *Billboard* called it 'a socko album debut for the younger set by one of the most popular of the new rock vocal teams.'* Another reviewer enthused,

> Having turned in three smashes in the singles area, the Shangri-Las can't miss with their first LP effort, which includes "Remember," "Leader of the Pack" and their latest deck, "Give Him a Great Big Kiss." The second side features six tunes taped live, most of which need no introduction to the teens who will turn out in droves for this set. If these gals could displace the Britishers on the best-seller

---

* Note that the biggest music trade journal of the day used the terminology 'new rock vocal team' in 1965 to describe the Shangri-Las ('Album Reviews,' *Billboard*, 20 February, 1965, 64).

145

charts, this group has a tremendous selling power, and tunes like "Maybe" and "Twist and Shout" provide still more appeal.[3]

Barely six months into the Shangri-Las' tenure as teen sensations, their 'tremendous selling power' and 'ability to displace the Britishers' was being commented upon. As noted in the review, Side B consists entirely of a 'taped . . . live performance at one of the Shangri-Las recent shows in the New York City area.'[4] From a practical standpoint, this was a quick way of assembling enough material for an album, with the added advantage of saving on studio costs. It seems likely that this live material was recorded late in 1964, as it included three of the four songs on the two singles that were released simultaneously in December of that year.[5] The live set included "Twist and Shout" and "Shout," both of which had been big hits for other artists and were teen dance favourites,* so their inclusion in a live set is not surprising. These live versions were the B-sides of "Give Him a Great Big Kiss" and "Maybe," respectively; this is also consistent with the practice noted earlier of throwaway B sides.

"Maybe" was originally recorded by the Chantels on George Goldner's End label in 1958; the Shangri-Las recorded a studio version for their single release, and a different, live version was included in the material on the B-side of the album. Just after the release of "Give Him a Great Big Kiss" in late 1964, the Shangri-Las told journalist June Harris that "Maybe" was issued as a single at the same time in an effort to deflect interest away from "Simon Says,", which had been re-released by Smash to capitalise on the Shangri-Las' newfound fame. Margie Ganser explained:

> "'Simon Says" is a horrible record. It's really bad. We had a contract with Smash about a year ago, and they released this as our first and only disc. I suppose at the time, being very new in the field, we figured it was going to be a great big hit, and didn't see anything wrong with it technically. Today, of course, we can see great big gaps in it. We would have given anything not to have seen it on the market again.

---

*"Shout" had been a *Billboard* top 50 hit for the Isley Brothers in 1959 and had remained a dancefloor favourite (Lulu had a UK top ten hit with her version in 1964); the Isley Brothers also had a *Billboard* top 20 hit with "Twist and Shout" in 1962/63, before their recording was overshadowed by the Beatles version in early 1964 (#2 *Billboard*).

It was our manager—Larry Martire—who suggested that "Maybe" should be released, so that we could squash "Simon Says". We don't even care if it doesn't sell, as long as it takes the interest off this one.'[6]

As early as the end of 1964, the group and its management were attempting to distance themselves from Artie Ripp and Kama Sutra Productions.

Three additional songs were included in the live material on the first Shangri-Las album: "So Much in Love," "You Can't Sit Down" and "Good Night, My Love, Pleasant Dreams." Taken together, these songs offer a fascinating snapshot of a very early Shangri-Las performance. "So Much in Love" was a hit in 1963 for doo-wop group the Tymes and, quite amazingly, features seagull and wave sounds at the very beginning to locate it at the beach.[7] "You Can't Sit Down" was also a hit in 1963, for the Dovells, with whom the Shangri-Las had performed at the Brooklyn Fox.[8] The Tymes and the Dovells both recorded for the Philadelphia-based Cameo-Parkway label, whose roster included many doo-wop groups (Rod McBrien, the engineer with whom George 'Shadow' Morton recorded the demo version of "Leader of the Pack," sang in doo-wop group the Valrays, who recorded several singles for Cameo-Parkway).[9] "Good Night, My Love, Pleasant Dreams," was originally recorded by Jesse Belvin in 1956.[10] Many artists subsequently covered it: in 1963 there were versions by the 4 Seasons, Bobby Vinton, the Tymes, and the Fleetwoods (for whom it was a hit), so it was definitely a popular song of the day.[11] The Shangri-Las' live material falls broadly into two categories—up-tempo rock numbers, and doo-wop-style vocal harmony material—but no real division existed between them. So much so, in fact, that the Shangri-Las arrangement of "Shout" segued into "Goodnight, My Love," and then back into "Shout." The live material on the Shangri-Las' first album emphasised that, for the group and their teen audience, these distinctions did not exist.

Another point to note is that all this material was relatively straightforward to perform live, given its emphasis on vocal harmonising and rock beats. This is in contrast to the Shangri-Las' first two hit singles, which were complex studio productions with elements and a 'feel' that would have been impossible to reproduce exactly live—with sound effects, for instance.[12] Of course, they *did* perform their hit singles live, but a version of "Leader of the Pack" recorded at the Brooklyn Fox the-

The Shangri-Las onstage at the Brooklyn Fox Theater. The motorbike onstage suggests they
were performing "Leader of the Pack" at Murray the K's Xmas Show in December 1964.
Photos courtesy of Gillian McCain, who found them at a flea market.

atre demonstrates the manner in which the dramatics of the studio version were subsumed by the limitations of playing with a workman-like
backing band which also had to accompany a dozen other artists (as
discussed previously), not to mention compete with a theatre full of
screaming teenagers (about half way through this recording, one can be
heard yelling 'Hi Mary!!!'). It does seem that on some occasions at the
Brooklyn Fox, a real motorbike was used during "Leader of the Pack";
certainly, this version contains motorbike sounds.[13]

The unreliability of the pick-up bands with which the Shangri-Las
were obliged to perform would eventually force them to assemble their
own group to back them on the road. As Mary Weiss recalled,

> You never knew what you were getting as far as backing . . . some of
> the backup used to sound like Bill Murray lounge lizard music, which
> used to drive us up the wall. It was unacceptable. Toward the end we
> got our own band and we were traveling by ourselves.[14]

It is unlikely that the band accompanying the Shangri-Las' on Tuesday, August 10th, 1965, in Harbor Springs, Michigan, sounded anything like 'lounge lizard music.'* The Iguanas, billed on this occasion
as 'the Fabulous Iguanas,' were a popular local teenage R&B–based
garage-rock band featuring one Jim Osterberg on drums. Osterberg

---

* Nor could this be said of the Sonics, who backed the Shangri-Las at a Seattle Center
Coliseum show in April, 1966 (see photo on p. 169).

would later (in)famously and permanently be known as Iggy Pop; his moniker derived from his tenure in the Iguanas. On this occasion, the Shangri-Las were performing at Club Ponytail, an alcohol-free teen club which boasted 'the largest patio in Northern Michigan' and 'continuous entertainment' from 8 p.m. to 1 a.m.[15] Iguanas guitarist Jim McLaughlin's reminiscences offer a telling window into the shambolic nature of pick-up band logistics:

> 'I was terrified,' says McLaughlin, 'but Jim said, this is going to be great, screw the practical side, man, we're on with the Shangri-Las.' After an hour of practice in the afternoon with the band's 'greasy lead-guitar-player slash manager slash roadie-guy' they hit the stage, with McLaughlin babbling, 'Which one is the candy store one, what are the chords, this is going to be a disaster!' But: 'Jim was perfect. He had the confidence, he knew no one would notice if we made any mistakes. And they didn't.'[16]

According to Faith Whitehill, who wrote the liner notes for the group's first album, the live material was included

> to prove again that the group's appeal is not entirely dependent on tricky studio work and recording gimmicks. The girls are not just record artists, they are fully-fledged entertainers, with talent, poise, stage presence, warmth, individuality—in short, all the qualifications to keep a live audience cheering and begging for more.[17]

The perception of the Shangri-Las as 'gimmicky' is discussed in more detail in chapter 6. But underlying this notion of 'tricky studio work' is the idea that a recording should essentially be an 'authentic' document of a performance, which is a hangover from the earliest days of recording.[18] As producer Virgil Moorefield has explained: 'Originally, the aim of recordings was to create the illusion of a concert hall setting . . . to bring to the living room the sensation of being at a live performance, a metaphor of presence.'[19] As discussed earlier, this was largely due to the limitations of recording apparatus in the first half of the twentieth century.[20] However, along with many other aspects of the music industry, the recording process was rapidly being upended in the early/mid 1960s:

There came into being a new conception of making records, developed separately and in stages, most notably by Phil Spector and [long-time Beatles producer] George Martin. While different in many ways, both of their approaches to production involved replacing the quest for the ability to present the illusion of physical reality with a new aesthetic. The new sonic world they sought to create was the appearance of a reality that could not exist—a pseudo-reality, created in synthetic space.[21]

This was, of course, what 'Shadow' Morton was creating too, and it is an indication of how recent this conception of record making was that it was regarded with some suspicion as gimmick-laden trickery, as somehow inauthentic. George Martin was also accused of this:

'This leads to the whole question of what you are aiming to produce when you make a record . . . one argument that is frequently levelled at me is: "You're not being very honest." I say, to hell with that. We have a different form of art here.'[22]

Faith Whitehill was anxious to assure the Shangri-Las' audience that the group indeed possessed 'all the qualifications to keep a *live audience* cheering and begging for more.' In other words, they were *authentic* because they could *perform live*—and implicit in this is a pre-emptive rebuttal of the notion of the Shangri-Las as merely putty in the hands of a genius producer. Furthermore, the separation of the songwriter from the *performer*, which was (just) still the norm at this point, meant that their performance was the standard an artist was judged by, not whether they had written their own material, and there is correspondingly no mention of songwriters in Whitehill's notes. Ironically, however, the only mention of the group members by name is in the body of the notes:

Mary, who is sixteen and blonde and the lead singer, and Maryann [sic] and Margie, who are seventeen and brunette and identical twins . . . [23]

The individual members of the Shangri-Las received no credit anywhere else on the album; their ages and hair colour were evidently more important to mention than their surnames. This is part of what Jacqueline Warwick has identified as a sublimation of individual identities in a group, the members of which 'were considered by many record producers to be replaceable as long as the look of the group was maintained more or less intact.'[24] The group was a vehicle for the songs; the components of the group were perceived as less important than the group itself.[25] Similarly, the last recording released under the name Frankie Lymon and the Teenagers, "Creation of Love," did not actually feature the Teenagers, since it was recorded after their split with Lymon; the Ray Charles Singers performed on it instead. This interchanging of performers was not something that only occurred with young *female* singers, it was standard industry practice.[26]

In keeping with this hierarchy, the largest credit on the cover is 'Produced by Shadow Morton' directly under the name of the group; in smaller print, engineers Brooks Arthur and Rod McBrien were credited. The photographer and cover designer were also named; it is noteworthy that these occupations received an official credit, whereas the instrumentalists who played on both the live and the studio material did not. This would be absolutely unthinkable today, but in 1964 it was standard. Session musicians were hired hands: they did their jobs, got paid, and a credit on a teen pop record was not particularly consequential.

REPRESENTATIONS OF REBELLION

Following the great success of "Leader of the Pack," and before the release of their first album, the Shangri-Las' 'image,' for want of a better term, underwent a quite radical transformation.[27] In mid-November 1964, the group performed "Leader of the Pack" on television quiz show *I've Got a Secret* wearing matching ultra-modest knee-length pleated skirts and blouses.[28] A month later, a full-page colour advertisement for their two new singles, "Give Him a Great Big Kiss" and "Maybe," featured the trio in matching two-toned pants and sleeveless sweaters with black knee-high boots.[29] The cover of the group's first album (February 1965) further reflected the success of "Leader of the Pack," with Mary Weiss and the Ganser sisters dressed in black pants, waistcoats and boots, flanking a leather-jacketed motorcyclist on a bike. Cynthia Cyrus has asserted,

> The Shangri-Las, a white group, evoked their bad-girl image with consistently slinky outfits, usually paired with go-go boots. They spin

out variants of tight dark pants in leather, knit and woven fabrics. The shirts can be ruffled or button-down, worn with vests or abandoned altogether for soft but sleeveless sweater tops. They flaunt the sophistication of the in-crowd. It comes as little surprise when they appear on an album cover alongside a motorcycle-riding leather jacketed hunk: he is, as the title above his head confirms, the 'Leader of the Pack.'[30]

On the contrary, as late as 26 December 1964 the Shangri-Las were pictured in *Cash Box* (after being named '#1 New Vocal Group 1964') in knee-length skirts and dressy heels, smiling cheerfully and affecting carefully staged mid-dance move poses.[31] There is nothing 'slinky' about their attire, nor is there anything even slightly subversive, as Cyrus seems to be suggesting, about their sleeveless tops. In the latter part of 1966 and early 1967, when they were signed to the Mercury label, the group was photographed in a consciously glamorous manner, in sophisticated white pant-suits and sporting big smiles and bouncy hair.[32] The cover of the first Shangri-Las album, on which Cyrus based her generalisations, was another matter entirely, but it is wrong to state that the group was 'consistently' photographed in this manner.[33]

The 'look' and image of the Shangri-Las is nevertheless an important subject for discussion, since it is almost always commented upon, usually in terms of how different it was from that of other 'girl groups.' So codified are perceptions of the 'genre,' however, and so rigid the Shangri-Las' placement within it, that few critics have considered alternate perspectives from which to view them than that of 'girl groups.' The opening sentence of Richie Unterberger's *All Music* entry is typical:

> Along with the Shirelles and the Ronettes, the Shangri-Las were among the greatest girl groups; if judged solely on the basis of attitude, they were the greatest of them all.[34]

As noted above, the cover of the Shangri-Las' first album, released in February 1965, is approximately the point at which the Shangri-Las began to be marketed as somewhat rebellious, tough bad-girls. The front cover is a stark and powerful image. Mary Weiss stands in the foreground, just off-centre, feet apart, hands behind her back, staring with sullen defiance at the viewer. Behind her, a motor cyclist, her

The "Leader of The Pack" girls now have their third hit in a row

SHANGRI-LAS MAKE IT BIG

Above: feature in *Music Business*, 31 December 1964.
Below: cover of the Shangri-Las debut album.

"Leader of the Pack," looks off camera to his right, warily, as if watching for potential assault. Mary stands between him and the viewer, protectively, defending him and her choice, daring anyone to open their mouth in opposition. To Mary's left, Marge and Mary Ann reinforce and restate her position, literally and emotionally, similarly defiant, and their physical likeness as identical twins adds another dimension to their support.

Much has been made of this image, and many have conflated the personalities of the group members with what has become the enduring image of the Shangri-Las. At the time, it was seen by some as something of a novelty; one review stated, 'they match the gimmicks on their records with their stage gear of tights, boots and suede waistcoats.'[35]

A convincingly marketable image was (and remains) an important component of the business of selling records. As Keith Richards once observed, 'In the early 60s nobody took the music as serious. It was the image that counted.' The Rolling Stones, he noted, were 'very hip to image and how to manipulate the press . . . a lot of PR went into it, consciously.'[36] Their first manager, Andrew Loog Oldham, was responsible for the famous "Would You Let Your Daughter Go with a Stone?" campaign in the English music paper *Melody Maker*. Oldham constructed the Rolling Stones as 'bad boys,' setting them up in threatening delinquent opposition to the Beatles. This worked at least in part because the Rolling Stones looked (and later acted) the part—handsome, sullen, brooding, and safely but tantalisingly dangerous.*

Something similar was at work with the Shangri-Las.[37] Mary Weiss has played down their 'tough girls' image, noting that she had 'a huge fight' about "Leader of the Pack" because

> I wasn't so sure I wanted to record it. I had my doubts, not that it would be a hit, I had more doubts that it would put me in a direction I didn't want to go . . . Everything I've read about myself from there on said how tough I was! If you look at those old clips, you tell me where you see tough![38]

On the other hand, Ellie Greenwich, who worked closely with the Shangri-Las, as a songwriter, and rehearsing material, described them

---

* By 'safely' I am referring purely to the relationship between spectator and image.

as 'very nice street urchins ... street classy ... and ... tough yet very vulnerable' which was, she thought, 'part of the appeal.' Greenwich recalled

'At the beginning we did not get along—they were kind of crude,
and having to deal with them on a daily basis used to get me very
uptight—with their gestures, and language, and chewing the gum,
and the stockings ripped up their leg. We would say, 'Not nice, you
must be ladies,' and they would say, 'We don't want to be ladies,'
and we had a couple of rough times there until ... we had a really
big blowout in the ladies room of the Brill Building one night. We
were screaming and yelling and ranting and raving. I cried and it was
just horrible. After that, it was wonderful. We got along. They were
on time. They wouldn't chew the gum so much. They controlled
their language to a reasonable level. But they were tough girls—they
really, really were.'[39]

This actually suggests that the Shangri-Las' *earlier* image of neat knee-
length pleated skirts, blouses and cheery teen smiles was in fact the
more contrived one. Mary Weiss has said on more than one occasion,

I used to get my slacks on Eighth Street in the Village in a Men's
Store. People would look at me like I was gay because I like low rise
pants. I don't get it, quite frankly.

She added,

I like those outfits on the LEADER album. That was my thing . . .
that was us. It's funny, because it created such a hoopla, like we were
tough, whatever, and all it is, is a white shirt, a vest and a pair of black
pants.[40]

Little wonder that the point at which image stopped and reality
began was not completely obvious. As Greenwich observed, on another
occasion,

Mary Weiss [had] the sweetest long straight hair, an angelic face,
and then this nasal voice comes out, and this little attitude—the

best of both worlds. They also knew they had a look, and they played into it.[41]

Clearly this struck a chord with their audience. 'A prom dress just wasn't me,' said Mary. 'I liked slacks and vests and boots. A lot of kids related to that.'[42] One of Weiss's contemporaries who certainly did was Suzi Quatro, whose musical career began at fourteen playing bass in all-female band the Pleasure Seekers.[43] The group formed in Detroit in 1964 and quickly achieved enough success to be out on the road performing from a young age, like the Shangri-Las.[44] When Quatro interviewed Weiss for her BBC radio show in 2007, she told her that in 1965

I saw you on Club 1270 in Detroit, I was one of the regular dancers on the TV show, OK—you came out with the Shangri-Las, I can't remember what song you did but you had on the leather waistcoat and the tight trousers. And you affected me! And I didn't realise until I was setting up this interview with you that you were probably image-wise and attitude-wise very much a role model for me. And I had no idea![45]

The Shangri-Las' teenage audience may also have related to the tension between the group's don't-mess-with-us image and their vulnerability to hurt and pain, evident in the emotional honesty of their music. A photo of the group that captures this with spectacular success was taken by David Dalton. More famous as a rock journalist and author of multiple music biographies, Dalton's involvement in music began as a fan taking photos at shows he attended; he then found he was able to sell them. In the mid-60s he worked at teen magazine *Hullabaloo* and in its early days wrote regularly for *Rolling Stone*.[46]

Dalton liked to photograph musicians in what he called 'rock tableaux'—setting up shots to suggest a particular situation that viewers would identify with the group and 'illustrate what the song was about.'[47] When he photographed the Shangri-Las for *Hullabaloo* in, he thought, late 1965 or 1966, he placed Mary in the foreground, facing the viewer but looking off to one side with an expression of deep, resigned sadness. To her right, in the background, Betty stands side on, hands in pockets. She speaks quietly, confidentially, inches from the ear of one of the Ganser sisters, likely Mary Ann, who simultaneously inclines her

om the *Hullabaloo* photo shoot by
avid Dalton, 1965. *Used with permission.*

head to hear and smiles conspiratorially at what Betty is telling her. Dalton's idea was to suggest a "Leader of the Pack" / 'Is she *really* going out with him?' scenario, which audiences familiar with the teen dialogue that regularly appears in Shangri-Las' songs would certainly recognise. Dalton remembers Mary commenting, at the conclusion of the shoot, "You're just like Bernard of Hollywood!" Bruno Bernard, better known as Bernard of Hollywood, was a photographer renowned for his highly stylised and carefully set-up shots of Marilyn Monroe, Jayne Mansfield and other screen stars in the 1940s and 50s.[48]

This compelling photograph conveys much more, however—it bristles with tension. Dalton has used several noteworthy techniques to convey this. Mary, Betty, and Mary Ann are dressed identically, signalling (even to a viewer with no knowledge of their identity) that a unity exists between them; yet they are opposed to one another in a two-versus-one formation that suggests an imbalance in their power dynamic. In addition, there are no props, and no backdrop. Like sculptured figures, the group members are isolated from pictorial narrative in an insular, cocoon-like space, so there is nothing to focus on except the expressions and movement of bodies. This is both minimal and relentlessly vertical, relieved only slightly by the tilt of Mary Ann's head and the bend in her leg, which is gently complemented by Betty's angled elbow. Mary's pain is completely focused in her pillar-like stillness, while her almost business-like stance, hands behind her back, simultaneously conveys strength and vulnerability. And all this in a form instantly recognisable to its target audience, for is there a teenage girl anywhere who has not been whispered about behind her back by her friends?

It is tempting to speculate that at least some of the Shangri-Las' teenage fans were attracted to the group's music and image because they related to them as fellow outsiders; certainly, the following the group has enjoyed in subsequent years would seem to bear this out. However, the Shangri-Las occupied an interesting position in relation to conformity and the expected social and career trajectories for young white women in mid-60s America. Laurie Stras has articulated a broad understanding of these: 'Marriage and domestic competence (if not aptitude) were expected, women's first responsibility was to home and family, and if as wives they had to work, they should strive to do so in strictly segregated jobs that did not compromise their respectability.'[49]

Performing, touring, and recording with a pop group did not fulfil any aspirational requirements in this direction, and the Weiss and Ganser sisters clearly had their own issues with expectations of 'ladylike' and 'respectable' behaviour, as their clashes with Ellie Greenwich indicate. Discussing the Shangri-Las' audience in 1966, Mary Weiss stated,

> 'They may buy the Supremes, but they listen to us. Because the Supremes come on very feminine and chic, but we come on like the average American girl, who just isn't slinky and sexy. We couldn't do all those oozy 'baby babys,' but the Supremes couldn't get away with "Leader of the Pack."'[50]

Did the 'average American girl' wear black pants and boots, crave the company of delinquent biker-types, fight with her parents and reject their values? Almost certainly not, but on some level, the Shangri-Las perceived themselves as 'average American girls,' and, it seems, had this reflected back to them by their audience. As Stras suggests, their 'songs could well have helped make teen angst seem normal—not just allowed but de rigueur if you were to be a real teenager.'[51]

There is a further implied dichotomy in Weiss's statement: the Shangri-Las were normal or 'average,' an important and assumed component of which was being white. The Supremes, on the other hand, were 'feminine and chic,' glamorous, an unattainable fantasy of young womanhood that the Shangri-Las saw as inappropriate for themselves, and implicitly non-average, non-normal, and non-white. This comparison with the Supremes is an apt one to take up at this point, because part of why the Shangri-Las could play at being 'bad girls,' in a way the Supremes certainly could not, was because they were white.

REBELLION AND WHITENESS

A significant body of literature now exists which undermines notions of whiteness as the norm, something assumed, unquestioned and invisible.[52] As Richard Dyer has argued, 'as long as race is something only applied to non-white peoples, as long as white people are not racially seen and named, they/we function as a human norm. Other people are raced, we are just people.'[53] An integral component of the invisibility of whiteness is that 'white people don't see their white privilege,' a complex and interconnected set of advantages and entitlements that allows the enjoyment of 'conferred dominance.'[54] Of particular relevance here are Gayle Wald's comments on the equation of 'white subjectivity with a social entitlement to experiment with identity.'[55] In Mary Weiss's first long interview in many decades—to promote her 2007 *Dangerous Game* album—Billy Miller remarked that, in contrast to the Shangri-Las' pants and boots, 'when you'd see the Supremes on *Ed Sullivan*, they'd have evening gowns on, old people's clothes.'[56] The Supremes, unlike the Shangri-Las, did not have the option of *not* appearing respectable, which adds another dimension to Mary Weiss's understanding of the Supremes as 'slinky and sexy' and unlike the 'average American girl.' This was to a large extent due to prevailing notions associating delinquent behaviour with non-white teenagers, and deeply held assumptions about the sexuality of Black women.[57] As Gayle Wald puts it,

> In a patriarchal context in which women's social value is conflated with their sexuality and sexual conformity, middle class white women are deemed 'naturally' virtuous, whereas black women, especially poor black women, are deemed 'naturally' degraded or corrupt or are removed from the realm of adult sexuality altogether.[58]

Motown's famous 'charm school,' overseen by Maxine Powell, ensured that the artists on its roster presented themselves in a way that would not leave them open to the ridicule and belittling that characterised prevailing middle-class white attitudes to Blacks.[59] In order for Motown artists, male and female, to be taken seriously musically and appeal to a multi-race and class audience, it was imperative that they project an air of glamorous, confident, well-groomed, middle-class respectability and modesty.[60] Mary Wilson of the Supremes remembered that as the fame of the group increased, they were criticised by some for being 'too "glamorous"':

> Knowing we were black girls from the inner city, many of our colleagues, especially those from England who liked to romanticize the plight of the disadvantaged, were surprised to discover that we dressed well off stage and comported ourselves like ladies. I shuddered to think what they were expecting.

Wilson was referring particularly to the Beatles, who she described as stoned and mumbling incoherently about Motown when they met the Supremes. The Beatles were apparently completely disarmed by the sophisticated, immaculately groomed Supremes, who they later described as 'square.'[61]

George Lipsitz has analysed this phenomenon with particular reference to Robert Johnson, the Black blues musician who supposedly sold his soul to the Devil in order to acquire exceptional skill as a guitarist. Johnson, whose entire body of recorded work dates from 1936-37, has been idolised by successive generations of white musicians (particularly male guitarists) including Eric Clapton, Keith Richards, John Mayall and Jack White.[62] Lipsitz noted,

> The romanticism that guides the circulation and reception of the story of Robert Johnson at the crossroads hides the hard facts of life and labor in the segregated South in Johnson's day. It obscures the ways in which unquestioned assumptions about artistic expression keep us wedded to the very practices our art ostensibly deplores. This romanticism contributes to the possessive investment in whiteness by maintaining the illusion that individual whites can appropriate aspects of African American experience for their own benefit without having to acknowledge the factors that give African Americans and European Americans widely divergent opportunities and life chances.[63]

As Jacqueline Warwick has observed, 'the gritty authenticity of soul music and black urban culture' was just what the Supremes and other Motown groups with upwardly mobile aspirations sought to distance themselves from.[64] This was in turn reflective of Berry Gordy's broader civil rights agenda for Motown, which, in Mark Anthony Neal's assessment,

> surmised that that the mass consumption of 'soul,' via an efficient mass-production process, was a natural corollary to broader efforts by blacks to integrate American society in general and corporate boardrooms in particular.[65]

Of course, being able to attract this market would also lead to mainstream success and correspondingly greater record sales, but there is no doubt that Gordy was acutely aware of the statement that Motown artists were making in a civil rights context.[66] He also released a recording of the Reverend Martin Luther King's *Great March to Freedom* on Motown subsidiary Gordy Records, in October 1963.[67] Mary Wilson remembered performing with the Supremes one night in Miami, after which 'a middle-aged Jewish woman came up to us and said, "You know, I usually don't let my children watch negroes on television, but the Supremes are different."'[68]

The sophisticated presentation and elegant comportment that were integral components of the Motown artist package could provide access to social worlds that were otherwise closed to Blacks in the early 1960s, and can be viewed in the context of forms of non-violent protest practiced by the civil rights movement.[69]

The advantages conferred by their whiteness worked in a very literal manner when the Shangri-Las were chosen in May 1965 to publicise Revlon's 'Swingstakes' competition, a promotion for their Natural Wonder line of cosmetics. Natural Wonder was aimed at teenagers and younger women, and its medicated make-up claimed to cover 'every little flaw' while working 'to help clear your skin.'[70] The Natural Wonder range did not include make-up for young Black women, however; Revlon would not develop a line that catered to the 'ethnic market' until the early 1990s.[71] As a direct response to 'the refusal of white cosmetics mavens' to cater for Black women, the Flori Roberts range was launched in 1965, and Fashion Fair, the first Black-owned range to be stocked in department stores, was introduced in 1973.[72] Prior to this, cosmetics designed for Black skin tones and colouring were predominantly sold through Black-owned and operated beauty salons and sales-people, rather than being widely available in supermarkets and drugstores.[73] The opportunity to endorse Natural Wonder make-up (its very name perpetuates the notion that white skin is 'natural' and normal) and enjoy all the promotional benefits of this association was not available to any groups of young Black singers of comparable popularity or hit-making ability.

With their youthful teen following, clear skin and photogenic looks, the Shangri-Las made perfect sense as a vehicle for promoting Natural Wonder to acne-prone teenage girls. Their 'bad girl' image was evidently not 'bad' enough to prevent a huge cosmetics company, whose entire purpose is to sell an image, from utilising the considerable aesthetic power that the Shangri-Las possessed. They recorded a Natural Wonder jingle in a Shangri-Las-style, as well as endorsements extolling the virtues of Natural Wonder's different make-up formats.[74] The promotional-only record containing these recordings, which was pressed for radio stations that participated in this national competition, proclaimed proudly on its cover, "Words and Music to Sell Teens By."[75] First prize in the competition was a trip to London to spend a weekend with the Dave Clark Five, who were enormously popular in the US at this time, probably second only to the Beatles. That the Shangri-Las' considerable selling power was used to promote a competition with this prize suggests an interesting kind of equality with the Dave Clark Five. While their roles were different—the Shangri-Las did the promoting, while the DC5 were 'the prize'—the cachet of both groups was effectively being utilised to sell make-up for the same promotion. Given that entrants were required to 'tear off the words "Natural Wonder" from any "Natural Wonder" package (or 'hand print the words "Natural Wonder" in block letters on a 3" by 5" piece of paper'), this likely resulted in significant sales for Revlon.[76]

WORK

On Monday 17 May 1965, the Shangri-Las appeared as part of the Dick Clark Caravan of Stars at the Melodyland Theatre in Anaheim, California. They shared the bill with '15 of the nation's top recording acts,' including Del Shannon, the Zombies (who were British), Jewel Aken, the Larks, Tommy Roe, Dee Dee Sharp, Mel Carter, the Ad Libs, the Velvettes, Jimmy Sole, Mike Clifford, the Ikettes, the Executives, and Don Wayne.[77] There were two performances, at 5pm and 9pm.

Stories abound of the cramped and chaotic conditions on the Dick Clark tours; indeed, of touring generally in the mid-60s.[78] The Supremes' first Dick Clark tour was in the summer of 1964, and Mary Wilson has spoken of the 'cramped, dirty bus' on which 'sleeping was usually impossible, and so the three of us would stay up and practice our tunes.'[79] Fellow Supreme Florence Ballard remembered that the members of the band also travelled on the bus: '[They] would get happy blowing their horns in your ear, but after a while you'd get so tired and you'd get on the bus and—I don't care how much noise they were making—you'd go to sleep, you'd just go to sleep.'[80] The Zombies' Colin Blunstone recalled,

Above: the four-piece Shangri-Las and backing band onstage at Valdosta State College, Georgia, probably early 1966 (*Valdosta State University Archives*); *left*: announcement of spring tours in *Music Business*, April 24, 1965.

Spring POP-ROCK Tours Kick Off

TOURS BLOSSOM. Pop record star tours blossomed out like Washington's cherry trees last week, with one already on the road, two others due to kick off at week's end and two more due for a May first launching.

Most active in the tour derby was the Dick Clark office in Hollywood, with three editions of Dick Clark's "Caravan of Stars," set for a total of 120 dates. One of the tours was booked by the William Morris Office (this one's known as the Gene Pitney Shower of Stars) and the Clark office booked the other two.

Of major importance too is the Shindig tour, on the road already through the aegis of Selmur Productions, the production firm for the well-known weekly TV show. The Shindig tour started on April 2 and will be out until May 29.

British groups again will be in the spotlight for tours of their own. The Rolling Stones arrive for a Montreal tour debut on April 23 and will be on their cross-country trek until the end of May. Also in line for tours are the Moody Blues, the Kinks and the Dave Clark Five. The complete wrap-up follows:

SHINDIG TOUR

Features Gerry and the Pacemakers (starting April 29); Bobby Sherman, Donna Loren, Shirley Ellis, Roosevelt Grier, the Dixiecups, Jim Doval and the Gauchos, the Shindig Girl Dancers, the Shindig Band and emcee, Jimmy O'Neill.

Memphis, April 19—Mid South Coliseum 8 pm

LaFayette, April 20—LaFayette Municipal Aud., 8:15 pm

Houston, April 21—Music Hall, 2:30 & 8 pm

Austin, April 22—Municipal Auditorium, 8 pm

DICK CLARK CARAVAN UNIT 1

Features Del Shannon, Jewel Akens, Dee Dee Sharp, the Ikettes, Mel Carter, the Ad Libs, Mike Clifford, Major Lance, the Zombies, the Shangri-Las, Tommy Roe, the Larks, Jimmy Soul, the Executives, Don Wayne and the Velvelettes.

April 19—Rockford, Illinois
20—Des Moines, Iowa
21—South Bend, Indiana
22—Bowling Green, Kentucky
23—Louisville, Kentucky
24—Evansville, Indiana
25—Nashville, Tennessee
26—Paducah, Kentucky
27—Memphis, Tennessee
28—Springfield, Missouri
29—Lincoln, Nebraska
30—Sioux City, Iowa

May 1—St. Joseph, Missouri
2—Omaha, Nebraska
3—Salina, Kansas
4—Wichita, Kansas
5—Dallas, Texas
6—Austin, Texas
7—Waco, Texas
8—Corpus Christi, Texas
9—Houston, Texas
10—San Angelo, Texas
11—Fort Worth, Texas
12—Lubbock, Texas
13—Amarillo, Texas
14—Denver, Colorado
15—Albuquerque, New Mexico
16—Las Vegas, Nevada
17—Anaheim, California
18—Santa Barbara, California
19—Reno, Nevada
20—Fresno, California
21—Sacramento, California
22—San Francisco/Oakland California
23—San Jose, California
24—Travel
25—Seattle, Washington
26—Vancouver, British Columbia, Canada
27—Calgary, Alberta, Canada
28—Edmonton, Alberta, Canada
29—Saskatoon, Saskatchewan, Canada
30—Minot, North Dakota
31—Fargo, North Dakota

June 1—Winnipeg, Manitoba, Canada
2—Minneapolis, Minnesota

DICK CLARK CARAVAN UNIT 2

Features Little Anthony, Herman's Hermits, Bobby Myron

Lee, Brenda Holloway, Billy Stewart, Little Junior Man, Bobby Vee, Freddie Cannon, Reparata and the Delrons, Round Robbin, George McCannon, and The Detergents.

April 30—Johnstown, Penn.

May 1—Philadelphia, Penn.
2—Bluefield, W. Va.
3—Prestonburg, Ky.—Pikeville
4—Richmond, Ky.
5—McComb, Ill.
6—Connersville, Ind.
7—Muncie, Ind.
8—Vincennes, Ind.
9—Ashland, Ky.
10—Jackson, Tenn.
11—Atlanta, Ga.
12—Panama City
13—Jacksonville, Fla.
14—Mobile, Ala.
15—Columbus, Ga.
16—Tallahassee, Fla.
17—
18—Augusta, Ga.
19—Columbia, S. C.
20—Winston-Salem, N. C.
21—
22—Charleston, W. Va.
23—Erie-Youngstown
24—
25—Syracuse, N. Y.
26—
27—Troy, N. Y.
28—Hershey, Pa.
29—New Haven, Conn.
30—Hartford, Conn.
31—Utica, N. Y.

June 1—Ottawa, Canada
2—Montreal, Canada

DICK CLARK CARAVAN UNIT 3
(GENE PITNEY SHOWER OF STARS)

Features Gene Pitney, Tim Tormey (emcee), Chad and Jeremy, Bobby Goldsboro, Bill Black Combo, the Reasons, Vic Dana, Darin D'Anna, Gary Lewis and the Playboys, the Crystals, the Reflections, the Rag Dolls, Bryan Hyland, Ronnie Cochran and Susan Wayne.

April 19—Boston, Mass.
20—New Haven, Conn.
21—Providence, R. I.
22—Hartford, Conn.
23—Poughkeepsie, N. Y.
Aft 24—Utica, N. Y.
Eve 24—Syracuse, N. Y.
25—Rochester, N. Y.
26—Sharon, Pa.
27—Clarksburg, W. Va.

we only stayed in a hotel every second night. On alternate nights, we drove through the night . . . and all the acts would sing . . . all the way through the night, and play music. Then the next night you'd get a hotel, but you want to go out to a party or something. So we didn't really get much sleep.[81]

By the end of the six-week tour, everyone was exhausted. The Zombies' guitarist, Paul Atkinson, was apparently almost delirious when collected from the airport by his parents, having lost a substantial amount of weight while touring.[82] Mary Weiss's experience echoed those of the other performers:

I didn't get to pal around with anybody. We were so busy. It was very different then. Now these singers say how rough they have it. They don't have a clue. Not a clue. Ride in a bus every night. Sleep every other night. See how *that* feels. People don't realize how hard it was back then. There were no monitors at the time. Sometimes you were screaming just to hear yourself singing. The Dick Clark Caravans, they were gruelling shows. Every other night you'd sleep in a hotel. Sleep on the bus, then you'd have to get up and look perky. It's exhausting.[83]

Brenda Holloway, another Motown artist who toured extensively on package tours at this time, concurred:

'Being on the road was tedious. We were younger, but it was very tedious because it took all of our day. We didn't have any social life when we were performing. It took the better part of the day and the evening. All we were ready for was bed whenever we got finished . . . It seemed to be harder for us than for the men. We had so many wigs and so many costumes . . . we were basically together all day long; learning make-up tricks from each other, just being with each other. We were with each other *a lot*.'[84]

Far from being a trivial conceit, wigs were a practical way of dealing with the fact that a busload of people might be sharing one bathroom, and washing and styling one's hair might not always be possible. Wigs made it possible to spend all night on a bus with no sleep and still look glamorous while performing.[85]

Added to this already considerable pressure on the Shangri-Las was the strain of attempting to keep up with their schooling. Mary Weiss, the youngest member of the group, has said, 'I missed out on doing any real high school stuff. I went to professional school where you could leave if you had to tour. It was necessary.'[86]

She attended Quintano's School for Young Performers, which was then located on West 56th Street opposite the back entrance of Carnegie Hall, within easy access of Manhattan's theatre district and about six blocks (a short walk) from the Brill Building. Quintano's had been established in 1951 by Leonard S. Quintano, known as 'Dr. Q.,' as a high school for teens with showbusiness aspirations, or who were already performers and for whom attendance at a standard high school was difficult.[87] Its students in the mid-60s, along with Mary Weiss, included Mitch Margo and Jay Siegel of doo-wop group the Tokens, and actors Bernadette Peters and Patty Duke; among earlier students were Tuesday Weld and Frankie Lymon.[88] At the outset, Quintano's School seems to have been reasonably reputable, but by the mid-60s, its educational standards were being called into called into question.[89] A June 1965 letter from New York's Division for School Regulation and Supervision observed pointedly that '"there is no science laboratory, no library, and no gymnasium,"' and noted further that '"Mr. Quintano . . . is not really interested in expanding his facilities or making extensive changes to meet state requirements."'[90] Furthermore, it seems that from some time in the mid-60s, the school became something of a haven for teenagers who had been expelled from their high schools for non-attendance or anti-social behaviour. As one former student put it, 'you had the students who were there because they had real careers, and you had the fuck-ups.'[91]

As long as the 'incredibly inexpensive' tuition fees were paid, teaching staff turned a blind eye to questionable activities, and in the latter part of the 60s drug use and dealing were rife. It is difficult to see how the students could have received anything equating to a formal high school diploma, and it later transpired that the diplomas it issued were in fact worthless.[92]

The pressures of touring and being recording artists caused others to drop out of school altogether. Rita Ganser had grave concerns about Mary Ann and Margie's schooling:

I wanted them to finish high school. They wouldn't finish high school. They had another year to go, and they cried and they cried, because this talent scout came after them, he heard them, and he wanted to right away sign them up, and of course I had a fit, I didn't want them to do it. But they carried on, so they got their way . . . [93]

This was not uncommon. The music teacher at Inkster High School, Dr. Phillips, maintains that the Marvelettes were encouraged, if not pressured, to leave high school so that they could tour and promote their debut record.[94] Three members of the group, Katherine Anderson, Georgeanna Tillman and Wyanetta Cowart, were all in their final year of high school when "Please Mr. Postman" became a huge hit. As Anderson saw it, 'we had the choice of going out there or staying in school, and all of us ended up making the choice that we made the record, we made it popular, and we were going out there representing ourselves.'[95] Unfortunately, this meant

we had to leave school, get schoolwork, and almost do independent study. Contrary to what has been said through the years, we did have chaperones; however, we did not have tutors . . . we were assigned a certain amount of homework or work that we would do on the road, but time did not always allow for us to get that work done. When we came home we turned in as much of it as we possibly could. You knew that there were any number of things that you could have done but you didn't have the time to do it.[96]

Not surprisingly, given what we have seen of the chaotic and gruelling nature of touring, the difficulty of balancing competing commitments became too much. Dr. Phillips remembered,

'After "Postman" hit, they began to miss classes; or if they did show up on Monday, they were just *dog* tired. Then sometimes they wouldn't make it at all til Wednesday. Of course, I had problems. I couldn't give credit for two students who weren't there. Then eventually, they just dropped out . . . That bothered me. That bothers me to this day.'[97]

A major interruption to their schooling, in some cases breaking it off completely, along with the concomitant instability of constant touring had major ramifications for many young performers. Katherine Anderson of the Marvelettes was only able to return to study relatively recently in order to gain her high school diploma: 'I was able to go back, but, unfortunately, I didn't go back early enough in my life that I could've made something of my life after showbusiness.'[98]

Like Murray the K's Brooklyn Fox shows, these tours were the music industry equivalent of sweatshops, with long hours, punishing conditions, and the expectation that these teenagers would unquestioningly sacrifice all other aspects of their lives to this treadmill, including, as we have seen, education, eating regularly and well, and getting sufficient sleep, in an environment that made it virtually impossible to maintain a healthy lifestyle. There were other dangers, too. Alan Betrock's chapter on the Shangri-Las in his *Girl Groups* book contains a long interview with Joseph (Joey) Alexander, who was seventeen when he left high school to play drums in the Shangri-Las' backing band:

> We did Dick Clark tours and a lot of Murray the K shows. On the Clark tours we would be on the road for three, maybe four months at a time—all one-nighters. At least the tours were routed out properly so we didn't have to travel too far between shows. Sometimes we'd do two a day, something like a state fair in the afternoon, and then drive a bit and do a show at night. Four days on, one day off, for week after week. We did bowling alleys, halls, dances, anything from four hundred to four thousand people. The equipment would be there when we arrived—we just carried baggage. We'd do a twenty-minute set, just four or five songs. The night time shows would start at around 6.30 and run for two hours or so. There was always wildness when the girls came on stage, with kids rushing and pushing up against the stage. They would grab Mary, and try to pull her hair.[99]

Security at venues where the groups performed was often inadequate or non-existent. Mary Weiss remembers,

> A lot of times it was very frightening. One time at an aquarium there was no security and I just about had my clothes ripped off. And the fans with pens almost poking your eye out. There was no security then. We were just winging it. When there's a lot of them and one of you, it gets scary.[100]

The Shangri-Las at the Seattle Center Coliseum, backed by legendary Pacific Northwest garage rockers the Sonics, 30 April 1966. Photographs by Jini Dellaccio (*University of Washington Libraries, Special Collections, UW42529, UW42532*)

This was compounded by an almost total lack of supervision and guidance while the group was travelling between shows. Mary Weiss has recounted harrowing stories of being out on the road in an era in which there were 'no cell phones,' 'hotels didn't have camera systems the way they do today,' and 'there were no police around.' As she put it, 'you were *out there*.'[101] Nominally, the group had a chaperone, but as she pointed out, this was quite ludicrous:

> If you can call an eighteen-year-old a proper chaperone. Maybe nine-teen, but that's as grown up as it got. We had a road manager, Fat Frankie, for a while . . . that wasn't much supervision. One of our other road managers was a black belt in karate. Once, there was a car full of drunken guys weaving all over a bridge, waving beer bottles and stuff and it was getting very dangerous. They kept swerving into our car and it was very scary. I was so petrified, my heart was in my throat. It was as if they thought they had the right to do this. They could have killed us all. Louie stopped the car and took them all on. They were flying everywhere, all over the bridge. You had no choice in the matter. It was a dark road with nowhere to go, there were no cell phones then. I'm glad he was there. I could see the headlines now, JIMMY KILLS MARY ON BRIDGE. It was much different than now. It's very hard to explain. Nothing was organized. It was, "Here's a list of shows, get on the road." I was only fifteen.[102]

This barely contained chaos is indeed hard to comprehend. After one particularly harrowing incident, Weiss took matters into her own hands:

> I bought a gun after someone tried to break into my hotel room. There were glass panels on the side of the door and all of a sudden I see this arm coming through. Not only was I scared to death, there were large amounts of money in the room. You're on the road with no protection. But, I was a little kid. I didn't know. Back then you could walk in anywhere and buy a gun. But the FBI came to my mother's house and said, "Will you please tell your daughter she'll be arrested if she gets off the plane with her gun?"[103]

That a teenage girl was obliged to buy a gun to protect herself while at her job speaks volumes about the extent to which the Shangri-Las' 'employers' failed on multiple levels to provide a safe working environment for them. Aside from the physical dangers that the young performers faced, there was also the considerable psychological strain coping with a high degree of stress on an ongoing basis.

Under these unnatural circumstances, it was absolutely impossible to relax, sleep, or in any way function normally. According to Mary,

> I toured so much I would put my head on the pillow and wake up and not know what state I was in. That's no way to live. And it's not a life. You're either at a radio station, a TV station, out to dinner for some PR, a show, more rehearsals, and then when you're not doing that and you're in New York and you're doing rehearsals, and studio and . . . I had no life.[104]

And Joseph Alexander remembers,

> There was always a lot of booze . . . and pot. Five dollars worth of pot would last for a whole week back then—we'd smoke it in these little cornpipes. A bunch of people would take pills too, either to wake you up or put you to sleep, or both, sometimes both. There'd be a lot of card playing and informal parties—not wild orgy-like parties—just good times where we could unwind and keep our spirits up. It was like being drafted. We were altogether in the same boat, so we made the best of it.[105]

At this time, there was little knowledge and no education about the dangers of using pills to wake you up or put you to sleep, but their use was common in various areas of showbusiness. Another child star, Patty Duke, who attended Quintano's at the same time as Mary Weiss, remembered routinely being given 'antipsychotic medications, as well as phenobarbital and Percodan' by her carer-managers when she was a teenager:

> Though I was never given enough to become addicted, it certainly wasn't a healthy practice . . . No one was educated then about how dangerous that stuff could be, so they probably weren't acting from malice, just a combination of ignorance, greed and bad judgement.[106]

Others young performers, including Frankie Lymon, Wanda Young (the Marvelettes), Florence Ballard (the Supremes) and Mary Ann Ganser developed drug and alcohol problems as a direct result of their experiences in showbusiness and on the road. Mary Ann and Marge Ganser's mother, Rita, was brutally frank about the consequences of her daughters being on the road without appropriate supervision. Initially, she had travelled with the group:

> A couple of times I went with them, they did a show, Dick Clark [Caravan of Stars]...and I met George Morton there and a couple of times we travelled together, and he was very nice, and I came home and told my husband, well, I think the girls have good people to travel with, I don't think I need to travel any more.

She later regretted this decision, calling it her 'big mistake':

> I never should have done that. Because they started drinking, probably got into drugs...I hate to see anybody get on the road with their music today, because...they always wind up taking drugs. You know *why* they take drugs? My daughter Marge told me that they *can't cope* with all what goes on in front of them, like when they're up on stage, and the kids are carrying on, she said they go *wild*! And I guess it plays on their nerves...so that's what they do...try something to calm their nerves.[107]

The extremes of wild adulation and the adrenalin rush that accompanies performing every day (sometimes twice a day), in conjunction with tedious and gruelling travel conditions, became a recipe for physical and psychological disaster.

On several occasions while relating anecdotes about touring conditions in the mid-60s, Mary Weiss refers to herself as a 'little kid' or otherwise emphasises her age. In one interview, she reflected, 'obviously, if I had been older at the time I would not have agreed to do so much.'[108] The age of the performers was what allowed this tremendous exploitation to take place, but also enabled the majority of them to 'cope' with it as well. They were young and famous, so it was very exciting. As the Marvelettes' Katherine Anderson put it,

'When you start out as a kid, you look at how much fun it is. The fun still exists, but then as you get older, you realise even more so that this is your job. Once you begin to look at things as being a job, it ends up being a lot more challenging to deal with and you lose some of the fun of it because the demands on you are so high.'[109]

Anderson's gradual awakening to the reality of labour is telling, and was likely accompanied by the realisation that her job's hourly rate and working conditions were far from equitable. Jacqueline Warwick has astutely observed that 'hegemonic understandings of singing and dancing as pleasurable activities that come "naturally" to women make it difficult to identify singers as artists, much less workers.'[110] In conceptual terms, Warwick likened this to the 'houswifization' of domestic labours, including the care of children, that are perceived to be biologically 'natural pastimes' for women, and therefore not classified as work.[111] This is further complicated by the contradictory messages women, particularly mothers, received about working, which was actively encouraged during WWII to address an acute labour shortage, but actively discouraged once the war ended.[112]

The idea of 'singing and dancing as pleasurable activities' and therefore not work has broader applications and can be extended to include teenaged performers in the music industry in the mid-60s. Paul Atkinson, the Zombies guitarist mentioned earlier, had a brother who worked as an accountant in London. Paul had just arrived back from the airport after the gruelling Dick Clark tour suffering from acute exhaustion, and Zombies bass player Chris White related that 'Paul's mother would say, "Oh, can you go outside and get the coal, Paul? Keith's had a hard day in the city today. He's working, you know." They never considered what we were doing to be work. And so therefore in the end you get fed up with fighting it . . .'[113]

The notion that young performers were just having fun and not taking their musical activities particularly seriously has been repeatedly invoked to evade accusations of exploitation. Ellie Greenwich commented,

The girls gave, and the girls took. They'd get fancy clothes, expensive dinners, all of that. Most of them didn't think in terms of a 'career.' It was just fun, and better than their alternatives, and they took what

The Shangri-Las performing at Brown University Spring Weekend, Providence, Rhode Island, April 22, 1967. Photos © Greg Lloyd.

they could get. Most of them only wanted their couple of years, and then they wanted to get married and raise a family. They knew there were trade-offs, but it wasn't a one-sided exploitation, that's for sure.[114]

What Greenwich failed to acknowledge was that the vast majority of these 'benefits' the young performers supposedly 'took' were claimed back as expenses from their already miniscule royalties—this was absolutely standard practice according to the contracts they had signed, or that their parents had signed on their behalf.[115] To claim this somehow made the labour transaction less one-sided is, at the very least, wishful thinking.

Mary Wilson of the Supremes recalled her sense of enormous pride in the Supremes' achievements—they'd had a number one record and been on the road for months playing Dick Clark Caravan shows that were mostly sell-outs. She 'couldn't wait to get back to Hitsville and find out how rich we were.' When she did, however, she was told by Motown's accountant Esther Edwards (Berry Gordy's sister, incidentally) that there was no money:

> "You were paid only six hundred dollars a week. Deduct from that the price of room and board and food for yourselves and Mrs. Ross and that leaves nothing." Then, as if to add insult to injury, she added, "It probably cost the company, but you needed the exposure." I tried to figure it out; where could the money have gone, especially when we so rarely stayed in a room anywhere? I left the meeting crushed.[116]

The costs of producing and promoting records were also deducted from the artist's royalties. In the majority of cases, the artists were only earning royalties for performing, not songwriting, which meant even less money coming their way.[117] Nevertheless, the artist footed the bill for the majority of 'expenses,' and since the calculation of 'costs' was largely at the discretion of the label owners, fraud was easy, common and rife. Mary Wilson never saw a tax return during her entire tenure at Motown.[118] She also commented, with reference to some particularly lucrative later engagements at the Copacabana, 'because we never saw the accounts, we had no idea how much of the Supremes' fee was spent on drinks, complimentary tickets, and other promotional items.'[119] According to mobster Sonny Franzese, it was at his behest that Copacabana manager Jules Podell booked the Supremes, which ensured (if it wasn't already certain) that Wilson would absolutely never see the accounts.[120]

The recouping of 'promotional costs' was a particularly notorious area for fraudulent accounting, as Artie Ripp explained:

> Who is to say I spent thirty minutes promoting this record and five minutes on this one? It's just simpler: Charge everyone $1000. So in fact if you were paying for the promotion trips, you were paying for the advertising, you were paying for this, that and the other thing, you were paying for the recording costs, traditionally the artists were getting fucked . . . And the black artist and the young white kid artist, what would they know? They would just be happy making records.[121]

Until they began to realise, as Mary Wilson did, that the wealth generated by *their* labour was, to put it mildly, being redirected. Attempts to redress the situation at the time were often futile, as Wilson found: in a clear conflict of interest, the brother of Motown's accountant owned the company. The efforts of Herman Santiago and Jimmy Merchant of the Teenagers resulted in threats to their lives, and taking their grievances to court ultimately availed them nothing.

For groups like the Shangri-Las, who had the misfortune to be involved with someone like Artie Ripp, recoupable promotional costs that came under the umbrella of 'this, that and the other thing' included parties and prostitutes for influential radio and industry figures: 'Every party was charged to the artist. "I've got a hundred hookers. Charge them to the artist."'[122]

In the days when he worked for George Goldner, Ripp has related, he would

> go on the road with George, which meant I had to get the broads to the hotel and then make sure the disk jockey who had just finished with the redhead knew that the blonde was down the hall. Back in those days, I saw bags of money going out and bags of money coming in. You could sell 100 records over the table and 1000 records under the table.[123]

Advertisements in the trade press. *Above: Billboard,*
19 December, 1964; right: Music Business, 20 March
1965; below: Billboard, 29 January, 1966.

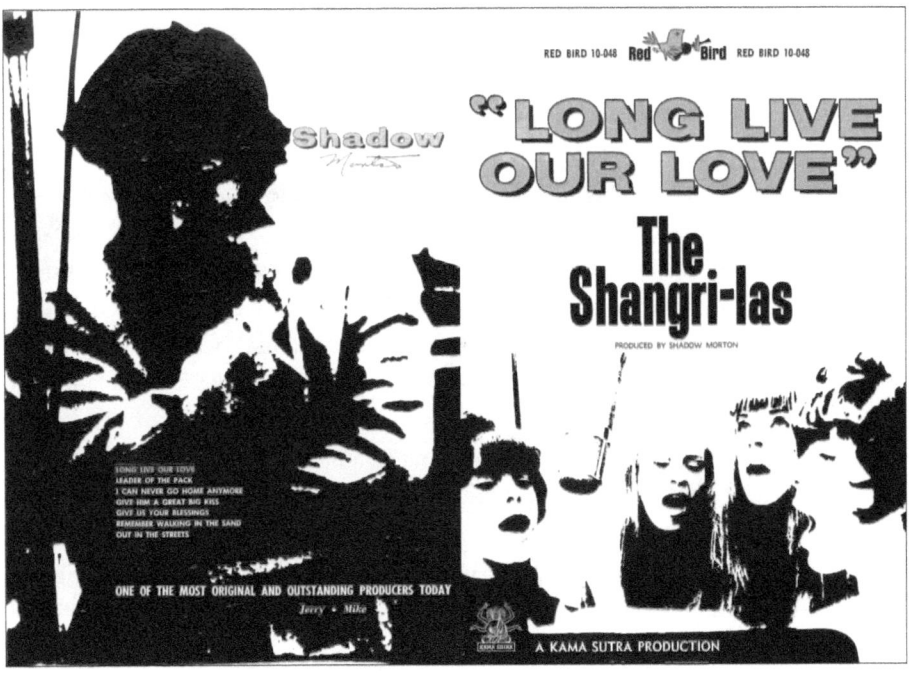

This was a practice that seems to have continued at Red Bird. Factor in Goldner's chronic gambling problem, and it becomes painfully clear just what a combination of vices the teenaged Shangri-Las (and many others like them) were being exploited into funding through their endless touring, in the name of 'promotion.'

Despite being on the road for much of 1965 and 1966, the Shangri-Las managed to record and release seven singles, as well as an album, *Shangri-Las 65!*, including some of their finest material. Among the singles were "Out in the Streets", "I Can Never Go Home Anymore", "He Cried", "Dressed in Black" and "Past, Present and Future" (all produced by George 'Shadow' Morton), and although none of them quite matched the chart impact of their first two Red Bird singles (only "I Can Never Go Home Anymore" cracked the *Billboard* top 20), all were at least lower-level hits and maintained the group's standing and chart presence.*

RED BIRD AND THE MOB

On 16 April 1966, an article appeared in *Billboard* entitled 'Goldner Buys Out 2 Labels.' Although it was not obvious at the time, this move would have dramatic and far-reaching ramifications for the Shangri-Las' ability to continue as a functioning group:

> George Goldner has bought out the interest of Jerry Leiber[124] and Mike Stoller in Red Bird and Blue Cat Records, two pop independent labels. Goldner is now the sole owner of the labels. The move was made to allow Leiber and Stoller to devote more time to writing and publishing and to work on film and Broadway show properties. Under the previous arrangement Lieber and Stoller, as an independent record production firm, earmarked its entire output to Red Bird and Blue Cat. Under the new set-up, Leiber and Stoller will still turn out masters for the two labels; they will also do work for other labels. According to Leiber, the Red Bird–Blue Cat arrangement resulted in the production company being swamped with work for the two labels and could not take on any outside work. Goldner said that he

---

* For a complete list of the Shangri-Las' US singles and albums (not including later reissues), see pages 371–72. Many of these tracks are discussed in detail in later chapters.

will depend exclusively on the output of independent production firms for his product and devote his time primarily to sales and promotion. The office set-up will be unchanged, with the Leiber and Stoller headquarters next to the Red Bird–Blue Cat offices.[125]

This all sounds plausible enough on the surface, but the reality was rather more complicated. The 'buy out' effectively spelled the end of Red Bird and Blue Cat (a subsidiary label for releasing more R&B-styled material), as operating entities and had devastating consequences for the artists on their roster, particularly for the most successful of its groups, the Shangri-Las.

The roots of the split between Goldner and his Red Bird partners go back at least to a 1965 lunch meeting in the Oak Room at the Plaza Hotel, Manhattan, attended by Leiber, Stoller, their attorney Lee Eastman, Goldner, and the top executives from Atlantic Records, Ahmet and Nesuhi Ertegun, and Jerry Wexler. The meeting was ostensibly to discuss a possible merger between Red Bird and Atlantic, which at the time was not enjoying the same level of chart success as Red Bird.[126] Before the creation of Red Bird, Leiber and Stoller had had a long association with Atlantic, working as songwriters and producers—they co-wrote and produced "On Broadway" (1963) by the Drifters, for example.[127] Reports vary regarding the impetus for the luncheon and the discussions that took place, but the stated motivations of Jerry Leiber and Mike Stoller are significant here. They had apparently discovered that Goldner was 'pressing, shipping and selling records off the books for personal profit' through a parallel business he had set up.[128] Mike Stoller recalls,

The idea [of a merger] was exciting for more than one reason: George Goldner, despite his extraordinary ability to pick and push hits, was someone we could never trust. Some employees claimed he was selling our records out back of the warehouse and pocketing the cash. There were rumors that he was back at the track, where his losses were piling up. A merger with Atlantic would mean close supervision over George's practices, something that Jerry and I, who stayed busy in the studio, weren't able to handle. If Goldner was stealing, as we strongly suspected, Wexler would quickly catch him.[129]

This carefully worded version of events appeared in the official Leiber and Stoller biography, published early in 2009. In 1993 Jerry Leiber had been rather more forthright:

> We were trying to use Atlantic to drive Goldner out. Goldner was involving us with guys with faces you'd only see at fights at the old Madison Square Garden. We were afraid of George and thought of Ahmet and Jerry as executives strong enough to control him. We thought of Goldner as crass and Atlantic as class.[130]

As discussed in the previous chapter, Goldner's chronic gambling had led to him losing a series of pioneering labels that he had established. As Leiber put it,

> Goldner was practically singlehandedly responsible for some of the greatest hits of the day. His labels were legendary—Tico, Gone, End, Gee, Roulette, Rama. The word was that Goldner was hooked on the horses. In spite of his success on the charts, he'd find himself so deeply in debt that his "friend" Morris (Moishe) Levy, bailed him out by buying his labels for a song. Goldner had lost them all at the track.[131]

According to Leiber and Stoller, Goldner sabotaged the Atlantic/Red Bird merger talks by drinking heavily and behaving belligerently at the lunch, knowing that if the merger took place, he would be held accountable and could no longer get away with his underhanded moneymaking practices. In the short term, he was successful—Goldner was able to continue as a partner in Red Bird for the time being.[132]

Matters apparently came to a head, however, after Jerry Leiber was accosted on Broadway, probably early in 1966. Josh Alan Friedman, whose book contains a lengthy description of this incident, names the accoster as Roulette employee Nate McCollough (aka Nathan McCalla), 'Morris Levy's right hand enforcer,' 'a highly decorated former marine officer' and 'an outside hitter connected to the Genovese mob.'[133] McCalla had his own subsidiary label at Roulette, Calla Records, which released recordings by soul singers including Bettye Lavette and J.J. Jackson; he also had his own publishing company, JAMF.[134] According to Leiber, he was 'escorted' by the man Friedman

named as McCalla to a room at the back of a deli near the Brill Building, where (again according to Friedman) John 'Sonny' Franzese, the
capo in the Colombo Mafia family who was involved with Artie Ripp
and Kama Sutra, was waiting with a number of his offsiders. Exactly
what took place at this meeting remains unclear. According to Leiber, Franzese indicated that Red Bird's partnership with Goldner now
included Franzese, because 'Goldner brought us into the business
when he needed some funding.' Franzese also apparently made it clear,
in a terrifying manner, that he knew Leiber had young children.[135] Leiber and Stoller's account of this incident names neither the 'enforcer'
nor the mobster, who is referred to as 'Sal,' with a note that 'Sal isn't his
real name.'[136] Friedman then notes,

> Whatever happened next is deeply buried within the shadows of
> music business lore ... I've heard tall tales, like one about Jerry being
> hung outside the Brill Building penthouse by his ankles. Jerry and
> Mike made a pact never to discuss it, and remain paranoid forty-five
> years later.[137]

According to Leiber, the situation at Red Bird became unwork-
able: 'guys started showing up in our office, brutes who could barely
fit through the door.' Confronted about the situation, Goldner apparently responded, "'It's only temporary. Once I pay them off, they'll be
out of here. It's nothing to worry about.'"[138] It seems that Goldner had
yet again run up gambling debts, borrowed money from questionable
sources (almost certainly involving Morris Levy), and used Red Bird
shares as collateral.[139] When Goldner was unable to 'pay them off,' the
'debt collectors' moved in.

Sonny Franzese was a silent partner in Buddah Records, an arm
of Artie Ripp's Kama Sutra company. He had almost certainly partially funded the establishment of Kama Sutra as well; he was a close
acquaintance of Phil Steinberg, who had founded the production
company along with Artie Ripp and Hy Mizrahi. In the early 1990s,
his son Michael Franzese, also a Mafia boss, became a born-again
Christian while serving a prison sentence for racketeering, turned
informer, and wrote a book called *Quitting the Mob* (1992), and followed it with a second, entitled *Blood Covenant* (2003). This *began*
with an anecdote about Kama Sutra, Phil Steinberg, the Shangri-Las,

and Morris Levy. He related that (according to Steinberg) in 1964, when "Remember" was in the charts, Morris Levy had visited the Kama Sutra offices at 1650 Broadway (an address that was home to a host of music publishing houses including Aldon Music, where Ripp had once been employed). Morris Levy had apparently walked in and said to Steinberg,

> The Shangri-Las, nice kids! Great group! Great song! . . . They're mine, and I want my cut.

According to Michael Franzese,

> Steinberg knew the streets: Levy was an associate of Gaetano "Tommy the Big Guy" Vastola, a vicious soldier in the DeCavalcante Mafia family. He was also the childhood friend of Vincent "the Chin" Gigante, a menacing hood on his way to becoming the boss of the Genovese family. In short, Levy was big trouble.[140]

Levy was renowned for shaking down performers and songwriters for royalties, so this was quite regular behaviour for him. As we have already seen (in chapter 2), he was not a songwriter, yet his name appears on songwriting credits for an extraordinary amount of material, including "Why Do Fools Fall in Love" by Frankie Lymon and the Teenagers.[141] Furthermore, both Goldner and Levy had long histories of siphoning off record company monies and artist royalties into their own pockets. According to Michael Franzese, his father Sonny 'enjoyed popping into the record company [Kama Sutra] as he made his Manhattan rounds' and did so quite regularly.[142] When Steinberg told Franzese senior about Levy's visit, Sonny told him not to worry about it, and the next time Steinberg saw Levy, there was no mention of him getting a cut, nor was there ever again. In other words, Sonny Franzese had sufficient mob clout to be able to successfully call Levy off this particular shakedown over the Shangri-Las.[143]

It is likely that matters were somewhat less straightforward than Michael Franzese has presented them, however. Artie Ripp's version of why Sonny Franzese was a frequent visitor to Kama Sutra's offices is quite different. He maintains that Kama Sutra was started by Mizrahi and Steinberg with dubious outside funding *before* Ripp was 'invited to become a partner.'[144] That dubious funding included $60,000 worth of insurance money following a fire—'Italian lightning', as Ripp put it:

> The partners were shamed into confessing they had borrowed $10,000 from mobsters, then greater amounts when that ran out—in return for shares in the company. 'It was rather disturbing,' says Ripp. 'I took it upon myself to figure out how I was going to get mercy from what was supposed to be a merciless group of people—people who now had a piece of this hot, happening rock-and-roll production company.'[145]

Ripp had apparently been so busy 'making records with groups like the Shangri-Las and the Critturs' that when he finally 'had time to relax and look around' he was horrified to find his offices being haunted by mobsters. George Morton and Ellie Greenwich have both emphatically denied that Ripp ever worked with the Shangri-Las in the studio, at least not on any of the Red Bird material—he received production credits from Red Bird in lieu of the Shangri-Las previous 'commitment,' whatever form that took, to Kama Sutra. According to Ripp, he solved the problem by telling Sonny Franzese he didn't want him involved, paying him off, and getting really drunk with him.[146] This account exonerates Ripp, paints him as the innocent victim of mob figures, and, to put it mildly, strains credulity. What *is* likely to be largely accurate in Ripp's version of the story, though, is that Sonny Franzese paid regular visits to the Kama Sutra offices because he had a stake in the company and was checking on his investment—visits that Michael Franzese whitewashed as pleasant family outings.

It is unlikely that the details of all this will ever be accurately determined, but this tangled web of mob involvement is significant because it goes some way toward explaining the tremendous obfuscation surrounding the demise of the Shangri-Las and the wall of silence around those events that exists to this day. It also shows how the established business practices of George Goldner, Morris Levy, and Artie Ripp, which had existed for years before the Shangri-Las were involved with any of them, played out on the fortunes (literally) of the group in a devastating way.

MERCURY RECORDS

The upshot of the alleged Franzese and McCalla shakedown of Jerry Leiber, which was almost certainly only one of a number of factors involved, was that Leiber and Stoller sold their share of Red Bird and Blue Cat to Goldner, as indicated in the *Billboard* article cited earlier. Among the many details *not* reported in the article was the price—one dollar.[147] Leiber and Stoller effectively walked away from Red Bird, and the label collapsed soon afterward. Before it did, two final Shangri-Las singles were released: "He Cried" b/w "Dressed in Black" in April 1966, and "Past, Present and Future" b/w "Paradise" in July 1966. The group was reaching new heights of sophistication in their material, particularly "Past, Present and Future" (which is discussed at length in chapter 7), making the timing and consequences of these events all the more disastrous.

While all this was taking place, one notable performance by the Shangri-Las was as part of the Spring Spectacular at the Seattle Center Coliseum on 30 April 1966. This was one in a series of multi-performer events organised by local KJR radio identities Pat O'Day and Dick Curtis. The bill included the Lovin' Spoonful, the Mamas and the Papas, Dino, Desi and Billy, along with locals Merrilee (Rush) and the Turnabouts, Don and the Goodtimes (featuring Kingsmen keyboardist Don Gallucci) and the Sonics, who also acted as backing group for the Shangri-Las on this occasion.[148] The Spring Spectacular is unusually well-documented thanks to the presence of Jini Dellaccio, a local painter-turned-photographer whose fashion shoots and portraits of musicians from and touring through the Pacific Northwest during the 1960s are now legendary.[149] Dellaccio photographed the Shangri-Las performing with the Sonics (see page 169) and also took a series of backstage shots (see pages 188 and 214) that allow a striking insight into the group dynamic at this time, made all the more poignant with knowledge of the machinations happening back in New York while the group was out on the road.

According to John Grecco, as a consequence of Red Bird's demise,

> Many things, including master tapes, were sold to various scavengers, scattering most, but not all of them to at least three different companies, possibly more. Other master tapes either reverted back to some

Las To Merc

Mercury president Irving G. Green (seated) adds his signature to contracts bringing the Shangri-Las to the label. Shown standing are (left to right) Shadow Morton, who produces the girls, Betty Weiss, personal manager Larry Martire, Mary Weiss and Marianne Ganser. A single, "Sweet Sounds Of Summer" and a "Golden Hits" LP were recently released on Mercury.

Cash Box, 17 December 1966.

lessors or may simply have been discarded. File cabinets, literally filled with promotional pictures, records, demos, contracts and the like were sold off, intact, for pennies on the dollar. Other items were sold, repossessed or just simply abandoned.[150]

In Jerry Leiber's recollection,

George attempted to keep Red Bird going. Within a few months, however, he sold all the master recordings to record company owner Shelby Singleton in Nashville.[151]

These masters included the Shangri-Las' Red Bird recordings. Singleton worked for Mercury Records, which by this time had grown into an international recording conglomerate.

Mercury was founded in Chicago in 1945 by Irving Green, owner of a record pressing plant, and Berle Adams, a booking agent whose clients included Louis Jordan. Initially Mercury signed Black performers ignored by other major labels but soon began releasing pop records; by the end of 1945 it 'ranked sixth in national sales.'[152] By the late 1950s, Mercury was a fully-fledged major label, recording and releasing pop, jazz, classical, and rhythm and blues records, and in 1961 was taken over by the North American arm of the European recording giant Philips. In short, by the mid-60s Mercury was big business, an international enterprise with all the impersonal industry mechanisms and operating systems of a powerful company.

Late in 1966, following the collapse of the Red Bird label and Mercury's acquisition of their back catalogue, the Shangri-Las signed contracts with Mercury Records. A photo of this occasion appeared in *Cash Box* on 17 December 1966; significantly, George 'Shadow' Morton and Larry Martire are also present, listed as their producer and manager respectively.[153] They signed as a trio—Mary and Betty Weiss, and Mary Ann Ganser—by this point, according to John Grecco, Marge Ganser had 'had it with being overworked, underpaid and under-appreciated,' and wanted to obtain her high school diploma.[154]

Mercury hastily issued a compilation of Red Bird material called *Golden Hits of the Shangri-Las*.[155] *Billboard* encouragingly reported,

> There's absolutely no risk in stocking this LP. The Shangri-Las are constant chart toppers in both singles and LP's. This contains some of their big hits like "I Can Never Go Home Anymore," "Walkin' the Sand," and "Leader of the Pack." It will be one of their biggest LP's to date.[156]

Mercury issued the first of two new Shangri-Las singles in January of 1967, "Sweet Sounds of Summer" b/w "I'll Never Learn." It was produced by Morton, who continued briefly to work with the group at Mercury, while increasingly devoting himself to future trends with Janis Ian and Vanilla Fudge. The Shangri-Las' second and final Mercury single was "Take the Time" b/w "Footsteps on the Roof," released in May of 1967. These four Mercury recordings are discussed more in more detail in chapter 8.

The Shangri-Las languished at Mercury, where their two releases failed to chart, after which the label did not see fit to make any further investment in recordings. The contrast between Mercury and Red Bird—a small label where the owners, producers, song-writers and artists all knew each other and worked together in close proximity—was considerable. The Shangri-Las had been the biggest-selling act on Red Bird; at Mercury they were a minor concern, lost in the greater and more impersonal mechanisms of a corporation. The group continued to be popular on the live circuit though, apparently performing for the rest of 1967 and into 1968. However, with little support coming from Mercury, and no new material imminent, the group disbanded.

The exact circumstances of and impetus for their break-up remain murky and unclear, and Mary Weiss consistently refused to discuss the subject except to remark that 'the litigation was thicker than the music;' beyond this she would not elaborate.[157] The fallout, however, was immense, and would play out for years afterward as the full extent of the contractual exploitation to which they had been subjected became apparent. Worse still was the toll that life in the Shangri-Las had taken on the personal circumstances of its four members.

Betty and Mary Weiss,
photographed by Jini
Dellaccio, 30 April 1966
(*University of Washington
Libraries, Special
Collections, UW42528*)

CHAPTER FIVE
Aftermath

The eventual implosion of the Shangri-Las as a performing and recording entity remains shrouded in mystery. The group members were prevented by an exploitative contract from recording with any other group or label, which effectively closed off other musical projects as options. The Shangri-Las were involved with three recording entities—Kama Sutra, Red Bird, and Mercury. By the time the group disbanded, Red Bird had collapsed, but from the glimpses that can be obtained into the shady business practices of some of its key figures, mob involvement and the circumstances surrounding the label's demise, it is not difficult to imagine that multiple parties pursued conflicting claims on the Shangri-Las recorded legacy.

As we have seen, this had been happening almost since the group's inception, and it seems that the Shangri-Las' affairs, through no fault of the group's, were in considerable disarray. Mary Weiss told Miriam Linna in 2006 that when the group disbanded, 'everybody around us was suing each other. Basically to me, the litigation just got so insane it wasn't about the music anymore.'[1] Weiss was always unwilling to elaborate on any of the litigation she refers to here, although she did go on to say in this particular interview that

> It was hard to get into the record industry and even harder to get out. I couldn't go near another record company for ten years . . . it was absolutely insane. And that was also how long I was still recognised on the street, which made it even more difficult.[2]

Even if she had chosen to, Weiss was contractually prevented from pursuing a singing career, solo or otherwise. In the short term, Mary said, she moved out 'on my eighteenth birthday. I moved into a hotel in Manhattan, then Gramercy Park, and then I moved to San Francisco for a while.'[3] Here, perhaps in an attempt to make up for some lost teenage time, she roller-skated a lot and immersed herself in the city's 'peace and love' hippy culture.[4] Eventually Weiss returned to New York City and began to work in commercial interior design. For seven years, she worked for an architectural firm, and ultimately 'ended up in the technical end, running crews of men around and analysing electrical and layouts, making sure your project's going to stand.'[5]

Weiss says she never went to college or trained formally to do this work, but said that she had 'a natural talent' for architecture inherited from her father, who she described as 'self-taught' and 'an exceptional builder':

I found a complete set of blue prints in my mom's attic, after she died. He designed and built the first house they ever lived in, from the ground up ... I could read blue prints from day one. I ended up running multi-million dollar projects (commercial interiors) ... There is no other explanation, other than that talent came from my father. There are certain strengths that I have, that my mother never did.[6]

MARY ANN GANSER

Before the Shangri-Las signed with Mercury as a trio in late 1966, Marguerite Ganser left the group and returned to study in order to gain her high school diploma. Her twin Mary Ann saw a future with the group and stayed on; she also registered an original composition (one page of sheet music) with the (perhaps working) title "No Words" on 26 December 1967.[7] At some point, almost certainly while on the road with the Shangri-Las, Mary Ann had developed drug-related health problems. From what we know of the pressures of hellish tour schedules, the disorganisation and lack of supervision, and drug use that took place on the road, this is not particularly surprising and was certainly not uncommon. Tragically, Mary Ann Ganser died as the result of complications connected with drug use sometime on the night of Saturday 14 March or in the early hours of Sunday 15 March, 1970. Her funeral was held on Thursday 19 March at Sacred Heart Roman Catholic Church in Cambria Heights, close by the associated school of the same name that she had attended as a child.[8] She was buried at St. Charles Cemetery in East Farmingdale, Long Island.[9] A few months after Mary Ann's death, her sister Marguerite re-registered the piece of instrumental music that Mary Ann had registered in 1967. The copyright entry noted its previous registration, that Marguerite had revised the melody, added words and a new arrangement, and that the work was now entitled "Lost Love."[10]

The date and circumstances of Mary Ann's death have been consistently obfuscated and inaccurately reported. It remains one of the biggest historiographical black spots concerning the Shangri-Las, but can be clarified to some extent here. In 2008 Jerry Simmonds stated in his *Encyclopaedia of Dead Rock Stars*:

> The facts behind Mary Ann's sudden death in 1970 still, to this day, divide her fans, friends and family. For a long time, it was believed that she might have suffered from encephalitis brought on by a malignant mosquito bite, and that she died following an untreated seizure while visiting a friend. Others—including, allegedly, the Ganser's mother—suggest that Mary Ann had battled heroin addiction for the last two years of her life, an overdose of barbiturates causing her death at just twenty-two.[11]

Over the years, accepted authorities on rock, including music scholars, have consistently stated that Mary Ann died from encephalitis, contracted from a mosquito bite—and in 1971, not 1970.[12] Rock journalist Kurt Loder conducted in 1985 what was at the time a rare interview with Mary Weiss. The resulting short piece, part of a larger 'Where Are They Now' feature on former pop stars, was published in *Rolling Stone*. In it, Loder noted that 'Mary Ann Ganser died in 1971 (of encephalitis, not a drug overdose, as is sometimes reported).'[13] This gave the strong impression that Mary was putting the record straight, as it were.[14]

In 2001, highly respected rock writer and Velvet Underground authority Phil Milstein interviewed Margie and Mary Ann's brother Robert and their mother Rita Ganser for a piece he was researching on the Shangri-Las' 1977 reunion.[15] Rita told Milstein,

> In the sixties and seventies . . . they were all into the drug thing, and that's what she got into. She was taking barbiturates and that's what

killed her, hanging out with these people. My husband and I, we never knew it, we never thought about it. And then one day she was sitting around the table having a meal with us, and all of a sudden she took a seizure, and we didn't know what it was all about and we had to rush her to hospital, and they told us there that it was an overdose she had.[16]

That it took an overdose for Mary Ann's parents to become aware that their daughter was struggling with drug problems is an indication of the extent to which addicts can conceal their addictions and manage to keep the symptoms from their closest relatives. Rita's account also indicates that neither she nor her husband had any knowledge or experience with the signs of and issues surrounding drug addiction. This is entirely consistent and to be expected; the common knowledge that we take for granted now was simply not available to Rita and Herman Ganser's generation.

On this occasion, prompt medical intervention enabled Mary Ann to recover. Rita continued:

She got over that fine, then she came home, and she was doing good for a while and then she went to one of her friend's, one of the girls in the singing group, Betty Weiss, she went to her house with my other daughter, her sister, and that's when she got into the drugs again. That night. And Betty didn't know what to do, and she passed right out in her house. That was a terrible shock, that she wasn't even *home*, oh! At least if she was home, we would have been able to help her, but here she was, up at Betty's house, and Betty didn't even have a telephone in the house, so how could she get help?[17]

Mary Ann's problems may have been more complex than Rita Ganser's account suggests. On 17 March 1970, under the headline '4 Teenagers Die from Heroin Here,' the *New York Times* reported,

Five addicts over 21 years old were also reported dead from acute reactions to heroin … Margaret [*sic*] Ganser was found dead at 105-24 64th Road in Queens Sunday afternoon.[18]

Although the *New York Times* writer named the wrong twin (as well as misnaming the wrong twin Margaret), this article is clearly referring to the death of Mary Ann Ganser. The *Long Island Press* published an obituary for Mary Ann Ganser on Wednesday 18 March 1970, and in the 'Death Notices' on the same page reported that Mary Ann had died 'suddenly, on March 15, 1970,' which was the previous Sunday.[19] The obituary does not state a cause of death, but noted:

> Miss Ganser died on Sunday while visiting a friend in Rego Park. The reason for her death is not yet known. She lived at 116-19 219th St.[20]

This address, 116-19 219th Street (in Cambria Heights, Queens), was that of her parents, Rita and Herman Ganser. It is likely that Mary Ann was living at home with her parents while trying to recover; Rita had said, 'she came home, and she was doing good for a while.' The address at which Mary Ann died, 105-24 64th Road, is a seven-storey early-1950s apartment block in the Rego Park/Forest Hills section of Queens.[21]

There is some evidence that Mary Ann had in fact developed a heroin addiction. The *New York Times* report cited above described Mary Ann as one of 'five addicts over 21 years old . . . reported dead from acute reactions to heroin,' and the description of Mary Ann as an 'addict' is significant, as is the repeated reference to 'the Medical Examiner's Office' as the source of the information contained in the article.[22] In the late 1960s, New York was grappling with a widespread and rapidly worsening heroin epidemic that was reported on almost daily in the press. Recent deaths were listed with names, ages, and (if available) addresses, in many cases along with tragic details and horrifying statistics.[23] A study of opiate use in New York City in the 1960s noted,

> According to the U.S. Bureau of Narcotics Report, fifty-two percent of the nation's active addicts lived in New York State, and 94 percent of the State's "active" addicts lived in New York City as of December 31, 1967.[24]

Moreover, heroin use was becoming particularly problematic in Queens. On the day Mary Ann Ganser's obituary was published in the *Long Island Press*, the same newspaper ran an article about the rapidly rising incidence of heroin usage in New York. Of the five boroughs,

4 TEEN-AGERS DIE FROM HEROIN HERE

Youths Are Among 8 Addicts Killed Over Weekend

Four more teen-agers have died from acute reactions to heroin, the Medical Examiner Office reported yesterday. They were among eight narcotics victims who died between Friday night and yesterday.

The total number of addicts dead so far this year from acute reactions to heroin and from infections caused by hypodermic needles is 179. Including 11 heroin addicts who were slain and seven narcotics users killed in accidents while under the influence of heroin, according to the Medical Examiner's Office, the total this year is 197 deaths. Of these, 55 were teen-agers.

A 16-year-old boy, Thomas Jesel, was found dead at his home yesterday at 115-24 Myrtle Avenue in Richmond Hill, Queens, and three other teen-agers died over the weekend. They were: José Torres, 15, who lived at 1013 Fox Street and was pronounced dead Saturday at Lincoln Hospital; Frederick Sanders, 19, who died at 691 Gerard Avenue Saturday, and Diane Cantey, also 19, who died Sunday at Trinity Hospital in Brooklyn of hepatitis. She was said to be 36 weeks pregnant.

15-Year-Old Girl Dies

A 15-year-old girl, Barbara Montabono, who died Saturday night at Brooklyn Hospital after she took 80 nembutal tablets—barbiturates used as "goofballs," was not listed among the heroin death totals for the weekend.

Five addicts over 21 years old were also reported dead from acute reactions to heroin. One, an unidentified young man, was found Saturday in a vacant apartment at 245 West 11th Street and Joseph Jackson, 41, was found in front of 2114 Eighth Avenue Friday.

Two died on Sunday; Margaret Ganser, was found dead at 105-24 64th Road in Queens Sunday afternoon and Arcello Roman, 46, was found dead at 176 West 88th Street on the same day. The Medical Examiners Office also reported that Samuel Henderson, 38, had died over the weekend as the result of an acute reaction to heroin. No address was given for him.

LONG ISLAND PRESS,

WEDNESDAY, MARCH 18, 1970

Mary Ann Ganser, Singer, Dies at 22

Mass for Mary Ann Ganser, 22, of Cambria Heights, who had sung with the "Shangri-Las" rock-and-roll television and recording performers, will be offered tomorrow at 10:15 a.m. in Sacred Heart Catholic Church of Cambria Heights.

Burial in St. Charles Cemetery, Farmingdale, will be under the direction of the Thomas J. Sheipe Funeral Home of Elmont. Miss Ganser died on Sunday while visiting a friend in Rego Park. The reason for her death is not yet known. She lived at 116-19 219th St.

A twin, Miss Ganser teamed in 1964 with her sister, Marguerite, and two neighborhood sisters, Betty and Mary Weiss, and within two months scored with a million-record song, "Remember."

In the same year, three months before Miss Ganser was to graduate from Andrew Jackson High School in Cambria Heights, she left with the group for England. There the Shangri-Las performed on the Dusty Springfield show with the Beatles and the Rolling Stones.

The Shangri-Las appeared on stage, such as the Mary Kay Show in the Fox Theater in Brooklyn; on radio, many times on television, and at Las Vegas. They were on the same bill with such singing groups as Diana Ross and The Supremes.

Some of their better known songs were "Walking in the Sand," "Leader of the Pack" and "Twist and Shout." They made five albums of songs before they stopped singing in 1968 when one member married and another became engaged.

Miss Ganser was born in Laurelton and graduated from Sacred Heart School in Cambria Heights.

Her parents have a musical background. Her father, Herman, a mechanical engineer, is from Vienna, Austria. Her mother, Rita, formerly of Brooklyn, is a pianist. She also leaves two brothers, Robert of Babylon and Alfred of Queens Village.

Queens had the highest rate of newly registered heroin users, a staggering 83.9% increase between 1967 and 1968.[25] In June 1970, journalist
Lawrence Altman reported,

> Deaths from the epidemic of narcotics use are still rising from the
> highest levels in the city's history—with no abatement in sight. Nar-
> cotics, chiefly heroin, now is the leading killer in the 15-35 age group,
> according to statistics provided by the office of the Chief Medical
> Examiner. About one fourth of the 950 narcotics deaths in 1969
> occurred among teen-agers and 53 per cent among those under 25
> years of age. These percentages are about double what they were ten
> years ago, meaning that more addicts are now dying at younger ages.[26]

It was not automatically assumed that any person who died a drug-
related death was an addict; there are plenty of news stories about inexperienced students at parties experimenting with substances and dying
as a result.[27] It was often noted if the deceased had any prior record
of drug use (or not), so for Mary Ann to be described as an addict,
although not conclusive, does suggest a history.

This likelihood is further strengthened by an *Identification of Body*
report by the Medical Examiner's office for Mary Ann Ganser that
makes reference to heroin problems going back (at least) two years.[28]
This document is probably the one being referred to in a 2003 post by a
researcher for the Google Answers platform, who had been tasked with
finding the cause of Mary Ann Ganser's death.[29] The researcher wrote,

> I got the tel. # from the operator for the brother [i.e., Robert Gan-
> ser], he gave me his mom's tel. #. I called [Rita Ganser] & she was
> very gracious & sent me Mary Ann's death papers and answered all
> my questions . . . When I mentioned a mosquito bite, she was taken
> aback. She said her daughter died of a barbitu[r]ate overdose. Her
> death papers confirmed she had battled heroin addiction for 2 yrs.*

---

* This post dates from 8 March 2003, see http://answers.google.com/answers/
threadview/id/173707.html (accessed 4 November 2021). I have made multiple
attempts to trace the person who made this post, to no avail; almost twenty years
have elapsed, and the platform no longer operates. Nevertheless, there are consistencies with Milstein's interactions with Rita Ganser that point to the accuracy of
what this researcher has relayed. Two years earlier, in 2001, Milstein also was given
Rita's number (which appears to have been unlisted) by Robert Ganser after being

In the early 1970s in New York City, an *Identification of Body* report
was one of several forms completed by the Medical Examiner's office
when a person died. Others included a *Report of Death*, which detailed
the circumstances of how, when, where and with what evidence (if any)
the body was found; and a *Notice of Death*, which recorded some of
the same information (date, time, location) but more succinctly.[30] The
'death papers' referred to by the Google Answers researcher are likely
to have included this *Identification of Body* report, a document that has
been incorrectly labelled elsewhere* as 'a copy of a coroner's inquest
from the collection of Mrs. Rita Ganser (Mary Ann's mom).'†

The report for Mary Ann Ganser is a one-page form headed *Office
of the Chief Medical Examiner of the City of New York: Identification of
Body*.[31] This is a standard form that is completed by the Medical Examiner in charge; in this case, since it was early in 1970, the office was still
using the forms designed for the 1960s, on which the first three numbers of the year were already input as 196_. Mary Ann's report records
that Herman Ganser, of '116-19 219th S.,' a private house in Cambria
Heights, Queens,

---

to some degree vetted by him; Rita also mailed Milstein some material (photos)
to use for the article he was writing. Rita's statements to Milstein, as well as her
forthrightness and willingness to clarify what happened to her daughter are also
consistent.

* Although both investigate causes of deaths and identify deceased people, a coroner
is an elected public servant, while a Medical Examiner must be a doctor in order to
be appointed (not elected) to this position. Medical Examiners can (but not always)
have additional training in forensic pathology, and their job is to prepare a report
based on available medical records, testimony from witnesses and/or family members and in some cases, an autopsy, in order 'to reach a conclusion regarding the
cause of death.' See Ron M. Aryel and Michael M. Wagner, 'Coroners and Medical
Examiners' in Michael M. Wagner, Andrew W. Moore, Ron M. Aryel, *Handbook of
Biosurveillance*, 179–181. This is consistent with the *New York Times* reports cited
earlier which contain multiple references to the 'doctors' and 'pathologists' at 'the
medical examiner's office'; Lawrence K. Altman, 'Deaths Attributed to Narcotics,
Mainly Heroin, Increase Here,' *New York Times*, 21 June 1970, 1.

† This document was uploaded to a post in a thread entitled 'Has anyone ever heard
of the Shangri Las'; see note 28 above. Again, I have attempted to contact the poster
via the forum to no avail. Although I am unable to confirm that it came 'from the
collection of Mrs Rita Ganser,' there are consistencies with other evidence, including
the testimony of Rita and Robert Ganser and newspaper reports, that persuade me
to treat it as genuine. Furthermore, Rita Ganser's phone number is written in pencil
on the top left-hand side of the document; this is the same phone number provided
by Robert Ganser to Phil Milstein in 2001.

Rita Ganser
631-843-9533

IDENTIFICATION OF BODY

TREATED BY DCR BERGER
516 354-6453
6/68 ———— 11/68
INJECTION OF B12

STATE OF NEW YORK
CITY AND COUNTY OF NEW YORK, ss.:
BOROUGH OF

HERMAN GANSER .... age.... 21 PLUresiding at

PVT. HOUSE

116 -19 219th St. QUEENS .... in the .... CAMBRIA HEIGHTS

being duly sworn, deposes and says: That he is a .... FATHER

of the person whose body was found at .... 105-24 64 ROAD 3/15/70 ......, 196....,

and subsequently sent to the Office of Chief Medical Examiner; that deponent has seen the .... REMAINS

of said deceased, and has every reason to believe that the body now recorded at the Office of Chief Medical

Examiner as ..... MARY ANN GANSER

is .... SAME .... who was last seen or heard from by deponent on

.... 3/14/70 ...., 196.......

Deponent therefore prays that HIS identification of said deceased person be accepted by the Chief

Medical Examiner of The City of New York.

Age: 22 .... Sex FEMALE .... Color WHITE ....

Marital Status: ...... SINGLE

Occupation: .... SINGER

Residence: ..... 116-19 219th St. CAMBRIA HEIGHTS.

FATHER STATES THAT HE XXXX
HE HAD HISTORY OF OVERDOSE
OF HEROIN 2 YEARS AGO.
WAS WARNED BY HER DOCTOR
BERGER NOT TO USE DRUGS AGAI

WAS HOSPITALIZED AT DEEPDALE
HOSPITAL 7-8 DAYS.
ENCEPHALOGRAPH DONE .SWELL ING
OF BRAIN

Sworn to before me this

16 day of MARCH 19x70

1;30 PM

H.R. REID

Identified to :........

X Herman Ganser
HR 3/16

HISTORY OF TWO EPISODES OF CONVULSIO
WAS TOLD NOT TO CONSUME ALCOHOL
HAD TWO OR THREE BEERS 3/24/70

Death Ctf. issued by :........ Date :........

R 3/16/70

FATHER of the person whose body was found at 105-34 64 ROAD 3/15/70 and subsequently sent to the Office of the Chief Medical Examiner; that deponent has seen the REMAINS of said deceased, and has every reason to believe that the body now recorded at the Office of Chief Medical Examiner as MARY ANN GANSER is SAME who was last seen or heard from by deponent on 3/14/70.[32]

Also recorded is that Mary Ann Ganser was '22, female, white, single,' her occupation was 'singer' and her residence '116-19 219th St. Cambria Heights.' Herman Ganser's signature is at the bottom; the date is recorded as (Monday) 16 March 1970, the time 1:30 pm.[33]

Additional typewritten notes in the margins of this document shed further light on the state of Mary Ann's health in the years immediately preceding her death. All are in uppercase letters. In the top righthand corner of the document, it was noted that Mary Ann was

TREATED BY DOR [Doctor] BERGER
516 354-3453
6/68- - - - - 11/68
INJECTION OF B12*

Then further down on the right-hand side, it was recorded that

FATHER STATES THAT [S]HE XXXXX XX [words struck out] HAD HISTORY OF OVERDOSE OF HEROIN 2 YEARS AGO. WAS WARNED BY XXX [word struck out] DOCTOR BERGER NOT TO USE DRUGS AGAIN.†

---

* 'Mary Ann Ganser: Identification of Body.' In the discussion that follows, I refer to this as note 1.

† 'Mary Ann Ganser: Identification of Body.' It appears that the medical examiner had started typing in block letters 'FATHER STATES THAT HE *KNEW* [*SHE?*— there are only two struck-out letters of this second word] HAD HISTORY' etc. but then struck out the word that appears to be 'knew' to make the statement more emphatic. The examiner then neglected to go back and add an 'S' before 'HE' to make the statement read 'SHE HAD HISTORY OF OVERDOSE . . . ' In the discussion that follows, I refer to this as note 2.

Just below these sentences, in the next block of available space, above Herman Ganser's signature, more typewritten notes record that Mary Ann

WAS HOSPITALIZED AT DEEPDALE HOSPITAL 7-8 DAYS. ENCEPHALOGRAPH DONE .SWELLING OF BRAIN.*

And below Herman's signature:

HISTORY OF TWO EPISODES OF CONVULSION. WAS TOLD NOT TO CONSUME ALCOHOL
HAD TWO OR THREE BEERS 3/14/70 †

It is not immediately obvious how to interpret these notes and how they relate to each other, nor is it clear precisely what bearing the events recorded here had on Mary Ann's death. However, as noted earlier, one of the chief functions of the Medical Examiner's office was to determine a cause of death, as well as to provide official identification of the deceased person. So by implication these notes were recorded for the purpose of explaining why an otherwise apparently healthy 22-year-old woman had died. A plausible reading, arrived at in conjunction with Robert and Rita Ganser's testimony and newspaper reports, is as follows.

The overdose referred to by Rita Ganser in her conversation with Phil Milstein is the 'overdose of heroin 2 years ago' that the medical examiner was informed of by Herman Ganser (note 2). If this had occurred two years earlier, it happened in 1968, and this is likely the time that Rita and Herman 'had to rush her to hospital'; it is also likely that this was when Mary Ann was 'hospitalized at Deepdale Hospital 7-8 days' (note 3). Deepdale General Hospital opened in 1959 at 55-15 Little Neck Parkway in Flushing, Queens, and was a short drive (10 to 15 minutes) from the Gansers' house in Cambria Heights.[34] If what I have suggested above is correct, then Mary Ann probably underwent heroin detoxification during her '7-8 days' at Deepdale Hospital; at this

---

* 'Mary Ann Ganser: Identification of Body.' In the discussion that follows, I refer to this as note 3.
† 'Mary Ann Ganser: Identification of Body.' In the discussion that follows, I refer to this as note 4.

time detoxing took place in hospitals (if a bed was available, which was not at all a given) and was usually allocated 'about 10 days.'[35]

Although it is not certain that Mary Ann's encephalograph was done during her stay at Deepdale, the placement of this information immediately below the note about her hospitalisation suggests that it was (note 3). This encephalograph—essentially, a brain scan—could have been carried out because of Mary Ann's 'history of two episodes of convulsion' (note 4), since seizures are a common result of cerebral edema (brain swelling). It is not clear, however, whether these convulsions date from before the overdose and hospital stay, or if they happened afterwards, in the months before her death, although Rita Ganser's account would indicate that the first she and Herman knew of Mary Ann's problems was her major overdose/seizure, so if there were others, they were likely after this. Either way, the scan showed that Mary Ann had some form of cerebral edema; what caused this is undetermined, as is (at least from this document) the extent to which it may have contributed to her death.

Depending on the severity of Mary Ann's overdose, an encephalograph may have been done as a matter of routine. This is especially likely if Mary Ann suffered a hypoxic overdose, that is, if she convulsed and/or passed out during which a loss of oxygen to the brain occurred, which would cause cerebral edema.[36] In a near-contemporary study of the effects of drug and alcohol abuse on the brain, Igor Grant and Lynn Mohns noted, 'abuse of intravenous narcotics has been associated with case reports of transverse myelitis and encephalitis. It is not known whether this pathology is a direct or hypersensitivity effect of narcotic drugs, of adulterants, or of infection.'[37]

At a time long before harm-minimisation strategies such as needle exchange programs and safe injecting rooms were developed, the illicit nature of heroin addiction meant that syringe sharing and poor hygiene, as well as the uncertain strength and composition of the drug itself ensured that even the most careful user was extremely vulnerable to infection and/or drug-related brain injury. It is not possible to be certain about what caused the swelling in Mary Ann's brain, but it does seem clear that it was not related to a mosquito-borne infection, which is only one of many possible causes of cerebral edema. When Phil Milstein interviewed Robert and Rita Ganser in 2001, neither mentioned a mosquito bite in relation to Mary Ann's death but both did refer to drug use. This is consistent with what the Google Answers researcher who spoke with Rita Ganser in 2003 reported: Rita was 'taken aback' at the mention of a mosquito bite and 'said that her daughter died of a barbitu[r]ate overdose.'

It is likely that Mary Ann left hospital detoxed and somewhat recovered and went back to her family home; as Rita put it, 'she got over that fine, then she came home, and she was doing good for a while.' Presumably it was during this time that she was treated by Dr Berger (notes 1 and 3) for follow-up care after being hospitalised. A Doctor Arnold L. Berger had (or worked at) a practice at 444 Elmont Road, Elmont, Queens, again a short distance from the Ganser's home on 219th Street.[38] The Medical Examiner noted that Berger treated Mary Ann from June to November of 1968, and that this treatment included 'injection of B12' (note 1). It was also noted that Berger had 'warned' Mary Ann 'not to use drugs again' (note 2). The Examiner included Dr Berger's phone number (note 1), which suggests that he was called and provided this information, with his number noted for the record and in case further clarification was required.[39]

In the course of Phil Milstein's interview with Robert Ganser in 2001, Robert described Mary Ann as being 'under some kind of medication' and as having occasional problems, but she 'was OK on the medication.' He was unable or unwilling to be more specific about Mary Ann's drug issues: 'I really don't know because I never got into drugs—I was always against that. It's more or less what killed my first sister, she was involved, she was like 22 when she died.'[40] Robert continued,

> My sister was under some kind of medication, we don't know, we never got the report on why, what happened when she died. She had an epileptic fit, that's what she died of, she was alone and she just suffocated.[41]

The medication that Robert referred to may have been Dr Berger's Vitamin B12 injections; if Mary Ann was receiving any other medication, it was not recorded here. At this time, Vitamin B12 was most commonly prescribed in women for anaemia and general malnourishment, but was also used in the treatment of alcoholism, all of which could of course be interconnected. Mary Ann had apparently been 'told not to consume alcohol' (note 4); given that (illicit) drugs are very often used in conjunction with alcohol, Mary Ann may have been struggling with issues relating to both.[42] Vitamin B12 was also understood to have applications for cognitive function and depression, all of which would be consistent given Mary Ann's cerebral edema diagnosis. Regular visits to Dr Berger and the resulting consistent medical supervision also may have been as helpful for Mary Ann as any actual medications she received. In any case, it seems that Dr Berger stopped treating Mary Ann in November 1968. Perhaps, after six months of consultations, he deemed her sufficiently recovered and no longer requiring treatment.

Rita Ganser's brief description of the circumstances of Mary Ann's death suggests that she had been recovering well until 'she got into the drugs again' on the night she died. John Grecco writes, in his lengthy piece on the Shangri-Las,

> All was quiet for some time as the girls got back into the swing of everyday life. In 1970 Mary Ann was experiencing some pretty serious health problems that led to her being susceptible to seizures. With her determination to get better, the full support of her family, and following doctor's orders, she was well on the road to recovery. Recuperating for quite some time and starting to feel her old self again, Mary Ann decided to pay a visit to a friend one night. During this visit she was beset by another seizure, and unfortunately by the time her friend had summoned help, Mary Ann was gone.[43]

Although this is a considerably more guarded account than the one Rita Ganser gave to Milstein, it is nevertheless consistent. So where does this leave us in terms of establishing the cause of Mary Ann Ganser's death? The New York Times reported a heroin overdose; Rita Ganser stated on two occasions a barbiturate overdose; and Robert Ganser cited a seizure which he described as an epileptic fit. The likelihood is that all three contributed to Mary Ann's death, the immediate cause of which was a seizure brought on by something she took that night—alcohol, pills, heroin—one or a combination of these. Why then did Rita Ganser state emphatically to Phil Milstein that Mary Ann died of a barbiturate overdose? There are several plausible possibilities. The first is that this was in fact the cause of her death. After all, the New York Times did get Mary Ann's name wrong, and it is entirely possible that Mary Ann had been treated previously for heroin addiction, and/or was, at the time of her death, a registered addict participating in a treatment program. The Department of Health's implementation of the New York City Narcotics Register in 1966 increases the likelihood that Mary Ann would have been on record as an addict.[44] When she then *died* of an overdose, it is conceivable that it was inaccurately reported by the *New York Times* as a heroin overdose. Or, even more likely, the Medical Examiner decided that there was enough evidence of prior use to rule Mary Ann's death as an accidental overdose and this information was reported by the *New York Times*, as it was in countless other similar reports. On the other hand, the *New York Times* article did differentiate between drugs for one of the other deaths listed; 15-year-old Barbara Montabono died 'after she took 80 Nembutal tablets—barbiturates used as "goofballs."' It was explicitly stated that her death 'was not listed among the heroin death totals for the weekend.'[45]

Furthermore, recovering heroin addicts often use other substances to dull the pain, both physical and psychological, of heroin withdrawal, which, depending on the length of time a person has been an addict, is lengthy and severe. It is also common for addicts to use other substances if for some reason (lack of money, erratic supply) heroin cannot be obtained. A Canadian study published in 1968 noted a significant increase in numbers of 'dual abusers' of heroin and barbiturates; the multiple reasons for this included 'potentiation' of heroin (i.e., using barbiturates simultaneously to heighten the effect of heroin, especially if the heroin was of poor quality and/or heavily cut) and, significantly, 'to obtain heavy sedation during heroin withdrawal, in order to reduce awareness of withdrawal symptoms.'[46] The same study also noted of barbiturates:

> Another characteristic of this class of drugs is that while there may be considerable tolerance to the sedative and intoxicating effects, the lethal dose is not much greater in addicts than in normal individuals. Consequently acute barbiturate poisoning may be accidentally or wilfully superimposed on chronic intoxication at any time. Thus barbiturate abuse is markedly more dangerous than is abuse of heroin, the lethal dose of which increases as tolerance increases.[47]

To make matters even more complex, withdrawal from barbiturates, which are extremely addictive, was almost as dangerous as overdose, and could result in 'delirium and grand mal convulsions, coma and death.' As a consequence, 'withdrawal from barbiturates is potentially considerably more dangerous than withdrawal from heroin and requires prolonged medical care with special nursing facilities to guard against delirium, convulsions and death.'[48]

A 'grand mal convulsion' is the type normally associated with epilepsy, which would explain Robert Ganser's description of his sister's seizure as 'an epileptic fit' in his interview with Phil Milstein. This also raises the possibility that Mary Ann's 'episodes of convulsion' resulted from attempts to *stop* using barbiturates. One New York study from the early 1970s noted that anecdotal evidence from health care workers suggested that barbiturate addiction or abuse seemed to be 'more troublesome among females,' occurring in women at higher rates than for other drugs.[49]

However, as Rita Ganser made so painfully clear in the interview, she was not present when the seizure/overdose that claimed Mary Ann's life occurred. It could just as easily have been the result of a heroin overdose, especially if, as Rita indicated, 'she was doing good for a while,' not using heroin, and her tolerance was lowered. This would also be consistent with her brother Robert's understanding that Mary Ann was 'under some kind of medication.'[50] This could indicate a heroin-substitute treatment program, such as methadone, which was in use in New York at this time.[51] While this prevents heroin withdrawal, and allows the addict to manage their addiction legally, it does not produce a 'high.' Despite its benefits, methadone is nevertheless a highly addictive opiate and if Mary Ann had been warned not to use drugs, it seems unlikely that she would be prescribed methadone. It was (and is) so common as to be a cliché, for addicts to reward themselves for all their hard work of staying 'straight' with a hit of heroin from which they then overdose because of their reduced tolerance. In yet another tragic parallel, this occurred with Frankie Lymon, whose tolerance was much reduced after a stint in the army in the mid-60s.[52] It is entirely possible that this is what happened to Mary Ann, especially if she was in the company of someone doing the same.

It is equally possible that, as a result of Mary Ann's previous drug use and/or her 1968 overdose, serious damage resulting in cerebral edema had occurred, and this was significant enough for her to be warned not to drink alcohol (note 4) or use drugs again (note 2).[53] She reportedly had 'two or three beers 3/14/70' (note 4) which, since Herman had last seen his daughter on this date (Saturday), was either observed by him (before Mary Ann went to Betty's) or reported to him by someone who had been there. The beers may have been enough for Mary Ann to let her guard down, especially if she had been feeling better, and take something else (barbiturates, according to Rita Ganser) that her now fragile system was simply unable to tolerate.

The circumstances surrounding the death of Mary Ann Ganser will probably never be completely clarified. That Mary Ann's death took place at Betty Weiss's apartment was difficult and painful for all concerned and remains so to this day. Robert Ganser commented that Mary Ann's sister Marge

> used to watch out after her, but that one time her sister left, and left her alone, and she was with this girl Betty, and nobody ever got the story on what happened. My mother asked her, and she won't talk about it.[54]

Robert Ganser was certainly of the opinion that Betty Weiss was having drug issues of her own at this point.* On 9 February 1970, Betty Weiss had married Jeremy Storch, the former organ player with the Vagrants, a Long Island rock band with whom the Shangri-Las shared management at some point in the mid-1960s.[55] By the late 1960s he was signed to RCA Victor as a solo artist; his 1970 album *From a Naked Window* is an acclaimed cult-psychedelic favourite with liner notes by "S/He Cried" composer Ted Daryll and a cover that includes a tiny inset photo of Storch and Betty Weiss projected onto the pupil of an eye.[56]

By 2006, Jeremy Storch was a rabbi with the Tabernacle of Praise Ministries, and the biographical section of his website located his decision to pursue this career path in the context of his earlier rock lifestyle:

> Once "The Vagrants" disbanded, in 1968, RCA Records picked up Jeremy to record and release two solo albums, "From a Naked Win-

---

* On several occasions throughout the interview with Phil Milstein, Robert Ganser stated that Betty was 'heavy into drugs,' but when pressed for details about what type(s), said that he didn't know because he had never been interested in drugs himself.

dow" and "Forty Miles Past Woodstock." This popularity and success led him further into the rock culture of the sixties—including
all the trappings of a typical rock star: experimentation with and
heavy use of various drugs and plunging into wild parties and illicit
affairs. In short, he became a prodigal son.

In 1970, Jeremy's excessive lifestyle caught up with him and he
died of a drug overdose on the way to the hospital. In this death
experience, God spoke to Jeremy saying, "I am giving you back your
life to do some work for Me!" As soon as that was spoken, Jeremy
awoke in a hospital bed.[57]

Neither Rita nor Robert Ganser mentioned an overdose incident
involving Jeremy occurring on the day/night that Mary Ann died, so it
must be presumed that this occurred on a different occasion. It is not
clear whether he and Betty were living together at this time (they did
subsequently divorce), but in 1970 Storch's drug use was clearly at its
peak. In any case, Robert Ganser felt that the only way that he and his
family might learn more about the circumstances of his sister's death
was if Betty 'ever came forward with it, but I don't think she ever will.
She's got some guilt over what she did, or something, I don't know.'[58]

What does seem clear is that the details of Mary Ann's death have
been obfuscated to elide Betty's involvement. This is evident in Mary
Weiss's comment in a 2007 interview with Michael Martin for *New York*
magazine:

> As for her former bandmates, Mary Ann Ganser died in 1971; con-
> flicting accounts cite a drug overdose or a seizure. "And I'll leave
> it that way. It doesn't much matter anymore," pronounces Weiss,
> sounding a bit like an intro to one of her old songs.[59]

Mary Ann's death remained off-limits in any interviews with Mary
Weiss, along with the subject of Betty's departure from the group in
1964 and the litigation that followed the demise of the group. In an
interview with Mike Schneider on the US television talk show *Night
Talk* to promote Weiss's 2007 album, *Dangerous Game*, Schneider asked
Mary Weiss about her sister Betty: 'There was a lot of talk back in the
old days, that she didn't show up all the time on the album covers, right?
And what was that . . .' At that point, Schneider, glancing off-camera and

clearly warned off the subject by someone, interrupts himself and says, 'But now you are well represented, right?'[60]

REFORMATION

Betty Weiss worked for a time at Rheingold Breweries, then later for a cosmetics company in Manhattan, according to John Grecco. She split from Jeremy Storch in the late 1970s, remarried and is known as Liz Weiss Nelson. Marge Ganser married Bill Dorste in 1972.[61] Mary also married and used the name Mary Weiss Stokes ; she later married again, and at the time of her death was married to Edward Ryan.

The three surviving members reformed the Shangri-Las for at least one show in the early 70s, at the New York Academy of Music in Manhattan. Billed as Gus Gossert's Rock and Roll Revival Show, it featured, along with the Ronettes, a selection of doo-wop groups including the Mystics and the Tokens.[62] Gossert was a disk jockey whose 'Doo Wop Shop' radio show on WCBS in New York won a loyal following in the early 1970s, despite the unfashionability of street corner vocal harmony at the time.[63] Ironically, the Shangri-Las found themselves labelled a 'revival' or nostalgia act, despite the fact that all members were still only in their early twenties. They were also pigeonholed within a category, but significantly it was not 'girl group,' but vocal harmony, or doo-wop.

In 1977 the three remaining Shangri-Las reformed for a lengthier period. This episode is one of the few periods of the Shangri-Las' career that has been chronicled in any depth, in a lengthy piece by Phil Milstein entitled 'Shangri-Las 77!'[64] The group made some recordings for Sire, a label owned and run by Seymour Stein, who knew the Shangri-Las from his time working at Red Bird in the mid-1960s. Stein and songwriter/producer Richard Gottehrer started Sire in 1966, initially licensing British progressive rock records (by the Deviants, Twink, and Stackridge, to name a few) for release in the US.[65] By the mid-70s Sire was issuing seminal early US punk records, including by the Ramones, Richard Hell and the Voidoids, the Dead Boys and Talking Heads. Sire also licensed for US release the debut albums of Australian groups the Saints ((*I'm*) *Stranded*, in 1977) and Radio Birdman (*Radios Appear*, in 1978) and released Madonna's debut album in 1983.[66]

Andy Paley was the producer who worked on the Shangri-Las' Sire sessions.[67] He recalled,

The Shangri-Las contacted Seymour, and they were old friends because Seymour used to work for Leiber and Stoller at Red Bird . . . Seymour told me about this and that the Shangri-Las wanted to make a record and they wanted to talk to different producers.[68]

It is unlikely that the timing of this decision is a coincidence, given that Mary Weiss has repeatedly stated that, around the time of the group's demise, she was contractually prevented from recording with another label for ten years. This suggests that it was the Mercury contract signed by the group late in 1966 that contained this stricture. If this were the case, this contract would have expired by late 1976, leaving them free to record again, and they approached Stein 'in late spring or early summer of 1977.'[69]

The sessions were ultimately successful but did not progress beyond those initial recordings, for reasons Andy Paley did not completely understand. At least four original songs were composed, for which copyrights were lodged:

"Our Song" w (words) Mary L. Stokes [Weiss], w & m (words and music) Marge Dorste [Ganser], 2 p. (pages) © 12 October 1977;[70]

"Municipal Parking Lot" w Marguerite Dorste, w & m Elizabeth A. Storch [Weiss]. 1 p. © 8 November 1977;[71]

"Wonderful You" w Mary L. Stokes, w & m Marguerite Dorste, 1 sound tape reel, © 10 April 1978;[72]

"On and On" w & m Marge Dorste, w Mary L. Stokes, 1 sound tape reel, © 26 May 1978.[73]

Despite the fact that Stein was apparently happy with the standard of the material, it was never released, and there seem to be no extant copies of the master recordings. When asked about the sessions, Mary Weiss commented that, in her opinion,

it wasn't there, material-wise. I don't want anything released that I don't believe in . . . it just wasn't right. I welcomed the opportunity from Seymour Stein, but it just didn't work out.[74]

At this time the Shangri-Las also played a spontaneous, one-off gig at CBGB, the legendary bar/music venue (now closed) on the Bowery in lower Manhattan. This was the epicentre of New York City's punk scene from the mid-70s well into the 80s. The show was a resounding success, since the Shangri-Las were great favourites of and a central influence on the Bowery punk scene groups, including the New York Dolls, Blondie and the Ramones. The band that backed the Shangri-Las included Andy Paley on guitar, with Lenny Kaye and Jay Dee Daugherty of the Patti Smith Group playing bass and drums respectively.[75] Kaye is a long-time fan and collector of group vocal harmony music, and had written a piece called 'The Best of A Cappella' for *Jazz and Pop* magazine in the late 1960s.[76] Furthermore, the records Sire was releasing at this time made this milieu a logical choice for the Shangri-Las to perform in.

According to Paley, the CBGB gig was the climax of his work with the Shangri-Las; after that, he said, it was the end of summer, and everything just fizzled out. He was at a loss to explain this but suspected that the group chose *him* over more experienced and famous producers at their disposal at least in part so that they would be under less pressure. Paley surmised that their thinking may have run along the lines of,

> We're gonna go make some records maybe, but really we're just gonna sing together and just hang out in the studio, which is this kind of funky little studio . . . why don't we just use this guy, cos if we use Stephen Galfus or Richard Gottehrer, then it's all of a sudden more big-time, then there's more pressure. They might well have thought, well, here's this guy in his twenties, let's use him instead.[77]

According to Paley, they did a lot of hanging out and just having fun, eating pizza and playing pool. Furthermore, they reconnected with the whole reason it all happened in the first place, as Paley explains,

> That is the magic thing about it. That would make everyone smile, no matter what the hell was going on . . . and the funny thing about them is that . . . they had these chips on their shoulders, and they were kind of tough. You know, the Long Island thing . . . but as soon as they started singing and got down to work, it was just all about sounding good, and they all started smiling and everything was really fun and loving and really, really good. And they could be hilarious, they were hilarious people just to hang around with, because they were all really smart and all really funny. They could cut somebody

down to size really quick if they wanted to, and I saw them do that a few times. Part of this was almost like they had a club. And I was allowed into that club. For that summer, and it was just like, it was really, really fun.[78]

The contrast between these conditions and their gruelling schedules and tours in the mid-60s could not be greater. They did material of *their* choosing, including one of Margie's songs (although, according to Paley, they did not record it).[79] Given what we know of the group members' experiences as teen stars in the mid-60s, it seems quite possible that, in some way, the Shangri-Las were reconfiguring their memories and asserting control. Once that had been achieved, it was no longer necessary to do anything more, like release a record. Had they gone ahead and done that, they would certainly have been required to do concert performances and tour to promote the record; it is little wonder if there was reluctance on their part to revisit that world. Paley repeatedly commented on how 'great' they sounded, reiterating,

> If somebody said that they found them on a street corner singing harmony I would believe it because that is the essence of what I heard . . . whenever they wanted to they could just break into three-part harmony and they were really, really good. They were *really* good at that.[80]

A number of Roberta Bayley's photos taken during these sessions are of the Shangri-Las singing a cappella in the street outside the Sire studios at 165 West 74th Street in Manhattan.* It is tempting to speculate that the Shangri-Las had taken their voices back to the street, back to their doo-wop origins. They had made it fun again, and that was enough.

In 1989 the Shangri-Las fought and won an extraordinary case over the name of the group. They had been booked to make a rare appearance at an 'oldies' show, Cousin Brucie's Palisades Park Reunion Show, on 3 June 1989. The show was to have an early-60s revue format, similar

---

* Roberta Bayley is a New York photographer most famous for her shots of rock figures from the 70s, particularly Blondie and the Ramones: see her official website. There is a fantastic collection of photos by Bayley of the recording sessions and the CBGB's show on the Getty Images website.

to those in which the Shangri-Las performed early in their career, and featured Lesley Gore, Little Anthony, the Tokens, the Chimes, Freddy Cannon and Bobby Rydell.[81] It turned out that the name 'Shangri-Las' had never been officially registered, and enterprising oldies/nostalgia promoter Richard (Dick) Fox, having realised this some years earlier, had registered the name and put together a fake Shangri-Las group to perform concerts and shows.[82] At what point Fox did this is unclear. Juan Casiano, who grew up in Cambria Heights, had known the Shangri-Las personally as a teenager and has been an obsessive fan ever since, recalled seeing a fake group perform in New Jersey as early as the mid-70s.[83] Joseph Alexander, drummer in the Shangri-Las' backing group in the mid-1960s, is quoted in Alan Betrock's book, published in 1982, saying,

> Later on, it got crazier, with all these lawsuits flying around, and people came in and told them that they had no rights to the name 'the Shangri-Las'—that they couldn't get work and play under that name. Can you believe that?[84]

Whether this was connected to the contractual strictures that prevented Mary Weiss from recording for ten years after the demise of the group is not clear. In any case, in 1989, after being booked to perform at the aforementioned Cousin Brucie show, the Shangri-Las found themselves the subject of an injunction from Richard Fox and his fake Shangri-Las, preventing the *real* group from performing on the basis that, according to Fox, the name had not been used in years and Fox was now its legal owner. Outraged, Marge Ganser and Mary and Betty Weiss took the matter to court. In an interview on *Entertainment Tonight*, Marge (Ganser) Dorste, visibly livid after viewing footage of the fake group, said,

> That is ... what *we* worked so hard for, what *we* went on the road for ... what we did the one-nighters for, and stayed in the lousy hotel rooms ... [85]

This ludicrous situation speaks volumes about the lasting effects of the contractual mechanisms implemented in the 1950s and 60s to exploit teenaged performers. And beyond, for that matter—alarming parallels exist between the Shangri-Las and the Runaways, a teenaged Los Angeles band that formed in the mid-70s, as lead singer Cherie Currie's biography attests.[86]

Knowing how events played out for the Shangri-las, the *Entertainment Tonight* feature on their case makes for difficult viewing, particularly the staggering entitlement displayed by Fox. Nor was the Shangri-Las' an isolated case; surviving members of the Marvelettes have been threatened with legal action if they perform under their name, which is now owned by Dick Fox's partner, Larry Marshak. Marshak has also caused similar problems for other groups, including the Coasters, the Platters and the Drifters.[87] What makes the situation even more galling is that many of the performers, having been prevented by exploitative contracts from receiving any substantial earnings in their heyday, now find the costs of pursuing legal action prohibitive. Promoters like Fox and Marshak have gleefully exploited this situation while holding the performers responsible for being somehow complicit in their own oppression. According to Fox:

> You can talk to them today, and they didn't care! They say, 'We wanted to hear ourselves on the radio. We were driving in our car, we heard ourselves on the radio,' and that was it. Money? What was money? . . . They signed these contracts that said, 'You turn over all your royalties, you turn over your first-born, you turn over your house, you turn over your parents.' They care now, but they didn't care then.[88]

As we have seen, many of the performers in question were minors, meaning that their parents or adult guardians had to sign their contracts for them; this is in itself an acknowledgement that the performers were not considered to yet possess the requisite knowledge, judgement and maturity to sign legal documents. Furthermore, many of them, like Frankie Lymon and the Teenagers, the members of the Marvelettes, and the Shangri-Las, were poor, as Mary Weiss has pointed out:

> I come from an extremely poor family. The Gansers were relatively poor. Nobody had any money. No money for attorneys. So considering where the four of us came from, with no support, no guidance, and nothing behind us, we didn't have proper outfits on stage. I mean

nothing. It's a miracle in itself to come from those circumstances and have hit records.[89]

The Shangri-Las took Marshak and Fox to court over the group's name and won the right to perform their 1989 engagement. Betty Weiss commented tellingly, 'We're not teenagers anymore, and we don't have to take it anymore. And we're not taking it anymore.'[90] A settlement was reached through which the surviving members of the Shangri-Las received a percentage payment whenever the Marshak/Fox group performs.[91]

This 1989 engagement turned out to be the Shangri-Las' last performance together; Marge Ganser Dorste died from breast cancer on 28 July 1996. As she had instructed, her ashes were divided between her sister Mary Ann's grave and Hampton Bays.[92]

In 2007, Mary Weiss released a solo album, *Dangerous Game*, on Norton Records, a small Brooklyn-based label run by rock stalwarts Billy Miller and Miriam Linna (Miller died in 2016).[93] Weiss was backed by the Reigning Sound, a garage rock band from Memphis usually fronted by singer/songwriter Greg Cartwright, who also wrote several of the songs on the album. The release of the record and accompanying live shows generated considerable radio, press and television coverage, in the course of which Weiss spoke more openly than she had for decades about her experiences with the Shangri-Las and her excitement about being back in the recording studio. Weiss toured and performed extensively with the Reigning Sound, and both her album and the shows were critically well received. *Dangerous Game* was her only solo recording.

Betty Weiss, Mary Ann Ganser, and Mary Weiss, photographed backstage at the Seattle Center Coliseum by Jini Dellaccio, 30 April 1966 (*University of Washington Libraries, Special Collections, UW42525*)

CHAPTER SIX

Hmmm, He's Good-Bad, but He's Not Evil: "Leader of the Pack," Shadowy Guys, and Rebellion

> As I wrote the song, I heard Mary singing and I saw Mary. This song was written about the girl on the street corner. Her, I touched on in a personal way, allowed her to open up . . . but *him*, he's the mystery.
> —George 'Shadow' Morton[1]

Rebellion—against parents and the moral codes of a conservative society—is a theme that runs through much of the Shangri-Las' oeuvre. The most famous and spectacular expression of this is "Leader of the Pack," which reached number 1 on the *Billboard Hot 100* on 28 November 1964.[2] The subject matter of the song, its dramatically compelling performances, and its innovative production techniques catapulted the Shangri-Las to international fame and controversy.

The central figure in the song is Jimmy, a motorcycle rider whose teenage girlfriend is forced by her parents to end their relationship. Distraught, he rides off into the rainy night, crashes his bike and dies. On the surface, it seems that Jimmy could have ridden straight out of *The Wild One*[3] to pick up Betty after school, but closer examination reveals a far more complex character, unfixed and malleable. Musicologist Jacqueline Warwick has observed that Jimmy functions as 'a shadowy male figure' to give the girls something to talk about, noting that this 'is a strategy common to soap opera writing.'[4] Jimmy is certainly this, but also much more. As a silent, partially sketched figure, Jimmy is able to act as a symbol for a range of white, postwar, generational, gendered, and class-based conflicts.

By 1964, the motorcycle rider was an established icon of white
American masculinity and, together with his bike, a figure with tremendous cultural resonance—a solo traveller, a man-machine. Although the
initial inspiration for the figure of Jimmy seems to have been a real-life
biker, I would suggest that George 'Shadow' Morton infused more of
his fantasy of himself into his songs than has previously been acknowledged.[5] The figure of the rider, who re-appears as an anti-hero archetype
in later songs, shares significant features with Morton, who acquired the
nickname 'Shadow' (apparently bestowed by Jerry Leiber) as a response
to his elusive, mysterious persona.[6] In "Leader of the Pack," both the
rider and his bike are transformed through the complex processes at
work in this intricately constructed pop song.

"Leader of the Pack" is credited to three songwriters—Jeff Barry,
Ellie Greenwich and George 'Shadow' Morton.[7] As noted in chapter
3, Greenwich and Barry were already signed to Trio Publishing and
employed as professional songwriters at Red Bird before Morton
arrived there. Morton has claimed sole authorship of the song, which
both Greenwich and Barry have denied vehemently. There is some
evidence to support his case, however, even if one acknowledges his
considerable ability to mythologise his own past. Rod McBrien, the
engineer with whom Morton recorded the original demo track (without vocals) at Ultra-Sonic Studios in Hempstead, Long Island, certainly
supported Morton's claim. McBrien told me that Morton came to him
with the idea for the song; McBrien then helped get the players together
for the session. These were not New York studio musicians but rather
friends of McBrien's from Long Island. His recollection was that they
included Sal DiTroia, Morton's former bandmate from the Markeys.[8]

By his own account, Morton grew up in Brooklyn, and moved with
his mother (and presumably, step-father and younger step-sister) to
Hicksville, Long Island, in the mid-50s at the age of about fourteen. He
claimed to have already had some exposure to gang culture by this point:

> By the time I moved out of Brooklyn, I'd already been stabbed
> once—nothin' serious but you know, it was over nothin', for no rea-
> son. It was common . . . I'd been shot at, I was tossed through a candy
> store window because I would take no bull. And this was a good
> neighborhood, just south of Flatbush Avenue. My gang was The Red
> Devils. There was The Little Red Devils and there was The Big Red

Devils. One night there was a big fight and the next night, they came to me and asked me to become the youngest member of The Big Red Devils. That's when it was exit time.[9]

Elements that later appeared in "Leader of the Pack" are present in this narrative: candy stores, gangs, urban street culture—Morton himself, apparently negotiating his way his way through this dangerous milieu by accepting and responding to its violent terms, growing up fast on 'the wrong side of town.'[10] According to Morton, a more specific inspiration for the song stemmed from an incident that took place after Morton and the Grimaldis had left Brooklyn—a move motivated, at least in part, by the desire to remove young George from the lure of street gangs. Morton commented that his parents 'had the theory, "my boy's gonna get in trouble so we're gonna move him out of Brooklyn."'[11] Other wayward teenagers seem to have found themselves in Hicksville for similar reasons, however:

My mother . . . gave me a few dollars and said, "Go down to the diner and get yourself a cup of coffee. Get out of the house, you're driving me crazy." . . . I came over the hill and . . . I couldn't believe what I saw . . . at least 150, 200 kids at this diner. Bikers, hot rodders, gum smacking ladies—not careful at all about their language and what they had to say . . . I found in Hicksville the toughest gang you could ever imagine. All the kids were . . . yanked from Queens, The Bronx, Brooklyn—and a lot of them because they'd been in trouble, they were going the wrong way. They all gathered around this diner, mostly hot rods . . . about a dozen bikes. Bumpy was the man. He was the head guy. He was my inspiration for "The Leader of the Pack." He took me under his wing as I was one of the newest kids around . . . I became like his little brother . . . [12]

As described by Morton, this scene conjures up a postwar parental and governmental nightmare of wayward, rampaging youth. The popularity with teenagers of motorbikes, hot-rods and gangs was one of many causes of consternation among middle-class parents and authority figures, since this was generally seen as evidence of the 'infiltration of lower-class and criminal values into youth culture.'[13] It is also significant that the figure of 'Bumpy' made such an impression on Morton, and that the young Morton to some extent identified with him and 'became like his little brother.'[14]

As discussed in chapter 3, Morton was in a 'high school' doo-wop group called the Markeys, who released two singles on RCA in 1958. The first of these, credited to 'the Markeys featuring George Morton,' was "Hot Rod." [15] Co-written by Morton, it is a revealing precursor to "Leader of the Pack." On the surface, "Hot Rod" is a not particularly spectacular twelve-bar-blues-based song in which the protagonist takes his 'turtle-dove' on a date in his hot rod, but it contains several significant elements that would manifest themselves in Morton's later writing in a far more developed manner. The first is the presence of vehicles with delinquent associations, reflective of Morton's account of the 'bikers' and 'hot rodders' he recalled at the diner. This song features a hot rod; "Leader of the Pack," of course, features a motor bike. "Hot Rod" also contains what is likely to be Morton's earliest attempt at utilising sound effects; it opens with his guttural vocal imitation of a hot rod engine, brass instruments approximating car horns, and a motor-revving electric guitar. This is restated by the complex doo-wop backing vocals which imitate the chugging of a motor. All this accompanies the lyrical subject matter, which is replete with mildly sexually suggestive motor imagery—'going for a ride' and 'turned my motor over, threw it into first,' for instance. About two-thirds of the way through the song, however, Morton intones,

> She looked at me with those big big eyes
> And says honey I have a sad surprise
> Our romance, it is through . . .

At this point, Morton makes a screeching tyre noise, clearly indicating the skidding of the hot rod to an abrupt halt, and explodes, 'Out with you!' Peaking at this angry climax, the song then tapers into an existential plateau:

> And now I ride all night til the dawn's early light
> For my mind is crazy and my eyes are hazy
> Til my wheels burn out and my motor's dead
> I got a girl that I want to forget . . .

The breakup of this romance is aligned with the screeching of tyres, and the protagonist responds to being rejected by abandoning his 'turtle-dove' on the side of the road and roaring off into the night:

Well now it's in third and I really really move
Doing 65, 75, 105 man alive!
Baby . . . oh little baby why'd you go and make me cry
Oh oh my honey we're going for a ride.

The song then concludes with a *spoken* couplet that is delivered in a delirious, accusatory, sadistic tone:

So long honey, tonight I'll cry
Tonight I might even die . . .

The elements and imagery that would make the Shangri-Las second single for Red Bird, "Leader of the Pack," such a complex and compelling song are present in "Hot Rod" in embryonic form, but performed here from the perspective of the rejected male. Throughout the entire song, the protagonist is allied with his hot rod—he causes it to move and moves with it, speaks its noises. He is at one with his vehicle. Rejected by his date, his response is to violently eject her from the car/himself, and then drive around all night, speeding and delirious. Finally, the death of the male protagonist as a result of this sexual rejection is suggested in the final line of the song, which quickly fades out after Morton has delivered it. These elements are realised with greater sophistication and complexity in "Leader of the Pack," and both songs reflect the teenage delinquent gang-related behaviour that authorities in mid-century USA found so worrying and problematic.

Perceptions of class are central to this discussion, but also notoriously slippery.[16] The robust post-war US economy offered some increase in opportunities for social mobility, and suburban developments allowed white Americans with middle-class aspirations to own their own homes at affordable rates, as discussed earlier.[17] Markers of middle-class identity included home-ownership, a family composed of a hard-working, industrious male breadwinner with a steady income, a supportive and morally virtuous wife, children, and a lifestyle that embodied 'family values.' Maintaining class boundaries was understood to be central to

respectability, however, while respectability was in turn 'a powerful sig-
nifier of class.'[18] As we saw in chapter 2, restrictive covenants endorsed
by the Federal Housing Association aimed to keep white neighbourhoods free of 'undesirable,' that is, Black residents, thus preserving the
economic value of white ownership, and through this exclusion offering
greater opportunities for upward mobility to poorer or working-class
whites.[19] This in turn fostered the myth that

> this period of growth, individual success, and some class mobility
> [was] exclusively . . . the result of individual industriousness and
> merit. By this interpretation, those worthy and virtuous individuals
> pulled themselves up by their own bootstraps to achieve class mobil-
> ity and some measure of economic success.

According to this logic, those who did *not* achieve such success were
lazy, lacked industriousness and motivation, were even unwilling to suc-
ceed; their failure was personal and of their own making.[20] Jean Halley,
Ashley Eshleman, and Ramya Mahadevan Vijaya trace the origins of
this idea to the unease of white workers about

> whether workers who did not own their own land and depended
> on wages could really be considered free . . . against the backdrop of
> slavery . . . To overcome this complex fear of comparison between
> wage labor and slave labor, a class identity emerged where white
> working-class people identified themselves as hardworking, inde-
> pendent-minded people as opposed to their perception of enslaved
> Black people as lazy and dependent.[21]

From these formulations, it is possible to see the manner in which
young white males who eschewed 'industriousness,' belonged to gangs
and rode motorbikes could be perceived as adopting lower-class behav-
iours, thereby contributing to a weakening of class and racial boundaries.

The fear of 'respectable' society being infiltrated by so-called
lower-class characteristics fuelled an intense scrutiny of teen culture in
the mid-twentieth century, and various panics over the juvenile misbe-
haviour many felt was inextricably linked with it.[22] This was reflected
in a veritable explosion of academic treatises examining juvenile delinquency, gang warfare, street culture, and urban offenders and attempt-

ing to develop theories on how to prevent these social problems.[23] In his 1955 sociological study, *Delinquent Boys*, Albert K. Cohen noted,

> the hallmark of delinquent subculture is the *explicit and wholesale repudiation of middle-class standards and the adoption of their very antithesis* . . . the delinquent is the rogue male. His conduct may be viewed not only negatively, as a device for attacking and derogating the respectable culture; positively it may be viewed as the exploitation of modes of behavior which are traditionally symbolic of untrammeled masculinity, which are renounced by middle-class culture because incompatible with its ends, but which are not without a certain aura of glamour and romance.[24]

Marlon Brando's character in *The Wild One*, Johnny Strabler, certainly inhabits this dual territory that Cohen describes, but Lily Phillips has argued persuasively that the *age* of Brando's Strabler was crucial to the development of his iconic status. He was not merely a biker, he was a *young* biker—the sullen, defiant leader of the Black Rebels Motorcycle Club, and the poster boy for post-war juvenile biker delinquency.[25] As Norma Coates has observed, the clean-cut teen idol pop singers who came to prominence in the years following *The Wild One*, such as Frankie Avalon and Fabian, were marketed in opposition to more 'authentic masculine' rock figures, foreshadowed by Strabler's delinquent anti-hero.[26]

How does Jimmy, the rider in "Leader of the Pack," who seems at least partially influenced by Morton's familiarity with a real-life juvenile delinquent biker, compare with the Strabler-type figure as characterized by Cohen? In the spoken introduction to "Leader of the Pack," which takes the form of seemingly vacuous schoolgirl chatter, the listener is immediately alerted to a problem with Jimmy, before we even know his name. The opening question is not, 'Are they really going out together?' but 'Is she *really* going out with him?' There is something odd, unusual, problematic about *this girl* going out with *this boy*. We soon learn ('Gee it must be great riding with him . . .') that Jimmy rides a bike.[27] It's also implicit in the question 'Is he picking you up after school today?' that sometimes he does—so Jimmy is not at work, at least not at a regular nine-to-five job. Nor would he be likely to be coming from school, as the submission to authority required by school attendance is also incompatible with Jimmy's soon-to-be revealed 'occupation.'[28] Finally, Betty bursts into song, proclaiming:

> I met him at the candy store
> He turned around and smiled at me . . .
> You get the picture?
> (Yes, we see . . .)
> That's when I fell for
> The Leader of the Pack.[29]

The revving of a bike, this time a real one, leaves the listener in no doubt that Jimmy is the leader of a pack—a gang—of motorcycle riders. That Betty met Jimmy 'at the candy store' is also noteworthy—far from being neutral public territory, candy stores were spaces often known to be frequented by gang members. Eric Schneider, in his study of post-war gangs in New York, described them as

> Typically small storefronts, with a counter, a soda dispenser, maga-zine racks, and perhaps a jukebox and some stools or a small table, candy stores provided a place where gang members could meet, gos-sip, and, if space permitted, dance with their debs.[30]

Particular candy stores were known to be the headquarters of specific gangs; rival gangs knew where to find the leaders of their opponents, police knew which candy stores to raid, and street workers attempting to reform gang members hung out and made contact with them at a given gang's candy store.[31] Not all candy stores were gang hangouts, of course, but the location is significant in the context of this song.

Betty's family is none too pleased about her choice of boyfriend, who not only lacks some core middle-class values, but possesses char-acteristics clearly recognisable to the average white middle-class par-ent as delinquent. Betty complains to her girlfriends about her family's response to Jimmy, lamenting,

> My folks were always putting him down
> They said he came from the wrong side of town.[32]

This loaded lyric introduces a class element: whether he is literally or metaphorically 'from the wrong side of town,' as far as her parents are concerned, Jimmy is *not* suitable for their daughter. Implicit here is the common assumption in mainstream society at the time that juvenile delinquency, and its gangs of leather-jacketed motorcyclists that were part of it, was a product of working-class neighbourhoods. The perceived spread of this 'problem' into 'nice' middle-class families was a source of great anxiety, as parents became 'fearful that their children were adopting the form and substance of working-class alienation in their music, dress, slang, and attitudes.'[33] Through her alliance with Jimmy, Betty is effectively contributing to a weakening of class boundaries, a source of great alarm to her parents' generation. Betty is unconcerned—on the contrary, this is one component of Jimmy's attractiveness.

All this locates Betty in the realm of delinquent girls, since dating a rebel itself constituted an act of rebellion.[34] As Jacqueline Warwick has pointed out, the 'juvenile delinquent' discourse concerning 'bad girls'

> differed significantly from the perceptions of male teens in trouble . . . while bad boys were more easily understood as individuals, responsible for their wrongdoings, bad girls at mid-century were seen as evidence of inadequate patriarchal control, and they threatened an entire social order. Taking up with a bad boy was often understood as the first step on a slippery slope away from father's loving control and towards a life of adolescent and eventually adult disrepute.[35]

It is significant, then, that Betty's *father* is the one to deliver the blow. Betty tells her girlfriends,

> One day my dad said "Find someone new."
> I had to tell my Jimmy "We're through."[36]

The way the song contextualises Betty's parents' handling of *her* implied delinquency is revealing. According to the moral code of the period, Betty has a model dad: he is present and involved enough in the life of his teenage daughter to be concerned for her welfare, and so to insist and ensure that she ends her relationship with the undesirable biker/delinquent Jimmy.[37] This is categorically *not* where the song's sympathies lie, however; instead it creates a critique of Betty's father and the particular brand of middle-class, conservative and conformist patriarchy that he espouses.

It is a mark of the song's complexity that it is possible to miss this. Ian Inglis, discussing in 2004 a group of eleven 'teenage death discs' released between 1959 and 1964, argues,

> in those songs where there is parental opposition, it is made abundantly clear that resistance to their instructions will inexorably lead to tragedy ... in "Leader of the Pack" the girl's disagreement with her parents results in the boyfriend's death.[38]

In fact, precisely the opposite takes place. Jimmy dies because he rode off into the rainy night distressed after Betty ended their relationship *in accordance with* her father's directive. It was Betty's obedience to her parents' instructions that resulted in Jimmy's death, not her defiance of them.

"Leader of the Pack" walked a fine line, as those involved in its creation were acutely aware. Morton claims that, when asked about a follow-up single for "Remember," he took the idea for the song to Jerry Leiber, the lyricist half of the Leiber and Stoller songwriting team, and co-owner of the Red Bird label. "Leader of the Pack" would ultimately become the Shangri-Las' second single on Red Bird,[39] but according to Morton, he was initially told not to produce it and that the label would not pay for it:

> It was dangerous. They were afraid of the repercussions. "Radio stations aren't going to play it! Parents aren't going to let their daughters go out and buy it!" I mean, it's a song about a young girl falling in love with a motorcycle man ... clearly a bad girl.[40]

In a 2007 radio interview, Mary Weiss, whose impassioned singing contributes enormously to the song's compelling narrative, revealed her own trepidation about "Leader of the Pack":

> I really had to sit down with this one. I took it [the demo] home and listened to it for a very long time before I agreed to do it ... even at the time, it was pretty much out there. There was a very rigid environment, even globally ... I mean, the record was banned in England the first time it came out.[41]

"Leader of the Pack" reached #1 in the US, but the song was banned from BBC radio in the UK, igniting a storm of controversy and triggering the cancellation of a planned English tour.[42] As journalist Iain Aitch noted,

> Some radio stations refused to play the record, feeling it would fuel the violent clashes between mods and rockers, and the TV music show *Ready, Steady, Go* would not show the girls performing it.[43]

British society was undergoing a moral panic of its own at the time. This was in response to uncontainable developments in youth culture that had come to a head with riots in English seaside towns over Easter 1964 between smartly dressed scooter-riding mods and motorbike-riding rockers. This, together with its focus on death, may have contributed to the decision to ban "Leader of the Pack."[44] It was not the only biker-themed song to suffer this fate: "Terry," written and performed by 16-year-old English pop singer Lynn Ripley under the name Twinkle, was also about a girl whose motorcycle-riding boyfriend dies in a crash,[45] and it too was banned by the BBC and independent television's influential live music show *Ready, Steady, Go*. Like "Leader of the Pack" would a few weeks later, however, "Terry" received enough airplay on radio stations broadcasting into the UK from elsewhere (Radio Luxemburg and the newly formed pirate radio stations) to generate considerable sales.[46] It entered the UK charts on 26 November 1964, peaking at #4; "Leader of the Pack," released in the UK some time after its US release, entered the UK charts almost two months later, on 14 January 1965, and reached #11.[47]

There is some speculation as to whether Twinkle could have heard "Leader of the Pack" *before* she wrote "Terry"—her sister worked as a pop music reporter and could have acquired a promotional copy before the record was commercially available in Britain, but this remains conjecture. Ripley claimed that she wrote "Terry" when she was 14, which would date the song to 1962.[48]

In January 1965, *New Musical Express* (*NME*) ran an article by Keith Altham entitled 'Nobody Objected to Shangri-Las in States,' which essentially downplayed the hullabaloo.[49] What is striking is that, despite the concerns expressed by the song's creators, neither British nor US audiences seem to have particularly objected to the notion of a young girl falling in love with a biker.

In his *NME* article, Altham noted that 'one of the greatest criticisms of "Leader of the Pack" was the inclusion of a motorbike used virtually as a musical instrument.'[50] Today, George 'Shadow' Morton is hailed as a pioneer in the field of record production techniques, but at the time his innovative use of sound effects was perceived in some quarters as gimmicky rather than ground-breaking. Given the similarities in subject matter of the two songs, Twinkle was called upon for her opinion of "Leader of the Pack," and responded,

> People in this country tend not to go for gimmick records and I thought that the sound of the motorbike on the disc might put people off. I say good luck to them with their musical motorbike.[51]

The idea that "Leader of the Pack" was 'gimmicky' is one that recurred frequently; this was evidently a common way to understand the use of sound effects, and led to the perception of the song as a novelty record. In an extremely positive review of the Shangri-Las' first LP which praised their singing, 'fascinating sound-patterns' and the 'most exciting, restless sound—with an organ' of the live material featured on the record, *NME* reviewer Allen Evans nevertheless noted that 'the girls do some lines in speaking voices, which adds to the novelty.'[52] The Shangri-Las never completely escaped this tag, which persisted well into the 1980s. Monica Syrette, writing in 1996, noted that she knew "Leader of the Pack" as 'a staple of AM radio when I was growing up, played as a gimmick song like "The Monster Mash."'[53]

This was brought into stark relief on an episode of the New York-based TV panel quiz show *I've Got a Secret* on 16 November 1964. An elaborate charade was performed by some of the adult contestants, and lines from "Leader of the Pack" acted out as a prelude to a studio performance of the song.[54] The Shangri-Las then mimed the song to a leather-jacketed 'Jimmy' figure on a bike, played by Robert Goulet, who had already played an active role in the charade. By 1964, Goulet was a well-established theatre and television performer who had achieved considerable fame on Broadway for his role as Sir Lancelot in *Camelot* (1960), alongside Richard Burton and Julie Andrews.[55] Introducing Goulet, the compère promoted his upcoming TV special 'on the CBS network,' *An Hour with Robert Goulet.*

During the Shangri-Las' performance on *I've Got a Secret*, Goulet pretended to rev the bike in time with the motorcycle sounds, throwing it around in pseudo-comedic attempts at wheelies. All the while, he pulled faces and acted the fool, eliciting laughter from the audience. The song was relentlessly sent up, the rider caricatured into a ridiculous, laughable figure.[56] Mary Weiss—15 years old, intent on her performance, completely inhabiting the song (albeit in ultra-modest knee-length skirt-and-blouse combo) —occasionally looked unsure but maintained extraordinary professional composure, stayed in character and did not laugh. Goulet clearly had the star power here; the Shangri-Las were treated as a foil for his antics, virtually dismissed at the end of their performance while the compère fussed over Goulet.

Ultimately, the attempts to make a joke of the song seem incongruous; the spectacle is unintentionally riveting. There are several reasons for this. It has already been noted that although "Leader of the Pack" was a hit, it also generated considerable debate and discomfort. To send the song up and parody the intense emotion and alienation experienced by its protagonist, as performed by Mary Weiss, is a particularly adult response to teen angst. There is a deep tension between the ironic, emotionally distant, somewhat patronising adult world and the all-or-nothing emotional vortex of the distraught teenage girl. Added to this is the difficulty of 'performing' such a sonically and narratively complex piece of music in a studio and in front of an audience that is expecting quizshow laughs, not operatic emotional intensity. Furthermore, Jimmy's shadowy complexity, left vague and only partially sketched in the song, is rudely and ham-fistedly stamped with the imprint of a cavorting Robert Goulet, which leaves little scope for audience imagination and robs the song of much of its mystery.

"Leader of the Pack" was also parodied as "Leader of the Laundromat" by a group of male singers calling themselves the Detergents. Their version was in the charts concurrently with "Leader of the Pack"; it peaked at #19 on 9 January 1965.[57] In this version, the gender of the protagonist was changed to a girl who was doing her washing— 'I met her one day at the Laundromat.' "Murray" was told by his dad to break it off with "Betty" 'because her laundry came back brown,' and, distraught at this news, Betty ran into the street and was hit by a garbage truck. Although certainly meant in fun, it is interesting to note that the Jimmy/

rider figure was converted into a female character whose inability to fulfil basic expectations of feminine behaviour (produce clean washing) mirrored Jimmy's rejection of middle-class patriarchal norms. Again, the power of the biker figure was negated, especially since the feminised version had no association with motorbikes whatsoever. Nevertheless, the revving noises were retained in "Leader of the Laundromat"; this is partly because they were such a distinctive part of the original version, but they also have a greater significance which I will discuss shortly.

"Leader of the Laundromat" also constituted a successful attempt to cash in on a popular song with minimal original input. The 'authors,' Lee Pockriss and Paul Vance, were successful professional songwriters who tended to work in the spoof/novelty area—they also wrote "Itsy Bitsy Teenie Weenie Yellow Polka Dot Bikini," a hit in 1960 for Bryan Hyland. One of the Detergents, Danny Jordan, was Vance's nephew. Pockriss and Vance are listed as sole writers of "Leader of the Laundromat" by the American Society of Composers, Authors and Publishers (ASCAP); it seems odd, given that this song was clearly based on an existing one, that the writers of the original received no songwriting credit.[58] (In a later comparable example, Weird Al Yankovic's version of "Beat It," titled "Eat It," is simply listed as a variation of the Michael Jackson song; Yankovic is not credited as writer.[59]) Given what we have seen of Morris Levy's behaviour, it is also worth noting that "Leader of the Laundromat" was released on his Roulette label. Vance apparently challenged Levy about unpaid royalties for the song after being told that 'all the records had been sent back unsold,' which was of course impossible for a record that reached #19 on the *Billboard* charts. John 'Sonny' Franzese told journalist Sandra Peddie that he was present when this took place:

> "I hung him out a window," Franzese said, telling him that if he didn't give up the royalties, "I'd drop him right there." In very short order, Vance said, "You got it," Franzese said.[60]

On the other hand, when "Leader of the Pack" *was* taken seriously, it was seen as morbid and death-obsessed. Vicki Trent, writing in the British magazine *Pop Weekly* in 1965, said of "Leader of the Pack":

> To me the disc, which describes in those awful pseudo-sad tones the leader of a motor-cycle gang being killed, is just about the very

bottom of the barrel as far as records go . . . to anyone who has had a teenage son, brother, or sweetheart even, killed on a motorbike (and that must be quite a few) it must be sickening . . . No wonder people, especially parents, are always condemning teenagers for being "juvenile delinquents." Why shouldn't they when records are sold by the thousand which deal with death and nothing else? [61]

Trent's explicit linking of songs about death with juvenile delinquency reflected an assumption that became widespread during the 1950s. This was the perception that the mass media, which included television, movies, comics, radio, and records, were having a negative effect on youth, encouraging juvenile delinquency and contributing to family breakdown.[62] This popular perception was shaped most famously by psychiatrist and neurologist Fredric Wertham, author of *Seduction of the Innocent* (1953). In his book and in numerous public appearances, Wertham argued that a strong causal link existed between mass culture, particularly comic books, and juvenile delinquency.[63] His 'articulate and coherent explanation for the rise of juvenile misbehavior' had tremendous popular appeal among worried adults seeking explanations for what they perceived to be unfathomable teenage conduct.

The wider implications of Wertham's argument are evident in a letter from an irate mother to the editors of *Modern Teen* magazine, a copy of which apparently made its way into the house through a friend of her daughter's. *Modern Teen*, the first issue of which was published in spring 1957, was one of the earliest of what its publishers called "'a new publishing field. It's a break for you teenagers . . . now there will be magazines edited exclusively for you.'" These magazines were marketed at teenagers of both sexes, with a heavy emphasis on teen idols (Sandra Dee, Elvis Presley and Annette Funicello graced early covers), and their readers were also encouraged to write letters to the editors for advice on teen issues: parents, shyness, dating and the like.[64]

The mother's letter conflated comic books with a number of other features of teen culture, which she perceived as tasteless, alarming and harmful:

I have never seen such a collection of tripe in my entire life. Don't you realize what you are doing? You are encouraging teenagers to write to each other, which keeps them from doing their school work

and other chores. You are encouraging them to kiss and have physical contact before they're even engaged, which is morally wrong
and you know it. You are encouraging them to have faith in the
depraved individuals who make rock and roll records when it's common knowledge that ninety percent of these rock and roll singers
are people with no morals or sense of values.

I can just picture a cross-section of your readers, complete with
acne, black leather jackets, motorcycle boots, comic books and all.
Any fan of yours spends his time failing at school, talking back to his
parents, sharpening his switchblade for the next gang fight, wearing
sensual revealing clothing, and last and certainly not least, feeding
his curious mind with the temptations put forth on the pages of
your lewd and demoralizing publication.[65]

For this parent, mass teen culture, as epitomized by *Modern Teen*,
was a checklist of perceived lower-class attributes and items that sig-
nified rebellion, delinquency, and a fundamental rejection of 'decent'
middle-class standards. These included black leather jackets and motorcycle boots, which were here explicitly linked with, among other things,
switchblades, gangs, and rock and roll. As Eric Schneider noted,

parents, journalists and public officials mistook the stylistic affecta-
tions of rebellion for its substance. They saw the spread of leather
jackets, Levi's, and rock 'n' roll as proof that juvenile delinquency was
like a contagious disease spreading outward from the slums, rather
than as the expression of clever marketing.[66]

This is not to say that these symbols were meaningless. Rather, their
meanings had been transformed; wearing a 'gang' or leather jacket
'became the symbol of youthful rebelliousness, guaranteed to worry
parents and teachers,' instead of an indication of gang membership, as
it had been previously.[67] And 'clever marketing' included profession-
ally composed songs like "Leader of the Pack," which captured and
expressed aspects of a certain zeitgeist that ultimately transcended its
original milieu of mid-60s New York City.

It is also important to note that "Leader of the Pack" was the latest
in a long line of what were termed 'teen death' records. This did not go
unnoticed at the time—Phyllis Lee Levin, writing in the *New York Times*

in 1965, discussed "Leader of the Pack" in the context of 'certain teen-age fads,' in this case, 'the sick songs, or, more politely termed, tragedy songs. The heroes and heroines of these songs issue last messages—or noises—from foxholes, coffins, motorcycles, and even garbage trucks.'[68]

Some of the more famous 'teen death' records include "Endless Sleep," a hit in 1958 for Jody Reynolds, and two 1960 hits, "Tell Laura I Love Her" by Ray Peterson and "Teen Angel" by Mark Dinning.[69] In 1955, the Cheers had a hit with a 'death disc' about a biker and his girl-friend, "Black Denim Trousers and Motorcycle Boots."[70] It was written by Leiber and Stoller, who were now Morton's superiors at Red Bird, and who had objected at first to his proposal of "Leader of the Pack." Part of their objection, as reported by Morton, was that 'you can't make a hero out of that situation,' that is, portray the "Leader" in a sympa-thetic light.[71] So it is noteworthy that in "Black Denim Trousers" the biker is a clichéd thug—he is cranky, dirty and treats his pretty girlfriend Mary-Lou so badly that

everybody pitied her because everybody knew
He loved that dog-gone motorcycle best.[72]

He is a resolutely unsympathetic figure, and when he roars off, imper-vious to Mary-Lou's pleadings that 'if you ride tonight I'll grieve' and crashes into a 'screaming diesel that was California bound,' the strong sense is that he will not be sorely missed and his death will in fact liber-ate the long-suffering Mary-Lou.[73] Although the subject matter is sim-ilar and the songs undeniably have common elements, "Black Denim Trousers . . ." has none of the narrative complexity and emotional impact of "Leader of the Pack." (Morton's association with Leiber, Stoller and Red Bird began almost ten years after this release, so it is by no means a given that he would have been aware of the song.)

Nor was "Leader of the Pack" alone in its use of sound effects. A real motorbike belonging to one of the sound engineers at the recording session, Joe Venneri, was used for the revving noises.[74] The skid and crash effect was a generic one from a sound effects record—the exact same effect was used on "Transfusion" by Nervous Norvus (1956), "Car Crash" by the Cadets (1960), "Two-Hour Honeymoon" by Paul Hamp-ton (1960, written and arranged by Burt Bacharach), and "Dead Man's Curve" by Jan & Dean (1964).[75] The use of sound effects in "Leader of the Pack" nonetheless struck reviewers as completely inappropriate. According to one UK review,

> If you like Twinkle's "Terry," then you'll dig The Shangri-Las' smash American hit, "Leader of the Pack" in a big way . . . the rumbling, reverberating Spector-like sound, and the absorbing harmonies by the girls are great. But they're interspersed by a sugary monologue, revving noises, and even the sound of the crash. Personally, I think it's obnoxious and tasteless, but I'm sure it'll be a walloping hit.[76]

It was indeed, and most of this discomfort apparently came from adult listeners. As Mary Weiss later commented of "Leader of the Pack,"

> I don't think teenage years are all that rosy for a lot of people—they certainly weren't for me. They are the most confusing time of people's lives and there is a tremendous dark side to the record, which I think teenagers related to.[77]

Seemingly, the teenagers who were its main buyers identified directly with its intense emotionality and themes of parental conflict.[78]

One significant role played by the motorcycle sounds has been lost in this discussion, however. It is important to note that Jimmy is voiceless in the song; before the song begins, Jimmy is already dead. He comes to us as a shifting mirage—a memory glimpsed through Betty's tears, the stunned awe of her girlfriends, and the blinkered authoritarianism of her father. The revving of the bike is his leitmotif, his signature melody, his voice. There is a long tradition associating masculinity with machinery and technology, and the revving sounds simultaneously announce Jimmy's presence and identify him as a rider at one with his vehicle, hyper-masculine, a man-machine.[79] As Hunter S. Thompson put it in *Hell's Angels*,

> The whole—man and machine together—is far more than the sum of its parts. His motorcycle is the one thing in life he has absolutely mastered. It is his only valid status symbol, his equalizer . . . without it he is no better than a punk on a street corner.[80]

When Jimmy and his bike crash, the sounds of the accident invite the listener 'to imagine all its horrors for themselves.' As film critic Jack

Sargeant has noted, during the final part of the song an 'extended skid is replayed and faded out' and 'never allowed to culminate in an impact.' This has the effect of eternally suspending Jimmy in oblivion, the looped skid his requiem.[81]

Parallels can be seen with Kenneth Anger's 1963 'silent' film *Scorpio Rising*,[82] in which there is no dialogue—all the riders, including Scorpio, are voiceless. In a sort of cinematic inversion of Jimmy's role, the soundtrack of the film is entirely popular songs from the late 50s and early 60s, very much of the vocal group milieu from which the Shangri-Las emerged, which segue into each other like a long sequence played by a disc jockey on the radio. These include "He's a Rebel" by the Crystals and "My Boyfriend's Back" by the Angels, both from 1963. It is tempting to speculate that if "Leader of the Pack" had been recorded and released just a little earlier, it would have been a strong candidate for inclusion. Anger also uses sound effects, predominantly those of motorcycles. Tellingly, the first time this occurs is several minutes into the film, after a series of slow, lingering shots that fetishize the machinery of the bikes and their accoutrements. The capped head of a biker appears at the bottom of the screen, rising until the studded words on the back of his leather jacket are visible: SCORPIO RISING—KENNETH ANGER. He turns around, a lingering shot of his open jacket and bare abdomen. All the while, the bike revs—flesh and gears, the man-machine.[83]

"Leader of the Pack" was not attempting anything like the mythic apocalypse of *Scorpio Rising*, which its director famously described as 'a death mirror held up to American culture.'[84] But Anger used a careful selection of the popular music of the day, bike sound effects and voiceless riders who appear as a series of images, to achieve his particular ends. *Scorpio Rising* also concludes with a violent motorcycle accident, complete with skidding noises, crash sounds, sirens, flashing lights—all while "Wipe Out" by the Surfaris hammers the point home. Anger's innovative use of music is central to *Scorpio Rising*, and Juan Suárez has argued compellingly that the film's engagement with pop songs, comic books and images of teen idols is at least as important to its artistic success as the avant-garde tradition within which it is usually discussed.[85] As *Scorpio Rising* straddles 'high' and 'low' culture, the barriers between these traditions are dissolved—Jesus walks down the street to "He's a Rebel" by the Crystals,[86] and shots of Brando in *The Wild One* are juxtaposed with images of Christ and Hitler—all this forms part of Anger's technique, as Carel Rowe put it, of reducing religion, political history and popular culture into 'sets of systems which destroy one another . . . different dogmas are equalized (and subsumed by) their structural and ideological parallels.'[87] The 'black-leathered motorcyclists who exist outside and in defiance of the prevailing culture' become symbols—they are the catalysts for revolution and the fall of an epoch.[88] Their blank voicelessness is central to their ability to function in this way, just as Jimmy's emptiness enables him to function as a complex symbol of post-war anxieties and teenage desire. That *Scorpio Rising* and "Leader of the Pack" were made within a year of each other, and both in New York, is a further indication of their cultural connectedness. *Scorpio Rising* was at least partly shot in Brooklyn, and, given Morton's background, it is tempting to speculate that he may have seen *Scorpio Rising* before writing "Leader of the Pack."[89]

GIVE HIM A GREAT BIG KISS

The Shangri-Las' next single, "Give Him a Great Big Kiss," featured another, differently sketched version of a 'Jimmy' figure, who in this song remains nameless.[90] Nothing overtly indicates that he is a biker, but there is plenty to suggest at least the trappings of gang involvement. The early lines of the song,

> Here comes my guy
> Walking down the street
> Look how he walks
> With a dancing beat

locate him in the street, *the* gang locale. That he walks 'with a dancing beat' is not mere affectation, but a territorial assertion. Walking 'bop style,' or using the 'diddleybop walk,' was part of the language of the street and functioned as a 'direct challenge' to others who might lay claim to a particular piece of turf or street. Israel Narvaez of the Mau Maus, a Brooklyn-based gang, described walking 'down the street like we owned it—doing the slow easy walk of the jitterbug, loosely swinging our shoulders, hips and knees, bobbing and weaving to our own individual rhythm.'[91]

In gang culture, the walk functioned as a statement that commanded respect. What's more, it was directly related to music, and the music of gangs was predominantly doo-wop, performed by street corner groups who often shared this terrain with neighbourhood gangs.[92] Dion DiMucci (Dion and the Belmonts) and Anthony Gourdine (Little Anthony and the Imperials) both started out as gang-associated street corner singers.[93] In the next lines of "Give Him a Great Big Kiss," we find that the 'Jimmy' figure is 'in the street' and singing 'his song' 'all day long,' which strongly suggests that he has ties to doo-wop singing. Furthermore, he is 'always wearing shades,' has 'dirty fingernails' and wears

> Tight tapered pants, high button shoes
> He's always looking like he's got the blues . . . [94]

This 'Jimmy' figure is moody, sullen and mysterious, but he is contextualised quite differently here. Whereas "Leader of the Pack" exuded dark intensity, "Give Him a Great Big Kiss" is light-hearted and playful; nevertheless, these resonances inform the persona of the object of the 'great big kiss.' In a live performance on the pop music TV show *Shindig!*, the group addressed the song to Ian Whitcomb, an US-based English singer who had a hit in 1965 with the self-penned "You Turn Me On." Whitcomb wore a leather bike jacket, dark pants, boots, sunglasses and a peaked black cap—a very clear reference to the protagonist of the Shangri-Las' previous single.[95] At the very least, he is an outlaw figure—like Jimmy, not gainfully employed and resisting the standards of 'order and decorum imposed by the dominant society.'[96] And in the final couplet of a section of mid-song dialogue, the lead singer's friends express concern about her boyfriend: 'Yeah? Well I hear he's bad,' to which she replies, 'Mmm, he's good-bad, but he's not evil . . . '[97] Good negates bad, and bad good. He's not evil—but he *is* a silent prop, rendered by complex processes of production, narrative and performance into a blank page—nothing, and therefore everything.

This figure, introduced in "Leader of the Pack," was established remarkably rapidly (by the end of 1964) as the Shangri-Las' archetypal 'guy' by his reappearance in "Give Him a Great Big Kiss." Morton explained,

> I had an image of the guy . . . but not trying to paint the picture of him allows everybody else to create whatever image or fantasy they want.[98]

He added that a lot of people had made the mistake of thinking that the "Leader" was based on a particular person:

> People were asking me, and rather than give an explanation, after a while, when they said, "Well, who's the motorcycle guy? Is it you? Is it this?" I would just simply say, "It's anybody you want it to be." I have my image, why should I give you my image? Create your own.[99]

With the proceeds of "Remember" under his belt, Morton, by his own admission, had motorbikes on his mind and was crafting his persona:

> When Leiber asked me in the hallway, what do you have, what he did not know was that morning, since I was now a big writer, I had a hit record, I was up on 11th Avenue looking to buy my first Harley.[100]

The production of "Remember" was credited to Jeff Barry and Artie Ripp, but the labels of both "Leader of the Pack" and "Give Him a Great Big Kiss" credit production to 'Shadow Morton.' By the time "Leader of the Pack" was released, George had metamorphosed himself into 'Shadow.'

In order to create the 'Jimmy' figure that became the signature Shangri-Las 'guy,' Morton drew on events with which he was familiar, and used a loose amalgam of his own personal experiences. Morton had extensive exposure to gangs (or claimed to), perceived the biker figure as 'a solo man,' and acted and saw himself as an outsider, an outlaw hustler who had grown up fast and learned how to fight and survive at a young age.[101]

The 'Jimmy' figure can thus be understood as a fantasy of Morton himself, biker-gang tough, but underneath it all sensitive and alluring enough that beautiful young women would intone his paeans of doomed love back in his direction. In 1975 Greil Marcus observed (not solely in relation to the Shangri-Las) that

> The songs most often celebrated a shadowy male of wondrous attractiveness, and on a superficial level, such figures surely represented the producer's or the lyricist's fantasy of himself.[102]

By keeping this character as 'a *shadowy* male figure' (as Jacqueline Warwick also put it) with just enough detail sketched in to make him real, he could remain vague enough to function as a cipher and operate as a larger than life, archetypal figure.

Consciously or unconsciously, using similar techniques to those that found expression in his songs, Morton constructed an elusive, 'shadowy' persona for himself. As discussed earlier, Morton has persistently played down his pre-Shangri-Las musical experience and presented himself as an untutored novice who accidently found himself in the music industry. He became 'Shadow,' a mysterious figure, unable to be pinned down. British journalist Ian Aitch, expressing frustration in 2007 after several failed attempts to contact Morton, reported:

> Back at my hotel, the bedside phone is flashing—a message from Morton asking me to call him back at the same, non-existent New York number. Shadow was so-named after staff at Red Bird were trying to track him down to finalise the credits on Leader of the Pack. When no one could find him, he was credited on the record as 'Shadow' Morton. He has lived up to his name ever since. The next day, as I prepare to fly home, the phone rings.[103]

This has been so completely absorbed into legend that such behaviour is expected of Morton; anything less would be a disappointment. Although, in Morton's defence, I didn't have any trouble reaching him on the phone number he gave me in 2007.

OUT IN THE STREETS

"Out in the Streets" was the Shangri-Las' fifth Red Bird single; it is credited to Jeff Barry and Ellie Greenwich as writers, with Morton as producer.[104] In this song, another complex exploration of a young woman's relationship with a delinquent anti-hero figure, the protagonist's boyfriend is a "Leader of the Pack" type, but he has reformed his ways to be with his 'respectable' girlfriend:

> He don't hang around
> With the gang no more
> He don't do the wild things
> That he did before

He used to act bad
Used to, but he quit it
And it makes me so sad
Cause I know that he did it for me
And I can see
His heart, is out in the street . . .
He don't comb his hair
like he did before
He don't wear those dirty old
black boots no more . . .

Along with the 'wild things,' hairstyle and 'dirty old black boots' that have been shed, an intrinsic part of himself has been lost too. This time, it is not parental strictures that prevent the success of the romance, but what Jacqueline Warwick has called 'the futility of love across social boundaries.'[105] Again, the anti-hero is misunderstood, has had it tough, and is at home in the streets:

He grew up on the sidewalk
Streetlight shinin' above
He grew up with no-one to love
He grew up on the sidewalk
He grew up running free
He grew up and then he met me . . . [106]

The Shangri-Las performed this song on *Shindig!* in 1965, miming to the record (as was the case for most pop music TV performances). Betty was absent from the group on this occasion, so it features Mary Weiss, with backing vocals by Mary Ann and Marge Ganser.[107] *Shindig!* was still being shot in black and white at this point, and all three are dressed in shiny black 'catsuits' and stand on individual pedestals, a few metres apart from one another. In addition to emphasising the impending loneliness of the protagonist, the pedestals place the group members above the street level to which the boyfriend of the protagonist must be returned. She is quite literally on a pedestal, unreachable for him, despite his efforts at class mobility—not wearing his dirty old back boots, or combing his hair like he did previously.[108] As the clip begins, the group members appear in silhouette, then are lit briefly. The

The Shangri-Las performing "Out in the Streets" on *Shindig* in 1965.

lights quickly fade again and the entire song is performed with minimal illumination. In conjunction with the catsuits, their bodies disappear into the darkness as the camera zooms slowly in, causing the remaining light to highlight their faces and their hands. These are further emphasised by close-ups, including an astonishing tracking shot during the middle-eight 'he grew up on the sidewalk' section that moves across the faces of Marge and Mary Ann, landing and resting on Mary's as she sings 'me ...' at the end of the phrase. All this is accentuated by minimal movement elsewhere—throughout the entire performance, the group members are virtually motionless from the waist down. This stillness heightens the effect of the 'performative choreography' (discussed earlier) with which the lyrics are emphasised.

The effect is intense, unnerving and emotionally charged. The viewer is drawn into the emotional world of the protagonist and removed from visual narrative—there are no distractions, no studio props clumsily attempting to 'illustrate' the song. A powerful sense of disembodiment is created that metaphorically emphasises the loss experienced by the anti-hero, who has sacrificed key parts of himself in the process of trying to become 'respectable.' These developments in turn have resulted in the demise of the protagonist's relationship with him, and she is obliged to 'set him free.' As the song fades out, the two opposing forces in the song, the protagonist and the streets, fight it out musically: 'he don't hang around with the gang no more' is antiphonally placed against 'out in the streets' (this approximately thirty-second outro is part of the recording but not present in the *Shindig!* performance). The entire song is drenched in reverb, adding to the effect of the otherworldly backing vocals.

This two minutes and twenty seconds of footage, shot for a teenage television audience in 1965, is a powerful cinematic experience that transcends the purpose for which it was created. Similar lighting and close-up techniques are observable in *Vivre sa vie* (1962) by French New Wave director Jean-Luc Godard, whose 1960s films display an ongoing fascination with the processes of popular music. The protagonist in *Masculin féminin* (1966) is a pop singer played by actual pop singer Chantal Goya, who is shown in one lengthy sequence in a recording studio making a single,[109] while *Made in U.S.A.*, also from 1966, features a still-teenage Marianne Faithfull performing an a cappella version of her 1964 hit "As Tears Go By" while seated in a café.[110]

In *Vivre sa vie*, however, Godard makes reference to an earlier Western artistic tradition, also observable in the Shangri-Las' *Shindig!* performance, in which hands and faces were understood to be direct conduits of feeling and expressive intensity. In late medieval devotional art, hands and faces were often magnified, or depicted in close-up, to heighten the emotional impact—Christ's crucifixion agony and Mary's grief at this torture of her son were two of the most common subjects to which this treatment was applied. This is part of what is known as affective piety, the forging of an emotional connection with the Christian story in the viewer via art that was specifically designed to elicit an emotional response. Such an understanding was central to Christianity in Western Europe in the late Middle Ages and part of a comprehensive belief and knowledge system that positioned intense emotionality as the path to devout piety.[111] A connection to this is explicitly present in *Vivre sa vie* when the protagonist Nana (Anna Karina) visits the cinema to see Carl Theodor Dreyer's *Le passion de Jeanne d'Arc* (1928), a silent epic which makes use of extended facial close-ups in order to convey the agony of Joan's (Maria Falconetti) impending martyrdom, a cinematic technique which clearly evokes this late medieval artistic tradition, current at the time of Joan of Arc's execution in 1431.[112] At the conclusion of this short scene, the camera cuts to Nana's face, making a specific connection between Joan's tears and those of Nana. Her body is then swallowed into the blackness of the cinema in which she sits, leaving only her face visible in a screen-filling close-up, just as the bodies of the Shangri-Las disappear into the blackness of the television studio, emphasising their faces and hands.

The powerful artistry of the Shangri-Las' extraordinary *Shindig!* performance and the cinematic techniques used to film it were acknowledged by British visual artist Elizabeth Price in her video work *The Woolworths Choir of 1979*, which won the prestigious Turner Prize in 2012. Price is also a musician; she was a member of mid-80s Oxford band Tallulah Gosh, and her works often include musical elements and/or sophisticated sonic landscapes.[113] Both are present in *The Woolworths Choir of 1979*, a 20-minute work that links three seemingly unconnected elements—a lecture on 13th-century Gothic (i.e., medieval Catholic) church architecture, with a particular focus on the choir section; the aforementioned footage of the Shangri-Las performing "Out in the Streets" on *Shindig!*; and news clips of the 1979 fire at a Woolworths department store in Manchester in which ten people died.[114] Significantly,

> The shared element, identified by the nameless narrators about a third of the way into the film, is a 'twist of the right wrist'—a gesture that can be found in all three strands.[115]

In this manner, Price constructed what she calls 'a fabric of relations'[116] so powerful that British art historian and critic Richard Dorment called *The Woolworths Choir of 1979* 'not only a visual tour de force, it is 20 of the most exhilarating minutes I've ever spent in an art gallery.'[117] Sonically, the film also uses loud handclaps and finger-clicks crisply recorded, hanging in space and drenched in reverb to create, in Dorment's words, a 'musical beat so insistent that I found it hard to sit still.' He went on to say,

> The second half of the film tells the grim story of how and where the Woolworths fire started, with the same immediacy and throbbing energy. This section lasts only about 10 minutes, but you will never forget what you learn about the tragedy in that time, including the layout of the store and how the fire spread.[118]

The fact that this knowledge is transferred so effectively is also noted by Blake Williams, who described *The Woolworths Choir of 1979* as

a work of experimental historiography that, to my mind, not only represents the most precisely calibrated challenge we have seen this century to time-based storytelling and meaning-making, but is effectively a manifesto against orthodox delivery systems of information and knowledge.[119]

Part of what makes the *Shindig!* footage of "Out in the Streets" so appropriate for this work of art—and central to its success—is that the visual component conveys meaning in a non-narrative way. The group members are like sculptures, isolated from narrative by carefully constructed lighting and studio techniques. That 'twist of the wrist'—along with the facial close-ups—conveys feeling and intensity of emotion which, as we have seen (and will see more in the next chapter), was the Shangri-Las' trademark.

I CAN NEVER GO HOME ANYMORE

"I Can Never Go Home Anymore" was released on Red Bird in November 1965.[120] In this deeply emotional song, a teenage girl refuses to end a relationship her mother disapproves of and runs away from home, causing her inconsolable mother to die, in an unspecified manner, from loneliness. On one level, the song functions as a paean to the sacredness of the American home, and a warning to teenagers to take their loving moms and homes for granted at their peril. But viewed within the context of the group's oeuvre, this song contains several well-established themes— parental conflict, an inappropriate love interest, and death—that function in a more complex manner than is initially apparent. Like Betty in "Leader of the Pack," this teenage girl has been compelled by parental strictures to embark on a course of action that ends in disaster, giving rise to an implicit critique of the middle-class home values the song appears to espouse. Furthermore, there are indications that the 'home' in question is a single-parent one, headed by the protagonist's mother. All this makes "I Can Never Go Home Anymore" a valuable window into idealised behaviour in the USA in the mid-1960s, especially given that it has been claimed, as recently as 2003, that 'forty years ago, digressions from the traditional nuclear family were omitted from popular culture.'[121] On the contrary, the digressions are there if you look for them.

"I Can Never Go Home Anymore" was the Shangri-Las' biggest hit since "Leader of the Pack," reaching #6 on the US charts. It was written by George 'Shadow' Morton and is one of the most emotionally charged in their repertoire. The main character in the song, like lead singer, Mary Weiss, is a teenage girl. She and her mother fight over her choice of boyfriend, with her mother insisting that 'the boy and I would have to part.' Instead, the daughter packs her clothes and leaves home, only to find that the relationship fails with the boy, who remains nameless. As a result of the girl leaving, her mother dies, lonely and broken-hearted; the protagonist is left wracked with remorse, lamenting that she 'can never go home anymore.'

Conflict with parents is a recurrent theme in the recordings of the Shangri-Las. In "Give Us Your Blessings" (1965), disquiet and foreboding are established immediately with the sound of a thunderstorm, which hangs over the whole song.[122] This is an established literary tradition for establishing tension, and as a metaphor for various forms of disharmony, both internal and external. Shakespeare regularly employed storms in this manner, one of the most famous instances being the tempest that dominates *King Lear*. In Act III, Lear, (significantly for this discussion) in a raging fury with his daughters, rushes out into a similarly furious storm to excoriate them.[123] Lear was aligned with the storm but 'his little world of man' was also pitted against it; his humanity against the cosmically far more powerful elements.[124] In "Give Us Your Blessings," the weather is a significant presence interacting with the demise of the protagonists, a metaphoric counterpart to the tension and conflict between Jimmy and Mary and their parents. As the thunderstorm booms, the vocals begin:

Run, Run, Run,
Mary Run, Run, Run

The storms fades out temporarily (it reappears toward the end of the song), replaced by booming piano, and

Run, Run, Run,
Jimmy Run, Run, Run

The narrator (Mary Weiss), employing a spoken delivery, explains that Mary and Jimmy's parents refuse to allow them to marry, and this has forced the young lovers to elope:

> Their *folks* just laughed
> And called them kids
> So Mary said
> Give us your blessings
> Please don't make us
> Run away ... [125]

Which they did, crashing the car because their vision was blurred by tears:

> The next day when they found them
> Mary and Jimmy were dead
> And as their folks knelt beside them in the rain
> They couldn't help but hear
> The last words Mary had said:
> Give us your blessings ... [126]

In a similar technique to that used in the closing bars of "Leader of the Pack," the song ends with ghostly cyclic choral backing vocals. 'Give us your blessings ... on our wedding day,' along with the thunderstorm, and 'Run, run, run,' all operate simultaneously in a conflicted counterpoint, which eventually fades out; this in turn is reminiscent of the final bars of "Out in the Streets." The use of names (Jimmy, Mary) personalises the narrative, but also suggests a continuity with "Leader of the Pack," which of course also features a 'Jimmy.' In "Give Us Your Blessings" Jimmy is not an anti-hero figure; nevertheless, he and Mary pay a heavy price for their defiance, as do their parents, condemned to hear Mary's pleas on repeat, eternally haunted by their refusal to endorse her love.

In the most famous of their songs dealing with parental conflict, "Leader of the Pack," it was also Betty's *folks* that were always putting Jimmy down, but, as noted earlier, it was Betty's *dad* who said 'find someone new.'[127] By contrast, "I Can Never Go Home Anymore" is unique in the Shangri-Las catalogue as a representation of *mother/ daughter* conflict. There is no mention of 'folks,' or 'my dad' in this song, only 'mom.' The song opens with a D minor chord that barely has time to be heard before we are plunged into the protagonist's world, into a conflict about which we know nothing:

> I'm gonna hide
> If *she* don't leave me alone
> I'm gonna run
> Away . . . [128]

The effect is disorienting, disarming, and compelling. The sense of immediacy this creates is heightened by the first-person narration—not simply in reference to the narrative voice, but also because of lead singer Mary Weiss's intimately personal style, which is here more spoken than sung, by this time a Shangri-Las trademark. Mary speaks *directly, personally*, to an audience that can safely be assumed to be teenage girls, counselling them—'if that's happened to you, don't let this . . .'—unlike "Leader of the Pack," in which the audience essentially eavesdrops on a conversation between 'Betty' and her girlfriends. It renders "I Can Never Go Home" almost confessional, as if the protagonist is desperately seeking to forgive herself and receive absolution. This intimacy is further enhanced the placement of Mary's vocals high up in the mix, so that they float, cloudlike, over the rest of the instrumentation and harmonies. This is particularly apparent during the verses; the accompaniment is sparse and drenched in Morton's (and engineer Brooks Arthur's) signature reverb. A sense of cavernous space is created, adding to the desolation and despair conveyed by the protagonist. All this makes the middle section of the song, with its strings and Mary's anguished cries of 'Mama!' all the more climactic, powerful, and intense.

'Intense' seems an appropriate way to describe the relationship between this mother and daughter. After nostalgia-ridden assurances that

> My mom is a good mom
> And she loves me with all her heart

We are told that

> *She* said I was too young to be in love and
> the boy and I would have to part . . .

She told me it was not really love
But only my girlish pride.[129]

And when, despite her mother's pleading, the protagonist leaves home to be with the boy, the memories she is wracked with all revolve around her mother: home = mom. This comes to a climax in the anguished middle section of the song, which lyrically evokes a lullaby, but is juxtaposed with a haunted, string-laden lament:

Hush little baby
Don't you cry
Mama won't go
Away . . .

Unlike her father, it is implied, who for whatever reason—divorce, death—is not present in this household. This is further reinforced toward the end of the song:

Don't do to your mom what I did to mine.
She grew so lonely in the end,
Angels picked her for a friend.

For this to occur, the mom is clearly alone in the house, deserted by her only companion, her daughter. And her daughter can 'never go home anymore' quite literally—because with the death of her mother, 'home' no longer exists. This would not be the case if her father was present, but he is completely absent from the picture.

This is significant on a number of levels. The first is that in a culture suffused with images of the nuclear family, it is a notable deviation. TV sitcoms like *Leave It to Beaver* and *Ozzie and Harriet*, as well as movies like *Marty* (1955), certainly presented the white suburban nuclear family as an ideal, the norm.[130] In the famous 'kitchen debate' of 1959 between Richard Nixon and Nikita Khrushchev, Nixon promoted the idea that

American superiority rested on the ideal of the suburban home, complete with modern electrical appliances and distinct gender roles for family members. He proclaimed that the 'model' home, with a male breadwinner and a full-time female homemaker, adorned with a wide array of consumer goods, represented the essence of American freedom.[131]

During the 1950s and 60s those in charge of television, which sociologist Ella Taylor has described as 'the most relentlessly domestic of our mass media,' adopted a policy of the 'least objectionable programming' that denied race, class, and structural diversity.[132] In doing so, 'they reproduced . . . not the reality of most American family lives, but just the kind of consensus desired by advertisers.'[133] Elaine Tyler May has demonstrated conclusively the manner in which the nuclear family, as the lynchpin of domesticity, was embraced as a bastion of security during the Cold War. As part of this strategy, mothers were deemed responsible for everything from stocking the bomb shelter to keeping their husbands sexually satisfied (in order to prevent sexual deviancy, which could lead to communism) and, significantly for this discussion, were charged with not lapsing into 'momism' by making their children weak and passive through overprotection.[134]

This song also reflected the reality of some of the performers' lives, if not that of its author as well. As we saw in chapter 2, sisters Betty and Mary Weiss had what Mary described as a 'difficult' upbringing in a single-parent household, their father having died when Mary was six weeks old.[135] She said later,

> I think most kids have a more structured home than I did. Years ago I remember people having like two parents, and finishing school . . . we kind of raised her [their mother], as much as we could.[136]

Their mother 'had periodic jobs on occasion, but nothing really substantial.'[137] The family was 'pretty poor' and struggled to make ends meet, a situation Mary later described as 'a hell of a way to grow up. I always kind of supported myself—it was a question of survival.'[138] Mary also alluded to experiencing a great deal of 'personal pain' that she channelled into her performances.[139] As she put it,

> I'm kind of a shy person, but I felt that the recording studio was the place that you could really release what you're feeling without everybody looking at you . . . I had enough pain in me at the time to pull off anything and get into it and sound believable.[140]

In specific reference to "I Can Never Go Home Anymore," Mary said that she 'had to turn the lights down in the studio for that one . . . I don't think I was even talking to my mother at the time' and commented further on what she called 'that love/hate thing' between daughters and their mothers. She added that for her the song was 'very real,' to the point where she had been crying while she recorded her parts.[141]

The author of the song was well aware of the ability of the group to be emotionally convincing and particularly of Mary's capabilities as the lead singer. In a 2007 interview, Morton commented,

> 'I had no idea until years later how fortunate I was to have Mary Weiss on the microphone. I made demands of her that Scorsese wouldn't make of his actresses. I would plead with her, threaten her, hug her; I'd do whatever I had to do, and she would end up nailing it. I was so lucky.[142]

By the time "I Can Never Go Home Anymore" was released, late in 1965, Morton had been producing and writing material specifically for the Shangri-Las for at least a year and a half. He was not the kind of songwriter who churned out songs for groups to which he had no personal connection. According to Morton, there had been a clash early on at Red Bird over this exact issue, when he had been told not to record "Leader of the Pack" because it was too controversial. He went ahead and recorded it anyway, using his old Long Island contacts, Rod McBrien and Billy Stahl at Ultrasonic, and using a group called the Goodies to sing on it, who were under the impression that it would be released as *their* first single, as discussed earlier. Management apparently insisted that Morton write/give material only to one group—the Shangri-Las:[143]

> Four girls, out of Cambria Heights, who fell into my lap from the get-go, and I never realized how much talent I had on my hands. Mary and the others had the ability to make my stories believable. I don't know too many actresses out there who could do it. If you took them off the screen and told them, "By word alone, convince people," they'd fail. The Shangri-Las were capable of pulling that off.[144]

Morton wrote material *specifically* for the Shangri-Las—and he wrote highly emotional teen mini-operas because they could deliver his material completely convincingly and with the requisite intensity.

Nor could Morton have been ignorant of the Weiss sisters' family situation, given that *all* the group members were minors (being between the ages of 15 and 17 in 1964) and had to have their parents sign contracts on their behalf. In fact, in one of the few comments Mary Weiss has made about the litigation the group found itself embroiled in during and after its demise, she stated,

'My mother kind of signed my life away when I was 14. I'm laughing. Thirty years of litigation. There's a storeroom of litigation up to the ceiling ... That's one of the reasons I walked away. The litigation was much thicker than the music. I couldn't go near another record label for ten years.'[145]

When I interviewed Morton in 2007, he told me that

at sixteen I found out my real name wasn't Morton, and my grandfather wasn't my grandfather ... but he did love me like a grandfather, he took care of me, and he gave me the name Morton ... [146]

He did not elaborate on this, and although it must remain inconclusive, there is enough evidence—the death of his mother Irene's parents

George Morton
and the author,
New York, 2007

and subsequent fracturing of that family that appears to have resulted in her being placed in an orphanage, her later divorce from George's father and remarriage while he was a child—that Morton's family situation was not completely straightforward either. Telling interviewers that he was born in Richmond, Virginia (his mother's birthplace, not his) and the adoption of 'Billy Kell(e)y' as one of his songwriting/arranging aliases suggests a conscious alignment/solidarity with the maternal 'Kell(e)y' side of his family; perhaps he felt the name 'Morton' no longer really belonged to him. He also told me,

> probably of all of the songs, "I Can Never Go Home Anymore" touches on my life more than the others . . . they were just things that came to me.[147]

That Morton wrote "I Can Never Go Home Anymore" specifically for the Shangri-Las is not open to question. It seems highly probable that his inspiration for the song was an amalgam of his own experiences and those of the Weiss sisters, and it was written with the expectation that it would touch raw nerves in such a way that Mary could completely inhabit the song and deliver an emotionally charged, compelling performance.

The 1965 Christmas edition of *KRLA Beat*, a Californian music paper named after a local radio station, contains a quite extraordinary reference to "I Can Never Go Home Anymore." A number of pop singers are pictured, accompanied by captions indicating what they would like for Xmas. The captions were penned by the *KRLA Beat* writing staff, and were largely humorous references to their recordings, clothing, hair, reputation and other things associated with the artists in question. In what was clearly a reference to their current hit, "I Can Never Go Home Anymore," Mary Weiss was pictured, with a caption that read 'A NEW HOME and a new mother.' The personal resonances are telling, to say the least.[148]

The Shangri-Las, Romanticism, and the Western Artistic Tradition: "Remember (Walkin' in the Sand)" and "Past, Present and Future"

"Remember (Walkin' in the Sand)" and "Past, Present and Future" were the Shangri-Las' first and last singles for Red Bird. They were released almost exactly two years apart, in the summers of 1964 and 1966 respectively, and both made reference to the beach. With no prior knowledge of either the group or the song, one might easily assume that "Remember (Walkin' in the Sand)" was yet another of the many songs released in the early to mid-60s that revolved around the beach and surfing. At this time, surf-themed singles and albums were being churned out by record companies anxious to cash in on this teen craze; they celebrated the sunny southern Californian coast of Dick Dale, Jan and Dean, and the Beach Boys, reinforcing the notion that this was indeed, Shangri-la—paradise. "Remember (Walkin' in the Sand)," on the other hand, is two minutes and fifteen seconds of desperate and intense teen anguish, a young woman's haunting lament for her lost love, in which the symbolism of the beach and the sea have an altogether different significance. In 1974, Mitchell Cohen noted,

> the commercial success of the Shangri-Las began and ended on the beach. One can only assume that the swain who used and abused the protagonist of 'Remember (Walkin' in the Sand)' is the cause of her defensive frigidity in 'Past, Present and Future,' where she warns a boy who walks with her along the shore, 'Don't try to touch me, 'cause that will never ... happen ... again.'[1]

In contrast to other, more obviously market-driven beach-themed pop music, the Shangri-Las' profoundly emotional 'beach' songs tap into the deep Western artistic traditions of Romanticism. This invests these songs with considerable gravitas, enabling them to transcend their mid-60s pop music milieu and find a place within an established artistic tradition that elevated emotion and depth of feeling over rationality and reason.

"Remember (Walkin' in the Sand)" was released in August 1964,[2] when the dominant image of the beach in US popular culture was as a sun-drenched spot filled with teenage girls and boys surfing and having fun. Surfing originated in Hawaii, where it was known as the sport of Hawaiian kings; the first European description of men surfing dates from 1779.[3] By the early 1960s, however, it was firmly and famously associated with Southern California. *Time* magazine reported in 1963 that

> surfing was until recently the private passion of a few bronzed dare-devils. But in the past few years, surfing has become something like a way of life for thousands of devotees all along the Southern California coast. Every weekend an estimated 100,000 surfers paddle into the briny on 7-ft. to 12-ft. balsa or polyurethane boards, struggle upright into a precarious balance with nature, and try to catch the big breakers coming in.[4]

The adoption of surfing as the 'private passion of a few bronzed daredevils' had links to the beat aesthetic of hedonism and the pursuit of thrills, kicks and danger. The 'surf bum' can be understood as a descendent of the free-spirited non-conformist beatnik, and the beach as a locale conducive to an accompanying resistance to and distaste for traditional notions of work and responsibility. The beach was a place to pursue pleasure and fun.[5]

Teen movies, including *Gidget* (1959), which featured Sandra Dee as a tomboy surfer, helped to redefine surfing as young person's pursuit, a teen phenomenon.[6] In the process, as Carol Cooper has explained, *Gidget*

> replaced the spooky Zen-hobo aura of the actual surf community with the clean-cut glow of a varsity letterman. Fusing the weedy, dissipated hipster with the sun-bronzed high school jock to make a new,

improved heterosexual male was as tricky a maneuver as desexualizing intimate friendships between half-naked boys and girls.[7]

Surfing/beach films, like those starring Frankie Avalon and Annette Funicello, presented and reinforced an image of clean white teens having harmless fun at the beach, and were immensely popular at the box office.[8] Joan Ormrod has estimated that around 70 surf-themed films were produced by Hollywood and independent producers between 1959 and 1966.[9] The films often starred actors, like Avalon and Funicello, who had already made a name for themselves as pop singers, thereby capitalising on their existing popularity in another teenage market.[10] This worked in the other direction too. The music that grew out of and came to be inextricably associated with surf culture—instrumentals with echo-laden guitar and booming drums (Dick Dale, the Surfaris, the Ventures) and songs about the beach featuring distinctive doo-wop inspired falsetto harmonies (the Beach Boys, Jan & Dean, the Rip Chords)—was hugely popular in the early 60s.

Dick Dale was one of the most important innovators in what came to be known as the 'surfer sound.'[11] Born Richard Monsour to Lebanese-American parents, Dale was a passionate surfer and guitar player who worked closely with Leo Fender to create an amplifier that would not blow up when he played extremely loudly.[12] This became known as the Dual-Showman Piggy Back Amp; its 2x15 inch speaker cabinet and 100 watt transformer (which peaked at 180 watts, according to the Official Dick Dale Website) revolutionised the power with which the electric guitar could be amplified.[13] Significantly, when questioned by Fender about the necessity of playing at such high volume, Dale listed, among other reasons, that he wanted to recreate 'the roar of mother nature's creatures and the roar of the ocean.'[14] Importantly, Dale was also responsible for developing (again with Leo Fender) the Fender Tank Reverb, an effects unit that gave his guitar playing an echoey sound that was simultaneously thick, wet, piercing and twangy. The original impetus for this was *not* to create a guitar effect, but rather so that Dale could run his vocal microphone through it and 'correct' his voice, which he perceived as being flat and lacking vibrato.[15] Since reverb quickly became inseparably associated with the sound of the 'surf guitar,' its original development as a vocal effect has a significance which will become apparent shortly.

The speedy popularisation and commercialisation of beach/surf music resulted in considerable revenue for record companies. On July 11, 1964, Capitol Records ran a full-page advertisement in *Billboard* headed 'CATCH THIS GIANT WAVE OF SUPER-SELLING SUMMER SURFING SOUNDS FROM CAPITOL.' Surrounded by pictures of nine album covers, including the Beach Boys' *All Summer Long* and Dick Dale's *Surfer's Choice*, the ad continued,

> The hottest, sellingest, chart-bustingest stable of surfing stars on any label. The Beach Boys! Dick Dale and his Del-Tones! The Super Stocks! Jerry Cole and his Spacemen!

It then roared in huge letters 'FREE BONUS SINGLES,' announcing,

> Included with four of these great new Capitol albums is a free 45 rpm surfing single—different one with every album. And, that's just one of Capitol's many fantastic merchandising aids! Other Capitol albums have free colour Hot Rod pictures included. Or motorcycle pictures . . . And more! It's going to be a HOT summer . . . with a Capitol "H."[16]

Several things are apparent from this advertisement. Capitol, anxious to maintain the popularity of surf music and the careers of the Beach Boys in the face of the 'British Invasion,' had decided that an additional promotional push was required, giving away singles as an extra incentive to buy LPs. It also demonstrated that surf culture was closely associated with hot rods, drag racing, and motorbikes, which were in turn understood by record company executives as a set of interlinked teen crazes. To maximize their revenue, record companies needed to capitalise on the popularity of such trends before others arose to take their place. By purchasing these records, so the marketing logic went, you could obtain your own piece of California sun no matter where you lived in the USA, which effectively extended the appeal of what could otherwise have been a localised market. Those unlucky enough to live elsewhere felt it too. As Gene Sculatti observed,

> So complete was the idealized California portrait as sung by the Beach Boys, Jan & Dean, Hondells, etc., everybody wanted in. Surf

bands sprang up in Colorado (the Astronauts), Minnesota (the Trashmen of 'Surfing Bird' fame) and Michigan (the Rivieras with 'California Sun'). In California, the influx of teenagers eager to join the in-crowd overcrowded the public beaches and kicked sand over the once noble surfer image.[17]

In a letter to the editors of *Teen* magazine in October 1964, Bob Oxley wrote:

Us Michigan surfing bugs think California is tops, and the kids are too, but how do we get out there to enjoy it? Hang onto your boards you California surfers! Dearborn, Michigan has a Surf Club!

We watch as many surfing pictures as possible and have beach parties, a dance band and two Woodys, but **WHERE'S THE SURF?** We have the Surfin' disease and just have to get out to California and see all the great kids that live out there at those swingin' beaches.

We are looking for jobs, anything in Southern California. We want a chance to live among all those surfin' guys and gals. California, here we come!!!!

Bob Oxley
23050 Sheridan
W. Dearborn, Mich[18]

Furthermore, in 1965, the Mamas and the Papas famously lamented, 'I'd be safe and warm/If I was in LA/California dreamin'/On such a winter's day.[19] It may not be stated explicitly in the song, but there is an implied dichotomy between a cold, gloomy East Coast and a sunny, joyous West Coast in "California Dreamin."

Right in the middle of the summer that Capitol Records had declared would be so 'HOT' with surf music, the Shangri-Las' "Remember (Walkin' in the Sand)" was released, in early August 1964.[20] As previously discussed, it was written by George 'Shadow' Morton, who maintains he hastily penned it on the way to the recording studio when he realised he did not have a song for the singing group that he had inveigled into recording with him. Given that the original demo version was over seven minutes long, this strains credulity, but his version of this story seemingly never wavered.[21]

"Remember" is, on the most basic level, a teenage girl's lament for her lost lover—he has gone away and, instead of returning, has sent a letter ending their relationship. The sea plays a number of roles simultaneously here, both literal and metaphorical, and is an integral component of the heightened sense of drama and emotion created in the song. This is established immediately, as it begins with a descending third, leading into a thundering D minor chord—a cadential figure which would normally be used to close, rather than open, a song. Musically, it's the ending, before the song has even begun, and thus an ominous foreshadowing of what lies ahead.[22] At this point the vocals begin, delivered with piercing emotional intensity by Mary Weiss:

> Seems like the other day
> My baby went away
> He went away
> 'cross the sea . . . [23]

Here the ocean is established as the separator/remover of the protagonist's absent lover—he has travelled somewhere unspecified, but it involves an ocean, which now keeps the two lovers apart. But what began as a physical separation has deepened into an emotional and psychological one:

> It's been two years or so
> Since I saw my baby go
> And then this letter came for me
> It said that we were through
> He found somebody new
> Oh! Let me think . . . let me think . . .
> What can I do?[24]

He is not coming back; the ocean between them is now eternal, as is the ocean itself. This is reinforced by the backing vocals throughout this verse, which consist of even measures of ooooh cascading into aaaaah-hh,[25] which mimic the rhythmic push and pull of the tide, waves receding, crashing, receding, crashing, a 'movement' which is also sexual. The motion of the ocean is inevitable, unstoppable, and controlled by the moon, long associated in literary symbolism with altered states, emotional instability, and in extreme cases, lunacy.

As the reality of her situation hits the protagonist, she and the song come to an abrupt halt. 'Oh no,' she half-sings, half-speaks, in distracted disbelief: 'Oh no. Oh no no no no no.' The instrumentation has dropped away, except to punctuate her 'nos'—sharp dabs of piano and double bass. These few bars act as a prelude to the chorus, which, in contrast to the standard pop song structure of understated verses and climactic choruses, is a study in emptiness. There are no backing vocals—the singer's words echo in space accompanied by handclaps, finger-snaps, and accentuating stabs of bass and piano. The most distinctive aspect of the chorus, however, lies in the use of sound effects—the sound of seagulls that squeal and cry overhead. In this musical context of utter desolation, located on the beach, the protagonist escapes the emotional turbulence of her new reality by hurling herself back in time to the early stages of her romance:

(Remember) Walkin' in the sand
(Remember) Walkin' hand in hand
(Remember) The night was so exciting
(Remember) His smile was so inviting
(Remember) Then he touched my cheek
(Remember) With his finger tips
(Remember) Softly, softly we'd meet with our lips . . . [26]

The dramatic intensity of this chorus is heightened by its slower, incantational, repetitive nature. The rhythmic exhortation to 'Remember!' at the beginning of every line has a devotional quality reminiscent of ancient Catholic religious practices like the use of rosary beads, or the meditative contemplation of key moments in the Christian story like the Stations of the Cross. The original impetus for such devotional practices was as aids to the memory; they also demanded a high degree of emotional involvement.[27] Given that the Shangri-Las were from Catholic families and attended Catholic schools in suburban Queens, New York, and that George 'Shadow' Morton had an Irish Catholic background and had attended St. Thomas Aquinas School in Brooklyn, this may not be too long a bow to be drawing.[28] The Chantels, who were signed to George Goldner's Gone label in the late 1950s, met while at St. Anthony of Padua School in the Bronx. Lead singer Arlene Smith, who wrote much of their material, was heavily influenced by Gregorian chant. The Shangri-Las would record a version of the Chantels' "Maybe," soon after the chart success of "Remember." [29]

The modal quality of the chorus of "Remember" is emphasised by the fact that there is no chord change—it remains on D minor—and the 'walkin' in the sand' melodic phrase is repeated six times in succession, creating tension and suspense. This stands in complete contrast to the heavy, thick and rhythmically ponderous verses. The emptiness of the chorus, its incantational vocals, harmonic minimalism, and sounds of seagulls (which *suggest* fluttering whether or not we actually hear their wings) evokes an altered mind-state. The protagonist is in shock: distracted, floating, unmoored, as she relives an encounter firmly located (by the sand and the seagulls) at the beach. Instead of the sunlit locale of teenage surfing and fun, however, this is taking place place *at night*— mysterious, "so exciting"—fraught with the danger of sexual frisson. That danger is realised as the beach is transformed from a sunny carefree teenage hangout into a dark place of desolation, empty but for the cries of seagulls echoing in space overhead.

'Space' is a crucial concept here. The instrumentation is minimal— just piano, double bass and drums—but the entire song is saturated with echo and reverb. This is particularly noticeable on the snare drum in the verse, the stabs of piano and bass in the pre-chorus, and the handclaps in the chorus. It is equally evident on the vocals, especially in the last line of the second verse, 'What will I do with it now,' in which the 'now' lingers on palpably in space after the singing has stopped. As noted earlier, the reverb effect was at this time firmly associated with the amplified guitars of surf music. Having turned the prevalent conception of the beach on its head, Morton underscored this by doing the same with reverb. Rather than evoking fun in the sun, in his hands it summons up emptiness, desolation, and darkness.

In this manner, the song invokes a much older set of literary and metaphoric associations with the beach, ocean and sea. The sea has had manifold and ever-changing metaphoric significance in the Western artistic tradition, but one of the most common metaphors, very relevant for this discussion, is that of the commotion of the sea mirroring internal emotional turbulence (an idea still present in current use of the term 'at sea' to describe confusion or bewilderment). It occurs fre-

quently in Greek myth, drama, and poetry, along with other sea, fish-
ing, shipping and sailing imagery—not surprising given that the sea was
central to everyday life in ancient Greece—and this is the likely origin
of the notion in Western culture.[30] In *The Iliad*, Homer described Achilles wracked with insomnia, mourning the death of his close friend and
fighting companion[31] Patroclus:

> The memories flooded over him, live tears flowing,
> and now he'd lie on his side, now flat on his back,
> now facedown again. At last he'd leap to his feet,
> wander in anguish, aimless along the surf, and dawn on dawn
> flaming over the sea and shore would find him pacing.[32]

At *night*, over and over, 'dawn on dawn,' Achilles was drawn by his
anguish to the beach. In 409 BCE, Sophocles dramatized the tragic tale
of Philoctetes, bitten on the foot by a snake on his way to fight in the
Trojan War, and subsequently abandoned on the island of Lemnos with
a festering and excruciatingly painful wound. The chorus sang,

> Such suffering my eyes have never seen . . .
> I have never beheld or heard of another
> Whose fate was harder than this man's . . .
> I cannot understand how he
> Ever was able to live all alone
> And hear the waves around him,
> Enduring a life so full of tears.[33]

The sound of the waves echoed and emphasised his loneliness and
mirrored his watery tears.

More particularly, the sea has been understood as symbolic of passion and of love itself. In the mythic tale of Tristan and Isolde (or Isolt),
dating from around the 12th century, the ocean is an omnipresent
force which acts as a vehicle for voyages of separation and reunion.[34]
In a modern retelling of the legend, Edward Arlington Robinson's epic
poem *Tristram* (1927), a clear parallel with "Remember" is evident:

> Isolt of the white hands, in Brittany,
> Could see no longer northward anywhere

A picture more alive or less familiar
Than a blank ocean and the same white birds
Flying, and always flying, and still flying,
Yet never bringing any news of him
That she remembered, who had sailed away
The spring before—saying he would come back,
Although not saying when.[35]

Standing on the beach and staring at the ocean, Isolt waited and waited, as the seagulls continued to fly, echoing her seemingly endless desolation.

In Richard Wagner's version of the tale, the opera *Tristan und Isolde*, which premiered in 1865, the drama is bookended by voyages, and repeatedly the lovers' affinity for and with the sea is emphasised. Land is associated with stability, calm, and 'sterile half-life,' the sea with love and passion.[36] On the initial voyage, Tristan delivers Isolde to his uncle, King Mark of Cornwall (Isolde was to be Mark's bride); on this voyage Tristan and Isolde drink a love potion that destines them to be tragic lovers. In the lengthy extended love scene that is Act Two, the doomed lovers are repeatedly aligned with the night, as Tristan sings,

Oh, now we are night
consecrated!
Malevolent day,
disposed to envy,
though it part us through fraud
can trick us no more by lies! . . .

Mid the day's idle fancies
he has only one longing,
a longing for
the holy night,
where forever,
solely true,
love and rapture await![37]

In the final act Tristan lies wounded and dying in his castle, separated from Isolde by the sea and waiting for the ship that is bringing her. She arrives in time for him to die in her arms and in the final part of the *Liebestod* (literally, love-death) she sings,

> In the billowy surge,
> in the ocean of sound,
> in the World's Spirit's
> infinite All,
> to drown now,
> descending,
> void of thought –
> highest bliss![38]

Here, the ocean and drowning are used metaphorically to convey the idea of love in death—and transfiguration. Unable to be together in the earthly realm, the lovers will be united for eternity in death, as the lovers would be in a later song by the Shangri-Las, "Give Us Your Blessings."[39] The ocean and its endless cycles are likewise eternal. Another of the sea's inherent attributes that makes it such a powerful metaphoric symbol is its dual nature—it is regenerative and life-giving as well as destructive and deadly. Similarly, love and passion hold great promise, but are fraught with danger, uncertainty and the potential for physical and emotional violence.[40]

I am not suggesting that Morton modelled "Remember" on the *Liebestod*, but I do want to argue that these established conceptions of the sea in Western culture contribute to making the ocean such a powerful metaphor, and that its overtones permeate "Remember." These resonances have significant implications for another song by the Shangri-Las that makes reference to the beach: "Past, Present and Future," released in June 1966.[41] It was the Shangri-Las' last single for the Red Bird label, which collapsed shortly after its release, and their last (albeit modest) commercial success, reaching #59 on the US singles chart.[42] Its authorship is credited to George 'Shadow' Morton, Jerry Leiber, and Artie Butler.* Conspicuously absent from this list of songwriting credits is Ludwig van Beethoven.

---

* Leiber and Stoller were partners in the Red Bird Record label with George Goldner (see chapter 2). Artie Butler is an arranger who was responsible for the orchestral arrangements on many of the Shangri-Las' recordings.

Like "Remember (Walkin' in the Sand)," "Past, Present and Future" is an intense teenage lament, suffused with heartbreak and sadness. In this case, the listener is not given any great detail about the circumstances of the female protagonist's pain; there are no letters from across the sea. But again she has had her heart broken and is reeling from the blow. The musical accompaniment to the lyrics is based on the famous first movement of Beethoven's Piano Sonata No. 14 in C-sharp Minor (Op. 27, No. 2), the 'Moonlight' Sonata. There is a long tradition in popular music of borrowing and reworking themes from works in the Western classical music canon; the many examples include "A Lover's Concerto" by the Toys (1965), based on the *Minuet in G*, by J.S. Bach;[43] Serge Gainsbourg's homage to Brigitte Bardot, "Initials B.B." (1968), based on a motif from the first movement of Antonin Dvořak's Symphony No. 9 *(From the New World)*;[44] and Eric Carmen's reworking of the second *Adagio sostenuto* movement of Sergei Rachmaninov's Piano Concerto No. 2 in C Minor, Op. 18, as "All By Myself" (1975).[45] In choosing a recognisable piece of classical music on which to base a song for the Shangri-Las, Morton was not doing anything particularly unusual or ground-breaking. However, the Shangri-Las were well-established by mid-1966 as purveyors of intensely emotional, highly dramatic pop music, and the opening movement of Beethoven's 'Moonlight' Sonata was spectacularly appropriate raw material for this purpose.

Beethoven's Piano Sonata No. 14 was written in 1801 and published in 1802.[46] It only acquired its 'Moonlight' nickname after Beethoven's death (1827), when novelist and music critic Heinrich Rellstab likened its first movement to a boat gliding on the waters of a lake in moonlight.[47] The sonata was popular and famous in Beethoven's lifetime, to an extent that he himself found bewildering; he remarked to his pupil (later friend and fellow composer) Carl Czerny that 'Everybody is always talking about the C-sharp Minor sonata! Surely I have written better things.'[48] The work is a piece for solo piano consisting of three movements, identified by their playing instructions: the first, *Adagio sostenuto* (slow and sustained), is the movement on which "Past, Present and Future" is based. It is followed by the *Allegretto* (rather fast), which composer and virtuoso pianist Franz Liszt (1811-1886) famously described as a 'flower between two abysses.'[49] The final movement is the *Presto Agitato* (very fast, restlessly and with agitation).[50] The 'Moonlight' is one of 32 sonatas for solo piano composed by Beethoven over the course of his life.

The 'Moonlight' Sonata marked a revolutionary break with traditional sonata form in several ways. These have a direct relationship to the degree of emotional intensity created by the sonata itself, but also have implications for its use in 'Past, Present and Future'. Firstly, the "Moonlight" begins with a slow, quiet, and atmospheric movement, which was virtually unheard of; usually this would take place in the second of the usual *four*, rather than three, movements. Several commentators have observed that it was as if Beethoven simply dispensed with a first (normally fast and up-tempo *'Allegro'*) movement and leapt straight into the second movement, the *Adagio*; in doing so, he 'created a sonata opening unique in his output'.[51] In addition, this work was designated by Beethoven as '*Sonata quasi una fantasia*', that is, in the style of a 'fantasia', which is defined as 'a work with an unpredictable number of sections, all played without pause', so that they segue into one another. To emphasise this, the end of the "Moonlight" *Adagio* is marked *attacca*—a musical directive for the performer to begin the next movement or section of a composition immediately, without pause. The effect is to stress the unity of the entire composition, rather than presenting the individual sections as freestanding autonomous movements.[52]

These modifications to traditional sonata form need to be seen in the context of 19th-century Romanticism, with its elevation of human emotion over rationality and reason.[53] A crucial component of Romanticism was the breakdown of the traditional forms—in art, music, literature, poetry—that were a product of rational Enlightenment philosophical ideologies, in order to allow for a more unfettered expression of emotional sensibilities.[54] Beethoven was at the forefront of these developments in music, particularly in his piano sonatas; discussing those composed from 1799 through 1801 (which include the 'Moonlight'), Beethoven scholar Lewis Lockwood has noted,

> we find in these sonatas a clear sense of innovation and expansion of the genre of the piano sonata, of reshaping it in the service of a stronger and more personal expressivity. Part of this results from new ways of approaching the form of the work, its number and order of movements, and the balance of function between the movements in the formation of the whole.[55]

Beethoven's innovations further modified a form that was already understood to possess uniquely expressive capabilities. The specific qualities and function of the sonata were explicated in 1774 in an influential article by composer and music critic Johann Abraham Peter Schulze.[56] In it he argued,

> There is no form of instrumental music that is more capable of depicting wordless sentiments than the sonata. The symphony and overture have a somewhat more fixed character, while the form of a concerto seems suited more for providing a skilled performer the opportunity to be heard accompanied by many instruments than for the depiction of passions ... In a sonata, the composer might want to express through the music *a monologue* marked by sadness, misery, pain, or of tenderness, pleasure and joy; using a more animated kind of music, he might want to depict a passionate conversation between similar or complementary characters; or he might wish to depict emotions that are impassioned, stormy or contrasting, or ones that are light, delicate, flowing and delightful.[57]

This conception is also consistent with the Romantic notion of blurring the boundaries between different artistic disciplines—of merging painting, poetry, music—so that poetry sang, and music painted pictures.[58] More specifically, Kenneth Drake related that 'Czerny describes the opening movement of Op. 27, No. 2 as being "extremely poetic" and easy to grasp—"a night scene, in which a plaintive ghostly voice sounds from far off in the distance."'[59]

Carl Czerny was a close and trusted friend of Beethoven and had insights into his compositional methodology. Even though Beethoven himself resisted such literal interpretations, Czerny's comments are nevertheless indicative of how the 'Moonlight' Sonata was received and interpreted by some of Beethoven's contemporaries,[60] and his reading of the opening movement as a 'plaintive ghostly voice' is significant for this discussion, as we shall see.

During Beethoven's lifetime, piano sonatas were considered 'too heartfelt and internal, too dependent on the intellectual and emotional concentration [of the virtuoso] and the [listener's] undisturbed immersion in their ideal nature' to be performed outside the privacy of a room or salon, wrote composer and musical theorist Adolf Marx

(1795-1866).[61] Public concert performances were rare, and although they gradually infiltrated concert halls, this view of the piano sonata persisted well into the 1850s.[62] Music historian Glenn Stanley explains further:

> The identification of a sonata with a monologue or a dialogue, poetic genres that readily map onto solo or duo sonatas, suggests a personal and subjective intimacy, utterances *in the first person* directly expressive of the speaker's own feelings.[63]

This is relevant to our discussion for several reasons. The Shangri-Las' "Past, Present and Future" employs a piece of music that utilised a form (the sonata) that was understood at the time it was written to be personal, intimate, and uniquely capable of conveying emotion—a musical monologue. The song begins with unaccompanied minor arpeggios played on a piano—the first bar of the 'Moonlight' Sonata, which is then repeated when the vocal begins, with all group members speaking the word 'Past.' This introduces the first section of the song, which is a *monologue* delivered over a rearranged and compressed amalgam of the first fifteen bars of the sonata (although not a note-for-note rendition of the score, it is nevertheless instantly recognisable as an arrangement of the 'Moonlight' Sonata).

The lyrics of "Past, Present and Future" are delivered by lead singer Mary Weiss in a direct, *spoken*, personal tone of communication— defeated, world-weary and resigned—and the *entire* song is spoken; not a single lyric is sung.[64] This makes the song unique in the Shangri-Las oeuvre, and is also significant structurally, because the song has no verse/chorus configuration—a verse/chorus structure is unsuited to a monologue. Instead, it has three 'verse' sections—'Past,' 'Present,' and 'Future'—that, *attacca*, segue into one another. (The 'Present' and 'Future' sections are separated by a waltz-like middle eight—this will be discussed in more detail shortly). Here is where the use of Beethoven's sonata takes on an even greater significance, because structurally, as we have seen, the sonata was understood to be a *musical* monologue, so pairing it with a literal monologue is both conceptually logical and has a sound historical underpinning.

So much so, in fact, that in 1816 someone else had the same idea. The immediate and immense popularity of the 'Moonlight' Sonata resulted in a number of attempts to transcribe it into different media. These included not only an orchestral arrangement of the first (*Adagio sostenuto*) movement but also, most significantly for this discussion, an attempt to set this movement to words. The composer and author Dr. Georg Christoph Grosheim,[65] explained at the time how this came about:

'I had set [author and poet Johann Gottfried] Seume's poem "At the Grave of a Friend" to music. He was pleased with it and sent me his "Praying Girl." Now . . . the theme of this poem immediately determines the character that its musical accompaniment should assume . . . in view of the length of the poem, its necessarily slow movement, and its punctuating pauses and cesuras. Meanwhile I sought indefatigably among Haydn's, Mozart's, and Beethoven's instrumental works for a composition that I might fit to this poem, one of the most touching pictures of filial love I know. And how great was my joy when I found in the fantasia in C-sharp minor of the last-named composer a perfect composition for Seume's "Praying Girl." The praying girl kneels at the high altar; consequently the scene is a subject for churchly music. The harmonious notes, moving in slow figures, beginning with the composition itself, form a four-voiced Kyrie, with an accompaniment of triplets. The notes that come in at various pauses, beginning towards the end of the fifth measure and later expanded from the upper tones of the harmony, form the melody of Seume's poem . . . the first words of the poem ('On the steps of the high altar, Lina kneels in prayer') are spoken out masterfully up to the ninth measure . . . Beethoven probably did not foresee this . . . I should be delighted if he were to honor it with his attention, being himself informed of the matter. Perhaps then we shall receive the work from his own hand.[66]

This work never came to fruition, despite several further appeals to Beethoven by Grosheim.[67] Nevertheless, it is significant that as early as 1816 the particular qualities of the 'Moonlight' Sonata made it seem appropriate for use in conjunction with a poem—fundamentally, a song. Furthermore, the subject matter of the poem, "Die Beterin" ("The Praying Girl") was deeply intense and emotional; a young woman praying at an altar in a church, for her dying father:

On the stairs of the great altar kneels
Lina praying, her visage aglow,
Carried by her anguished soul,
To the holiest of feet.

Her hands, wrung hot, tremble,
Her anxious, wet gaze wavers,
Beseeching the saviour's crown of thorns,
For mercy at the foot of the Father's throne:

Mercy for her father, for his pain,
For her kind, sorrowful heart
In which life's beautiful years of bloom
Bitterly gnaw away the seeds of any joy.

Salvation for the father of her virtue
For the only guide of her youth,
For him alone she lives her life
Over which the breath of death hovers.

Her sighs from deep within her blow
Her pleas burning with devotion
Over to the incense; cherubim
Stand ready to attend the imploring maiden.

Convey, o angels, her angel's tears
Pray to appease the father!
None have wept more piteously to the crown of thorns
Not even Mary for her dead son.

See, O friend, in the visions of transfiguration
There radiates a quiet, blessed joy;
Lina wipes the tears from her cheeks,
And leaves full of sweet hope.

A tear wets my eyelids, too.
O Father, restore her father to her again.
I would approach death gladly
If she could pray so fervently for me.[68]

The poem's emotional and anguished language employed the imagery of fevered passion that became a staple of later Romantic poetry (Christina Rossetti's 'Goblin Market,' for example). However, the fervent emotional engagement with the Passion of Christ (the crown of thorns) and the evocation of the *pietà* (Mary holding the dead Christ and weeping over his body) locate "The Praying Girl" within a long-standing tradition of Christian devotional literature, including poetry, stretching back to at least 1300.[69] There is very little action or movement in the poem; its somewhat ponderous length is part of an overall technique for creating stasis, which is why it is quoted here in full. This is a depiction of feeling and an emotional state, of a young woman's desperate pain and anguish, intense and fervent. While the subject matter is very different to "Past, Present and Future," the poem focuses on the anguished state of a young woman and love—in this case, for her dying father.

These historical resonances situate the emotional intensity and heart-break experienced and conveyed by the protagonist of "Past, Present and Future" firmly within the context of 19th-century Romanticism.[70] The song is highly emotional and intimate. The protagonist begins by nostalgically evoking an idyllic past, with images of childhood and innocent play:

> The past . . . well now let me tell you about the past
> The past is filled with silent joys and broken toys,
> laughing girls and teasing boys . . . [71]

Lurking in the background, however, are hints of the darkness to come, projected in hindsight; the joys are silent, toys broken. Into this world has intruded the event that caused the pain and heartbreak she will shortly evoke in her shattered present:

> Was I ever in love? I called it love . . .

Unmoored, on shaky ground, she is no longer sure about the reality of this love. Was she taken for a ride, duped? Was it real?

> I mean, it felt like love,
> There were moments when,
> well, there were moments when . . .

She trails off, and lands in the brutal present. Engaging in an imaginary dialogue with, it is assumed, a boy, she asks herself questions that he could be expected to ask, and answers them:

Go out with you? Why not.
Do I like to dance? Of course.
Take a walk along the beach tonight? I'd love to.[72]

To go out, to dance, and to walk along the beach—these are staples of mid-60s teen dating activity that would generally be understood to send a teenage girl in 1966 into paroxysms of excitement. But the protagonist is capable only of listless resignation; just as the young woman who is the subject of 'The Praying Girl' has her youth gnawed away by anguish. Numb, devastated, it's easier just to agree—it's all hopeless and pointless anyway, so indeed, why not go out with you? But ominously, she continues,

But don't try to touch me, don't try to touch me
'Cause that will never happen again.

After a detached, rhetorical, almost sarcastic 'Shall we dance . . . ,' the song then launches full tilt into a middle eight that is a whirling, almost psychotic wall-of-sound waltz. Not the Shing-a-Ling, the Monkey, or the Sophisticated Boom Boom, but a *waltz*, a dance form that reached its peak of popularity in the 19th century and is inextricably associated with Romanticism. As Ruth Katz has explained, the waltz broke down the formality of earlier dance forms (much like Beethoven was breaking down the sonata form):

The waltz not only made it possible for different kinds of individuals to come together on an egalitarian basis, it also made possible a kind of 'escape' from reality through the thrilling dizziness of whirling one's way in a private world of sensuality. The 'letting go' function of a waltz seems relevant to a world without clear standards, in which the individual stood alone having to find his own way.[73]

As indeed the protagonist of "Past, Present and Future" must also find her own way. But structurally, within this song, the waltz also acts as a breaking pause, an interlude between the 'Present' and the 'Future.' There are hints that this may be reflected psychologically in the mind of the protagonist—that despite the devastation of the past and her bleak view of 'the future,' the waltz may perform a liminal function, allowing her to break with the past, and move forward:

> Tomorrow? Well tomorrow's a long way off
> Maybe someday I'll have somebody's hand
> Maybe somewhere someone will understand . . .
>
> But at the moment it doesn't look good
> At the moment it will never happen again
>
> I don't think it will ever happen again.

"Past, Present and Future" ends bleakly with an evocation of an idealised past and a shattered future, but our protagonist has at least moved from 'that will never' to '*I don't think* it will ever' happen again.[74]

In a 1966 interview with Richard Goldstein in the *Village Voice* just after the release of "Past, Present and Future," Mary Ann Ganser took aim at listeners who were unable to take the group's emotional intensity seriously:

> 'They say our stuff is corny, well a lot of people eat corn. Besides, if that were true, then we wouldn't sell. Which we do. Our lines are realistic and frank. Take our latest single. The girl who's talking in it has had one tragic affair, and is obviously hung up on it. Well, we never say she's hung up because she let herself go. We don't put her down for it.'[75]

This renders Ada Wolin's previously noted assertion that 'Weiss was able to find genuineness in a song that was never meant to be genuine' patently ludicrous, not to mention patronising.[76] Mary Ann Ganser made it clear that as far as the group members were concerned, the Shangri-Las spoke to their teenage audience with sincerity and directness, and took the pain of their heartbreak seriously. The author of the article, Richard Goldstein, commented further,

Their heroines are the victims of high tragedy and negligent parents, intense loyalty and exotic romance. The teens in these songs have never heard of the "cool" generation; they are actively, passionately, hopelessly involved. Crying is a sign of tragic involvement in Shangri-La ballads; it never implies cowardice or effeminacy.[77]

In August 1966, Californian music newspaper *KRLA Beat* ran an article entitled 'Three Shangri-Las: Grooving in Utopia,' in which they were described as

three young girls who are so different and refreshing that they are in a sort of utopian category all their own.

The Shangri-Las sound is offbeat. It is a weird, distinct sensation with taunting lyrics that contain sometimes-overlooked, deep-rooted messages. It is something you would expect to hear in Greenwich Village or in a smoke-filled room housing a conglomeration of beat poets . . .

Most of the songs by the Shangri-Las have that same element of beauty but all seem to contain the same degree of a serene sadness. Their latest release, "Past, present and Future," which also is a top seller, is probably their most hauntingly sad song yet.[78]

Neither Goldstein, writing in New York, nor the *KRLA Beat* journalist writing for a Californian audience, displayed any discomfort whatsoever with the Shangri-Las' emotionalism. Forty years later, reflecting on her performance in "Past, Present and Future," Mary Weiss said,

I had no conception of what love was at the time. But I really, I had to have almost every light in the studio out on that one, and I was crying my brains out . . . if you have a lot of issues in your life, and you've converted it into music, everything you're feeling, that's your release, that's where you put it, and that's what I did. It was a very helpful release, I think much like anybody that paints, or does anything like that.[79]

This calls to mind the notion of method acting, but also the Romantic idea of total immersion in art. Beethoven's close associate Carl Czerny had an understanding of a 'correct performance' of a Beethoven work as being characterised by 'an *attitude* toward the music.' As Beethoven scholar Kenneth Drake explained,

> Czerny was stating, as the one, all-encompassing rule of perfor-
> mance practice for the playing of Beethoven, total personal involve-
> ment . . . becoming possessed by the music, cerebrally, muscularly,
> and subjectively.[80]

I am not arguing that Mary Weiss's performance in "Past, Present and Future" constituted one that Czerny would recognise as 'the playing of Beethoven,' but I *am* suggesting that dimming the lights in the studio and crying one's brains out was a fair way along the road to 'total per-sonal involvement' and 'becoming possessed by the music.' As George 'Shadow' Morton marvelled,

> Here she was, this teenage girl with no experience in show-biz, and
> I made her act out all these crazy parts . . . Nobody else was doing
> anything like "Past Present and Future" and "I Can Never Go Home
> Anymore" . . . I musta been out of my skull . . . but no matter what I
> asked her to do, she delivered, each and every time.[81]

Mary Weiss was accessing personal anguish in order to achieve emo-tional conviction, and to enable a deep emotional engagement with the material she was performing. Keeping the events that were the source of the pain oblique rather than explicit ensured that any heartbroken teenager could relate to and share in the protagonist's grief.

Given the pain, heartbreak and emotional desolation that form the subject matter of "Past, Present and Future," the song's use of the 'Moonlight' Sonata takes on an even greater significance. While com-posing this sonata, Beethoven was in love with a young woman. He was also suffering increasingly from hearing problems—tinnitus and worsening deafness. For a musician and composer, especially one of Beethoven's stature, this represented a tragedy of unspeakable propor-tions. On October 6, 1802, in a letter to his brothers which has become known as the *Heiligenstadt Testament*, Beethoven wrote at length about the deterioration of his hearing:

But what a humiliation for me when someone standing next to me heard a flute in the distance and *I heard nothing*, or someone heard a *shepherd singing* and again I heard nothing. Such incidents drove me almost to despair, a little more of that and I would have ended my life—it was only *my art* that held me back. Ah, it seemed to me impossible to leave the world until I had brought forth all that I felt was within me. So I endured this wretched existence . . . [82]

Almost a year earlier, he had spoken of both his deafness and his love in a letter to Dr Franz Gerhard Wegeler (a physician and friend since childhood):

I am living more pleasantly now, since I mingle with more people. You will scarcely believe how lonely and sad my life has been for the last two years. My bad hearing haunted me everywhere like a ghost and I fled—from mankind. I seemed like a misanthrope, and yet am far from being one. This change has been wrought by a dear fascinating girl who loves me and whom I love. There have been a few blessed moments within the last two years, and it is the first time I feel that—marriage might bring me happiness. Unfortunately she is not of my station—and now—it would be impossible for me to marry.—I must still hustle about most actively. If it were not for my deafness, I should before now have traveled over half the world, and that I must do.[83]

This 'dear fascinating girl' was almost certainly Countess Giulietta Guicciardi, who was 17 when she met Beethoven in 1800 and became one of his piano students.[84] Beethoven dedicated the 'Moonlight' Sonata to her, and although the exact nature of their relationship remains unclear, it is generally accepted that Beethoven was for some time in love with Guicciardi, and was certainly in love with her in 1801.[85]

The dedication of the 'Moonlight' Sonata to Giulietta Guicciardi has been the subject of much critical discussion, and it has been suggested that it was in fact inspired by his love for her.[86] It has also fuelled speculation that an unaddressed, passionate love letter and two postscripts—all written but unsent by Beethoven, and only discovered after his death—were intended for her. In the second postscript, he addressed his 'immortal beloved'; the fact that all three missives were not dated

with a year resulted in well over a century's worth of critical speculation and discussion as to when Beethoven wrote them and the identity of the 'immortal beloved.'[87] Some of this, as Eric Blom put it, has
been 'sentimental commentators insisting on seeing [the 'Moonlight'
Sonata] as a musical counterpart to the love letter,' and consequently
Giulietta Guicciardi as a prime candidate for the 'immortal beloved.'[88]
The Beethoven/Guicciardi romance ended, however, when Guicciardi
married Count Wenzel Robert Gallenberg (a composer of ballet music)
in 1803 and relocated to Italy with him.[89] It has been suggested that
Beethoven's deepening realisation that the social gulf he referred to in
1801 ('she is not of my station') was unbridgeable contributed further
to the despair evident in the *Heiligenstadt Testament*.[90] Alexander Wheelock Thayer (1817-1897), author of the first scholarly biography of Beethoven, speculated,

> Beethoven at length decided to offer Countess Julia his hand; that
> she was not indisposed to accept it, and that one of her parents con-
> sented to the match, but the other, probably the father, refused to
> entrust the happiness of his daughter to a man without rank, fortune
> or permanent engagement; a man, too, of character and tempera-
> ment so peculiar, and afflicted with the incipient stages of an infir-
> mity which, if not arrested and cured, must deprive him of all hope
> of obtaining any high and remunerative official appointment and
> at length compel him to abandon his career as the great pianoforte
> virtuoso. As the Guicciardis themselves were not wealthy, prudence
> forbade such a marriage.[91]

Guicciardi's marriage with Gallenberg later broke down, and she
returned to Vienna in 1822. At some point she attempted to renew her
acquaintance with Beethoven; he reportedly said, 'she visited me weeping, but I scorned her.'[92] In the same conversation, he stated that Guicciardi had loved him more than she ever had her husband.[93]

From the moment of its publication, the 'Moonlight' Sonata was
bound up with doomed love and tragedy. It was dedicated by the composer to a teenage 'girl who loves me and whom I love,' a love that was
a temporary respite from the anguish, isolation and social exclusion
caused by his worsening deafness. This love could not be, however,
because Ludwig was not of the same 'station' as Guicciardi; for her, this

was the early 19th-century equivalent of dating a guy 'from the wrong side of town,' as the Shangri-Las famously sang in "Leader of the Pack," and Countess Giulietta accordingly married a count. This whole tragic affair was not merely of interest to a group of squabbling Beethoven obsessives, either; the story formed the basis of a major film, *Immortal Beloved* (1994), starring Gary Oldman and Valeria Golino.[94]

Small wonder, given all these factors, that the 'Moonlight' Sonata possesses, as Beethoven scholar Lewis Lockwood put it, 'a succession of intense emotional atmospheres unlike any other early Beethoven sonata.'[95] On the subject of 'intense emotional atmospheres,' "Past, Present and Future," like "Remember (Walkin' in the Sand)," is steeped in reverb and echo. These effects create a sense of cavernous space, which emphasises *sonically* the loneliness, devastation, and heartbreak of the protagonist. Amazingly, the *Adagio Sostenuto* movement of the 'Moonlight' Sonata comes with the playing instruction, 'the whole piece should be played very delicately and without dampers.'[96] This has resulted in decades worth of controversy about what Beethoven actually meant. Virtuoso pianist András Schiff has recorded and conducted master-classes on all 32 of Beethoven's piano sonatas.[97] Of this one, he noted,

> Consider the so-called 'Moonlight' Sonata . . . this is a fantastic sonata. The first movement is playable by amateurs, but they tend to think of "moonlight" instead of actually reading the score, in which Beethoven asks the player to hold down the pedal for the entire movement. Most players ignore this, saying it is not practical on today's instruments. But they never really give it a try. Beethoven was inventing sounds and sonorities that no one thought of before. Using the pedal—raising the dampers so that the strings continue to vibrate—allows sounds that do not traditionally belong together to blend into a cloud. He's going against the textbook.[98]

Beethoven's pedalling techniques raised eyebrows at the time—Czerny noted in the early 1800s that the 'partisans' of his rival, composer and pianist Johann Hummel

> accused Beethoven of mistreating the piano, of lacking all cleanness and clarity, of creating nothing but confused noise the way he

used the pedal, and finally of writing wilful, unnatural, unmelodic compositions.[99]

Schiff describes Beethoven as 'the first great composer of the pedal,' and has argued that 'he wanted a very special sonority, a very special sound,' so 'that the harmonies swim together like in a wash, and the overtones are strengthening each other.'[100] This sounds awfully like Beethoven was attempting to create some form of echo and reverb of his own.

The use of the first movement of Beethoven's 'Moonlight' Sonata as the foundation for "Past, Present and Future" created a whole series of resonances that lend the song a gravitas which enabled it to transcend its original milieu of mid-60s New York City. It paired an *actual monologue* with a piece of music that employed a form, the sonata, that was understood to function as a *musical monologue*—personal, intimate and uniquely capable of expressing emotion. It is not really so surprising that, as early as 1816, Dr Georg Grosheim had the idea of using the first movement of the 'Moonlight' Sonata as the musical setting for a piece of poetic anguish centred on a young female protagonist. As a composer and teacher himself, he would have been well-versed in the conventions of 18th- and 19th-century sonata theory. But it *is* quite extraordinary that a similar idea occurred to a wild young songwriter and producer from Brooklyn nicknamed 'Shadow' (because of his habit of disappearing, usually into bars) 150 years later and in a social, musical and historical context far removed from that of early 19th-century Vienna. In all likelihood this was largely accidental; Morton chose the 'Moonlight' Sonata because its melancholy—immediately apparent without any knowledge of its historical context—suited the Shangri-Las' deeply intense and emotional aesthetic. As Morton related:

> "Past, Present and Future" was an incredible session. The song came about at 3 o'clock one morning in Jerry Leiber's office. Artie Butler was there at the piano playing song after song while me and Jerry were doing the brandy. He played a tune, which I did not recognise. I asked him to keep playing it, and I wrote the song right there and then on a piece of paper. Later on, when I got my royalty cheque, it was for half the amount I expected. Leiber said, 'What about your

co-writer?' I said, 'What co-writer?' He said, 'Beethoven, for one.' I honestly did not know. I wasn't ignorant, just innocent.[101]

Nevertheless, its presence in "Past, Present and Future" links the Shangri-Las' intense emotionalism to 19th-century Romanticism, with its emphasis on immersion in emotion as fundamental to the creative process, just as references to deeply-rooted metaphorical associations involving the beach and the sea in "Remember (Walkin' in the Sand)" invoke themes of loneliness and desolation, love and death in the Western artistic tradition dating back over two thousand years. And the performance of this material by the Shangri-Las—in particular the passionate intensity of Mary Weiss—ensures that the emotionality conveyed in both songs is not only believable, but utterly compelling.

Mary Ann Ganser, Betty Weiss, and Mary Weiss (*Pictorial Press Ltd / Alamy*)

CHAPTER EIGHT

Four Last Songs

> Leaf after golden leaf
> Falls from the tall acacia.
> Summer smiles, astonished and drained,
> Into the garden's dying dream.[1]

When journalist Mitchell Cohen observed in 1974 that 'the commercial success of the Shangri-Las began and ended on the beach,' he was referring to the group's Red Bird material. "Remember (Walkin' in the Sand) is thematically linked, in part by beach references, to "Past, Present and Future," the last recording by the Shangri-Las to enter the Hot 100.[2] However, the Shangri-Las recorded another, final 'beach' song. Following the collapse of Red Bird, the group signed (as a trio) to Mercury Records and recorded two further singles; these would be their last releases as a group. "Sweet Sounds of Summer" b/w "I'll Never Learn" was released in late 1966, and "Take the Time" b/w "Footsteps on the Roof" early in 1967.[3] Neither was a commercial success: "Sweet Sounds of Summer" reached #123 and "Take the Time" failed to chart at all.[4] As a consequence, both singles are generally perceived to be embarrassing failures and rarely feature in discussions of the group and their recordings, except to be speedily dismissed.[5] Alan Betrock, for example, described these two singles as 'glossy, slick, dishonest pieces of plastic which were as misdirected as the girls themselves were.'[6] This derisive assessment does not recognise the value of these recordings as a window into the final months of the Shangri-Las as a recording entity. Their new label seemingly attempted to 'update' and reconfigure the Shangri-Las as a group with a young adult, rather than teen, appeal, which involved forcing them into inappropriate markets. Three of the four songs the group recorded for Mercury ("I'll Never Learn" was the exception) were self-referential in some way, quoting lyrics from earlier Red Bird material or using similar sound effects and lyrical themes, presumably in an attempt to manufacture some kind of continuity between the group's existing oeuvre and their new material.

"Sweet Sounds of Summer" was released in December 1966.[7] Billboard reported that 'the girls have a winner with this unusual material reminiscent of their "Remember (Walkin' in the Sand)."[8] From the outset, it was perceived as a companion piece to "Remember," and indeed, the beach setting, romantic subject matter and bird-noise sound effects seem to have been deliberately employed to encourage the listener to situate the song in this context. The song was written by Larry Martire, who had been listed as 'Personal Management' for the Shangri-Las since at least December 1964.[9] George 'Shadow' Morton was credited as arranger on the label of the record, which also read 'A Phantom Production by Shadow.' According to John Grecco, 'Phantom Productions' was a co-operative venture between Morton and Martire that included George Goldner; Mick Patrick states that it was a company that Morton set up with Tony Michaels and Vinny Gormann (authors of "Dressed in Black"), but the exact nature of its operations remains unclear.[10]

By late 1966, when "Sweet Sounds of Summer" was recorded, the landscape of popular music had undergone rapid and dramatic changes. Billboard's end-of-year "Top LPs" wrap-up included the Beach Boys' Pet Sounds, The Beatles' Rubber Soul and Revolver, and Bob Dylan's Blonde on Blonde, in amongst the Mantovani and Tijuana Brass records that were still a dominant presence in the charts.[11] These four albums are perhaps not a representative sample of the records released in 1966, but they show the direction in which popular music was evolving. They were written by the performers themselves, were in different ways introspective and psychedelic, containing various veiled and not-so-veiled drug references. Blonde on Blonde, for instance, contains "Rainy Day Women #12 & 35," with its lurching, drunken New Orleans-brass band feel and 'everybody must get stoned' refrain. On the West Coast, Ken Kesey was conducting his infamous Acid Tests, and the Grateful Dead became involved in this scene, taking LSD and playing a loose, freeform style of rock music.[12]

In April of 1966, the Byrds released "Eight Miles High," widely considered to be the first psychedelic hit.[13] Billboard made no mention of its references to drug use, of course, describing the song as a 'big beat rhythm rocker with soft lyric ballad vocal and off-beat instrumental backing.'[14] The song had its origins as a poem written by Gene Clark, and evolved into "Eight Miles High" with input from Roger McGuinn and David Crosby (the authorship of the song has been the subject of some dispute). Clark acknowledged in 1985 that it was initially inspired by an 'airplane trip to England,' but was also 'about drugs . . . because during those days the new experimenting with all the drugs was a very vogue thing to do.'[15] Mysterious and enigmatic, its clear acid-trip allusions were denied strenuously by group members in the face of a US radio ban over alleged drug references. Despite this, "Eight Miles High" reached #14 on the *Billboard Hot 100*. Years later, David Crosby admitted,

> Did I think "Eight Miles High" was a drug song? No, I *knew* it was. We denied it, of course. But we had a strong feeling about drugs, or rather, psychedelics and marijuana. We thought they would help us blast our generation loose from the fifties. Personally, I don't regret my psychedelic experiences. I took psychedelics as a sort of sacrament.[16]

In a July 1966 article in the *New York Times*, Richard Lingeman discussed at length the ways in which 'psychedelic culture has now made interpenetrations into public society,' but stated,

> It is difficult to see how the following (from "Eight Miles High") encourages drug-taking, or anything else:
> *Eight miles high and when you touch down*
> *You'll find that it's stranger than known*
> *Signs in the streets that say where you're going*
> *Are somewhere just being their own.*[17]

Lingeman's assertion highlights the pitfalls of discussing song lyrics without reference to their musical setting—because lyrics alone do not constitute a song. With music and or songs that might be termed 'psychedelic,' there are, as Russell Reising put it, 'common techniques that convey a musical equivalent of a hallucinogenic experience.'[18] Sheila Whiteley has referred to such techniques as 'psychedelic coding':

These include the manipulation of timbre (blurred, bright, over-lapping), upward movement (and its comparison with psychedelic flight), harmonies (lurching, oscillating), rhythms (regular, irregular), relationships (foreground, background) and collages which provide a point of comparison with more conventionalized, i.e. normal treatment.[19]

In "Eight Miles High" rhythms are fractured, instrumentation thick and layered, and Roger McGuinn famously attempted to emulate John Coltrane's free-jazz explorations while the overtones produced by his 12-string Rickenbacker simultaneously created a sitar-like effect.[20] Similarly, the Beatles' "Tomorrow Never Knows" (on *Revolver*) featured sitar, tape loops, irregular drumming, and Eastern-influenced mystical lyrics. As Reising has pointed out, one of the areas in which a 'psychedelic' influence is particularly obvious in music is with timing. Psychedelic music plays with time, emulating the manner in which 'the passage of time seems to slow down tremendously when under the influence of acid. A few minutes may seem like hours, a few hours may seem like days.'[21] Much psychedelic rock and pop music disrupts time in various ways—longer, more drawn-out songs, non-standard rock time signatures, and tempo changes—slowing down and speeding up. Sometimes this takes place in conjunction with more overt references to time. "Time Has Come Today" by the Chambers Brothers, originally recorded in 1966 but not released until 1968, opens with the simulated ticking of a clock, and features a long, spaced-out acid-rock middle section in which the ticking and tempo alter drastically.[22] Although "Eight Miles High" is contained within a short pop-song format, its middle section is slowed-down and sprawling, and the whole song is recognisably psychedelic.

That this was popular with a mainstream record-buying audience in mid-1966 is significant, because "Sweet Sounds of Summer" was quite clearly an attempt to 'psychedelicise' the Shangri-Las. The song opens with a repeated echo-laden piano motif that is vaguely reminiscent of "Remember," but not nearly as intense or ponderous. This is accompanied by twittering birds, but unlike the seagulls in "Remember," whose cries echo in space and emphasise the loneliness and desolation of the protagonist, these birds seem to perform no identifiable metaphoric function beyond representing a 'sweet sound of summer.' A wandering melodic flute line weaves through the verse, and snippets of fuzz-laden guitar give the song a slightly trippy, psychedelic feel. Another reference to "Remember" (with its repeated, incantational chorus) is present in the backing vocals, immediately preceding the chorus:

(*Remember*) Sweet sounds of summer
Guitars are strumming and
Sea breeze is humming with our song . . . [23]

Ostensibly, the lyrics revolve around a romantic liaison that took place at the beach but has now ended, which is familiar Shangri-Las territory. Instead of the emotional intensity and sophisticated use of metaphor found in "Remember," however, the opening verse of "Sweet Sounds" is grammatically clumsy and metaphorically heavy-handed:

Once I'd wake up, I'd reach out and take your hand
The sky was our blanket, our pillow was the sand
And on the beach, that's where we fell in love
The only one who shared our love were [*sic*] the bright stars up above . . . [24]

Locations and emotions are stated rather than suggested, in a manner that is completely at odds with the Shangri-Las' earlier material. Furthermore, the heartbreak experienced by the protagonist that is referenced in the lyrics is not matched by the musical accompaniment; the jaunty, upbeat, major-key tonality works against such lines as

Now all I have is my lonely room, and winter's call
The only sound that can be heard are [*sic*] my teardrops as they fall.[25]

This creates a great sense of contradiction. By not focusing the constituent elements of the song in a unified direction, its overall effect is weakened; it seems inconsequential rather than powerful.

"Sweet Sounds of Summer" also contains a psychedelic middle section which, although presaged by the flute and fuzz-guitar in the verses, is nevertheless a significant enough departure from the rest of the song to seem like a notable disjunction. As the protagonist describes how she was 'So very lost and in love/So very lost . . . ,' the song drops away into a droning high register organ motif, punctuated by backing vocals of 'Quiet!' followed by 'Don't Stop!' and 'More!' placed back in the mix to give the impression of distant voices. A formless organ motif is then regulated with percussive tambourine hits that unmistakably resemble the metronomic ticking of a clock. Handclaps, rumbling drums and snatches of fuzz-laden guitar are introduced as the organ fades in and out, and the overall effect metaphorically likens the headiness of a new summer love to an acid trip. The song then crescendos back into a (final) verse, and back into reality:

> Say life's a game and it hurries by so fast
> So if you find someone to love, do your best to make it last
> We were too young and the summer's come and gone
> Till the time we meet again the memory lingers on.[26]

Such neat, trite sentiments contrast sharply with the majority of the Shangri-Las' earlier material, which explored themes of emotional devastation and parental conflict in a complex but emotionally direct manner. As we have seen, the performative abilities of the Shangri-Las, particularly Mary Weiss, were particularly evident in material that required a deep level of emotional immersion; "Remember (Walkin' in the Sand)" and its ancient cultural resonances and ocean imagery are especially relevant here. "Sweet Sounds of Summer" possessed little scope for performative emotionality, and none of the deep cultural resonances of "Remember." The deliberate positioning by Morton and Martire of "Sweet Sounds of Summer" as its companion piece unfortunately ensured that "Sweet Sounds" appeared totally lightweight by comparison.

As noted earlier, Larry Martire is listed as the writer of "Sweet Sounds of Summer," but available evidence suggests that his music industry background involved little in the way of songwriting. Late in 1960, he was arrested in connection with a large-scale, Mafia-funded record bootlegging operation, the purpose of which had been to 'flood the pre-Christmas market with $1.5 million worth of bogus LPs by Frank Sinatra and Johnny Mathis.' Also arrested in the raids was Gaetano Vastola, an already notorious DeCavalcante Mafia figure with a stake in Roulette Records and close ties to Morris Levy.[27] Martire, Vastola and four others were indicted in March 1961; they finally pleaded guilty to charges of 'disk counterfeiting' in May 1962.[28] A series of FBI wire taps between 1961 and 1965 implicated Vastola in various fraud and extortion conspiracies; he was convicted and jailed for extortion in 1972.[29] Martire and Vastola maintained their ties for over twenty years: both were charged in 1986, along with Morris Levy, in a famous case involving the sale of 'cutouts' from the MCA catalogue to John LaMonte, a Pennsylvania record dealer who also had prior convictions for record counterfeiting.[30] 'Cutouts' were records a company had decided not to re-press, usually due to falling demand. The records were deleted from catalogues and the remaining copies sold at discount rates to record dealers, who then made them available for sale in stores at an attractive price (a hole was punched in the corner of the sleeve or the corner of the sleeve was snipped off to distinguish them from full-priced stock). Levy and Vastola were charged with making 'extortionate loans,' and Martire with 'teaming to obtain usurious interest payments ... "induced by wrongful use of fear and injury to the person and property" of LaMonte,' who was brutally assaulted and had his jaw broken by Vastola.[31]

The American Society of Composers, Authors and Publishers (ASCAP) has no entry for Larry Martire, but Broadcast Music Incorporated (BMI) has four songs registered under his name; "Sweet Sounds of Summer" is the only one for which he is credited as the sole writer.[32] He received a co-credit on "Dum Dum Ditty," which was written by Tommy Boyce, Bobby Hart and Steven Venet, professional songwriters most famous for writing much of the material performed by the Monkees. "Dum Dum Ditty" was originally recorded by the Goodies, and later by the Shangri-Las.[33] "Karate Man" was co-credited to Martire and Jerry Ciccone, a musician who played guitar on a Left Banke album (recorded after the departure of singer/songwriter Mike Brown) called *Left Banke Too* (1968).[34] Martire was also co-credited for "Eye for an Eye" with Joe Simmons, a prolific songwriter throughout the 1960s with over one hundred registered compositions.[35] It seems unlikely that these established songwriters would require assistance from Martire; it is far more likely that he received songwriting credits for reasons other than musical contribution. According to John Grecco, the ideas for the song were Martire's, but they were shaped into usable form by Ellie Greenwich and George 'Shadow' Morton, who apparently did not see fit to accept writing credits.[36]

It is tempting to speculate about why this recording was released as the A-side of an important single (with far better-quality material relegated to the B-side—more on that shortly). It is likely that Martire and Morton had some form of legal/financial arrangement (Phantom Productions) through which Morton could produce and work with the Shangri-Las at Mercury. The Shangri-Las were signed to the label; the arrangement (if any) that Morton had with Mercury is unclear, but he seems not to have been a staff songwriter in the way he was at Red Bird. That none of the four sides recorded by the Shangri-Las for Mercury were written by Morton would seem to bear this out. Morton was on board as an arranger and producer (as he was credited on the labels of the records), but perhaps embedded somewhere in the deal was an understanding that Martire would have *his* song recorded and released as the A-side, for which he would take the majority of the royalties, being listed as sole songwriter. If so, Morton would have worked with the material as best he could, adding some of his trademark sound effects and flourishes, as well as a psychedelic middle section. This was indicative of the direction he would shortly take with Vanilla Fudge, whose Morton-produced debut album, containing the hit version of "You Keep Me Hanging On," was released in mid-1967.[37]

Martire and Mercury may well have attempted to capitalise on a successful formula—the Shangri-Las, Morton, and the beach—updated with a contemporary spin, but Martire's inexperience as a songwriter resulted in substandard material that Morton and the group were obliged, contractually or otherwise, to record. That this song was released as an A-side at the expense of a far more sophisticated and well-written B-side, penned by an experienced and extremely talented songwriter, seems a decision made, yet again, on the basis of selfishness, avarice, with the hope of short-term gain rather than with the best interests of the group in mind.

The B-side of "Sweet Sounds of Summer" was "I'll Never Learn," written by 18-year-old Sandra Hurvitz, who would later be known as Essra Mohawk. Within a couple of years she would achieve cult fame as a short-term member of Frank Zappa's Mothers of Invention and begin to cement her reputation as a singer-songwriter with a series of critically acclaimed solo records.[38] By the time the Shangri-Las recorded "I'll Never Learn," late in 1966, Hurvitz had already enjoyed a brief but well-respected career as a songwriter and performer. In 1965 under the name Jamie Carter, she had released a single called "The Boy with the Way,"[39] which was a *Cash Box* 'Newcomer Pick' for the week of 7 August

1965. It featured in *Billboard*'s 'Pop Spotlights' the same week, where it was described by the reviewer as 'a ballad that starts simply and builds into a frenzy with screeching brass in full support. Watch this one!'[40] On the strength of this, Hurvitz was offered positions as a staff-song-writer at Koppelman & Rubin and United Artists; she declined both.[41] It is likely that this song is what brought her to Morton's attention; he was sufficiently impressed with the quality of her work to have the Shangri-Las record "I'll Never Learn," and later include two of her songs on *Renaissance*, the third Vanilla Fudge album, which he produced, in 1968. In short, unlike Larry Martire, Hurvitz was a young, talented and extremely competent songwriter.

With its themes of anguish, loss and regret, "I'll Never Learn" sits effortlessly alongside the Shangri-Las' Red Bird oeuvre. Like "Past, Present, and Future," with its clear links to the Western classical tradition, "I'll Never Learn" eschews standard pop music instrumentation and features stringed chamber instruments, predominantly violins and cellos. Mary Weiss's vocals are intense and despondent, soaring high in the mix as she sings of dreaming in pained delirium of her lost lover, in language that represents a clear shift in a more psychedelic direction:

> Here I am in a dream
> Immersed in liquid sea of love
> Shimmering rainbow bubbles
> From the sky above
> A looking glass that reflects
> The past . . . [42]

The instrumentation during the verses consists of delicate, lilting phrases with long notes and minimal, syncopated jazz-like drumming, with brushes. The unusually placed backing vocals are ethereal and heavily overlaid with echo, creating a slightly unsteady, dream-like atmosphere which complements the half-spoken, skat-like lyrics. All this drops away for the chorus (in the manner of "Remember"), during which the protagonist is awake in reality, rather than the dream-like state of the verse:

> But I wake up
> Sit here thinkin,' thinkin' about

The happy times we used to have
Now they're gone forever
I still have to wait for their return
No
I'll never learn, I'll never learn
My eyes they burn
From sleepless crying . . . [43]

This altered emotional state is reflected musically by minimal chamber instrumentation, a non-syncopated rhythm and a canon-like, cyclic four-chord repeated phrase with long notes that slow the tempo of the song momentarily. Mary Weiss conveys these contrasting states in a completely convincing manner, imbuing the material, which is a perfect vehicle for her strengths as performer, with her trademark emotional power. "I'll Never Learn" ends with an extraordinary staggered echo of the word 'hell,' and is as dark, impassioned, and bleak as any of the Shangri-Las finest Red Bird material.

What "Sweet Sounds of Summer" seemed to strain awkwardly towards, "I'll Never Learn" achieves with ease. It places the Shangri-Las in familiar territory of emotional anguish and lost love, achieving a seamless continuity with their existing body of work, giving the group material that highlights their strengths and enables them to shine in a different context. It also extends the experimentation with song structures that characterised recent work such as "Past, Present and Future" and continues the classically-styled instrumentation that helped locate the group within a wider artistic tradition. "I'll Never Learn" also functions as an elegant bridge between their earlier material and a more psychedelically oriented direction; if this had been pursued, it might well have led to a different outcome for the group, especially if their first outing on Mercury had been even a moderate success. Instead, in what was a clear conflict of interest, their management selfishly and short-sightedly relegated "I'll Never Learn" to the B-side of a single that had been 'penned' by their manager, who had never distinguished himself as a songwriter, either before or since.

The final release for the Shangri-Las was "Take the Time" b/w "Footsteps on the Roof," released by Mercury in March, 1967. Both sides were written by Sal Trimachi and Ritchie Cordell, two professional songwriters whose song "It's Only Love" was a hit for Tommy James and the Shondells in 1966.[44] Morris Levy, mobster and owner of Roulette Records, also received a songwriting credit; this was 'payment' for allowing James to record material for Roulette by Cordell and Trimachi, who had a contractual arrangement with (none other than) Artie Ripp.[45] In the next couple of years, Trimachi and Cordell would become famous as bubblegum writers for the Buddah label, an arm of Ripp's Kama Sutra company, and this is a likely explanation for the Kama Sutra credit on the record label of "Take the Time." Morton was again credited as producer and arranger, and George Goldner as musical supervisor, presumably as part of the Phantom Productions deal. It is almost inconceivable that the ensuing recordings were the results of a collaboration by such a collection of musical heavyweights; it is far more likely that—as had happened throughout the Shangri-Las' recording career—royalties and publishing shares were being parcelled out for reasons that had little, if anything, to do with the group.

Billboard reviewed "Take the Time" favourably, noting that 'tambourines shake out the driving rhythm lending solid, easy dance beat support to the girls' strong vocal workout.' The song also possessed what *Billboard* described as in a tellingly non-specific way as 'powerful lyrical content.'[46] The lyrics do not refer to the conflict by name, but it is quite clear that "Take the Time" is a patriotic statement of support for US involvement in the war in Vietnam. When asked by Billy Miller in 2006 about "Take the Time," which he referred to as 'weird, a pro-Vietnam record,' Mary Weiss replied,

> I never wanted to record that song. I was completely against the Vietnam War and I protested accordingly. Still, the Shangri-Las supported our servicemen and women and I've done many shows for them.[47]

Miller's comment demonstrates the degree to which hindsight informs perceptions of the relationship between the Vietnam War and the popular music released during that time. John Grecco has commented,

> Another single, "Take the Time," was finished and readied for release in 1967. A patriotic song, it unfortunately seemed to condone U.S. action in Viet Nam, at a time when many wisely disapproved of any

involvement. With a theme like this, the reason it didn't chart should be obvious.[48]

If this reasoning was accurate, and 'the reason it didn't chart . . . obvious,' it would indeed be a bewildering logic that governed the recording and release of such a single—tantamount to consigning the Shangri-Las to commercial suicide. A closer examination of the historical and musical context into which "Take the Time" was released reveals, in fact, a more complex set of circumstances than the two assessments cited above would suggest.

Kenneth Bindas and Craig Houston have described how the 1960s are remembered as 'an era of swirling change and social protest' with the perception that 'the decade's music fostered a social revolution and spoke for the ideals of young people.'[49] They point out, however, that rock and pop music, while perceived as anti-establishment, was by no means unanimous in its condemnation of the Vietnam War.[50] David James has also noted that 'what is remarkable about late 60s rock, not least in the San Francisco Renaissance, is that its central instrumentality in countercultural formation coincided with a virtual absence of any cogent analysis of the war or even critical attention to it.'[51] This assessment is supported by war veteran Lee Ballinger, who remembered,

> despite what some may choose to think, rock and roll was never fundamentally antiwar; it was a soundtrack for the entire process, of which opposition was only a part. Rock also served to let civilians forget about the war, just as it allowed those who were in Vietnam or had somebody there to make it through just one more day without doing anything about the situation.[52]

In his study of the relationship between popular music and the Vietnam War, Lee Andresen writes that 'those who supported the war were far from silent musically and there are many recordings, both well-known and obscure, that propagated the "hawkish" philosophy.'[53] Historically, popular songs recorded or published during the twentieth century largely supported US military policy; it was only during the Vietnam War that this began to change.[54]

Folk singers were amongst the earliest protestors against the Vietnam War. By 1963, older, more established performers, including Pete

Seeger, Peter Yarrow and Malvina Reynolds, openly questioned US involvement. Younger singers—Tom Paxton, Phil Ochs, Joan Baez, Bob Dylan—followed suit, but at this time spoke to a limited, non-mainstream audience.[55] This could not be said of Barry McGuire, however, whose single "Eve of Destruction"—written by P. F. Sloan, a 19-year-old West Coast singer/songwriter and session musician[56] —entered the *Billboard Hot 100* on 21 August 1965.[57] McGuire's gravelly voice bristled with frustration and anger as he spat out vitriol against a litany of issues. The song begins,

> The eastern world, it is exploding
> Violence flarin,' bullets loadin'
> You're old enough to kill, but not for votin'
> You don't believe in war, but what's that gun you're totin' . . .

The song also attacked impotent politicians, racial disharmony, nuclear war and religious hypocrisy, argued strenuously that 'this whole crazy world is just too frustratin,' and that ultimately, the world was apocalyptically 'on the eve of destruction.' It lacked subtlety, was rather heavy-handed, and was accused of attempting to cash in on the 'protest' bandwagon.[58] The strident lyrics were accompanied by ominous drums, steel-string acoustic guitar, and enough Dylan-esque harmonica to link the song musically to the folk/protest tradition and the trappings of authenticity this carried with it. Despite the objections raised about the song, McGuire was undeniably sincere, believed in what he was singing, and conveyed that convincingly, as he recalled:

> Phil [P.F. Sloan] wrote those songs that were just tailor-made for me. To have a songwriter that wrote so specifically what I felt to be true . . . I discovered a lot of truth in those songs.[59]

"Eve of Destruction" struck a chord with a large section of the record buying public and, unsurprisingly, ignited great controversy.

The lead article in the 21 August 1965 issue of *Billboard*, headlined 'Rock + Folk + Protest = An Erupting new Sound,' noted,

> With many notable exceptions, folk music has been more concerned with the message and the narration than the sound . . . the latest

development has been to take the rock sound and instrumentation and use folk oriented lyrics. The singer or group has something to say.

This 'hybrid,' noted *Billboard*, 'is selling across the board.'[60] Of particular note was

Barry McGuire's "Eve of Destruction," released last week on Dunhill. The beat is solid, but the lyric, aimed at teen-agers, deals with the dropping of a nuclear bomb.[61]

"Eve of Destruction" reached #1 on 25 September 1965, and as Richie Unterberger pointed out, its success was extraordinary:

Although "Eve of Destruction" was blunt in its delineation of civil rights clashes, war, and nuclear proliferation leading society to the brink of apocalypse, it was nonetheless remarkable to bring even the faintest discussion of such issues to commercial radio in 1965.[62]

There followed a significant backlash, resulting in considerable polarisation about overtly polemical releases. One San Francisco-area jukebox operator, Henry Leyser, said,

Out of personal conviction . . . I do not program this music. I wouldn't dream of programming it because, first and foremost, it is not entertainment. It's an indirect slap at the government. Let those who wish to hear it, listen to it at home.[63]

A significant number of explicitly patriotic releases followed in the wake of "Eve of Destruction," attempting to counter its success, influence, and 'message.' Almost immediately, a group called the Spokesmen released an 'answer' record called "Dawn of Correction."[64] The most famous and successful of the pro-military recordings was Barry Sadler's "The Ballad of the Green Berets," released early in 1966.[65]

On 22 January 1966, "The Ballad of the Green Berets" was the subject of a full-page colour advertisement (with type in two shades of green) in *Billboard*, announcing that this record was 'as timely as today's headlines!':

Backed by heavy consumer advertising, here is a hot new single with a ready-made market of millions who have read the bestselling book, "The Green Berets." Composed and sung by Staff Sergeant Barry Sadler who served with the Green Berets in Vietnam, here is the glory and heroism of the men who make up the U.S. Army Special Forces. Sadler's set for an appearance on the Ed Sullivan show January 30.[66]

It reached #1 on the *Billboard Hot 100* in March 1966 and remained there for five weeks.[67] As its title indicates, musically the song is a ballad, a form associated with traditional/folk music, which carries with it notions of directness and authenticity. The song was penned by Sadler, whose singing style is semi-spoken, with a marked lack of singerly flourishes; his delivery is syllabic rather than melismatic. This gives the song a speech-like air, that of a restrained but imploring directive. It begins with a militaristic rolling snare drum accompanied by clipped rhythm guitar that follows the beat closely. This minimal marching rhythm is maintained throughout, while the gradually introduced backing vocals and revivalist-style organ convey the sense of a divinely ordained call to arms. In the final verse, the addition of brass instruments brings the song to a rousing climax. In their analysis of the war song tradition, Les Waffen and Peter Hesbacher state,

> War songs are at their most stylized when they consist of spoken word against instrumental background. Conventionally, "America," "Battle Hymn of the Republic," "Onward Christian Soldiers" or "Taps" is performed with trumpet and fife and drum . . . this traditionally patriotic or "seasonal" arrangement of war songs is supplemented by other styles of popular music.[68]

The author, performers and arrangers of "The Ballad of the Green Berets" consciously situated this song within an existing genre of patriotic war songs by employing its conventions and reference points.

In one television studio appearance, Sadler's performance begins with the camera lingering on the insignia of the US Army Special Forces (the official name of the Green Berets), which consists of two crossed arrows, a sword, and the motto "De oppresso liber."[69] Sadler, in full dress uniform with green beret, then mimes the song while filmed in a series of carefully constructed placements. Sadler first stands next to and is studiously balanced with a large model of the insignia, the background black and stark to ensure that nothing distracts from the seriousness of the song's content. For the next verse, he is filmed from the shoulders up, centred against the black background. Together with Sadler's fundamentally motionless delivery, this recalls the iconic imagery of the sculptured bust, a staple of military representation that originated in the first-century Roman republic and included the shoulders and upper chest to enable the inclusion of armour and other indications of military prowess.[70] In this instance, it enables the viewer to focus on Sadler's face, the 'silver wings upon [his] chest,' his epaulettes and other indicators of military rank. For the next verse, the camera angle is a profile close-up, which evokes another form of imperial portraiture, the coin.[71] At times, Sadler turns and faces the camera in close-up, addressing his audience directly and intimately. The final shot places Sadler next to the insignia, restating his placement earlier in the performance clip.

Visually, this carefully stylised series of shots unequivocally reinforces the 'message' of the song, which is that the elite 'Green Berets' are 'fearless,' 'brave,' 'America's best,' with 'courage deep.' This imagery, along with the 'Latin' motto, was also designed to locate this soldier, and the ongoing war, within a history of military campaigns, thereby emphasising its supposed legitimacy and lending the conflict and its participants enhanced gravitas. The camera's repeated return to the insignia associates these men with 'liberation from oppression,' that is, the freedom of which Sadler sings:

> Silver wings upon their chest
> These are men, America's best
> One hundred men we'll test today
> But only three win the Green Beret.
>
> Back at home a young wife waits
> Her Green Beret has met his fate
> *He has died for those oppressed*
> Leaving her this last request

Put silver wings on my son's chest
Make him one of America's best
He'll be a man they'll test one day
Have him win the Green Beret.[72]

This was in line with standard government rhetoric about the war in Vietnam. In March 1964, President Johnson reviewed his first hundred days in office in a television interview. When asked if, like President Kennedy, he believed in 'the falling domino theory; that if Vietnam were lost that other countries in the area would soon be lost.'[73] he responded,

> I think it would be a very dangerous thing . . . the whole of Southeast Asia would be involved and that would involve hundreds of millions of people . . . We must do everything that we can . . . we must stay there and help them, and that is what we are going to do.[74]

He went on to emphasise the preservation of freedom as a guiding principle and justification for combat:

> We are very anxious to do what we can to help those people preserve their own freedom. We cherish ours and we would like to see them preserve theirs . . . we are patient people, and we love freedom, and we want to help others preserve it, and we are going to try to evolve the most effective and efficient plans we can to continue to help them. [75]

The rhetoric of freedom is also reflected in the State Department White Paper on Vietnam, *Aggression From the North* (27 February 1965), which described the war in Vietnam as 'a new kind of war . . . a totally new brand of aggression has been loosed against an independent people who want to make their way in peace and freedom.'[76]

As we have seen, this was reflected in mainstream pro-Vietnam War songs like "The Ballad of the Green Berets," but this same sentiment, although not explicitly stated, also underlies a song by the Shangri-Las that pre-dates "Take the Time."

Early in 1966, while still signed to Red Bird, the Shangri-Las had some success with "Long Live Our Love," a song that took the separation of lovers, a theme familiar from their earlier material, and located it within a current 'wartime' context.[77] A pair of young lovers, 'childhood sweethearts,' had 'vowed to love each other,'

> But something's come between us,
> And it's not another girl,
> But a lot of people need you,
> There is trouble in the world.[78]

A spoken section (a device familiar to the Shangri-Las' audience, associated with intimacy and directness) explicated the situation further:

> It's the fighting that has come between us
> And it's taken you far, far away.
> But please don't wonder if I'll be faithful
> You're in my heart both night and day.
> So, darling, I send my love to you,
> While you are fighting overseas,
> And I know one day if we are lucky,
> God will send you back to me.[79]

In a live TV performance of this song on *Hullabaloo* from 1966, Mary looks and speaks directly into the camera, as if personally reassuring her lover.[80] A similar sentiment is present in the Shirelles' 1962 hit "Soldier Boy," in which the protagonist assures her lover,

> You were my first love
> And you'll be my last love
> I will never make you blue
> I'll be true to you ... [81]

The young girlfriend or wife waiting at home while her soldier is fighting overseas is a well-established image in war songs; it is also employed by Sadler in the "Ballad of the Green Berets"('back at home a young wife waits ... ').[82] In an earlier example from 1917, "My Sweetheart Is Somewhere in France," the protagonist also maintained a vigil for her soldier:

'Every day I kiss his picture,
And tell him I'll be true,
Just as he is to his country,
And the old red, white and blue.'

"Long Live Our Love" is another in this long tradition of 'war' songs
that revolve around romantic separation; when the Shangri-Las performed the song on *Hullabaloo,* they were surrounded by life size cutout models of soldiers, simplified into cartoon-like figures, dressed in
uniforms from an earlier era. In this manner, they functioned as a form
of 'everysoldier' and positioned the song and the war it referred to in
a broader historical setting, keeping references to the Vietnam War
oblique rather than direct.

This is consistent with other techniques employed in this song,
which begins (and ends) with snatches of 'When Johnny comes marching home again, hooray . . . hoorah . . . ' in slow, sombre, and what can
reasonably described as mournful tones. Bookending the song in this
way underlines that the subject matter is serious and worthy of contemplation, since "Long Live Our Love" is upbeat and sprightly, with a
marching beat, and, ultimately, positive and hopeful. It is also another
means of locating the song within a wider historical context, since
"When Johnny Comes Marching Home" was first published in 1863
and was popular with both sides during the US Civil War.[83] The song's
origins are uncertain but it is credited to Patrick Sarsfield Gilmore, an
Irish-American bandmaster and composer who published it under the
pseudonym Louis Lambert. It is related to an Irish anti-war ballad,
"Johnny, I Hardly Knew You," but claims that this existed before the
Civil War version remain unsubstantiated.[84] It was regularly revived
during wartime, particularly during the Spanish-American War of 1898,
and was also a popular marching song with the US Army in France in
1918.[85] "When Johnny Comes Marching Home" is generally viewed as
a patriotic song that celebrates the return of the victorious soldier:[86]

When Johnny comes marching home.
Get ready for the Jubilee,
Hurrah! Hurrah!
We'll drink him a toast or two or three,
Hurrah! Hurrah!

The laurel wreath is ready now
To place upon his loyal brow
And we'll all feel gay
When Johnny comes marching home.

Lee Andresen has pointed out that the words 'When Johnny comes marching home again hurrah, hurrah' were used during the Vietnam War to headline a poster that depicted a soldier in full uniform, on crutches and missing a leg. The text at the bottom of the poster read, 'Stop the crippling. Stop the killing. Stop the war. Write, wire or call your congressman today.' The power of quoting this song here lies, of course, in the ironic contrast between the image of the mutilated soldier and traditional understanding of the song as representing a soldier's triumphant return.[87]

When the Shangri-Las quote 'When Johnny Comes Marching Home Again' in "Love Live Our Love," the use of the soldier's name encourages the audience to connect with their song on a more personal level.[88] Other Shangri-Las' songs also used names (Mary, Betty, Jimmy), as we have seen, and just before the final chorus of "Love Live Our Love," there is another short spoken section in which Mary implores, over a reprise of "When Johnny Comes Marching Home,"

Please Lord, don't let anything happen to him, please
I'm waiting for you, Johnny, I'm waiting . . .

This makes an explicit connection between the protagonist's 'Johnny' and the older 'Johnny' who presumably marched home after fighting in the Civil War. Mary is not just singing to her Johnny, she is singing for all the wives and girlfriends whose 'Johnnys' were and had been away fighting and would, Lord willing, come marching home. In this, it is unmistakably a patriotic song, locating this personal experience of war, and the (Vietnam) war itself, in the context of a longer tradition of heroic, self-sacrificing men and US military involvements. This is further reinforced by the use throughout the song of tin whistles in march tempo, and flourishes of brass reminiscent of a military band.[89] The brass arrangement used in the *Hullabaloo* performance (which, according to John Grecco, aired on 10 January 1966), is even more bombastic than on the recorded version.

The single sold well, but was not an enormous hit. Grecco suggests as an explanation that despite label advertising support and the TV appearance on *Hullabaloo*, 'it most likely didn't fare as well because the times were a-changing, with the teens rightfully questioning our involvement in Viet Nam.'[90]

It is reasonable to question this assessment, though, given that "Long Live Our Love" peaked at #33 on the *Billboard Hot 100* on 5 March 1966, when "The Ballad of the Green Berets" was at #1.[91] And a few months later, Californian music newspaper *KRLA Beat* felt confident enough in their assessment of the sentiments of their predominantly young readership to run a full-page cover photo of Sadler in uniform beside an US flag, with the headline 'Sadler Sounds Off.'[92] Inside, writer John Michaels reported Sadler saying it was 'draft card burning and dissent by American youth' that had prompted "Ballad of the Green Berets," and commenting, 'I don't think you have to have shoulder-length hair and shake dandruff over the first three rows to be able to sing.' This was a dig at 'long-haired groups' for which, observed Michaels, Sadler shared a similar 'distaste' to that he felt towards 'dissenters' and 'draft card burners.'[93]

Sadler's musical career was reported on in much the same way as those of Bob Dylan, the Beatles, the Beach Boys, the Mamas and the Papas and all the other 'long-haired groups' featured in *KRLA* (and seen on their covers, for that matter)—seriously and respectfully. Nor did the Sadler cover feature incite a barrage of angry letters to the editor from a readership furious at Sadler's placement in such musical company, at the respect accorded his views and at US participation in the Vietnam War. The one person who did write in about Sadler, Mary Jean Tragna, was not upset about the platform *KRLA Beat* gave to Sadler's pro-war fervour, but by his comments about dandruff and long hair:

> You never see the Stones or any other long-haired group go through all the bother to write an article to cut down short hair. Why doesn't everyone just mind their own business and stop this criti[ci]zing.[94]

What *did* incite a barrage of letters to *KRLA Beat* in the second half of 1966, on the other hand, was the 'butcher cover' controversy accompanying the Beatles' *Yesterday and Today* album,[95] followed in short order by John Lennon's comment about the Beatles being 'more popular than Jesus.'[96] Although it did not consist solely of teenagers, the record-buying public was, in fact, very much aware of the Vietnam War, and demonstrated this by making "The Ballad of the Green Berets" an enormous hit, a 'smash.' The simultaneous success, albeit more modest, of "Long Live Our Love," demonstrated that in early 1966, pro-war sentiment was certainly not a hindrance to mainstream record sales.

An article in *Billboard* in June 1966 entitled 'The Vietnam Conflict Spawning Heavy Barrage of Disk Tunes,' noted,

> Since January, well over 100 Vietnam records have been released, with five making the *Billboard Hot 100* and a dozen making Billboard's country charts . . .
>
> Reasons for the large number of Vietnam songs are largely political. While other U.S. wars have had a groundswell of public opinion behind them, *the Vietnam War has split the public into two camps— one the supporters, the majority*; the other, an articulate minority opposed to U.S. participation. And *the event songs about Vietnam fall into two categories—the patriotic song*, generally aimed at the country market, and the protest song, generally aimed at the draft age youngster with folk song leanings. *The first category leads by far in number of releases and in total sales.*[97]

At this point, it should be noted that ideas about the war were not as neatly polarised as the war-themed records—and this *Billboard* article—might indicate. Historian Paul Lyons has cautioned against lapsing into 'a dualism of doves and vets' and viewing the Sixties generation as 'divided into those who served their country and those who opposed its policies.' He points out there was 'a sizable group' of baby boomers who fit neither category, a 'silent majority' who 'stood on the sidelines.'[98] Nevertheless, later in 1966, Senator Everett Dirksen, a Republican from Illinois, had considerable success with a spoken-word album called *Gallant Men: Stories of the American Adventure*, with which he too sought to contextualise the Vietnam War as the latest in a long line of heroic battles fought for the USA by 'gallant men.' Dirksen explained of his collection of patriotic poems and stories, 'I feel it is an answer to the beatniks, draft-card burners, and those who are opposed to our efforts in Vietnam.'[99] It sold so well that in the week before Christmas, *Billboard* reported that Capitol Records had to 'rearrange its pressing schedule to accommodate consumer demand,' prompting Capitol's president, Alan Livingston, to comment that 'Senator Dirksen's album has taken off like a Beatles record.'[100] The single taken from it, "Gallant Men," was a Top 40 hit in January, 1967, and the album won the Grammy Award for Best Spoken Word, Documentary or Drama Recording in 1968. Clearly condemnation of the Vietnam War, although building, was yet to become mainstream at the end of 1966.

In this context the Shangri-Las' last single, "Take the Time," was released early in 1967.[101] The song begins with the sound of a clock ticking, but this notion of 'time' is very different to the psychedelic conceptions discussed earlier. Here the ticking clock creates a sense of anticipation and immediacy; it signals that what follows is timely, worthy of attention, and the audience should take note. This is heightened further by the introduction of a rolling snare drum which briefly suggests a march, after an understated strumming guitar. It is apparent almost immediately that this song will dispense with complex production values and emotional intensity in favour of a more minimal, easy-listening approach that hints at a folk aesthetic and allows the emphasis to be placed on the lyrics:

> Did you ever take the time
> A moment or more?
> To stop and thank the ones we left behind
> On some foreign shore
> To hear from no more.[102]

At this point, the narrative becomes more personal, although not to the same degree (first name basis) as "Long Live Our Love":

> I can picture one of many boys
> Very brave and so alone
> Giving up the life that he enjoys
> Protecting what he has back home.[103]

Military band-style brass flourishes and a jaunty march tempo summon up patriotic fervour. The common rhetoric of personal sacrifice for the greater good and the preservation of freedom is employed, recalling President John F. Kennedy's famous call to 'ask not what your country can do for you—ask what you can do for your country.'[104] The bravery of the boy who is 'giving up the life that he enjoys' is contrasted implicitly with those who 'shrink from this responsibility.'[105] A few months earlier, in August 1966, again in *KRLA Beat*, Gil McDougall had written an article entitled 'California: Gangs, Vietniks and Surfers.' McDougall, an English journalist, appeared to be sending up outsiders' supposed perceptions of California, facetiously describing protesters against the Vietnam War as 'Vietniks' who were

> usually college students, and [they] come in various sizes—with or without guitars . . . Vietniks dislike draft cards, the local police force, Barry Sadler, Lyndon B. Jo[h]nson, and Hell's Angels. Vietniks like beards, long hair, casual clothes (spelled s-l-o-p-p-y), Barry McGuire, folk music and the Beatles . . . Vietniks often organise protest parties—anyone welcome but be sure to bring a supply of well-worded protests—and the party will sometimes culminate with select members of the group burning their draft cards. After this ceremony the draft card burners will demonstrate their vocal capabilities as they are dragged away by the FBI. Colour them red.[106]

Young people protesting against the US presence in Vietnam and the draft were portrayed as sloppy, lazy and by definition aligned with the perceived communist enemy—'red.' Furthermore, the two top-selling musical Barrys—Sadler of the "Green Berets," and McGuire of "Eve of Destruction"—were pitched in opposition to one another .

The dominant ideological justification for the US presence in Vietnam, the Cold War threat of encroaching Communism and the necessity of its containment, was reflected in the next verse of "Take the Time":

> Don't you wish that you can do your part
> For this country proud and tall
> If we don't finish what we did not start
> There'll be no country left at all.[107]

The song is clearly a heavy-handed, jingoistic espousal of government justifications for the war in Vietnam:

> This country that we're living in
> Knows only that we've got to win

No matter what the cost may be
Our loss is keeping you and me
Free . . . [108]

As an attempt to perhaps take the Shangri-Las in a more 'meaningful' direction, the song was not a success. As the context of its release indicates, however, the reasons for its failure are more complex than its adoption of a pro-war stance. "Take the Time" was not an anomaly in a sea of protest music. It was not a success—on any level, neither artistically nor commercially—*not* simply because it supported the war in Vietnam; as we have seen, there were multiple examples of patriotic pro-war hits from this time. It failed mostly because it was musically unmemorable, heavy-handed and browbeating; such an approach worked well enough for a former Vietnam War soldier personally intoning his experiences of being a "Green Beret," but it was completely unsuitable and inappropriate for a group of young female singers whose reputation rested on impassioned renderings of complex narratives of teenage emotional desolation. The Shangri-Las were a pop group, with no history of folk/protest music involvement, or anything vaguely connected to any kind of political statement. The one previous exception had been "Long Live Our Love," a patriotic war/romance song that had been moderately successful but was thematically quite out of character with the rest of their material.

Arguably, "Take the Time" utilised enough elements—from the tradition of war songs as well as from the Shangri-Las' own oeuvre, including a refashioning of their anti-hero figure into a soldier—to place it in familiar enough territory to work. Moreover, mainstream public opinion had not yet turned against the war, and there was clearly an enormous market of record buyers who supported US involvement in Vietnam. From the perspective of a corporate record label, then, it probably seemed quite logical to think that a song like "Take the Time" *might* actually sell well, take the group in a new direction, give them something to say with 'powerful lyrical content,' and reconfigure the group as one with a more adult appeal. After all, the song built on and extended thematically the sentiment of "Long Live Our Love," while increasing the patriotic fervour, as other successful records were doing. Furthermore, the Shangri-Las had mainstream appeal—and mainstream sentiment supported the war. From the misguided perspective of the marketing department at Mercury in early 1967, when the full horrors of the war were yet to become apparent, "Take the Time" certainly would have seemed much less of a commercial risk than a 'Vietnik' protest record.

This reading is supported by attempts to reconfigure the image of the group during this period. Promotional pictures of Mary Weiss were taken for which her hair was styled by Monti Rock, a celebrity hairdresser who regularly made appearances on *The Tonight Show* with Johnny Carson (he later made disco records and appeared in *Saturday Night Fever* as a DJ).[109] Rock styled Mary's hair to appear very full and glamorous, reminiscent of 1940s film star Veronica Lake. This look was evidently not one Mary felt comfortable with, or chose for herself; she later told Miriam Linna 'I look stupid. I didn't like it at all.'[110] It suggests strongly that the group's management and/or Mercury may have been attempting to move the group away from their 'teen' image (especially its more rebellious iterations) towards one that they perceived to be more 'grown up' and sophisticated; a page from a 1966 magazine reproduced on the Norton Records website shows the three Shangri-Las in 'before' (from 1964) and 'after' shots.[111] It is likely that Monti Rock was responsible for all three 'after' hairstyles, given that the shot of Mary is identical to the 'Veronica Lake' photograph discussed above. Betty sports lustrous, bouncy, heavily styled curls, and Mary Ann a short but softening, slightly mussed-up look that seems more consciously 'feminine' than her previous styles.

Another contemporary photo shoot, with New York-based fashion photographer Kenn Mori, appeared in the October 1966 issue of *Teen Datebook*. This featured the 'Mad Mod' look, which comprised various forms of pantsuits and seemed to be a style they were far more comfortable with:

> "The pantsuit has become our trademark," say the Shangri-Las. "We love them, on stage and off." Here, Mary, Betty and Mary Ann model for you the kind of mad-mod wardrobe they might take on a cross-country tour. The suits travel smoothly through press conferences, performances, receptions, pack easily and need little ironing. In fact, they're ideal for any girl whether your scene is the public—or the private eye.[112]

THE MAD-MOD LOOK: SHANGRI-LAS

Fashion shoot for the October 1966 issue of *Teen Datebook*. Photographs by Kenn Mori. (*courtesy of Alex Moretti*)

The styles are decidedly grown-up, and their attire less figure-hugging and more understated—'mod but feminine and comfortable', the reader is assured—than their "Leader"-era outfits. Most tellingly, all three members wear broad, sunny smiles, as though they had been neatly laughing (not too uproariously) at a tasteful joke. These shots seem to be presenting a new, grown-up, happy Shangri-Las, who have moved on from teenage devastation and into an adult world in which they now perform songs about wholesome times by the sea and support for their country's war effort. While this was a plausible enough marketing strategy—and in keeping with the musical material they recorded at this time, which clumsily attempted to push the group into new markets—these efforts were ultimately unsuccessful.

Although he produced their two Mercury singles, George 'Shadow' Morton's partnership with the Shangri-Las appears to have run its course by early 1967. Through no fault of their own, many vocal groups like the Shangri-Las, who had formed in an earlier era dominated by doo-wop and vocal harmonising, found themselves quite suddenly out of vogue. Since their record label had no concept of the group as artists, and had them on a virtually non-stop treadmill of recording and touring, it is difficult to see how they could even have had the time to catch their breath and notice this happening. In a 1979 interview, Morton declared that he 'bowed out' of working with the Shangri-Las because 'it was boring.'[113] This is an easy way of closing off further discussion, but there were almost certainly other factors involved. Morton may well have been restricted by forces beyond his control, since only one of the four sides he recorded with the Shangri-Las at Mercury, "I'll Never Learn," is characteristic of their earlier, tremendously fruitful collaborations. Nevertheless, Morton had a history of closely observing and attempting to anticipate trends in popular music, and 'moving on' from the Shangri-Las can also be understood in this context.

The landscape of popular music had changed drastically since the Shangri-Las shot to fame in 1964; by 1967 it was increasingly dominated by singers and groups who played instruments and performed their own material. Singer-songwriters, most famously Bob Dylan, had achieved increasing prominence and the idea of the artist performing self-penned material as an artistic expression of introspection was becoming 'central to rock ideology,' as Jacqueline Warwick has put it.[114] The new directions pursued by Morton are entirely consistent with these trends, but they are at the same time in keeping with his earlier work with young female singers. He recorded and produced a teenaged singer-songwriter, Janis Ian, who had played him a song called "Society's Child."[115] It is narrated from the point of view of a young white woman forced by deeply entrenched racial mores to end her romance with a young Black man:

> When she was finished, I [Morton] said, "Do you believe that?" She said, "If I wrote it, I believe it." I said, "OK, you've got a deal. We're going into the studio with that. And make no mistake about it, this one's going to be tough."[116]

With her acoustic guitar and hair pulled back plainly, Ian unmistakably evoked the folk/protest song tradition, and "Society's Child" was a harmonically complex composition with sophisticated concerns. Ian recorded an entire album of her own material with Morton, which is significant, since the *album* was becoming established as the format of the artistic statement in rock music. At a time when the Civil Rights movement was steadily gaining momentum and gathering increasingly vocal support, this collection of material, but particularly "Society's Child," was socially relevant and made a political statement, so much so that Ian endured a range of extreme attacks including spitting, vitriolic abuse and death threats.[117] That Morton recorded this song, and Ian's album, in late 1966, while Red Bird was collapsing and the Shangri-Las were beginning to undergo Mercury's clumsy attempts at remodelling them, is surely telling.

Furthermore, "Society's Child" received considerable publicity, and its significance did not go unnoted at the time. Conductor and composer Leonard Bernstein was so impressed that he hosted Ian on his television show *Inside Pop: The Rock Revolution* in 1967, praising the song's 'astonishing key changes and even tempo changes, ambiguous cadences, unequal phrase lengths—the works!' Significantly for Morton, Bernstein also noted the production and arrangements of "Society's Child," effusing about the 'fascinating sounds, both natural and electronic, strange use of harpsichord and that cool nasty electric organ.'[118] Robert Shelton wrote in the *New York Times*:

> "Society's Child" marks a new boldness in popular music while also proclaiming the radiant new talent, Janis Ian. Those who care about

the upgrading of popular music and its freedom of expression will watch closely both Miss Ian's song and the issue of censorship that it has so forthrightly raised.[119]

In a manner entirely consistent with his earlier career, Morton was again looking ahead to capitalise on the newest developments in popular music, and Ian vindicated his championing of her and her self-penned songs. In 1974, Morton told Lenny Kaye that 'his favourite was Janis Ian, and to this day he maintains that the albums and singles he cut with her were the best records he ever made. Not the Shangri-Las. Not the Fudge . . .' Morton continued:

> She was writing ten years ahead of her time . . . she said more and intimidated more people in the world than most artists. And she made the greatest albums walking.
>   She wrote every conceivable scene in social life, and wrote it better than anybody else. What the public wasn't ready for was not Janis Ian's lyrics. They weren't ready for Janis Ian.[120]

Significantly for the Shangri-Las, Robert Shelton also noted in his *New York Times* write-up that due to the controversy surrounding the song and its subject matter, 'Larry Martire, an associate of the record's producer, George 'Shadow' Morton, said, "I've never had so much trouble promoting a record in my career."'[121]

It seems that Mercury's promotional efforts were going primarily into the hot and topical Janis Ian, not into the Shangri-Las. John Grecco reported that Mercury failed to promote either of the singles the Shangri-Las recorded for the label:

> There were no calls to come into the studio, no hype from Mercury on the girls, and it now seemed that Shadow was occupied producing two new acts, Janis Ian and The Vanilla Fudge.[122]

Vanilla Fudge was an all-male heavy psychedelic rock band, recorded and produced by Morton. Their debut album was released in 1967 and consisted entirely of dramatically slowed-down cover versions, including the Beatles' "Ticket to Ride" and "Eleanor Rigby," and yielded a top ten hit with their rendering of the Supremes' "You Keep Me Hanging

On."[123] This constitutes a fascinating bridge between an earlier vocal group/professional songwriter tradition, as examined in detail in the previous chapters, and the introspective, LSD-infused, sprawling psychedelic rock jams that would become common fare in the late 60s.

The B-Side of "Take the Time" was "Footsteps on the Roof," penned, as noted earlier, by the same pair of songwriters who wrote "Take the Time." It is a lively, upbeat song whose protagonist is

> Waiting here so patiently
> My love will soon be here for me . . . [124]

Like "Take the Time," it favours simpler, guitar-based arrangements rather than the complex productions George 'Shadow' Morton was best-known for. There are repeated references to 'the silence of my room,' but the musical accompaniment is so relentlessly cheery that no convincing sense of melancholy is conveyed. Just as "Sweet Sounds of Summer" was set up as a companion piece to "Remember (Walkin' in the Sand), so "Footsteps on the Roof" was linked with "Dressed in Black," a darkly intense Morton co-composition of devastation and lost love from mid-1966. "Dressed in Black" ends with a spoken coda over the barest accompaniment of double bass and minimal percussion:

> I climb the stairs
> I shut the door
> I turn the lock
> Alone once more
> And no one can hear me cry
> No one.[125]

In a clear and unmistakable reference to this, the spoken middle section of "Footsteps on the Roof" has Mary intoning,

> I climb the stairs
> I shut the door
> I turn the lock
> Alone once more
> I sit and stare
> At the stars up above

And dream of the moment
I'll run to my love
Come to me
Come to me . . .

The devastating realism for which the Shangri-Las were famous is reconfigured here into a trite and completely unconvincing happy ending. Since "Dressed in Black" had been the B-side of "He Cried," which peaked at #65 on the *Billboard Hot 100*, it is difficult to see this appropriation as a reminder of the group's earlier hit-making prowess. It may have been an attempt to manufacture continuity between their earlier material and current direction, or even a short-sighted recycling. Whatever the logic, it sat awkwardly with the group and failed to connect with their audience.

The four last songs the Shangri-Las recorded were, with the notable exception of "I'll Never Learn," crudely conceived and executed attempts at reconfiguring the Shangri-Las into a group with adult rather than teen appeal, in order to drive them into new and inappropriate markets. In order to achieve this, it was necessary to abandon their earlier image as angst-ridden, heartbroken teenagers, and the material foisted upon the group by their new label, Mercury, reflected this. The new songs were not chosen with the Shangri-Las' particular abilities and strengths—emotional intensity and unwavering conviction—in mind. Instead, an assortment of what were perceived to be winning formulas was haphazardly applied. The results were predictably unconvincing— the polar opposite of the emotional sincerity that the Shangri-Las had always reliably delivered in the past. An understanding of this 'logic' helps explain Mercury's otherwise bewildering choice of songs—bland, easy-listening material that was self-referential, superficially psychedelic, supporting the Vietnam War—and the label's decisions about the direction of the group. It is no coincidence that the only artistically persuasive song released during the Shangri-Las' tenure at Mercury, "I'll Never Learn," was written by a prodigiously talented young woman and was not a crass attempt to capitalise on inappropriate market trends.

The Shangri-Las' tenure as recording artists at Mercury was in many ways typical of the recorded music industry's treatment of young performers within the larger capitalist economy. Although the group recorded only four songs over a period of a few months, they remained contracted to the company for another ten years. Shackled to a label that had no particular interest in utilising their strengths, nor any realistic conception of how to record and market them in a rapidly changing musical environment, they were nevertheless unable to leave, ensuring that if Mercury could not enjoy revenue generated by new Shangri-Las material, no other label would either. This was purely and simply an economic decision; musicality, artistry and talent did not enter the equation.

Despite the structural disempowerment the Shangri-Las suffered while working, the group possessed tremendous cultural and aesthetic power, as reflected in their popularity, the sales of their records, and their enduring influence in a variety of musical and artistic contexts. Nevertheless, the Shangri-Las and their recordings have been repeatedly marginalised in traditional accounts of rock history, their substantial contributions, both subtle and striking, to their own work consistently overlooked. Critically examining and dispensing with the anachronistic categorisation of the Shangri-Las as a 'girl group' and employing wider social, economic, artistic and musical frameworks reveals hitherto unacknowledged qualities in the group's recordings and dismantles the false conceptions of authenticity and genre through which their work has been traditionally interpreted and misunderstood. In doing so, this book elevates the Shangri-Las—Mary Ann and Marguerite Ganser, and Elizabeth and Mary Weiss—to a position in the rock canon where their considerable artistic achievements can be clearly understood, properly acknowledged and genuinely celebrated.

Acknowledgments

This book is the culmination of an obsession that began in the early 2000s and encompassed a PhD, completed in 2012 in the Department of History at the University of Western Australia (UWA). The quantity of deep-dive research in the preceding pages was made possible only by generous scholarships and other funding (including travel) that enabled me to fully devote myself to this work from 2005–2010. Everything since has been squeezed in around full–time employment, which is partly why this book has taken so long! In addition to Rob Stuart and Andrew Broertjes at UWA, I would like to thank everyone who sought out and downloaded my thesis, particularly those who took the time to write to me with thanks, fervour, excitement and questions. It was this level of engagement that convinced me that there was in fact an audience for this book, so you have all played a part in bringing it to life.

I extend massive thanks to Steve Connell at Verse Chorus Press for immediately understanding the value and timeliness of my research, and for agreeing to publish it—over four years ago now—when I had largely given up on this ever happening. Steve has been incredibly patient while I worked in my unrelated day job and crammed editing and considerable further research for this volume into nights and weekends. His editorial direction has been thoughtful and thorough and his work on the images included in this book has saved me from tearing ALL my hair out. Steve, I can't thank you enough! Thanks are also due to fellow Verse Chorus author, friend of many years and writer of monumental music tomes David Nichols, who initially pointed Steve towards my PhD thesis and has maintained a keen interest in the progress of this book.

Monica Syrette remains a loyal and steadfast friend whose support has been invaluable. She has been on board with all iterations of this project since day one, and her enthusiasm for it is exceeded only by her love of the Shangri-Las (and perhaps the Carlton Football Club). Cat Hope is a brilliant conceptualist, composer and musician who I count myself extremely lucky to have as a friend and collaborator. I am tremendously grateful for her unwavering belief in my ideas and ability to execute them, often in conjunction with French cheese and Sicilian wine varietals, and to Karl Ockelford for endless delicious dinners. Although I don't see them nearly as often as I'd like, fellow historians Corinne West and Emily Booth are cherished friends and fantastically astute advisors, as is Juliet John—I'm thrilled to have all of you in my corner.

For their interest, enthusiasm and encouragement at various points over the years, I also thank Adam Spellicy, Edwina Preston, Caroline Kennedy, Michael Munson, Janelle Johnstone, Alison Huber, Jon Dale, Bruce Russell, Kate Reid, Molly Monro, Jenny Branagan, Penny Kelleher & Ian Epps, Emma Brady (who graciously let me stay for ages in NYC), Kurt Gottschalk, Lynne Barrow, James Hullick, Stuart Grant, Laila Costa, Robbie Egan, Jenny Griffiths & Kevin Robertson, Stina Thomas, Jan Pardy, Lauren Sanders, Cathy Alizzi and Simon McLean. Special thanks to Alex Moretti for generously sharing images and archival finds, and my nephew Jesse Steinfort for his awesome graphic design skills. I also extend thanks to Laurie Stras at the University of Southampton and Erik Richmond at the Queens Borough Public Library. I am especially grateful to Ruba Sadi and the Special Collections Team at University of Washington Libraries for helping me to navigate the extraordinary Jini Dellaccio photo archive from the other side of the world.

To my brilliant partner Evgeny Postnikov, trade agreement expert and academic extraordinaire (and super modest to boot), thank you for never doubting that this would happen, doing all the cleaning and for sharing countless marvellous meals and bottles of fine wine with me (a skill not to be taken lightly).

Sadly there have been many deaths since I began working on this book, and I'm very sorry that these people did not live to see it made manifest: Rowland S. Howard (1959–2009), Holly Anderson (1955–2017), Richard Minadeo (1948–2024), Saskia Sansom (1984–2024), Ollie Olsen (1958–2024), and my mother Margaret (Edith) MacKinney (1932–2024). Mum loved reading and composition, but was one of ten children in a family unable to afford the paltry administrative fee required for school attendance. Too embarrassed to admit this, she left at fourteen to join the workforce. I didn't really know or understand the ramifications of this until recently, and I still find it hard to come to terms with. Mum's death really emphasised the importance of the bond with those left behind: Dad (Rod), Jamie, Lyn & Stephen, Jesse & Olivia, Cooper, Charlotte, Quentin, Fern, William, Alex; thank you all for being my family.

Greg Kratzmann (1949–2021) co–supervised my Honours and Masters theses with Judith Richards (1938–2023), whose 1EE Elizabethan England was the first History subject I took at La Trobe University in 1992. This was the beginning of a very special relationship that would last decades and came to include teaching, mentoring, academic rigour, friendship, feminism, compassion, enormous respect, and very strong coffee. I know both Judith and Greg would be grinning from ear to ear, and I'm so sorry they're not here to enjoy this book.

Finally, but importantly, this book would not have happened without Phil Milstein, on whose Spectropop desk a tentative email about the Shangri-Las landed in 2005. Then and there, Phil decided that I might actually be the one to pull off writing a book about the Shangri-Las, something we both agreed was long overdue and criminal in its absence. Phil's support, friendship, enthusiasm, unstinting generosity in sharing source material, contacts and his impossibly intricate knowledge of musical minutiae was central to making this happen. So Phil, *Dressed in Black* is for you—I hope it's worth the wait.

Notes

INTRODUCTION

1 Suzi Quatro, 'Suzi Quatro's Heroes of Rock 'n' Roll: Interview with Mary Weiss,' BBC Radio 2, broadcast 24 Oct. 2007.

2 Alan Betrock, *Girl Groups: The Story of a Sound*, 98.

3 Betrock, 102; see also the Shangri-Las discography included in Miriam Linna, *Mary Weiss of the Shangri-Las: Good-Bad, But Not Evil* (online interview, part 8).

4 Betrock, 102; the Shangri-Las, "Leader of the Pack" (Barry/Greenwich/Morton), RED BIRD 014, Oct. 1964.

5 Betrock, 106–8.

6 John Grecco, *Out in the Streets: The Story of the Shangri-Las* (online article, part 2).

7 Grecco, *Out in the Streets*, part 2.

8 New York Dolls, "Looking for a Kiss," Live at Max's Kansas City, New York, 1973 (YouTube); the Shangri-Las, "Give Him a Great Big Kiss" on *Shivaree*, 1965 (YouTube).

9 Quoted in Kris Needs & Dick Porter, *Trash! The Complete New York Dolls*, 12.

10 Betrock was the author of *Girl Groups* (see note 1); Lester Bangs, *Blondie*, 40–41.

11 For a thorough discussion of the 1977 reunion, which included recording sessions for a never-released album, see Phil Milstein, *Spectropop Presents: Shangri-Las 77!* (online).

12 Milstein, *Shangri-Las 77!*

13 Aerosmith recorded "Remember (Walkin' in the Sand)," with Mary Weiss singing backing vocals, on *Night in the Ruts* (1979; live version from 1980 via YouTube). Bette Midler's live album *Divine Madness* (1980) contains a version of "Leader of the Pack" (YouTube). The Australian guitarist Rowland S. Howard, formerly of the Boys Next Door, the Birthday Party, and These Immortal Souls, included a version of "S/he Cried" on his 1999 album *Teenage Snuff Film* (live performance from 1999, YouTube). In the last conversation I had with Howard before his untimely death in 2009, he had been thrilled that I was working on this study, as he was a great fan of the Shangri-Las and cited them as a significant influence.

14 Mick Heggerty and C.D. Taylor, *Totally Go-Go's*, Live at Palos Verdes High School, LA, Dec. 4, 1981 (YouTube).

15 Sam Armstrong, "'Oh No! How a 60s Girl Group Anthem Took Over TikTok,' *Udiscovermusic* 21 July 2021 (online); see also Discogs entry for *The Best of Capone-N-Noreaga: Thugged Da F-Out* (online).

16 Cat Hope, 'The Wonderment of the Bleak: Sculpting the Static,' *Art Monthly Australia* 225 (Nov. 2009), 45–47.

17 In the years since that lightbulb moment, a volume has been published in Blooms-bury's 33⅓ series devoted to specific albums: Ada Wolin, *Golden Hits of the Shangri-Las*, 2019.

18 Lisa MacKinney, *Dressed in Black: The Shangri-Las and Their Recorded Legacy*, PhD dissertation, University of Western Australia, 2012.

19 See also Laurie Stras's comments in the introduction to *She's So Fine: Reflections on Whiteness, Femininity, Adolescence and Class in 1960s Music*, 23.

20 See the related comments of Steve Jones and Kevin Featherly in 'Re-viewing Rock Writing: Narratives of Popular Music Criticism' in *Pop Music and the Press*, ed. Steve Jones, 21.

21 Jacqueline Warwick also noted this issue, adding that 'girl group' music has been 'denounced by some feminists who embrace instead the apparently unmediated expressions of personal experience by individual singer/songwriters.' See Jacqueline Warwick, *I Got All My Sisters with Me: Girl Culture, Girl Identity and Girl Group Music*, Los Angeles: UCLA PhD thesis (Musicology), 2002, x. This has been revised and published as *Girl Groups, Girl Culture: Popular Music and Identity in the 1960s*.

22 See Warwick, *Girl Groups, Girl Culture*, 89–91.

23 Warwick discusses this issue in detail in a chapter entitled, 'He's Got the Power: Pro-duction and Authorship,' in *Girl Groups, Girl Culture*, 113–162, see esp. 117–121.

24 Those with particular application for this study include Susan Douglas, *Where the Girls Are: Growing Up Female with the Mass Media*; Norma Coates, 'Teenyboppers, Groupies and Other Grotesques: Girls and Women and Rock Culture in the 1960s and early 1970s,' *Journal of Popular Music Studies* 15:1 (2003), 65–94; and Lisa Rho-des, *Electric Ladyland: Women and Rock Culture*. Especially important is *She's So Fine*, ed. Laurie Stras; this will be discussed in more detail shortly.

25 Gavin Edwards, 'Mary Weiss, Who Sang "Leader of the Pack", is Dead at 75,' *New York Times*, 22 Jan 2024.

26 See Linna, *Mary Weiss of the Shangri-Las*, part 4.

27 See also Ken Emerson, *Always Magic in the Air: The Bomp and Brilliance of the Brill Building Era*, 225–6.

28 Lisa MacKinney, *Recovering the Late Medieval Devotional World of Margery Kempe and her Book*, unpublished MA thesis; 'Rosaries, Paternosters and Devotion to the Virgin in the Households of John Baret of Bury St. Edmunds,' *Parergon* 24:2 (2007), 93–114.

29 Where such material is represented in collections, for instance at Bowling Green State University, which has an extensive collection of popular culture material, it has rarely (if ever) been microfilmed, and libraries have understandably been reluctant to allow overseas borrowing.

30 Miriam Linna, *Mary Weiss of the Shangri-Las: Good-Bad, But Not Evil*.

31 Milstein, *Shangri-Las 77!*

32 Lisa MacKinney, 'The Book of Daughters and the Sonic aGender Guitar Project: Inclusivity as Guiding Principle' in *A Century of Composition by Women: Music Against the Odds* ed. Linda Kouvaras, Maria Grenfell and Natalie Williams, 327–345.

33 Cherie Currie with Tony O'Neill, *Neon Angel: A Memoir of a Runaway*; Viv Alber-tine, *Clothes Clothes Clothes, Music Music Music, Boys Boys Boys* and *To Throw Away Unopened*; Kim Gordon, *Girl in a Band*; Carrie Brownstein, *Hunger Makes Me a Modern Girl*; Laura Jane Grace, *Tranny: Confessions of Punk Rock's Most Infamous Anarchist Sellout*; Kathy Valentine, *All I Ever Wanted: A Rock 'n' Roll Memoir*; Cosey Fanni Tutti, *Art Sex Music*; Sinéad O'Connor, *Rememberings*.

34 Sini Anderson, *The Punk Singer: A Film About Kathleen Hanna*; Asif Kapadia, *Amy* & Marina Parker, *Reclaiming Amy*; Amy Berg, *Janis: Little Girl Blue*; Liz Garbus, *What Happened, Miss Simone?*; Liam Firmager, *Suzi Q*; Alison Ellwood, *The Go-Go's*;

Bobbi Jo Hart, *Fanny: The Right to Rock*; Vanessa Roth, *Mary J Blige's My Life*; Samantha Stark, *Framing Britney Spears*; Morgan Neville, *20 Feet from Stardom*.

35 Ronnie Spector and Vince Waldron, *Be My Baby: How I Survived Mascara, Miniskirts and Madness, or My Life as a Fabulous Ronette*; Erica Gonzales and Bianca Betancourt, 'Zendaya Is in Talks to Star in a Ronnie Spector Biopic—Here's What to Know,' *Harper's Bazaar* (online).

36 Tracey Thorn, *My Rock 'n' Roll Friend*.

37 Jennifer Otter Bickerdike, *Being Britney: Pieces of a Modern Icon* and *You Are Beautiful and You Are Alone: The Biography of Nico*, 1–2.

CHAPTER ONE: *Genre and Gender. The Shangri-Las and 'Girl Group' Mythology*

1 Greg Shaw, 'Leaders of The Pack: Teen Dreams and Tragedy in Girl Group Rock,' *History of Rock* 1982 (Rock's Backpages).

2 Duke Ellington, quoted by Nat Hentoff, *At the Jazz Band Ball: Sixty Years on the Jazz Scene*, 1.

3 Richard Goldstein, 'Pop Eye: The Soul Sound from Sheepshead Bay,' *Village Voice*, 23 June 1966, 7–8, 30–31, reprinted with substantial amendments in Richard Goldstein, *Goldstein's Greatest Hits: A Book Mostly About Rock 'n' Roll*, 8–14. See also Lisa Rhodes, *Electric Ladyland: Women and Rock Culture*, 43.

4 Goldstein, *Village Voice*, 8.

5 Goldstein, *Goldstein's Greatest Hits*, 9.

6 Goldstein, *Goldstein's Greatest Hits*, 9–11, 13.

7 Goldstein, *Goldstein's Greatest Hits*, 9, 12–13.

8 For a more detailed discussion of Goldstein's 'Pop Eye' column, and particularly this article, see Rhodes, 72–7, esp. 76–7.

9 Jacqueline C. Warwick, *Girl Groups, Girl Culture: Popular Music and Identity in the 1960s*.

10 Robert Palmer, *Rock and Roll: An Unruly History*, 35.

11 Timothy E. Scheurer, 'The Beatles, the Brill Building, and the Persistence of Tin Pan Alley in the Age of Rock,' *Popular Music and Society* 20:4 (1996), 90 (italics added).

12 Kembrew McLeod's discussion of gendered descriptors that are applied to rock and popular music functions also as an exploration of what is understood to constitute 'authenticity'; see 'Between a Rock and a Hard Place: Gender and Rock Criticism' in *Pop Music and the Press*, ed. Steve Jones, 93–113, esp. 102–105.

13 Leiber and Stoller, official website.

14 Rhodes, 41–88.

15 Rhodes, 42–3; see also the comments of Gestur Gudmundsson, Ulf Lindberg, Morten Michelsen and Hans Weisethaunet, in 'Brit Crit: Turning Points in British Rock Criticism, 1960–1990,' in *Pop Music and the Press*, ed. Steve Jones, 41–2.

16 Ellen Sander, 'The Journalists of Rock,' *Saturday Review*, 31 July 1971, 47; Rhodes, 43–4.

17 Sander, 47.

18 For a detailed survey of the major early developments in US rock journalism, see Rhodes, 41–9; Steve Jones and Kevin Featherly, 'Re-viewing Rock Writing: Narratives of Popular Music Criticism' in *Pop Music and the Press*, ed. Steve Jones, 19–40, esp. 32–4.

19 See Norma Coates, 'Teenyboppers, Groupies and Other Grotesques: Girls and Women and Rock Culture in the 1960s and early 1970s,' *Journal of Popular Music Studies* 15:1 (2003), 65–94, esp. 65–8; Rhodes, 41–8.

20 Rhodes, 72.

21 Brenda Johnson-Grau, 'Sweet Nothings: Presentations of Women Musicians in Pop Journalism,' in *Pop Music and the Press*, ed. Steve Jones, 205.

22 'Radio Action and Pick LP's,' *Billboard*, 17 Mar. 1973, 58.

23 Cherie Currie with Tony O'Neill, *Neon Angel: A Memoir of a Runaway*, 92.

24 Keaton Bell, 'How the Go-Go's Found their Beat: An Oral History,' *Vogue*.

25 Quoted in Aida Pavletich, *Sirens of Song: The Popular Female Vocalist in America*, 243.

26 See Mike Kelley, 'Cross Gender/Cross Culture,' *PAJ: A Journal of Performance and Art*, 22:1 (Jan. 2000), 1–9, esp. 3; Donna Gaines, 'Let's Talk About Sex,' *Rolling Stone* 773 (13 Nov. 1997), 91–94.

27 See Pavletich, 242–6; see also Johnson-Grau, 202.

28 Warwick, *Girl Groups, Girl Culture*, 95.

29 Rhodes, 18–21; Steve Chapple and Reebee Garofalo, *Rock 'n' Roll Is Here to Pay: The History and Politics of the Music Industry*, 77–8.

30 See Benjamin Filene, *Romancing the Folk: Public Memory and American Roots Music*, 76–132, esp. 122–127.

31 Rhodes, 19; for an explanation of 'rack-jobbing' and changes to the manner in which records were distributed in the 1960s, see Chapple and Garofalo, 89–92.

32 Rhodes, 19–20; Chapple and Garofalo, 109–111.

33 As noted, an extremely important exception is Warwick, *Girl Groups, Girl Culture*; other attempts to address and unpack various aspects of rock mythology include *Key Terms in Popular Music and Culture*, ed. Bruce Horner and Thomas Swiss, and *Pop Music and the Press*, ed. Steve Jones. I will discuss feminist scholarship and gender in more detail shortly.

34 See http://www.iaspm.net/ (accessed 1 Apr. 2021).

35 Robert Walser and Susan McClary, 'Start Making Sense! Musicology Wrestles with Rock,' in *On Record: Rock, Pop, and the Written Word*, ed. Simon Frith and Andrew Goodwin, 277–92, esp. 280–81. This deeply perceptive article is a succinct articulation of the complex issues inherent in the academic study of popular music. See also *Key Terms in Popular Music and Culture*, ed. Horner and Swiss, 2.

36 My case exemplifies this: I am a historian and musician but have never studied the discipline of music in an academic context. See, for example, William Mathews Hetzel, *Romanticism in Sixties Rock: Literary Traditions in Anglo-American Folk and Rock Lyrics (1963–1977)*, PhD thesis; John A. Jackson, *American Bandstand: Dick Clark and the Making of a Rock 'n' Roll Empire*; James M. Salem, *The Late Great Johnny Ace and the Transition from R & B to Rock 'n' Roll*; Laurence Coupe, *Beat Sound, Beat Vision: The Beat Spirit And Popular Song*; Elijah Wald, *How The Beatles Destroyed Rock 'n' Roll: An Alternative History Of American Popular Music*. Liverpool Hope University, in the Beatles hometown, introduced a Masters level subject in 2009 entitled *The Beatles, Popular Music and Society*; see 'First Master of Beatles Graduates,' (BBC online). I thank Andrew Broertjes for drawing this to my attention.

37 Jon Stratton, 'Jews Dreaming of Acceptance: From the Brill Building to Suburbia with Love,' *Shofar* 27:2 (2009), 102 (my italics); see also 113 where Stratton repeats his unsubstantiated assertion: 'The Shangri-Las were Jewish: sisters Mary and Betty Weiss and twins Marge and Mary Ann Ganser.' This article was reproduced without correction in Jon Stratton, *Jews, Race and Popular Music*, 37–58.

38 See John Grecco, *Out in the Streets: The Story of the Shangri-Las*, part 1, for a photo of the Ganser twins with a nun at Sacred Heart.

39 'Mary Ann Ganser, Singer, Dies at 22,' *Long Island Press*, 18 Mar. 1970, 47.

40 Henry Petroski, *Paperboy: Confessions of a Future Engineer*, 32.

41 See Linna, *Mary Weiss of the Shangri-Las*, part 2.

42 Stratton, *Shofar*, 119.

43 Linna, *Mary Weiss of the Shangri-Las*, part 3.

44 Ada Wolin, while backhandedly acknowledging Weiss's account ('the story goes that . . . the name was lifted from a local Chinese restaurant') nevertheless embarks

on a lengthy discussion of James Hilton's novel *Lost Horizon*, from which the name Shangri-La as an earthly paradise derives, without acknowledging Stratton's article, published in 2009. See Ada Wolin, *Golden Hits of the Shangri-Las*, 76–80.

45 Stratton's direct references to the Shangri-Las are not accompanied by footnotes or equivalent scholarly apparatus. On female singers, especially children and teenagers, as blank slates, see also Robynn J. Stillwell, 'Vocal Decorum: Voice, Body, and Knowledge in the Prodigious Singer, Brenda Lee,' in *She's So Fine: Reflections on Whiteness, Femininity, Adolescence and Class in 1960s Music*, ed. Laurie Stras, 57–87, esp. 60–65.

46 Warwick, *Girl Groups, Girl Culture*, 3.

47 Belinda Johnson-Grau is a notable exception, observing in 2002 that the 'girl group' descriptor 'derided and marginalised . . . many successful and influential female artists' but the wide-ranging scope of her excellent article did not allow for a detailed interrogation of 'girl group.' See Johnson-Grau, 'Sweet Nothings,' 202–218, esp. 204–5.

48 Quoted in Warwick, *Girl Groups, Girl Culture*, 5.

49 Frankie Lymon and the Teenagers, "Why Do Fools Fall in Love," *Frankie Laine Show*, 1956 (YouTube).

50 The Shangri-Las and Robert Goulet on *I've Got a Secret*, including a performance of "Leader of the Pack," 16 Nov. 1964 (YouTube). This performance is discussed in detail in chapter 5.

51 The Shangri-Las, *The Shangri-Las* (also known as *Leader of the Pack*) RED BIRD 20-101, 'Pop Spotlight,' *Billboard*, 20 Feb. 1965, 64. This album is discussed in detail in chapter 3.

52 Richard Green, 'Searchers talk about the Shangri-Las,' *New Musical Express*, 20 Nov. 1964, 13 (italics mine).

53 *Ebony* 20:8 (June 1965), 1, 4.

54 "The Supremes: Sweet-Sounding Detroiters Push To Top as New Rulers of "Rock,"' *Ebony* 20:8 (June 1965), 80–88, esp. 80, 81, 86.

55 'The Supremes' in *Ebony* 20:8 (June 1965), 81.

56 *16 Magazine Spectacular*, Summer 1965, 4–7.

57 *Ebony* 22:1 (Nov. 1966), 184–192. Johnson-Grau also mentioned these two *Ebony* features but did not note their implications for the 'girl group' label.

58 'The Ronettes: Rock 'n'roll girls trio teams up with the Beatles on a whirlwind, 14-city, U.S. entertainment tour,' *Ebony* 22:1 (Nov. 1966), 184.

59 Bobbee Barbee, 'Rocking Ronettes Rocket Toward Fame: Two Sisters and a First Cousin,' *Jet* 30:24 (Sept. 22, 1966), 60–1.

60 Palmer, 36.

61 'Employment Section: Help Wanted,' *Billboard*, 15 Apr. 1967, 67.

62 Greg Shaw, 'Charlie Feathers: The Minit-Stop,' *Phonograph Record*, July 1973 (Rock's Backpages).

63 Greil Marcus, 'How the Other Half Lives: The Best of Girl Group Rock,' *Let It Rock*, May 1974 (Rock's Backpages, italics mine). *Let It Rock* was a UK magazine; a different version of this article was published for a US audience as 'Girl Groups: How the Other Half Lived,' *Village Voice*, 8 Sept. 1975.

64 See Ian Inglis, 'Some Kind of Wonderful: The Creative Legacy of the Brill Building,' *American Music* 21:2 (2003), 214–235; Ken Emerson, *Always Magic in the Air: The Bomp and Brilliance of the Brill Building Era*.

65 The Motown house band was the subject of a 2002 documentary directed by Paul Justman, *Standing in the Shadows of Motown*.

66 Alan Betrock, *Girl Groups: The Story of a Sound*.

67 Betrock, 7.

68 Grecco, *Out in the Streets*; Ada Wolin, *Golden Hits of the Shangri-Las*.

69 Andy Schwartz, 'Remembering Alan Betrock,' *Village Voice*, 7 Apr. 2001 (Rock's Backpages).

70 Warwick, *Girl Groups, Girl Culture*, 90.

71 Betrock, 70 (italics added).

72 Barney Hoskyns, 'Transistor Sisters: Alan Betrock's Girl Groups—The Story of A Sound,' *New Musical Express*, 1982 (Rock's Backpages).

73 Greil Marcus, 'The Girl Groups,' *Rolling Stone Illustrated History of Rock and Roll*, ed. Jim Miller, 160.

74 See Warwick, *Girl Groups, Girl Culture*, 139–143; Mark Ribowsky, *He's A Rebel: Phil Spector, Rock and Roll's Legendary Producer*; Richard Williams, *Phil Spector: Out of his Head*.

75 Warwick, *Girl Groups, Girl Culture*, 97.

76 Charlotte Greig, *Will You Still Love Me Tomorrow: Girl Groups From the 50s On ...*, 8–9. Greig (1954–2014) was a musician, singer, songwriter and author working in multiple forms.

77 Warwick, *Girl Groups, Girl Culture*, esp. xii, 93–107, 121–35.

78 Craig Schuftan, *Hey! Nietzsche! Leave them kids alone: the Romantic Movement, Rock & Roll, and the End of Civilisation As We Know It*, 182–185.

79 Schuftan, 184.

80 A welcome exception is the discussion of Spector, Morton, and Motown founder Berry Gordy by Rhodes, 29–30.

81 Lenny Kaye, 'You Can't Make Heroes Out Of Guys in Black Leather Jackets, They Told George 'Shadow' Morton. He Did ... : Shadow Morton, Part 2,' *Melody Maker*, 9 Mar. 1974 (Rock's Backpages).

82 Paul Gripp, 'Party Lights: Utopic Desire and the Girl Group Sound,' in Diane Christine Raymond, *Sexual Politics and Popular Culture*, 59–67. Gripp misspells Ronettes (variously as 'Ronnette's' and 'Ronnettes') throughout his article.

83 Wolin, 25 (italics mine).

84 James M. Curtis, *Rock Eras: Interpretations of Music and Society, 1954–1984*, 85.

85 Curtis, 85–6.

86 Marcus, 'Girl Groups: How the Other Half Lived,' *Village Voice*.

87 Warwick, *Girl Groups, Girl Culture*, 3.

88 Barney Hoskyns also noted what he termed a 'nostalgic-fetishistic bent' in Betrock's writing about 'girl groups'; see Hoskyns, 'Transistor Sisters.'

89 Cynthia J. Cyrus, 'Selling an Image: Girl Groups of the 1960s,' *Popular Music* 22:2 (May 2003), 181.

90 Betrock's book is listed in Cyrus's bibliography (192–3).

91 See Betrock, 158–9.

92 See Betrock, 51.

93 'The Cookies at Mirasound Recording Studios, NYC,' Brooks Arthur, official website, Photo Gallery, photo #24. Brooks Arthur was an engineer who worked with many Brill Building groups, and on many Shangri-Las sessions. For the Shangri-Las in the studio, see Photo Gallery, photos #27–31; for the Chiffons in the recording studio, photo #2. See Richard Buskin, 'Classic Tracks: The Ronettes 'Be My Baby,' *Sound on Sound*, Apr. 2007 (online), for the Ronettes at Gold Star Studios with Phil Spector, photo #2.

94 Linna, *Mary Weiss of the Shangri-Las*, part 5. BM: Billy Miller, ML: Miriam Linna, then-owners of Brooklyn-based label Norton Records. This interview was conducted to promote Mary Weiss's first post-Shangri-Las solo album, *Dangerous Game*, released on Norton in 2007. Miller died in 2016: see William Grimes, 'Billy Miller, Curator and Historian of Fringe Music, dies at 62,' *New York Times*, 14 Nov. 2016. See also Dugan Trodglen, 'Who Says You Can Never Go Home Anymore?

The Shangri-Las Once Did. But Mary Weiss Is Proving That Wrong with a Swell Return to Rock,' *Stomp and Stammer*, Nov. 2008 (online).

95 Johnson-Grau, 209.

96 On the wider issue of the 'lumping together' of female artists in 'women in rock' books, see Coates, 88, n. 5.

97 Marcus, 'How the Other Half Lives ...'

98 Brian Ward, *Just My Soul Responding: Rhythm and Blues, Black Consciousness, and Race Relations*, 124.

99 Hoskyns, 'Transistor Sisters.'

100 See Theodor W. Adorno, 'On the Fetish-Character in Music and the Regression of Listening,' in Stephen Duncombe, *Cultural Resistance Reader*, 275–303; Coates, 65–6.

101 See also Rhodes, 70.

102 Shaw, 'Leaders of the Pack' (italics mine).

103 The Chantels, "He's Gone" (Smith/Goldner) b/w "The Plea" (Smith/Goldner), END E-1001, 1957. See also Betrock, 10; John Clemente, *Girl Groups: Fabulous Females that Rocked the World*, 49.

104 *Catalog of Copyright Entries*, Third Series, Vol. 11, Part 5, Number 1. Music, Jan.–June 1957, 180 ("He's Gone") and 385 ("The Plea"), both registered on 25 June 1957.

105 Greil Marcus, 'Girl Groups: How the Other Half Lived,' *Village Voice* (italics mine).

106 Charlie Horner and Pamela Horner, *The Musical Legacy of Richard Barrett Part Three: Richard and the Heroines of Harmony*, 1–9, esp. 2, 4 (online).

107 See Warwick, *Girl Groups, Girl Culture*, 46–8; Marc Taylor, *The Original Marvelettes: Motown's Mystery Girl Group*, 19–41, esp. 19–21.

108 See Russell A. Potter, 'Race,' in *Key Terms in Popular Music and Culture*, ed. Horner and Swiss, 78–9.

109 Greg Shaw, 'Leaders of the Pack,' (italics mine).

110 See also Gayle Wald's discussion of 'stereotypical assumptions of black artistic naïveté' in 'One of the Boys? Whiteness, Gender and Popular Music Studies,' in *Whiteness: A Critical Reader*, ed. Mike Hill, 159.

111 *Rolling Stone Illustrated History of Rock and Roll*, ed. Jim Miller.

112 Coates, 78.

113 See excerpt from the *Songmakers Collection*, a documentary about the Brill Building from 2001 (YouTube). It also contains rare footage of the Shangri-Las recording with Morton; the manner in which most of the interviewees describe the Shangri-Las in relation to Morton should be noted. See also the comments of Coates, 77–8.

114 Rich K., 'Beaches S/T,' *Terminal Boredom: Record Reviews*, Spring 2010 (online).

115 The Vivian Girls are an all-female rock trio from Brooklyn, New York City. Kim Gordon was the bass guitarist in experimental rock group Sonic Youth. The writer of this review was implying that, at 57 (in 2010), she was a 'mother-figure' for younger women who play in rock groups with experimental leanings.

116 Rich K., 'Beaches S/T.'

117 David Quantick, 'Leaders of the Teen Beat: Remember (Walkin' in the Sand) with the Shangri-Las,' *New Musical Express*, 17 Sept. 1983 (Rock's Backpages).

118 Marcus, 'How the Other Half Lives.'

119 Greil Marcus, 'The Girl Groups,' *Rolling Stone Illustrated History of Rock and Roll*, 160.

120 Anna Blumenthal, '40 Years Between Records: A Shangri-La Returns,' *New York Times*, 4 Mar. 2007, 25.

121 Johnson-Grau, 204.

122 Rhodes, 30.

123 At the end of 1964, after the success of "Leader of the Pack," the Shangri-Las tied with the Four Tops to win the Best New Vocal Group in the *R&B* section of *Cashbox* magazine's end-of-year survey: '#1 New Vocal Group 1964,' *Cash Box*, 26 Dec. 1964, 31; see also the discussion of 'black pop' by Ward, 123–169, esp. 146.

124 Josh Alan Friedman, *Tell the Truth Until They Bleed: Coming Clean in the Dirty World of Blues and Rock 'n' Roll*, 23.

125 Potter, 73–4.

126 See Potter, 71–84.

127 See Warwick, *Girl Groups, Girl Culture*, 189–92; Mina Carson, Tisa Lewis, and Susan M. Shaw, *Girls Rock! Fifty Years of Women Making Music*, 32.

128 Warwick, *Girl Groups, Girl Culture*, 2.

129 Steven Mintz, *Huck's Raft: A History of American Childhood*; Grace Palladino, *Teenagers: An American History*; Jon Savage, *Teenage: The Creation of Youth Culture*.

130 Barbara Ehrenreich, Elizabeth Hess and Gloria Jacobs, 'Beatlemania: Girls Just Want to Have Fun,' in *The Adoring Audience: Fan Culture and Popular Media*, ed. Lisa A. Lewis, 84–106. See also Sheila Whiteley, *Too Much Too Young: Popular Music, Age and Gender*.

131 Susan Douglas, *Where the Girls Are: Growing Up Female with the Mass Media*, 56–60, 83–98, 113–21. Other significant early studies include Barbara Bradby, 'Do-Talk and Don't-Talk: The Division of the Subject in Girl-Group Music,' in *On Record*, ed. Frith and Goodwin, 341–368.

132 Rhodes, Coates, Johnson-Grau.

133 *She's So Fine: Reflections on Whiteness, Femininity, Adolescence and Class in 1960s Music*, ed. Laurie Stras; Annie J. Randall, *Dusty! Queen of the Postmods*.

134 Laurie Stras, 'Voice of the Beehive: Vocal Technique at the Turn of the 1960s,' in *She's So Fine*, ed. Stras, 52–3.

135 Warwick, *Girl Groups, Girl Culture*, 93–107.

136 Warwick, *Girl Groups, Girl Culture*, 193.

137 Warwick, *Girl Groups, Girl Culture*, 118.

138 Warwick, Girl *Groups, Girl Culture*, 194.

139 'Melodrama,' *Oxford English Dictionary*.

140 Wolin, 69–72, esp. 71; see also Will Stos, 'Bouffants, Beehives, and Breaking Gender Norms: Rethinking "Girl Group" Music of the 1950s and 1960s,' *Journal of Popular Music Studies*, 24:2 (2012), 139, where "Past, Present and Future" is described as 'defensive posturing.'

141 Linna, *Mary Weiss of the Shangri-Las*, part 5; 'Suzi Quatro's Heroes of Rock 'n' Roll: Interview with Mary Weiss'; see also Goldstein, 'Pop Eye: The Soul Sound from Sheepshead Bay,' 30.

142 See also Warwick's (*Girl Groups, Girl Culture*, 118) characterisation of "Leader of the Pack" as 'histrionic' but 'nevertheless . . . an earnest and meaningful exploration of the heightened emotions of teenage girls.' Even so, Warwick still felt that the emotionality of the song had to be justified, by pointing out that 'Greenwich asserts that she and the Shangri-Las took the piece seriously and found it moving.'

143 Needs and Porter, 12–13.

144 Jay Warner, *American Singing Groups: A History from 1940s to Today*, 344.

145 *Billboard*, 24 July 1971, 38; *Billboard*, 7 Aug. 1971, 56; *Billboard*, 17 July 1971, 30.

146 Uncritical use of the term continues with Laura Flam and Emily Sieu Liebowitz, *But Will You Love Me Tomorrow: An Oral History of the '60s Girl Groups*, from 2023. The interviews Flam and Liebowitz have conducted constitute important new primary material for the historical record; nevertheless, their chapter on the Shangri-Las (225–234, which includes no new material from either of the Weiss sisters) does not challenge received understandings of the group.

147 Trodglen, 'Who Says You Can Never Go Home Anymore?'

148 Palmer, 37–8; Greig, 78–84; Donna Gaines, 'Girl Groups: A Ballad of Co-dependency,' in *Trouble Girls: The Rolling Stone Book of Women in Rock*, ed. Barbara O'Dair, 111–12; Ritchie Unterberger, 'Shangri-Las,' entry on allmusic.com.

149 Wolin, 20. I am not alone in having issues with Wolin's volume: see Mitchell Cohen, 'Good-Bad, Not Evil: *Golden Hits of the Shangri-Las*,' *Rock and Roll Globe*, 18 Apr. 2019 (online). Cohen has been a music journalist for decades and has written about the Shangri-Las: see Mitchell Cohen, 'Shangri-Las: A Teenage Melodrama,' in *Let It Rock*, Dec. 1974 (Rock's Backpages).

150 Stras, 6 (italics mine).

CHAPTER TWO: *Queens, Doo-Wop, and Two Pairs of Sisters*

1 Jeffrey A. Kroessler, *Building Queens: The Urbanization of New York's Largest Borough*, Unpublished PhD thesis, 7; see also Kenneth T. Jackson, 'Introduction,' in Claudia Gryvatz Copquin and Kenneth T. Jackson, *The Neighbourhoods of Queens*, xxi–xxvii.

2 For a detailed examination of the early agricultural history of Queens, see Kroessler, *Building Queens*, 7–39; for the relocation of industry, see 184–9.

3 Jeffrey A. Kroessler, 'Suburban Growth, Urban Style and Patterns of Growth in the Borough of Queens,' in *Long Island: The Suburban Experience*, ed. Barbara M. Kelly, 25.

4 Kroessler, *Building Queens*, iv–v, 2–3, and for a more detailed discussion of the rapid urbanisation of Queens and its context, 230–385; see also Sylvie Murray, *Suburban Citizens: Domesticity and Community Politics in Queens, New York, 1945–1960*, Unpublished PhD thesis, 15–16.

5 Kroessler, 'Suburban Growth,' 31.

6 Kroessler, 'Suburban Growth,' 32–3.

7 Murray, 18–22.

8 Murray, 26.

9 Carol Taylor, 'Queens has a street named Utopia,' *World Telegram*, 14 Oct. 1948, quoted in Murray, 27.

10 For a detailed discussion of Queens as an idyllic, affordable place to raise a family, see Murray, 26–34.

11 Henry Petroski, *Paperboy: Confessions of a Future Engineer*, 3; for Petroski's career and publications, see http://www.cee.duke.edu/fds/pratt/cee/faculty/petroski (accessed 6 Mar. 2023); see also Copquin and Jackson, 21.

12 Quoted in Kroessler, 'Suburban Growth,' 29.

13 Murray, 42.

14 Stephen Grant Meyer, *As Long as They Don't Move Next Door: Segregation and Racial Conflict in American Neighborhoods*; Kevin Fox Gotham, *Race, Real Estate and Uneven Development: The Kansas City Experience 1900–2000*; Thomas J. Sugrue, *The Origins of the Urban Crisis: Race and Inequality in Postwar Detroit*, esp. 33–88.

15 George Lipsitz, *The Possessive Investment in Whiteness: How White People Profit from Identity Politics*, 26, see also 24–33.

16 See Murray, 163–180.

17 Copquin and Jackson, 193.

18 Murray, 23–4.

19 John P. Dean, 'Only Caucasian: A Study of Race Covenants,' *Journal of Land and Public Utility Economics* 23:4 (1947), 429–30. His study covered the counties of Queens, Nassau and Southern Westchester.

20 Dean, 430.

21 Dean, 431.

22 Dean, 430–32.

23 Quoted in Ellen K. Feder, *Family Bonds: Genealogies of Race and Gender*, 30; on Levittown and whiteness, see also 25–44.

24 Murray, 83–88.

25 Meyer, 7–8; see also David Theo Goldberg, "'Polluting the Body Politic'": Racist Discourse and Urban Location,' in *Racism, the City and the State*, ed. Malcolm Cross and Michael Keith, 45–60, esp. 51–2.

26 Copquin and Jackson, 21.

27 See Sugrue, esp. 209–229; Olivia Frost, 'The Housing Market in Queens,' *The Crisis* 67:6 (June–July 1960), 349–354.

28 Copquin and Jackson, 21; see also Janet E. Lieberman and Richard K. Lieberman, *City Limits: A Social History of Queens*.

29 Murray, 25, n. 20.

30 *Social Security Death Index*, entry for Herman Ganser (familysearch.org).

31 In 2018, Gmünd had a population of 5,375.

32 The Ganser family plot at Friedhof Gmünd, Austria: https://www.findagrave.com/memorial/80318041/anna-ganser (accessed 2 Jan. 2024).

33 *Canada, Arriving Passengers Lists, 1865–1935*, Series: RG 76-C; Roll: T-14762 (ancestry.com). See Norway-Heritage website for the *Calgaric*: http://www.norwayheritage.com/p_ship.asp?sh=calga and the White Star Line: http://www.norwayheritage.com/p_shiplist.asp?co=white (accessed 2 Jan. 2024).

34 *Canada, Arriving Passengers Lists, 1865–1935*, Series: RG 76-C; Roll: T-14762 (ancestry.com).

35 *Canada, Arriving Passengers Lists, 1865–1935*, Series: RG 76-C; Roll: T-14762 (ancestry.com).

36 Ninette Kelley and Michael Trebilcock, *The Making of The Mosaic: A History of Canadian Immigration Policy*, 194–99, esp. 195; see also Laura A. Detre, 'Canada's Campaign for Immigrants and the Images in *Canada West* Magazine,' *Great Plains Quarterly*, Spring 2004, 113–29.

37 Jonathan F. Wagner, *A History of Migration from Germany to Canada, 1850–1939*, 164–6; see also *Canadian Museum of Immigration at Pier 21*, 'Railway Agreement, 1925' (online).

38 *Canadian Museum of Immigration at Pier 21*, 'Ship Arrival Database' (online).

39 See Michael John, 'Push and Pull Factors for Overseas Migrants from Austria-Hungary in the 19th and 20th Centuries,' in *Austrian Immigration to Canada: Selected Essays* ed. Franz Szabo, 55–82; see also Vadim Kukushkin, *From Peasants to Labourers: Ukrainian and Belarusan Immigration from the Russian Empire to Canada*, 30–80.

40 Wagner, 166–68.

41 *New York, New York, U.S., Marriage License Indexes*, 1907–2018, Borough: Manhattan; Volume Number: 6 (ancestry.com).

42 New Jersey State Archives; Trenton, New Jersey; *Marriage Indexes*; Index Type: Bride; Year Range: 1915–1919; Surname Range: T–Z, *New Jersey, U.S., Marriage Index, 1901–2016*, certificate number 06759 (ancestry.com).

43 *New York, New York City Marriage Records, 1829–1940*, Peter Conrad and Johanna Clancy, 01 May 1898, New York City Municipal Archives, New York; FHL microfilm 1,503,843 (familysearch.org).

44 *United States Census 1900*, Peter and Johanna Conrad, Borough of Manhattan, Election District 19 New York City Ward 3, enumeration district (ED) 57, sheet 2B, family 50, NARA microfilm publication T623; FHL microfilm 1,241,082 (familysearch.org).

45 *New York, New York City Municipal Deaths, 1795–1949*, FHL microfilm 1,322,975 (familysearch.org).

46 Peter and Johanna's third daughter Loretta was born 28 Oct. 1902 at 56 Leroy St and died 20 Nov. 1905 at 16 Clarkson St, the address at which the family was living at the time of the 1905 census. See *New York, New York, U.S., Index to Birth Certificates, 1866–1909*, Borough: Manhattan; Year: 1902 (ancestry.com). For the 1905 census see New York, U.S., *State Population Census Schedules, 1905*; Election District: A.D. 03 E.D. 16; City: Manhattan; County: New York; 46 (ancestry.com).

47 *United States Census 1910*, Peter Conrod [*sic*], Manhattan Ward 9, New York, New York, United States; citing enumeration district (ED) ED 176, sheet 8A, family 198, NARA microfilm publication T624, roll 1006; FHL microfilm 1,375,019 (familysearch.org).

48 Entry for Johanna Conrad, 14 Sept. 1912, *Episcopal Diocese of New York Church Records, 1767–1970*, 'Baptisms,' 608–9 (ancestry.com).

49 Death notice for Johanna Conrad, *New York Times*, 16 Sept. 1912, 13.

50 Peter Conrad, *New York State Census, 1915* (familysearch.org).

51 *U.S., Social Security Applications and Claims Index, 1936–2007* (ancestry.com).

52 Peter Conrad, *United States Census, 1920*, (familysearch.org); Peter Micheal (sic) Conrad, *U.S. World War I Draft Registration Cards 1917–1918*, 1918, Draft Card, New York, Manhattan City, 105, Draft Card C (ancestry.com).

53 Death notice for Mary Conrad, *New York Tribune*, 20 Feb. 1920, 4.

54 Wan Yang, Elisaveta Petkova and Jeffrey Shaman, 'The 1918 influenza pandemic in New York City: age-specific timing, mortality, and transmission dynamics,' *Influenza and Other Respiratory Viruses* 8:2 (Mar. 2014), 178.

55 Death Notices, *New York Tribune*, 20 Feb. 1920, 4.

56 *New York City Municipal Archives*; Borough: Manhattan; Volume Number: 6 (ancestry.com).

57 Peter Conrad, *United States Census, 1930* (familysearch.org).

58 Rita Conrad in household of John Martin, *United States Census, 1930*, Queens (Districts 1251-1500), Queens, New York, United States (familysearch.org).

59 Peter John Conrad, *United States Census, 1940*, Brooklyn, New York City, New York, United States (familysearch.org). Here Peter's middle name is listed as John; elsewhere it is recorded as Michael, or not recorded at all. It is possible Peter Conrad had more than one middle name, but in any case, it is clear from matches with other records that this is the same person.

60 The Federal census was taken every ten years in the first year of the new decade (1900, 1910, 1920 etc.); in New York a State census was often (but not always) taken every ten years but mid-decade; they exist for 1905, 1915 and 1925, but not 1935.

61 *United States Federal Census 1940* (ancestry.com).

62 *United States Federal Census 1940* (ancestry.com).

63 'Mary Ann Ganser, Singer, Dies at 22,' *Long Island Press*, Mar. 18, 1970, 47; *New York City Phone Directory 1964–5: Queens*, 441; Phil Milstein, interview with Robert Ganser, 14 Oct. 2001.

64 'Mary Ann Ganser, Singer, Dies at 22'; Jeremy Simmonds, *The Encyclopedia of Dead Rock Stars: Heroin, Handguns, and Ham Sandwiches*, 33.

65 Grecco, *Out in the Streets*, part 1.

66 Grecco, *Out in the Streets*, part 1.

67 Milstein, interview with Robert Ganser.

68 Phil Milstein, interview with Rita Ganser, 14 Oct. 2001; see also Grecco, *Out in the Streets*, part 1. Rita Ganser died on 31 Mar. 2004; *U.S. Social Security Applications and Claims Index, 1936–2007*, Rita Marie Ganser (ancestry.com).

69 Milstein, interview with Rita Ganser.

70 Milstein, interview with Rita Ganser.

71 Grecco, *Out in the Streets*, part 1.

72 New York, New York, U.S., *Marriage License Indexes*, 1907–2018 (ancestry.com); *Federal Census 1940*, New York, Queens, New York; Roll: m-t0627-02742; Page: 6B; Enumeration District: 41-1138A (ancestry.com).

73 *Federal Census 1940*; New York, Queens, New York; Roll: m-t0627-02742; Page: 6B; Enumeration District: 41-1138A (ancestry.com); Queens New York City Telephone Directory, Winter 1939–40, 381.

74 Harry Weiss's 1940 Draft Card lists the address of his workplace as 101 Willoughby St, Brooklyn: U.S., *World War II Draft Cards Young Men, 1940–1947* (ancestry. com); see also 'Long Island Headquarters of the New York Telephone Company,' *Landmarks Preservation Commission* (report) for a photo and extensive discussion of the building's architectural significance.

75 *Occupational Outlook Handbook: Employment Information on Major Occupations for Use in Guidance prepared in cooperation with Veterans Administration Office of the Assistant Administrator for Vocational Rehabilitation and Education*, 175, 470–71.

76 U.S., *Find a Grave Index*, 1600s–Current, George M. Weiss.

77 Elizabeth Anna Nelson, *U.S., Index to Public Records, 1994–2019* (ancestry.com).

78 New York, New York, U.S., *Birth Index, 1910–1965* (ancestry.com); Linna, *Mary Weiss of the Shangri-Las*, part 2.

79 Terry Gross, 'Mary Weiss comes back for a *Dangerous Game*,' interview for *Fresh Air* on NPR (National Public Radio), 6 Mar. 2007.

80 Petroski, 71.

81 Iain Aitch, 'The Leader's Back,' *The Telegraph*, 14 Apr. 2007.

82 'Rescue High in Air Brings Vail Award,' *New York Times*, 1 June 1940, 11.

83 'In What Ways Did Your Father Influence Your Life?: Mary Weiss,' *Growing Bolder*, 13 June 2008 (online).

84 *Federal Census 1950*, Record Group Number: 29; Residence Date: 1950; Home in 1950: New York, Queens, New York; Roll: 6235; Sheet Number: 74; Enumeration District: 41-1658 (ancestry.com).

85 Gross, 'Mary Weiss comes back for a *Dangerous Game*.'

86 Linna, *Mary Weiss of the Shangri-Las*, part 7; Kurt Loder, 'Where Are They Now? The Shangri-Las,' *Rolling Stone*, 12 Sept. 1985, 50; see also Ken Emerson, *Always Magic in the Air: The Bomp and Brilliance of the Brill Building Era*, 225–6.

87 For a former student's description, photos and anecdotes see Lee Somerstein, 'The Corner,' *LFS: The Storyteller* (online).

88 Petroski, 127–8.

89 Grecco, *Out in the Streets*, part 1.

90 Petroski, 128.

91 Walter B. Miller, 'Lower Class Culture as a Generating Milieu of Gang Delinquency,' *Journal of Social Issues*, 14:3 (1958), 5–19.

92 *Addisleigh Park: Report Prepared by Jane Cowan for the Historic Districts Council* 5–15; see also Robert A.M. Stern and John Montague Massengale, *The Anglo American Suburb*.

93 For details of the court proceedings, see *Addisleigh Park: Report*, 15–18.

94 See Andrew Weise, '"The House I Live In": Race, Class and African American Suburban Dreams in the Postwar United States,' in *The New Suburban History*, ed. Kevin Michael Kruse and Thomas J. Sugrue, 99–119, esp. 105–110; *Addisleigh Park: Report*, 18–21.

95 Addisleigh Park: Report, 21.

96 Addisleigh Park: Report, 21–2; James Gavin, *Stormy Weather: The Life of Lena Horne*, 184.

97 Copquin and Jackson, 193. On jazz and jazz musicians in Queens, see Nat Hentoff, *At the Jazz Band Ball: Sixty Years on the Jazz Scene*, 160–62.

98 Linna, *Mary Weiss of the Shangri-Las*, part 4.

99 Aileen Jacobson, 'Mary Weiss Is Trying To Get Back in the Rocker Pack,' *Los Angeles Times*, 6 Apr. 2007.

100 'Gospel Tent's "Screaming" Services Drive Neighbours to Court Protest,' *New York Times*, 11 Sept. 1951, 31.

101 See Davarian L. Baldwin, *Chicago's New Negroes: Modernity, the Great Migration, and Black Urban Life*, 155–192.

102 *Gotham Center for New York City History*, 23 Mar. 2007, http://www.gothamcenter. org/discussions/viewtopic.php?id=854&p=3 (accessed 23 Aug. 2010).

103 Leonard Buder, '40 Policemen Guarding Jackson High,' *New York Times*, 1 Mar. 1969, 28.

104 Loder, 50; see also Emerson, 225–6.

105 Linna, *Mary Weiss of the Shangri-Las*, part 2.

106 Milton Esterow, 'Summer Fetes Attracting Stars: Talent Converging on City in Version of the old Rush; Events at Randalls, Freedomland and Forest Hills Set,' *New York Times*, 29 June 1962, 13.

107 'Daily Events–1962' (20 Aug.), https://www.history-of-rock.com/daily_ events_1962.htm (accessed 2 Jan. 2024); Linna, *Mary Weiss of the Shangri-Las*, part 2.

108 'Suzi Quatro's Heroes of Rock 'n' Roll: Interview with Mary Weiss'; Linna, *Mary Weiss of the Shangri-Las*, part 2. Good examples of the Everly Brothers' harmonising include "All I Have to Do Is Dream" and "Cathy's Clown" on *The Alma Cogan Show*, 1961 (YouTube).

109 'Suzi Quatro's Heroes of Rock 'n' Roll: Interview with Mary Weiss.'

110 'Suzi Quatro's Heroes of Rock 'n' Roll: Interview with Mary Weiss.'

111 David Chiu, 'Cambria Heights Singer Returns to Music,' *Queens Chronicle*, 4 Oct. 2007.

112 Gross, 'Mary Weiss comes back for a *Dangerous Game*'; Linna, *Mary Weiss of the Shangri-Las*, part 2.

113 The De Villes, "Kiss Me Again and Again," *Billboard*, 5 May 1958, 118.

114 Anthony J. Gribin and Matthew M. Schiff, *Doo-Wop: The Forgotten Third of Rock 'n' Roll*, 14. See also Jeffrey Melnick, '"Story Untold": The Black Men and White Sounds of Doo-Wop,' in *Whiteness: A Critical Reader*, ed. Mike Hill, 137.

115 Jay Warner, *American Singing Groups*, 44–5.

116 Warner, 38–9.

117 Gribin and Schiff (1992), 25; Mike Evans, *NYC Rock*, 16–19; Philip Groia, *They All Sang on the Corner: A Second Look at New York City's Rhythm and Blues Vocal Groups*, 28–9.

118 Grace Palladino, *Teenagers: An American History*, 142.

119 See discussion of recording contracts by Hank Bordowitz, *Dirty Little Secrets of the Record Business: Why So Much Music You Hear Sucks*, 259–70.

120 Marc Taylor, *The Original Marvelettes: Motown's Mystery Girl Group*, 23–25.

121 Gribin and Schiff (1992), 24.

122 Eric C. Schneider, *Vampires, Dragons and Egyptian Kings: Youth Gangs in Postwar New York*, 35; on overcrowding and the racial politics of space, see Goldberg, 51–54.

123 Gribin and Schiff (1992), 25.

124 Bill Millar, 'Frankie Lymon: Why Do Fools Fall in Love?' *Pye Records*, 1972 (Rock's Backpages).

125 Gribin and Schiff (1992), 17, 20, 25.

126 Gribin and Schiff (1992), 21.

127 Gribin and Schiff (1992), 14.

128 Melnick, 137; Groia, 84–5.

129 June Bundy, 'R&B Disks Sock Pop Market; Major Firms Jump into Ring,' *Billboard*, 29 Jan. 1955, 56.

130 Susan J. Douglas, *Listening In: Radio and the American Imagination*, 222.

131 'The Billboard Music Popularity Charts, Rhythm & Blues, Review Spotlight on . . . Records: The Teenagers–Frankie Lymon,' *Billboard*, 4 Feb. 1956, 58.

132 Warner, 244.

133 Seymour Stein with Gareth Murphy, *Siren Song: My Life in Music*, 56–7; Stuffed Animal, 'Mambo Gee Gee: The Story of George Goldner and Tico Records, Part One' *Spectropop* (online).

134 Stuffed Animal, 'Mambo Gee Gee: The Story of George Goldner and Tico Records, Part Two' *Spectropop* (online).

135 Charlie Horner, Pamela Horner, and Val Shively, *The Musical Legacy of Richard Barrett—Part Two: Richard Barrett and the Teenagers*, and *The Musical Legacy of Richard Barrett—Part Three: Richard and the Heroines of Harmony*.

136 The Teenagers featuring Frankie Lymon, "Why Do Fools Fall in Love" (Lymon/Goldner) b/w "My Girl" (Harrington-Saffer), GEE 1002, 1956. See Horner et al., *The Musical Legacy of Richard Barrett—Part Two*, especially page 3 for the original Gee pressing naming Lymon and Goldner as authors.

137 Horner et al., *The Musical Legacy of Richard Barrett—Part Two*, 3–4. Mary Weiss also attended Quintano's; this will be discussed in more detail in the next chapter.

138 Horner et al., *The Musical Legacy of Richard Barrett—Part Two*, 7.

139 Horner et al., *The Musical Legacy of Richard Barrett—Part Two*, 7–8; Art Peters, 'Comeback of a Child Star,' *Ebony*, Jan. 1967, 46, 48

140 'Goldner Sells Out to Levy; Stays in Field,' *Billboard* 6 Apr. 1957, 16, 44.

141 For a thorough discussion of Morris Levy, his business practices and ties to the Mob, see Richard Carlin, *Godfather of the Music Business: Morris Levy*. See also Fredric Dannen, *Hit Men: Power Brokers and Fast Money Inside the Music Business*, 31–57; Justine Picardie and Dorothy Wade, *Atlantic and the Godfathers of Rock and Roll*, 41–47.

142 'N.J. Jury Issues Indictments in Cutout Probes,' *Billboard* 4 Oct. 1986, 1, 91; William Knoedelseder, *Stiffed: A True Story of MCA, the Music Business, and the Mafia*; see also Carlin, 197–224.

143 Dannen, 40–41.

144 Bordowitz, 259–70.

145 Peters, 48; Charlie Horner, Pamela Horner and Val Shively, *The Musical Legacy of Richard Barrett—Part Five: The Lewis Lymon and Jimmy Castor Stories*, 3; the Teenagers were described as 'reeling from the loss of Frankie Lymon going solo.'

146 David Edwards and Mike Callahan, 'End Records Discography,' (online); for a brief biography of George Goldner, see Edwards and Callahan, 'The George Goldner Story,' (online).

147 Peters, 43.

148 Peters, 43.

149 'Frankie Lymon Dies in Apartment Here,' *New York Times*, 28 Feb. 1968, 50; Mary Koval, *Opiate Use in New York City*, i.

150 Richard Perez-Pena, 'Here's Who First Asked Rock's Big Question,' *New York Times*, 19 Nov. 1992, A1, B8.

151 Perez-Pena, A1, B8.

152 '2 Members of The Teenagers Awarded Royalties for "Fools,"' *Billboard*, 28 Nov. 1992, 6, 96; see also Michael Goldberg, 'Lawsuit Over Lymon Song Settled,' *Rolling Stone*, 1 July 1993, 19.

153 Perez-Pena, A1, B8.

154 See Fredric Dannen, 'The Godfather of Rock and Roll,' *Rolling Stone*, 17 Nov. 1988, 88–97, 164.

155 Tommy James with Martin Fitzpatrick, *Me, the Mob and the Music: One Helluva Ride with Tommy James and the Shondells*, 62. Carlin details multiple instances of violence meted out by Levy and his henchmen: see, for instance, 107–110, 179–180.

156 *Jimmy Merchant and Herman Santiago, plaintiffs-appellees-cross-appellants, v. Morris Levy, Big Seven Music Corp. and Roulette Records, Inc., Defendants-appellants-cross-appellees, and Windswept Pacific Entertainment Co., intervenor-defendant-appellant-cross-appellee, 92 F.3d 51, 2d Cir. 1996*; for detailed coverage of the "Why Do Fools . . ." saga, see Carlin, 179–196.

157 BMI listing for Morris Levy. BMI (Broadcast Music Incorporated) and ASCAP (American Society of Composers, Authors and Publishers) record and manage authorship for the collection of publishing, performance and broadcast royalties.

158 Melnick, 134–150; see also *White Doo-Wop Collector* (website) on which there are hundreds of listings.

159 David Edwards, Patrice Eyries, and Mike Callahan, 'The ABC-Paramount Story,' (online); see also Bundy, 'R&B Disks Sock Pop Market, 56.

160 See *Singles Discography for ABC Paramount Records—9000 series*: "Cathy" b/w "Rock and Roll Baby" is # 9920. See BMI listing under "Ripp Arthur M" for songwriting credits for "Cathy" and "Rock and Roll Baby"; the other writers, Mario Scarpa and Stewart Silverman, do not appear on BMI as having composed other songs. They are listed among the group's personnel, along with a picture and discography: see 'The Four Temptations,' *White Doo-Wop Collector* (website) entry for The Four Temptations (online).

161 'Reviews of New Pop Records,' *Billboard*, 5 May 1958, 115.

162 See *45 Discography for Goldisc Records* (online) and BMI listing for Ripp, Arthur M. Artie Ripp's group is unconnected with the Motown group the Temptations, who released their first single, "Oh Mother of Mine," in July 1961; see Warner, 462–3.

163 'Reviews of New Pop Records,' *Billboard*, 22 Feb. 1960, 45.

164 Goldisc Advertisement, *Billboard*, 21 Mar. 1960, 42.

165 Ren Grevatt, 'Kama Sutra Productions: Is Twenty-Three too Young to Own a Record Company?,' *Hi Fi/Stereo Review* 15 (1965), 28.

166 Mark Ribowsky, He's a Rebel: Phil Spector—Rock and Roll's Legendary Producer, 92.

167 'Artie Ripp,' in Joe Smith and Mitchell Fink, *Off the Record: An Oral History of Popular Music*, 134.

168 'Artie Ripp,' *Off the Record*, 135.

169 Songwriter Jerome Solon Felder, better known as Doc Pomus, described Ripp as 'an obnoxious little shit,' (Ribowsky, 68); for an incident involving Ripp, Spector and two young women described by Ripp as 'crazy nymphomaniacs' upon whom he 'got the job done,' see Ribowsky, 72–3; Emerson, 77.

170 Emerson, 136.

171 Grevatt, 28.

172 Gross, 'Mary Weiss comes back for a *Dangerous Game*.'

173 Grecco, *Out in the Streets*, part 1; Richard Arfin, 'The "Shadow" Reappears—A Rare Talk With Producer George "Shadow" Morton,' *Goldmine*, 12 July 1991, reproduced by Long Island Music Hall of Fame (website), part 4.

174 Grecco, *Out in the Streets*, part 1.

175 Songwriting credits on BMI indicate that Tony Gianna, Tony Giannattasio, and Tony Michaels are the same person. This use of various publishing aliases seems to have been a common practice.

176 See listing for BMI listing for Tony Michaels. It is not clear when these were composed and who recorded them (if they were recorded at all).

177 Linna, *Mary Weiss of the Shangri-Las*, part 2; 'Suzi Quatro's Heroes of Rock 'n' Roll: Interview with Mary Weiss'; Warner, 462–3.

178 Linna, *Mary Weiss of the Shangri-Las,* part 2.

179 "Simon Says" (Michaels) b/w "Simon Speaks" (Mizrahi/Steinberg), SMASH 1866, Dec. 1963.

180 Quoted in John Broven, *Record Makers and Breakers: Voices of the Independent Rock 'n' Roll Pioneers,* 292-3; for the distribution benefits of subsidiary labels, see 46-7.

181 Linna, *Mary Weiss of the Shangri-Las,* part 3.

182 The Four Seasons could be a club, or the doo-wop group the Four Seasons, who had released a single on the Gone label (so there was a connection, however slight, via Ripp).

183 Grecco, *Out in the Streets,* part 1.

184 *Billboard,* 28 Dec. 1963, 14-15.

185 *Cash Box,* 28 Dec. 1963, 76.

186 "Wishing Well" (Monaco/Michaels) b/w "Hate to Say I Told You So" (Jackson/Steinberg/Steinberg), SPOKANE 4006, Apr. 1964.

187 See also Mick Patrick, liner notes for *Girls with Guitars: All Girl Bands, Axe Backed Babes and the Like,* which includes the Morton composition "Only Seventeen," about which more shortly. Morton reported to me that 'the studio in Hicksville was Dynamic Recording Studios, it was in the basement of a house, the house was owned by Joey Monaco.' Lisa MacKinney, interview with George 'Shadow' Morton, 24 Apr. 2007.

188 Linna, *Mary Weiss of the Shangri-Las,* part 3.

189 The Shangri-Las, "He Cried" (Daryll/Richards) b/w "Dressed in Black" (Michaels/Gormann/Morton) RED BIRD 053, 1966.

190 Linna, *Mary Weiss of the Shangri-Las,* part 2; Betrock, 98.

191 Douglas, *Listening In,* 229–33.

192 'Cousin Brucie' Morrow and Rich Maloof, *Doo Wop: The Music, the Times, the Era,* 119.

193 Gross, 'Mary Weiss Comes Back for a *Dangerous Game.*'

CHAPTER THREE: *The Shangri-Las, George 'Shadow' Morton, and Red Bird Records*

1 Richard Arfin, 'The "Shadow" Reappears—A Rare Talk With Producer George "Shadow" Morton,' part 1, lists the year of Morton's birth as 1944. However, the Wikipedia entry for Morton lists it as 1941; Richie Unterberger's entry for Morton for the All Music website listed it as 1942 in 2010 but now lists it as 1940; and Morton's Myspace page, which he personally administered, listed his age in 2010 as 63, which would require a birth date of 1947.

2 See photo of (Eleanor) Greenwich in *U.S., School Yearbooks, 1900–1999,* Levittown Memorial High School, 'Echoes,' 1955, scan 57 (ancestry.com); Richard Williams, 'Ellie Greenwich, 1940–2009,' *The Guardian,* 27 Aug. 2009; Ralph M. Newman, 'Only the Shadow Knows: An Interview by Ralph M. Newman, *Time Barrier Express* 26 (Sept/Oct 1979), 41.

3 *New York, New York, U.S., Birth Index, 1910–1965* for George F. Morton (ancestry.com).

4 *New York, New York, U.S., Marriage License Indexes, 1907–2018,* Brooklyn, 1936, July–Oct.; groom George F. Morton, 771 & bride Irene A. (? name listed as Irene Regina on Morton's 1940 Draft Card; possibly misread/transcribed as A instead of R) Kelly, 628, Marriage Licence No. 16823 (ancestry.com).

5 *1940 United States Federal Census,* New York, Kings, 24-1372 (ancestry.com).

6 *1930 United States Federal Census,* New York, Kings, Brooklyn (Districts 501-750), District 0623 (ancestry.com).

7 *1940 United States Federal Census, New York, Kings,* 24-1372 (ancestry.com). George and Irene are on 22 (Sheet 11A); Frank and Martha are on 22-3 (Sheets 11A & 11B).

8 U.S., *World War II Draft Cards Young Men, 1940–1947, New York (City)* for George Francis Morton (ancestry.com); this also confirms wife Irene Regina and their residential address of 219 13th St, Brooklyn. For W.W. Fitzhugh, see *Brooklyn, New York City, Telephone Directory, 1950* (online).

9 Parochial School of St Thomas Aquinas (picture), https://www.bklynlibrary.org/item?b=11150044 (accessed 28 Sept. 2021).

10 Arfin, 'The "Shadow" Reappears,' part 3.

11 Henry Petroski, *Paperboy: Confessions of a Future Engineer*, 24, 32–34.

12 Petroski, 32; Petroski, Henry (Snr), *Brooklyn, New York City, Telephone Directory, 1950* (online); St Thomas Aquinas Church Park Slope: https://holyfamily-stthomas-brooklyn.org/ (accessed 28 Sept. 2021).

13 *Sophisticated Boom Boom: The Shadow Morton Story* (CD), liner notes by Mick Patrick, 8.

14 See note 12 above for Park Slope; St Thomas Aquinas Church Flatlands: https://stthomasaquinasbrooklyn.com/ (accessed 28 Sept. 2021).

15 *United States Census 1950*, Record Group Number: 29, Kings, New York; Roll: 940; Sheet Number: 5; Enumeration District: 24-1657 (ancestry.com). In 1950 (unlike previous years) the census collector noted the household's apartment number: the Mortons were in Apartment 8.

16 *Virginia, Marriages, 1936–2014*; Roll: 101167344, Certificate No: 1948018686 (ancestry.com).

17 *Virginia, U.S., Select Marriages, 1785–1940* (ancestry.com).

18 *United States Census 1910*; Richmond Clay Ward, Richmond (Independent City), Virginia; Roll: T624_1644; Page: 8B; Enumeration District: 0070; FHL microfilm: 1375657 (ancestry.com).

19 Robert West Kelly, Certificate No. 1912015634, Virginia, U.S., *Birth Records, 1912–2015, Delayed Birth Records, 1721–1920* (ancestry.com); Irene Kelly, U.S., *Social Security Applications and Claims Index, 1936–2007* (ancestry.com).

20 Christina Kelly, Certificate No. 1918027838, Richmond, Virginia; *Virginia Deaths, 1912–2014* (ancestry.com).

21 *United States Census 1920*; Census Place: Richmond Madison Ward, Richmond (Independent City), Virginia; Roll: T625_1911; Page: 20A; Enumeration District: 143 (ancestry.com).

22 St Josephs is still operating, albeit in modified form: see *St Joseph's Villa: Mission & History* (online) and short film *The St Joseph's Villa Story* (via YouTube).

23 *United States Census 1920*, Census Place: Richmond Madison Ward, Richmond (Independent City), Virginia; Roll: T625_1911; Page: 20A; Enumeration District: 143 (ancestry.com).

24 *United States Census 1920*, Census Place: Richmond Clay Ward, Richmond (Independent City), Virginia; Roll: T625_1909; Page: 22B; Enumeration District: 66 (ancestry.com).

25 *United States Census 1910*, Census Place: Richmond Clay Ward, Richmond (Independent City), Virginia; Roll: T624_1644; Page: 8B; Enumeration District: 0070; FHL microfilm: 1375657 (ancestry.com).

26 Richmond, Virginia; *Virginia Deaths, 1912–2014*, Robert Lee Kelly, Death Certificate No. 1927010973 (ancestry.com).

27 *United States Census 1940*, Census Place: New York, Kings, New York; Roll: m-t0627-02569; Page: 12B; Enumeration District: 24-919 (ancestry.com); see also Santo J. Grimaldi, *WWII Draft Registration Cards for New York City, 10/16/1940 – 03/31/1947*; Record Group: Records of the Selective Service System, 147 (ancestry.com).

28 New York, New York, U.S., *Birth Index, 1910–1965* (ancestry.com).

29 *United States Census 1950*, Record Group Number: 29; Residence Date: 1950; Home in 1950: New York, Kings, New York; Roll: 2865; Sheet Number: 75; Enumeration District: 24-1100 (ancestry.com).

30 *United States Census 1950*, Record Group Number: 29; Residence Date: 1950; Home in 1950: New York, Kings, New York; Roll: 2865; Sheet Number: 45; Enumeration District: 24-1073 (ancestry.com); Petroski, 32–34.

31 Lenny Kaye, 'Standing in the Shadow of Rock: Shadow Morton, Part 1,' *Melody Maker*, 2 Mar. 1974 (Rock's Backpages); Arfin, 'The "Shadow" Reappears,' part 2.

32 U.S., *School Yearbooks, 1900–1999*, Bethpage High School, 'The Blue Book,' 1956, scan 89 (ancestry.com). Mick Patrick also notes that Morton graduated from Bethpage High School in 1959; *Sophisticated Boom Boom*, liner notes, 11.

33 U.S., *School Yearbooks, 1900–1999*, Bethpage High School, 'The Blue Book,' 1956, scan 90 (ancestry.com).

34 Arfin, 'The "Shadow" Reappears,' parts 4 & 2.

35 Arfin, 'The "Shadow" Reappears,' part 2; Patrick, *Sophisticated Boom Boom*, liner notes, 9–11, which also includes a rare photo of the group from Morton's own collection.

36 *Catalog of Copyright Entries*: Third Series, Vol. 12, Part 5, Number 1. Music: Current and Renewal Registrations Jan.–June 1958, entry no. EU529555, 202.

37 The Markeys featuring George Morton, "Hot Rod" (George Francis Morton and Joseph J. Monaco) b/w "Yakkity Yak" (Jack Hammer), RCA 47-7256, 1958; and "A Time To Love" (George Francis Morton and Joseph J. Monaco) b/w "Make a Record, Man" (George Francis Morton, Joseph J. Monaco and Martin Monaco), RCA 47-7412, 1958. Of these, "Hot Rod" is included on *Sophisticated Boom Boom: The Shadow Morton Story*. "Hot Rod" is particularly significant and is discussed at length in chapter 6.

38 Patrick, *Sophisticated Boom Boom*, liner notes, 10.

39 Arfin, 'The "Shadow" Reappears,' part 4. Levittown and Bethpage are neighbouring suburbs, and 'off Bloomingdale Rd' is consistent with Billy Joel's cited recollection, which will be discussed shortly.

40 The Shangri-Las, "Wishing Well" (Monaco/Michaels) b/w "Hate to Say I Told You So" (Jackson/Steinberg/Steinberg), SPOKANE 4006, 1964.

41 The Shangri-Las, "Simon Says" (Tony Michaels) b/w "Simon Speaks" (Hy Mizrahi and Phil Steinberg), SMASH 1866, 1963.

42 Patrick, *Sophisticated Boom Boom*, liner notes, 10.

43 'Reviews of New Pop Records,' *Billboard*, 1 Dec. 1958, 44.

44 Patrick, *Sophisticated Boom Boom*, liner notes, 11.

45 The Lonely Ones, "My Wish" (Tony Gianna, Martin J. Monaco and George Francis Morton) b/w "I Want My Girl" (George Francis Morton and Joseph J. Monaco), SIR 270, 1959; see also 45 *Discography for Baton/Sir Records* (online).

46 'Reviews of This Week's Singles,' *Billboard*, 13 July 1959, 34.

47 Lisa MacKinney, interview with Rod McBrien, 10 Apr. 2008.

48 Georgie Morton, "Some of These Days" (Shelton Brooks) b/w "My Mammy" (Donaldson-Lewis-Young) SWIRL 103, 1961.

49 See "Some of These Days," https://secondhandsongs.com/performance/39802/versions#nav-entity (accessed 29 Sept. 2021).

50 See "My Mammy," https://secondhandsongs.com/work/129882/versions#nav-entity (accessed 29 Sept. 2021).

51 'Special Merit Spotlights,' *Billboard*, 1 May 1961, 23.

52 See BMI listing for George Francis Morton and Billy Kelly; Patrick, *Sophisticated Boom Boom*, liner notes, 10–11; for Sal DiTroia credits see his allmusic.com entry.

53 Morton George, "The Stretch" (Billy Kelley & Arthur Hilliard) b/w "Come On In" (Billy Kelley & Arthur Hilliard), AMY 858, 1962; Patrick, *Sophisticated Boom Boom*, liner notes, 10–11.

54 'Reviews of New Singles,' *Billboard*, 15 Sept. 1962, 27.

55 'Best Bets,' *Cash Box*, 8 Sept. 1962, 24.

56 Finger snaps, 'Where? Over there!' "Long Live Our Love" (Jackson/Barnes) b/w "Sophisticated Boom Boom" (Morton) RED BIRD 048, Feb. 1966.

57 Morton wrote only the A-Side of "I Feel Majestic" (Morton) b/w "Send Her Back" (Vince Benay) MALA 466, see BMI listing for George Francis Morton; *45 Discography for Mala Records* (online).

58 'Best Bets,' *Cash Box*, 28 Sept. 1963, 22.

59 See Teacho Wilshire (and variations) entries on allmusic.com and Discogs.

60 Newman, 41.

61 The Beattle-ettes, "Only Seventeen" (Billy Kelly/Joseph J. Monaco) b/w "Now We're Together" (Billy Kelly/Joseph J. Monaco) JUBILEE 5472 (1964), see *45 Discography for Jubilee Records* (online); for a brief history of the label, see *Jubilee Records* (online); see BMI listing for George Francis Morton AKA Billy Kelly.

62 'Pop Spotlights,' *Billboard*, 29 Feb. 1964, 43.

63 See also Patrick, *Sophisticated Boom Boom*, liner notes, 11.

64 Linna, Mary Weiss of the Shangri-Las, part 3.

65 Gil Faggen, 'Vox Jox,' *Billboard*, 9 May 1964, 12; also reproduced in Patrick, *Sophisticated Boom Boom*, liner notes, 11.

66 Andrew Hamilton, 'The Persianettes' (allmusic.com).

67 'Vera Carey of the Persianettes'(online); 'Timmy Carr,' *Sir Shambling's Deep Soul Heaven* (online).

68 The Beatlette's, "Dance Beatle Dance" b/w "We Were Meant to be Married" (JAMIE 1270), 1964; see Popsike listing (online) which includes photos of both sides and audio samples. Jamie/Guyden website listing spells it as Beatlettes; *45 Discography for Jamie Records* spells it Beatle-ettes (online).

69 See track listing for *The Jamie/Guyden Story* (1995) compilation (allmusic.com); see Bob Finiz (Discogs).

70 Jonathan Takiff, 'How a small Philadelphia record company gave an Oscar contender its sound,' *The Philadelphia Inquirer*, 20 Nov. 2018.

71 Jamie/Guyden website for The Beatle-ettes: http://jamguy.com/Beatlettes/ (accessed 27 Dec. 2023).

72 See Discogs for Les Beatlettes; Piers A. Hemmingsen, 'Across Canada with the Dave Clark Five,' which includes a newspaper advertisement for the Montreal show listing Les Beatlettes (online); R. Duane Cozzen, *Girl Bands of the '60s: Collector's Quick Reference*, 57–8.

73 The Beatlettes, "Yes!!! You Can Hold My Hand Part One" b/w "Yes!!! You Can Hold My Hand Part Two," ASSAULT 1893, 1964.

74 For a photo of the label and the review from *Cash Box* (15 Feb. 1964, 12), see http://www.45cat.com/record/18931894 (accessed 12 Oct. 2021); see also *Cash Box*, 15 Feb. 1964, 'Cash Box Top 100,' 4 & 'Top Hundred Albums,' 25.

75 Martin Lewis, 'Tweet The Beatles! How Walter Cronkite Sent The Beatles Viral . . . in 1963!,' *HuffPost*, 18 July 2009.

76 Richard Harrington, 'The Beatles' Helping "Hand"; She Triggered Beatlemania in 1963 But Prefers Her Role to Be Unsung,' *The Washington Post*, 16 Jan 2004, C.01; see also Bruce Spizer, *The Beatles Are Coming! The Birth of Beatlemania in America*, esp. 70–112.

77 Persianettes discography (online).

78 An album by yet another group called the Beetlettes, *Outside Carnegie Hall*, was released on the Assault label in 1964 (ASLP1001). The cover features three young

white women with guitars, so it is unclear whether there is any connection to the other Assault release: see *Popsike* listing (online) and Discogs entry for The Beetlettes.

79 See 'Music Response: An Overview of the Answer Record' (online).

80 Newman, 41.

81 Betrock, *Girl Groups*, 98–100; Arfin, 'The "Shadow" Reappears,' part 2; see also Kaye, 'Standing in the Shadow of Rock'; Lisa MacKinney, interview with George 'Shadow' Morton, 24 Apr. 2007.

82 Charlotte Greig, *Will You Still Love Me Tomorrow*, 78.

83 Richie Unterberger, 'Shangri-Las' (allmusic.com).

84 Bill Smith, *I Go to Extremes: The Billy Joel Story*, 55.

85 Suzi Quatro, 'Suzi Quatro's Heroes of Rock 'n' Roll: Interview with Mary Weiss.'

86 Margalit Fox, 'Shadow Morton, Songwriter and Producer, Dies at 71,' *New York Times*, 15 Feb. 2013.

87 *Sophisticated Boom Boom: The Shadow Morton Story*, liner notes by Mick Patrick, Ace Records, CDTOP1369, 2013.

88 Lisa MacKinney, *"Dressed in Black": the Shangri-Las and their recorded legacy*, PhD dissertation, 95–138.

89 Ada Wolin, *Golden Hits of the Shangri-Las*, 38, italics added.

90 Flam and Liebowitz, *But Will You Love Me Tomorrow*, 225–6.

91 Mick Patrick, 'Only Seventeen,' liner notes for *Girls with Guitars: All Girl Bands, Axe Backed Babes and the Like*.

92 Susan J. Douglas, *Where the Girls Are: Growing Up Female with the Mass Media*, 114.

93 Cash's version of Depeche Mode's "Personal Jesus" exemplifies this.

94 *The Continuum Encyclopedia of Popular Music of the World Part One, Vol. 2: Performance and Production*, ed. John Shepherd, Dave Laing, David Horn, Paul Oliver, and Peter Wicke, 196; see 196–7 for an excellent overview of the role(s) of the producer; see also Jacqueline Warwick, *Girl Groups, Girl Culture*, 93–5.

95 Virgil Moorefield, *The Producer as Composer: Shaping the Sounds of Popular Music*, 1–3; Theodore Gracyk, *Rhythm and Noise: An Aesthetics of Rock*, 51–55.

96 John Tobler and Stuart Grundy, *The Record Producers*, 7–8.

97 Shepherd, Lang et al., 196; Moorefield, 3–5.

98 Moorefield, xv. Moorefield is a musician, composer and producer who ran his own recording studio in New York City for thirteen years (xix).

99 Quoted in Tobler and Grundy, 18 (italics mine).

100 Tobler and Grundy, 18; for more detail about Spector and his early days with Leiber and Stoller, see Moorefield, 5–12; Mark Ribowsky, *He's A Rebel: Phil Spector, Rock & Roll's Legendary Producer*, 49–77.

101 Emerson, *Always Magic in the Air*, 214–17.

102 Quoted in Tobler and Grundy, 11.

103 Quoted in Tobler and Grundy, 11.

104 Shepherd, Lang et al., 196; Moorefield, 27.

105 Quoted in Tobler and Grundy, 13.

106 Quoted in Tobler and Grundy, 13–14.

107 Quoted in Tobler and Grundy, 19.

108 'Suzi Quatro's Heroes of Rock 'n' Roll: Interview with Mary Weiss.'

109 Arfin, 'The "Shadow" Reappears,' part 1.

110 Arfin, 'The "Shadow" Reappears,' part 1.

111 Murray Kaufman, *Murray the K Tells It Like It Is, Baby*, 28.

112 Charlotte Greig, 'Spectropop Presents Ellie Greenwich, interviewed by Charlotte Greig,' *Spectropop*; Betrock, 86.

113 Arfin, 'The "Shadow" Reappears,' part 4.

114 Arfin, 'The "Shadow" Reappears,' part 4; see also Betrock, 99–100.

115 Morton, quoted in Betrock, 99.

116 Arfin, 'The "Shadow" Reappears,' part 4; Betrock, 99; Tom Hibbert, 'Billy Joel: We All Make Mistakes . . .', *Q*, Sept. 1987 (via Rock's Back Pages).

117 John Grecco, liner notes for The Shangri-Las, *The Best of the Red Bird and Mercury Recordings*. Grecco's version is that the "Remember" demo was recorded at Ultra-Sonic; Morton and McBrien both told me that it was recorded at Joe Monaco's Dynamic studio, which is Billy Joel's recollection too. Furthermore, South Oyster Bay Road is very close to Bloomingdale Road (which, according to Morton, Monaco's Dynamic studio was just off) and not really anywhere near Ultra-Sonic.

118 Betrock, 99.

119 Hibbert, 'Billy Joel: We All Make Mistakes . . .'; see also Joel's more recent recollections in Flam and Liebowitz, *But Will You Love Me Tomorrow,* 229.

120 John Grecco, liner notes for The Shangri-Las, *The Best of the Red Bird and Mercury Recordings*.

121 Greig, 'Spectropop Presents Ellie Greenwich.'

122 Hibbert, 'Billy Joel: We All Make Mistakes . . .'

123 Betrock, 100; MacKinney, interview with George 'Shadow' Morton, 24 Apr. 2007. Morton told me that if a copy of this original still existed, it would be with 'Joey' Monaco in South Carolina, where, according to Morton, he then lived.

124 Arfin, 'The "Shadow" Reappears,' part 4; see also John Grecco, *Out in the Streets,* part 1.

125 MacKinney, interview with George 'Shadow' Morton.

126 Greig, 'Spectropop Presents Ellie Greenwich.'

127 Greig, 'Spectropop Presents Ellie Greenwich.'

128 Grecco, *Out in the Streets,* part 2.

129 Ellie Greenwich, quoted in Betrock, 100 (italics mine).

130 MacKinney, interview with George 'Shadow' Morton; italics added to indicate the words Morton emphasised as he spoke.

131 Linna, *Mary Weiss of the Shangri-Las,* part 3.

132 MacKinney, interview with George 'Shadow' Morton.

133 Michael Franzese, *Blood Covenant,* 22–4; Justine Picardie and Dorothy Wade, *Atlantic and the Godfathers of Rock and Roll,* 112–114; Sandra Peddie, 'Living the High Life,' *Newsday,* 3 Mar. 2020, 6.

134 The five New York City *Cosa Nostra* families were Colombo, Gambino, Genovese, Bonanno and Lucchese; see Franzese, 27; see also Fredric Dannen, *Hit Men: Power Brokers and Fast Money Inside the Record Business,* 164. Franzese was in the news again in 2010 and was described as a man 'who turned murder into an art form and whose name made foes shudder in fear'; see John Marzulli, 'Colombo underboss John (Sonny) Franzese betrayed by son, who'll testify against legendary mobster,' *New York Daily News,* 9 June 2010.

135 Betrock, 100.

136 Betrock, 100; see also Grecco, *Out in the Streets,* part 2.

137 'Kama-Sutra Productions thanks the music business . . .', *Cash Box,* 17 Oct. 1964, 23. 'Tender Tunes' was Ripp/Kama Sutra's publishing company.

138 Flam and Liebowitz, *But Will You Love Me Tomorrow,* 229–30.

139 The Shangri-Las (as a trio) did sign with Mercury after the demise of Red Bird in 1966; it is not clear whether there was any connection between this and their earlier Smash single, but it seems unlikely.

140 Artie Ripp, 'Kama Sutra: Past, Present and Future', *Cash Box,* 16 Nov. 1968, B9.

141 Giles Smith, 'Playing piano until the fingers get burnt: After 20 years in the music business, Billy Joel has a lot to teach about music. And a lot to learn about business', *The Independent,* 8 July, 1993. Equally eyewatering is the recent news, reported

by multiple outlets, that Artie Ripp's filmmaker son Adam is making a revisionist biopic about Joel that focuses on his early years with Ripp senior and for which Joel, unsurprisingly, is refusing to allow any use of his music or likeness. See Ethan Shanfeld, 'Billy Joel Biopic "Piano Man" Greenlit by Michael Jai White's Jaigantic Studios', *Variety*, 9 Mar. 2022; see also Roger Friedman, 'Ripp Off: Billy Joel's Early Career to Be Exploited on Screen by Sons of First Manager and Greedy Label Owner', *Showbiz* 411, 10 Mar. 2022.

142 Brian Wawzenek, 'Why Billy Joel Hated His First Album, *Cold Spring Harbour*,' *UCR: Classic Rock & Culture*, 1 Nov. 2016.

143 'Hot Pop Spotlights,' *Billboard*, 1 Aug. 1964, 18.

144 Linna, *Mary Weiss of the Shangri-Las*, part 3.

145 'Suzi Quatro's Heroes of Rock 'n' Roll: Interview with Mary Weiss.'

146 Marc Taylor, *The Original Marvelettes*, 122–3; see also Warwick, *Girl Groups, Girl Culture*, 51–56.

147 Taylor, 122–23; see also Warwick, *Girl Groups, Girl Culture*, 51–56.

148 Richard Goldstein, 'The Soul Sound from Sheepshead Bay,' *Village Voice*, 23 June 1966, 30; Betrock, 100. I have been unable to locate a date for this appearance, but it likely would have been Sept. or Oct. of 1964.

149 Adrian McCoy, 'Clark Race: Obituary,' *Pittsburgh Post-Gazette*, 28 July 1999.

150 Goldstein, 'The Soul Sound from Sheepshead Bay,' 30.

151 Richard Green, 'Searchers talk about the Shangri-Las,' *New Musical Express*, 20 Nov. 1964, 13.

152 Annie J. Randall, *Dusty! Queen of the Postmods*, 51.

153 Howard Thompson, 'Teen-agers Howl for the Animals,' *New York Times*, 5 Sept. 1964, 11.

154 'A Rock 'n' Roll Double Header,' *Hit Parader*, Mar. 1965, 34.

155 Green, 13.

156 A Rock 'n' Roll Double Header,' 37.

157 The Dovells, "Bristol Stomp" b/w "Out in the Cold Again," CAMEO-PARKWAY 827, 1961.

158 Irene Brodsky, who attended many Murray the K shows at the Brooklyn Fox when in her early teens, testified with wild enthusiasm about the Dovells and their popularity; Lisa MacKinney, phone conversation with Irene Brodsky, 27 Aug. 2009.

159 A Rock 'n' Roll Double Header,' 37.

160 Green, 13. To my knowledge, the only extant footage of "Remember" was filmed almost a year later for the *Where the Action Is* TV show and aired on 1 July 1965 (YouTube). It is possible that the group (in this case, minus Betty) had less choreographic freedom when filming for TV, as they seem largely limited to hand claps and finger snaps.

161 Green, 13.

162 Quoted in Warwick, *Girl Groups, Girl Culture*, 53.

163 Charlie Horner, Pamela Horner, and Val Shively, *The Musical Legacy of Richard Barrett Part Two: Richard Barrett and the Teenagers*, 5; Mary Wilson, *Dreamgirl: My Life as a Supreme*, 184; Warwick, *Girl Groups, Girl Culture*, 53; Taylor, 65.

164 The Shangri-Las may have received professional assistance with their choreography, but I have not located any evidence for this.

165 'A Rock 'n' Roll Double Header,' 37.

166 'A Rock 'n' Roll Double Header,' 52.

167 'A Rock 'n' Roll Double Header,' 52.

168 Green, 13.

169 Jim Dawson and Steve Propes, *45 RPM: The History, Heroes & Villains of a Pop Music Revolution*, 97–109.

170 Randall, 52.

171 MacKinney, telephone conversation with Irene Brodsky, 27 Aug. 2009.

172 Ronnie Spector, *Be My Baby: How I Survived Mascara, Miniskirts, and Madness, or My Life as a Fabulous Ronette*, 32–3.

173 Spector, 37.

174 Linna, *Mary Weiss of the Shangri-Las*, part 4; 'Suzi Quatro's Heroes of Rock 'n' Roll: Interview with Mary Weiss.'

175 Green, 13.

176 'Suzi Quatro's Heroes of Rock 'n' Roll: Interview with Mary Weiss.'

177 A notable exception was the Ronettes, of whom the reviewer noted that they were famous for "Be My Baby" and their 'bump and grind choreography.'

178 Randall, 52.

179 Susan J. Douglas, *Listening In: Radio and the American Imagination*, 222.

180 Douglas, *Listening In*, 230–232.

181 Kaufman, 25.

182 Spector, 36–7.

183 See also Bosley Crowther, 'A Theater Closes: And an Era too as the Paramount Goes Dark,' *New York Times*, 23 Aug. 1964, XI.

184 Gay Talese, 'Beatles and Fans Meet Social Set,' *New York Times*, 21 Sept. 1964, 44.

185 Talese, 44.

186 Jonathan Clarke, 'Mary Weiss interviewed by Jonathan Clarke on *Out of the Box*,' Q1043FM, New York City (YouTube).

187 Quoted in Barbara Ehrenreich, Elizabeth Hess and Gloria Jacobs, 'Beatlemania: Girls Just Want to Have Fun,' in *The Adoring Audience: Fan Culture and Popular Media*, ed. Lisa A. Lewis, 103.

188 Goldstein, 'The Soul Sound from Sheepshead Bay,' 30.

189 Grace Palladino, *Teenagers: An American History*, 143.

190 Spector, 36–7; see also Palladino, 143.

191 See for example Bill Cotter and Bill Young, *The 1964–1965 New York World's Fair*; Young also launched and continues to maintain a comprehensive New York World's Fair website; see also *The 1964 World's Fair* [videorecording], which contains many interviews with Fair workers and visitors.

192 *Remembering the Future: The New York World's Fairs from 1939 to 1964*, 16 Sept.–31 Dec. 31, 1989; *Highlights of Remembering the Future: The 1964 New York World's Fair*, 21 Jan.–30 June 1990; *Designing the Future: The Queens Museum of Art and the New York City Building*, Mar. 10–July 7, 2002; *The Seeing Eye: Art and Industry at the 1964 World's Fair*, July 18 2004–Oct. 24, 2004. See also the exhibition catalogue by Rosemary Haag Bletter, *Remembering the Future: The New York World's Fair from 1939–1964*.

193 Gay Talese, 'About the Fair: Blind Singers Sense the Excitement and Soak Up the Swirl of Sounds,' *New York Times*, 28 Apr. 1964, 31.

194 See *It's All the Streets You Crossed Not So Long Ago* (online). The author of this blog noted: 'I wanted to write a full-blown entry on bands that played the WORLD'S FAIR, 'cause I've always fantasized that it must have been a hotbed of mid-60s rock & roll action—after all, '64/'65 were the prime post-British Invasion years when garage bands sprouted like fungi. Truth be told I haven't had much time to research this topic, and what little time I have had hasn't yielded much info.' My own efforts to locate more information about the Shangri-Las' performance, which involved combing through many boxes of archival material at the *Queens Museum of Art* and the New York Public Library, were similarly fruitless.

195 Byron Lee and the Dragonaires, official website.

196 'Fair Calendar,' *New York Times*, 12 Oct. 1964, 59.

197 Grecco, *Out in the Streets*, part 2; Linna, *Mary Weiss of the Shangri-Las*, part 6. As I indicated in n. 194, despite extensive searching, I have been unable to locate any further information about this event.

198 There are several fantastic photographs of the Shangri-Las in England, dated 23 Oct. 1964, accessible through the Getty Images website.

199 'Shangri-Las Visit London Next Week,' *New Musical Express*, 16 Oct. 1964, 8–9.

200 Linna, *Mary Weiss of the Shangri-Las*, part 6.

201 Green, 13.

202 Betrock, 108.

203 Greig, 83.

204 See, for example, the Shangri-Las, "Give Him a Great Big Kiss," *Shindig!*, 1965 (You-Tube); "Right Now and Not Later," *Shivaree*, 1965 (YouTube). "Right Now and Not Later" was released late in 1965.

205 Richie Unterberger, 'The Shangri-Las,' (allmusic.com).

206 For a detailed discussion of sex, teenage girls, pregnancy and available options in the early 1960s, see Rickie Solinger, *Wake Up Little Susie: Single Pregnancy and Race Before Roe v. Wade*, esp. 20–40; Douglas, *Where the Girls Are*, 61–81; see also Ehren-reich et al., 84–106.

207 Patti Smith, *Just Kids*, 17–19.

208 Smith, 19–20.

209 Elizabeth Anna Weiss and Donald Gruntz married on 27 July 1964, see *The NYC Marriage Index* and associated records (online). Their daughter Tracy was born on 5 Feb. 1965 (familysearch.org).

210 See Grecco, *Out in the Streets*, part 4, for a photograph of Betty and Tracy at the final Shangri-Las reunion in 1989.

211 'Suzi Quatro's Heroes of Rock 'n' Roll: Interview with Mary Weiss.'

212 Arfin, 'The "Shadow" Reappears,' part 6.

213 The Goodies, official website.

214 Dave the Rave, interview with the Goodies on 'Relics and Rarities,' WQMA Oldies Radio 1520AM, date unavailable. Copy supplied by Phil Milstein.

215 For Nick and the Nacks, see entry on *White Doo Wop Collector* (online); see also the Goodies official website.

216 Dave the Rave, interview with the Goodies on 'Relics and Rarities.'

217 Dave the Rave, interview with the Goodies on 'Relics and Rarities.'

218 Gross, 'Mary Weiss comes back for a *Dangerous Game*,' (italics mine).

219 Dave the Rave, interview with the Goodies on 'Relics and Rarities.'

220 Dave the Rave, interview with the Goodies on 'Relics and Rarities.'

221 The Goodies, "Dum Dum Ditty," (Boyce/Venet/Hart/Martire) b/w "Sophisticated Boom Boom" (Morton) BLUE CAT 117, June 1965.

222 Dave the Rave, interview with the Goodies on 'Relics and Rarities.'

223 Alan Betrock actually stated, 'Shadow Morton produced the Goodies for Blue Cat, where he used two Shangri-Las songs, copied their vocal sound, and used some of their backing tracks.' Betrock, 109.

224 See Taylor, 57–8 for a similar situation with the Marvelettes and the Andantes.

225 'The Concerts and Tours,' (Rolling Stones), *The Telegraph*, 1 Jan. 2001; see also *The Rolling Stones' Opening Acts: A Partial List* (online).

226 See *Beach Boys Tour and Sesssions, 1964* (online).

227 The Shangri-Las and Robert Goulet on *I've Got a Secret*, including a performance of "Leader of the Pack," 16 Nov. 1964 (YouTube).

228 "Maybe" was originally recorded by the Chantels and released on George Goldner's End label in 1958.

229 Note: not "Girl Group"; *Cash Box*, 26 Dec. 1964, 31. This was in the R&B category.

CHAPTER FOUR: *Red Bird's Demise, the Mob, and Mercury Records*

1 Jimmy Bowen, quoted in Richard Carlin, *Godfather of the Music Business: Morris Levy*, 68.

2 The Shangri-Las, *The Shangri-Las*, RED BIRD 20-101, 1965.

3 'Album Reviews,' *Cash Box*, 6 Mar. 1965, 22, reproduced in Alan Betrock, *Girl Groups: The Story of a Sound*, 102.

4 *The Shangri-Las*, liner notes by Faith Whitehill, RED BIRD 20-101. My copy is an English reissue: London: CHARLY RECORDS CRM 2028, 1986.

5 The Shangri-Las, "Give Him a Great Big Kiss" (Morton) b/w "Twist and Shout" (Russell/Medley), RED BIRD 018, Dec. 1964; The Shangri-Las, "Maybe" (Goldner) b/w "Shout" (Isley/Isley/Isley) RED BIRD 019, Dec. 1964.

6 June Harris, 'Shangri-Las Make it Big', *Music Business*, 31 Dec. 1964–9 Jan. 1965, 11.

7 The Tymes, "So Much in Love" b/w "Roscoe James McClain," PARKWAY 871, 1963.

8 The Dovells, "You Can't Sit Down" b/w "Stompin' Everywhere," PARKWAY 867, 1963.

9 For the Valrays on Cameo-Parkway, see *White Doo Wop Collector* (online).

10 Jesse Belvin, "Goodnight My Love" b/w "I Want You with Me Xmas," MODERN 1005, 1956 (miscredited on the label as 'Jessie Belvin')

11 See "Goodnight My Love," https://secondhandsongs.com/performance/72961/versions (accessed 2 Nov. 2021).

12 See also Jacqueline Warwick, *Girl Groups, Girl Culture*, 94–7.

13 The Shangri-Las, "Leader of the Pack," recorded live (audio only) at the Brooklyn Fox Theatre, (listed as) 1964 (YouTube).

14 Dugan Trodglen, 'Who Says You Can Never Go Home Anymore? The Shangri-Las Once Did. But Mary Weiss Is Proving That Wrong with a Swell Return to Rock,' *Stomp and Stammer*, Nov. 2008.

15 See 'Get Down with Iggy Pop's High School Band the Iguanas', *Dangerous Minds*, 22 Oct. 2019, which includes a poster advertising the Shangri-Las/Iguanas show; Morgan Sherburne, 'Do You Remember Harbor Springs' Club Ponytail?', *Petoskey News-Review*, 11 Jan. 2014.

16 Paul Trynka, *Iggy Pop: Open Up and Bleed*, 45–46.

17 *The Shangri-Las*, liner notes by Faith Whitehill.

18 For a discussion of the recording versus performance dichotomy, see Theodore Gracyk, *Rhythm and Noise: An Aesthetics of Rock*, 37–67, esp. 38–42.

19 Virgil Moorefield, *The Producer as Composer: Shaping the Sounds of Popular Music*, xiv.

20 See also Walter L. Welch, Leah Brodbeck Stenzel Burt, and Oliver Read, *From Tinfoil to Stereo: The Acoustic Years of the Recording Industry, 1877–1929*.

21 Moorefield, xv.

22 George Martin, quoted in Gracyk, 53.

23 *The Shangri-Las*, liner notes by Faith Whitehill.

24 Warwick, *Girl Groups, Girl Culture*, 78; see also Cynthia J. Cyrus, 'Selling an Image: Girl Groups of the 1960s,' *Popular Music* 22:2 (2003), 182–3.

25 See Ken Emerson, *Always Magic in the Air: The Bomp and Brilliance of the Brill Building Era*, 233–4.

26 See Charlie Horner, Pamela Horner, and Val Shively, *The Musical Legacy of Richard Barrett—Part Two: Richard Barrett and the Teenagers*, 8.

27 See also Warwick, *Girl Groups, Girl Culture*, 189–91.

28 The Shangri-Las and Robert Goulet on *I've Got a Secret*, including a performance of "Leader of the Pack," 16 Nov. 1964 (YouTube); see also Warwick, 189–191. This performance is discussed in more detail in chapter 6.

29 *Billboard*, 19 Dec. 1964, 27; this photo is reproduced on p. 177.

30 Cyrus, 180.

31 *Cash Box*, 26 Dec. 1964, 31, reproduced in Betrock, 104.

32 See, for example, the photo captioned 'White boots go hi-style,' Linna, *Mary Weiss of the Shangri-Las*, part 6.

33 Cyrus, 180–181.

34 Richie Unterberger, 'The Shangri-Las,' *All Music* (online).

35 See press clipping reproduced at Linna, *Mary Weiss of the Shangri-Las*, part 4.

36 Quoted in Gracyk, 178.

37 See also Warwick, *Girl Groups, Girl Culture*, 147.

38 'Suzi Quatro's Heroes of Rock 'n' Roll: Interview with Mary Weiss.'

39 Ellie Greenwich, quoted in Betrock, 102–3.

40 Linna, *Mary Weiss of the Shangri-Las*, part 6.

41 Charlotte Greig, '*Spectropop* Presents Ellie Greenwich.'

42 Jim Farber, 'Leader of the Pack Is Back: Girl-group Legend Comes Home,' (online).

43 See Suzi Quatro, *Unzipped*, 29ff.

44 The Pleasure Seekers' 1965 single "What A Way to Die" is magnificent catchy garage rock that espouses a quite extraordinary catalogue of sentiments for a group of young women in the mid-1960s. Pleasure Seekers, "Never Thought You'd Leave Me" b/w "What a Way to Die," HIDEOUT 1006, 1965.

45 'Suzi Quatro's Heroes of Rock 'n' Roll: Interview with Mary Weiss.'

46 Lisa MacKinney, telephone conversation with David Dalton, 14 Dec. 2021. Sadly, Dalton died from cancer on 11 July 2022; see Neil Genzlinger, 'David Dalton, Rock Writer Who Lived the Scene, Dies at 80,' *New York Times*, 15 July 2022.

47 Lisa MacKinney, telephone conversation with David Dalton, 14 Dec. 2021.

48 Lisa MacKinney, telephone conversation with David Dalton, 14 Dec. 2021.

49 Laurie Stras, 'Introduction,' *She's So Fine: Reflections on Whiteness, Femininity, Adolescence and Class in 1960s Music*, ed. Laurie Stras, 13.

50 Richard Goldstein, 'The Soul Sound from Sheepshead Bay,' *Village Voice*, 23 June 1966, 8.

51 Stras, 18.

52 For the United States in the nineteenth century, see David R. Roediger, *The Wages of Whiteness: Race and the Making of the American Working Class*. See also Jean Halley, Ashley Eshleman, and Ramya Mahadevan Vijaya, *Seeing White: An Introduction to White Privilege and Race*; for the early twenty-first century, see Melanie E.L. Bush, *Everyday Forms of Whiteness: Understanding Race in a 'Post-Racial' World*.

53 Richard Dyer, *White*, 1.

54 Peggy McIntosh, quoted in Dyer, 9. McIntosh developed the concept of 'conferred dominance' in her pathbreaking essays 'White Privilege and Male Privilege' (1988) and 'White Privilege: Unpacking the Invisible Knapsack' (1989).

55 Gayle Wald, 'One of the Boys? Whiteness, Gender, and Popular Music Studies,' in *Whiteness: A Critical Reader*, ed. Mike Hill, 151–167, esp. 153–5; see also Warwick, 189–194; Cyrus, 180.

56 Linna, *Mary Weiss of the Shangri-Las*, part 6.

57 Warwick, 191–2; Ruth Frankenberg, 'Introduction: Local Whitenesses, Localizing Whiteness,' in *Displacing Whiteness: Essays in Social and Cultural Criticism*, ed. Ruth Frankenberg, Durham, NC: Duke University Press, 1997, 1–33, esp. 11–12.

58 Wald, 155.

59 Mary Wilson, *Dreamgirl: My Life as a Supreme*, 181–5; Warwick, 141–162; Suzanne E. Smith, *Dancing in the Street: Motown and the Cultural Politics of Detroit*, esp. 1–53.

60 Smith, 47–8; Mina Carson, Tisa Lewis, and Susan M. Shaw, *Girls Rock! Fifty Years of Women Making Music*, 30–31; Warwick, 158–162.

61 Wilson, 213–4, 259; Warwick, 146–7.

62 Nick Hasted, 'How Jack White and the White Stripes Breathed New Life into the Blues,' *Louder: Classic Rock* (online).

63 George Lipsitz, *The Possessive Investment in Whiteness: How White People Profit from Identity Politics*, 120; see also 118–139.

64 Warwick, 146.

65 Mark Anthony Neal, *What the Music Said: Black Popular Music and Black Public Culture*, 44.

66 Neal, 42–5; Smith, 21–53, esp. 21–25, for Gordy's release of recordings of Martin Luther King's speeches on a Motown subsidiary label.

67 Rev. Martin Luther King, *Great March to Freedom*, GORDY 906, 1963. For review, see 'Album Reviews,' *Billboard*, 5 Oct. 1963, 30.

68 Wilson, 259.

69 Warwick, 80; Neal, 42–5.

70 Natural Wonder advertisement, *Life*, 15 Mar. 1963, 17.

71 Caroline V. Clarke, 'Redefining Beautiful: Black Cosmetic Companies and Industry Giants Vie for the Loyalty of Black Women,' *Black Enterprise*, June 1993, 248.

72 Clarke, 246–8; Jessie Carney Smith, 'Cosmetics,' *Encyclopedia of African American Popular Culture* ed. Jessie Carney Smith, 4 vols., 373–6.

73 Skylar Harris, 'Cosmetics,' *The Jim Crow Encyclopedia* ed. Nikki L. M. Brown, Barry M. Stentiford, 191–195.

74 See Warwick, 190–91.

75 This promo-only LP is extremely rare; some good-quality photos are available on this listing: https://www.rootsvinylguide.com/ebay_items/dave-clark-five-shangri-las-music-to-sell-teens-by-rare-lp-10-poster-photos (accessed 2 Nov. 2021).

76 'Official Entry Blank for Revlon's Big 'Natural Wonder' 'SWINGSTAKES,' *KRLA Beat*, 12 May 1965, 3–4.

77 'Dick Clark Caravan of Stars,' advertisement in *KRLA Beat*, 12 May 1965, 2.

78 Tommy James with Martin Fitzpatrick, *Me, the Mob and the Music: One Helluva Ride with Tommy James and the Shondells*, 76–78; Warwick, 203–211.

79 Wilson, 172–4.

80 Peter Benjaminson, *The Lost Supreme: The Life of Dreamgirl Florence Ballard*, 48.

81 Quoted in Claes Johansen, *The Zombies: Hung Up on a Dream, A Biography 1962–1967*, 129.

82 Johansen, 129–130.

83 Linna, *Mary Weiss of the Shangri-Las*, part 4.

84 Taylor, 80.

85 Benjaminson, 49.

86 Linna, *Mary Weiss of the Shangri-Las*, part 3.

87 Tom Sinclair, 'School's Out!,' *Spin*, Sept. 2005, 90–96.

88 John Grecco and Phil Milstein, '*Spectropop Presents* Lavender Girl: the Patty Michaels Story,' (online); Patty Duke and Kenneth Turan, *Call Me Anna: The Autobiography of Patty Duke*, 126.

89 Sinclair, 96, 93.

90 Sinclair, 93.

91 Sinclair, 93.

92 Sinclair, 93–4.

93 Phil Milstein, interview with Rita Ganser, 14 Oct. 2001.

94 Taylor, 35–8.

95 Taylor, 36.

96 Quoted in Taylor, 34.

97 Quoted in Taylor, 36–7.

98 Taylor, 38.

99 Quoted in Betrock, 106.

100 Linna, *Mary Weiss of the Shangri-Las*, part 3.

101 'Suzi Quatro's Heroes of Rock 'n' Roll: Interview with Mary Weiss.'

102 Linna, *Mary Weiss of the Shangri-Las*, part 6.

103 Linna, *Mary Weiss of the Shangri-Las*, part 3.

104 'Suzi Quatro's Heroes of Rock 'n' Roll: Interview with Mary Weiss.'

105 Quoted in Betrock, 108.

106 Duke and Turan, 88.

107 Milstein, interview with Rita Ganser.

108 Iain Aitch, 'The Leader's Back,' *The Telegraph*, 14 Apr. 2007.

109 Quoted in Taylor, 182.

110 Warwick, *Girl Groups, Girl Culture*, 129.

111 See Warwick, 129–130; Maria Mies, *Patriarchy and Accumulation on a World Scale: Women in the International Division of Labour.*

112 Susan J. Douglas, *Where the Girls Are: Growing Up Female with the Mass Media*, 43–60, 57.

113 Johansen, 132; see also 128–133.

114 Ellie Greenwich, quoted in Emerson, 234.

115 See Hank Bordowitz, *Dirty Little Secrets of the Record Business: Why So Much Music You Hear Sucks*, 259–70; Taylor, 23–25; Wilson, 102–104.

116 Wilson, 178.

117 Wilson, 102–4.

118 Wilson, 202.

119 Wilson, 210.

120 Sandra Peddie, 'Living the High Life,' *Newsday*, 3 Mar. 2020, 6.

121 Artie Ripp, quoted in Emerson, 234.

122 'Artie Ripp,' in Joe Smith and Mitchell Fink, *Off the Record: An Oral History of Popular Music*, 134.

123 'Artie Ripp,' *Off the Record*, 135; for a similar scenario involving Golder recounted by Joey Dee (most famous for "Peppermint Twist," recorded with the Starliters in 1961), see Carlin, 122.

124 Leiber is incorrectly spelled 'Lieber' throughout the article.

125 'Goldner Buys Out 2 Labels,' *Billboard*, 16 Apr. 1966, 3.

126 Picardie and Wade, *Atlantic and the Godfathers*, 106–110; Emerson, 229.

127 See Emerson, 214–15.

128 Emerson, 229; Picardie and Wade, *Atlantic and the Godfathers*, 111.

129 Jerry Leiber, Mike Stoller, and David Ritz, *Hound Dog: the Leiber & Stoller Autobiography*, 210.

130 Jerry Leiber, quoted in Jerry Wexler and David Ritz, *Rhythm and the Blues: A Life in American Music*, 164, quoted by Emerson, 229.

131 Leiber, Stoller, and Ritz, 198.

132 For Leiber and Stoller's account of the merger luncheon, see Leiber, Stoller, and Ritz, 209–212.

133 Josh Alan Friedman, *Tell the Truth Until They Bleed: Coming Clean in the Dirty World of Blues and Rock 'n' Roll*, 10–17.

134 JAMF was an acronym for Jive-Ass Mother Fucker; Freidman, 15; Fredric Dannen, *Hit Men: Power Brokers and Fast Money Inside the Music Business*, 50.

135 For Leiber's account of the deli incident, see Leiber, Stoller, and Ritz, 212–214; Friedman, 15–17.

136 Leiber, Stoller, and Ritz, 212.

137 Friedman, 17.

138 Leiber, Stoller, and Ritz, 215.

139 Picardie and Wade, *Atlantic and the Godfathers*, 114.

140 Franzese, *Blood Covenant*, 22–23.

141 Fredric Dannen, 'The Godfather of Rock and Roll,' *Rolling Stone*, 17 Nov. 1988, 88–97, 164; see BMI listing under Writer/Composer for Levy, Morris which lists 349 songs under his name.

142 Franzese, 24.

143 Franzese, 24–5; this incident is also related by Richard Carlin in *Godfather of the Music Business: Morris Levy*, 201.

144 Picardie and Wade, *Atlantic and the Godfathers*, 112–113. Inexplicably, Kama Sutra is described as 'a record and production company based in Los Angeles' (112).

145 Picardie and Wade, *Atlantic and the Godfathers*, 113; see also Ripp's recent version of Kama Sutra's origin story as recounted to Flam and Liebowitz, *But Will You Love Me Tomorrow*, 229–30.

146 Picardie and Wade, *Atlantic and the Godfathers*, 112–114.

147 Emerson, 232; see also Seymour Stein with Gareth Murphy, *Siren Song: My Life in Music*, 60–69, esp. 67–9.

148 *1966 Spring Spectacular* (Seattle Center Coliseum) concert program, 30 Apr. 1966, reproduced in part on Gasoline Valley Antiques' Facebook page.

149 *Jini Dellaccio Photographs, approximately 1940-2013*, University of Washington Libraries, Special Collections, 'Biographical Note' (website); see also Karen White-head's documentary *Her Aim is True* (2013), which brought Dellaccio's work (and extraordinary musical background) to a wider audience.

150 Grecco, *Out in the Streets*, part 4.

151 Leiber, Stoller, and Ritz, 219. For Singleton's career at Smash and Mercury, see John Broven, *Record Makers and Breakers: Voices of the Independent Rock 'n' Roll Pioneers*, 287ff.

152 Robert Pruter, *Chicago Soul*, 293; Frank W. Hoffmann & Howard Ferstler, *Encyclopaedia of Recorded Sound*, v.2, 676; 'Tiny Hill Inked as Wax Star-Flacker of Disks and Dukes,' *Billboard*, 3 Nov. 1945, 14.

153 'Las to Merc,' *Cash Box*, 17 Dec. 1966, 51. An article with the same photo, almost identical text and a different heading ('Shangris' Signing') is reproduced by John Grecco (see *Out in the Streets*, part 4) but unfortunately no details about the origin of this clipping are included.

154 Grecco, *Out in the Streets*, part 4.

155 Grecco, *Out in the Streets*, part 4. This compilation is the subject of a volume in the Bloomsbury 33⅓ series: Ada Wolin, *Golden Hits of the Shangri-Las*.

156 'Album Reviews,' *Billboard*, 31 Dec. 1966, 31.

157 See, for instance Terri Gross, 'Mary Weiss comes back for a *Dangerous Game*,' interview for *Fresh Air* on NPR; Linna, *Mary Weiss of the Shangri-Las*, part 7.

CHAPTER FIVE: *Aftermath*

1 Linna, *Mary Weiss of the Shangri-Las*, part 7.

2 Linna, *Mary Weiss of the Shangri-Las*, part 7.

3 Linna, *Mary Weiss of the Shangri-Las*, part 7.

4 Michael Martin, 'The Leader of the Pack Is Back,' *New York*, 25 Feb. 2007.

5 Mike Schneider, *Night Talk interview with Mary Weiss*, 20 Apr. 2008, part 2 (online).

6 'In What Ways Did Your Father Influence Your Life? : Mary Weiss,' *Growing Bolder*, 13 June 2008 (online).

7 *Catalog of Copyright Entries: Third Series*, Vol. 21, Part 5, Number 2, Section 1. Music: Current and Renewal Registrations July–Dec. 1967, 2009. I thank archivist Alex Moretti for drawing this to my attention.

8 'Funeral Notices,' *Long Island Press*, 18 Mar. 1970, 47. For an image of the church interior, see the *Sacred Heart Cambria Heights* website.

9 Mary Ann Ganser (findagrave.com); see also Grecco, *Out in the Streets*, part 4.

10 *Catalog of Copyright Entries: Third Series*, Vol. 24, Part 5, Number 2, Section 1. Music: Current and Renewal Registrations July–Dec. 1970, 2080.

11 Jeremy Simonds, *The Encyclopedia of Dead Rock Stars: Heroin, Handguns, and Ham Sandwiches*, 34.

12 See, for example, Patricia Romanowski Bashe, Holly George-Warren and Jon Pareles, *The Rolling Stone Encyclopaedia of Rock & Roll, Revised Edition*, 876; Warwick, *Girl Groups, Girl Culture*, 213.

13 Kurt Loder, 'Where Are They Now? The Shangri-Las,' *Rolling Stone*, 12 Sept. 1985, 50, 52.

14 I suspect strongly that the incorrect date has been perpetuated, or at the very least, not corrected, to make the obtaining of accurate information more difficult, as I found during my own attempts (see also note 21 below).

15 Phil Milstein, 'Shangri-Las 77!,' *Spectropop*. Milstein founded the Velvet Underground Appreciation Society in 1977 and published its associated fanzine *What Goes On* for approximately twenty years. He continues to publish (regularly in *Ugly Things* magazine) meticulously researched work on the Velvet Underground and other areas of rock and popular music.

16 Phil Milstein, interview with Rita Ganser, 14 Oct. 2001. Copy supplied by Milstein.

17 Milstein, interview with Rita Ganser.

18 '4 Teen-agers Die from Heroin Here,' *New York Times*, 17 Mar. 1970, 40; reproduced on p. 194.

19 'Mary Ann Ganser, Singer, Dies at 22,' *Long Island Press*, 18 Mar. 1970, 47; reproduced on p. 194.

20 'Mary Ann Ganser, Singer, Dies at 22.'

21 I include all this to indicate the detective work involved in locating Mary Ann's obituary, which I never would have managed without the date provided by the article in the *New York Times*, which is digitised, unlike (at time of writing) the *Long Island Press*, and searchable by keyword. When dealing with microfilm without knowing a date, a year's difference (1971 instead of 1970) is significant. At the time of my first research trip to New York in 2007, when I located Mary Ann's obituary on microfilm in the Long Island Division of the Queens Public Library, Simmonds' book (which I cited earlier and which does list the date of Mary Ann's death correctly) had not been published.

22 '4 Teen-agers Die from Heroin Here,' *New York Times*, 17 Mar. 1970, 40.

23 See, for instance, Richard Severo, '28 Users of Heroin Die Here in 10 Days,' *New York Times*, 25 June 1969, 33; '4 More Persons Killed by Heroin Doses Here,' *New York Times*, 1 Mar. 1970, 65; '5 Heroin Deaths Recorded in Day; Koch Asks Increase in Federal Funds for Narcotics Programs Here,' *New York Times*, 8 Mar. 1970, 67.

24 Mary Koval, *Opiate Use in New York City* (report), i.

25 'Queens Tops All Boroughs in Heroin User Increase,' *Long Island Press*, 18 Mar. 1970, 3.

26 Lawrence K. Altman, 'Deaths Attributed to Narcotics, Mainly Heroin, Increase Here,' *New York Times*, 21 June 1970, 1.

27 See, for example, Richard Severo, 'The Scourge of Youth: Use of Heroin by Students Is Called Deadliest Fad Ever to Hit Campuses,' *New York Times*, 2 Feb. 1970, 24.

28 'Mary Ann Ganser: Identification of Body,' uploaded 26 July 2008 to *Scott Michaels' Find a Death: The Forum* (online). I thank Alex Moretti for drawing this to my attention.

29 Google Answers operated from 2002 to 2006 as a platform through which members of the public could request answers/research to be undertaken on their behalf for a flat fee (generally two or three dollars).

30 For another near-contemporary example, see author Marc Tyler Nobleman's blogpost on comic strip writer Milton 'Bill' Finger, about whom Nobleman wrote *Bill the Boy Wonder: The Secret Co-Creator of Batman* (Charlesbridge, 2012). Nobleman's blogpost reproduces copies of all three document types from Finger's death in 1974, and his discussion includes the difficulty he had obtaining them.

31 'Mary Ann Ganser: Identification of Body.'

32 'Mary Ann Ganser: Identification of Body.'

33 'Mary Ann Ganser: Identification of Body.'

34 Deepdale Hospital was renamed Little Neck Hospital in 1991 and closed in 1996, see *Where to Find Medical Records for Closed Hospitals in New York State.*

35 Barbara Campbell, 'West Side Marchers Seek More Addict Facilities: Mothers Lead Youths to Roosevelt Hospital to Obtain 40 new Beds,' *New York Times,* 24 Mar. 1970, 30.

36 See *Neurological Disorders Caused by Substance Abuse,* particularly 'Seizures' and 'Encephalopathy,' (online).

37 Igor Grant and Lynn Mohns, 'Chronic Cerebral Effects of Alcohol and Drug Abuse,' *International Journal of the Addictions,* 10:5 (1975), 915.

38 There is still a medical practice operating at this address.

39 Berger is listed with this same phone number at 444 Elmont Road, Elmont, NY 11003 in *Directory: Aviation Medical Examiners,* Department of Transportation, Federal Aviation Administration, Office of Aviation Medicine, June 1973, 187. He was appointed to this position in 1971 (Google Books).

40 Phil Milstein, interview with Robert Ganser, 14 Oct. 2001. Copy supplied by Milstein.

41 Phil Milstein, interview with Robert Ganser.

42 Grant and Mohns, 905.

43 John Grecco, *Out in the Streets,* part 4.

44 J.J. Fishman, Donald P. Conwell & Zili Amsel, 'New York City Narcotics Register: A Brief History,' *International Journal of the Addictions* 6:3 (1971), 561–569.

45 '4 Teen-agers Die from Heroin Here,' *New York Times,* 17 Mar. 1970, 40.

46 Malcolm C. Cumberlidge, 'The Abuse of Barbiturates by Heroin Addicts,' *Canadian Medical Association Journal* 98 (June 1968), 1045.

47 Cumberlidge, 1048.

48 Cumberlidge, 1048.

49 Robert T. Dale & Farley Ross Dale, 'The Use of Methadone in a Representative Group of Heroin Addicts,' *International Journal of the Addictions* 8:2 (1973), 293–308, esp. 300.

50 Phil Milstein, interview with Robert Ganser.

51 Richard Severo, 'Narcotics Addicts Find Aid Is Scarce: Acute Shortage of Medical Facilities Plagues City,' *New York Times,* 26 Sept. 1969, 1. Severo noted that 'experimental programs dispensing methadone . . . serve about 2000 addicts at present.'

52 'Dope Kills Singer Who "Broke Habit,"' *Washington Post, Times Herald,* 28 Feb. 1968, C11.

53 See also *Drug Abuse and Brain Damage (Encephalopathy)* (online).

54 Milstein, interview with Robert Ganser.

55 *NYC Marriage Index—Queens 1970,* (Bride) Elizabeth Weiss and (Groom) Gerald J Storch. It is unclear how long Liz/Betty remained married to Donald Gruntz, but clearly they were no longer married by this time.

56 See 'Jeremy Storch: From a Naked Window' (online).

57 Jeremy Storch, official website.

58 Milstein, interview with Robert Ganser.

59 Martin, 'The Leader of the Pack Is Back.'

60 Mike Schneider, *Night Talk: Interview with Mary Weiss Part 3*, 28 Apr. 2008 (online). Weiss has consistently refused to discuss any details of the litigation that accompanied the group's demise. Her comments to Suzi Quatro are typical: 'When the litigation started everybody was suing everyone. I won't go into any details,' in 'Suzi Quatro's Heroes of Rock 'n' Roll: Interview with Mary Weiss.'

61 Grecco, *Out in the Streets*, part 4.

62 Program Guide for sale at http://groovytunesday.com/fanzines.html (accessed 3 Jan. 2022), described as: '7th NOSTALGIC ROCK'N'ROLL SHOW—Program Guide styled artist overviews of Gus Gossert's NYC Concert w/ Johnny Maestro & The Crests; Nolan Strong & The Diablos; Schoolboys; Turbans; Moonglows; Ronettes; Shangra-Las [*sic*]; Mystics; Buddy Knox; Tokens; Diamonds & others, plus articles on Dick Clark & Rock & Roll.'

63 Simmonds, 88.

64 Milstein, 'Shangri-Las 77!'

65 Seymour Stein with Gareth Murphy, *Siren Song: My Life in Music*, 70–98.

66 Stein, 199ff. See Sire discography (online).

67 See Paley's website for his illustrious list of credits, which include recordings with Brian Wilson, Jonathan Richman, April March and Madonna; see the 'Experience' tab for some photos from the session(s) with the Shangri-Las. Paley died on 20 Nov. 2024; see Alex Williams, 'Andy Paley, 73, Composer and Producer Whose Imprint Was All Over Pop Music,' *New York Times*, 3 Dec. 2024, B10.

68 Phil Milstein, interview with Andy Paley, 20 Sept. 2001. Copy supplied by Milstein.

69 Milstein, 'Shangri-Las 77!'

70 *Catalog of Copyright Entries: Third Series*, Vol. 31, Part 5, Number 2, Section 2. *Music: Current and Renewal Registrations* July–Dec. 1977, entry no. EU831032, 2490. I thank archivist Alex Moretti for drawing these four entries to my attention.

71 *Catalog of Copyright Entries: Third Series*, Vol. 31, Part 5, Number 2, Section 2. *Music: Current and Renewal Registrations* July–Dec. 1977, entry no. EU847571, 2803.

72 *Catalog of Copyright Entries: Fourth Series*, Vol. 1, Part 3, Number 2. *Performing Arts*, Apr.–June 1978, entry no. PAu 17-436, 854.

73 *Catalog of Copyright Entries: Fourth Series*, Vol. 1, Part 3, Number 2. *Performing Arts*, Apr.–June 1978, entry no. PAu 22-723, 557.

74 Linna, *Mary Weiss of the Shangri-Las*, part 7.

75 See Andy Paley, official website. Kaye is still the guitarist in the Patti Smith Group, but on this occasion he played bass.

76 Reprinted as Lenny Kaye, 'The Best of Acappella,' *The Age of Rock II*, ed. Jonathan Eisen, 287–301.

77 Milstein, interview with Andy Paley.

78 Milstein, interview with Andy Paley.

79 It is likely that this was one of the songs for which a copyright was lodged (see page 208, above) but not certain.

80 Milstein, interview with Andy Paley.

81 Juan Casiano, *The Shangri-Las '89 Reunion Concert* (online).

82 Emerson, *Always Magic in the Air*, 233; Milstein, *Shangri-Las 77!*, n.8.

83 Casiano, *The Shangri-Las '89 Reunion Concert*.

84 Quoted in Betrock, 110.

85 'The Shangri-Las on *Entertainment Tonight*, 1989' (YouTube).

86 Cherie Currie, *Neon Angel: A Memoir of a Runaway*. Currie's memoir is the basis of the feature film *The Runaways* (2010), directed by Floria Sigismondi and starring Kristen Stewart and Dakota Fanning.

87 Taylor, *The Original Marvelettes: Motown's Mystery Girl Group*, 170–176; see also Karen DeMasters, 'Pop Music: There are Oldies, and there are New Oldies,' *New York Times*, 22 Aug. 1999, NJ9.

88 Dick Fox, quoted by Emerson, 233.

89 Linna, *Mary Weiss of the Shangri-Las*, part 7.

90 'The Shangri-Las on Entertainment tonight, 1989' (YouTube).

91 Grecco, *Out in the Streets*, part 4; Milstein, interview with Rita Ganser.

92 Grecco, *Out in the Streets*, part 4.

93 William Grimes, 'Billy Miller, Curator and Historian of Fringe Music, dies at 62,' *New York Times*, 14 Nov. 2016.

CHAPTER SIX: 'Hmmm, He's Good-Bad, but He's Not Evil'

A portion of this chapter has been published online as '"Mmmm, he's good-bad, but he's not evil . . .": The Shangri-Las, "Leader of the Pack," and the Cultural Context of the Motorcycle Rider,' *International Journal of Motorcycle Studies* 4:1 (Mar. 2008).

1 Lisa MacKinney, interview with George 'Shadow' Morton, 24 Apr. 2007.

2 The Shangri-Las, "Leader of the Pack" (Barry/Greenwich/Morton) b/w "What Is Love?" (Michaels/Morton) RED BIRD 014, 1964; *Billboard*, 28 Nov. 1964, 22.

3 *The Wild One*, dir. Laslo Benedek, 1954.

4 Jacqueline Warwick, *Girl Groups, Girl Culture: Popular Music and Identity in the 1960s*, 193.

5 See also Greil Marcus, 'Girl Groups: How the Other Half Lived,' *Village Voice*, 8 Sept. 1975.

6 See Flam and Liebowitz, *But Will You Love Me Tomorrow*, 228. Jeff Barry also noted, 'I grew up with The Shadow as a radio show. "Who knows what evil lurks in the hearts of men? The Shadow [knows]."'

7 The Shangri-Las, "Leader of the Pack" (Barry/Greenwich/Morton).

8 Lisa MacKinney, interview with Rod McBrien, 10 Apr. 2008; Ken Emerson, *Always Magic in the Air: The Bomp and Brilliance of the Brill Building Era*, 225, 227.

9 Richard Arfin, 'The "Shadow" Reappears—A Rare Talk with Producer George "Shadow" Morton,' part 3.

10 See Eric C. Schneider, *Vampires, Dragons and Egyptian Kings: Youth Gangs in Postwar New York*, 106–136 for a discussion of gangs and adolescent masculinity, and 126–8 for the cementing of junior gang members' 'reputations as masculine tough guys' through street violence.

11 Ralph M. Newman, 'Only the Shadow Knows: An Interview by Ralph M. Newman,' *Time Barrier Express* 26 (Sept/Oct 1979), 40.

12 Arfin, 'The "Shadow" Reappears,' part 1; see also Newman, 40.

13 James Gilbert, *A Cycle of Outrage: America's Reaction to the Juvenile Delinquent in the 1950s*, 18.

14 Schneider, 118–123.

15 The Markeys featuring George Morton, "Hot Rod" (George Francis Morton and Joseph J. Monaco) b/w "Yakkity Yak" (Jack Hammer), RCA 47-7256, 1958.

16 Linda Holtzman, *Media Messages: What Film, Television, and Popular Music Teach Us About Race, Class, Gender, and Sexual Orientation*, 104–6.

17 See above, 55–57; see also Holtzman, 113–14.

18 Warwick, 141; Beverley Skeggs, *Formations of Class and Gender: Becoming Respectable*, 1–4.

19 This is discussed above, with particular reference to Queens, 57–60; see also Jean Halley, Ashley Eshleman, and Ramya Mahadevan Vijaya, *Seeing White: An Introduction to White Privilege and Race*, 109–110.

20 Holtzman, 114.

21 Halley, Eshleman, and Vijaya, 101.

22 Gilbert, esp. 200ff; for an excellent examination of the impact of international politics on responses to the biker/juvenile delinquent in the USA, see Lily Phillips, 'Blue Jeans, Black Leather Jackets, and a Sneer: The Iconography of the 1950s Biker and its Translation Abroad,' *International Journal of Motorcycle Studies* 1 (2005).

23 These include Albert K. Cohen, *Delinquent Boys: The Culture of the Gang*; August Aichhorn, *Wayward Youth: A Psychoanalytic Study of Delinquent Children, Illustrated by Actual Case Histories*; Richard A. Cloward and Lloyd E. Ohlin, *Delinquency and Opportunity: A Theory of Delinquent Gangs*; for a useful survey see *Juvenile Delinquency: A Book of Readings*, ed. Rose Giallombardo, 108–188.

24 Cohen, 129, 140 (italics mine); Michael Barson and Steven Heller, *Teenage Confidential: An Illustrated History of the American Teen*, 51. For the historical background of these ideas, and fears of hyper-masculinity among the working classes, see Gail Bederman, *Manliness and Civilization: A Cultural History of Gender and Race in the United States, 1880–1917*, 16–31.

25 Phillips, 'Blue Jeans, Black Leather Jackets.'

26 Norma Coates, 'Teenyboppers, Groupies and Other Grotesques: Girls and Women and Rock Culture in the 1960s and early 1970s,' *Journal of Popular Music Studies* 15:1 (2003), 69–70.

27 'Riding' can also be understood as a metaphor for sex, given the common investment of motorcycles with feminine/sexual qualities and their role as an object of desire: see John Pigot, 'Symbolic Identities: Masculinity and the Motorcycle,' *Artlink* 16:1 (1996), 48.

28 See Schneider, 107–118 for the problematic relationship between school attendance and gang membership, and concomitant issues that arose later for gang members and the labour market.

29 "Leader of the Pack" (Barry/Greenwich/Morton).

30 Schneider, 153.

31 Schneider, 152–3.

32 "Leader of the Pack" (Barry/Greenwich/Morton).

33 Steven Mintz, *Huck's Raft: A History of American Childhood*, 295; Schneider, 138; Gilbert, 18; see also Walter B. Miller, 'Lower Class Culture as a Generating Milieu of Gang Delinquency,' *Journal of Social Issues* 14:3 (1958), 5–19.

34 Warwick, 197.

35 Warwick, 196.

36 "Leader of the Pack," (Barry/Greenwich/Morton).

37 On father/daughter relationships during this period, see Rachel Devlin, 'Female Juvenile Delinquency and the Problem of Sexual Authority in America 1945–1965,' in *Delinquents and Debutantes: Twentieth-Century American Girls' Cultures*, ed. Sherrie A. Inness, 83–106, esp. 84–6; see also Rachel Devlin, *Relative Intimacy: Fathers, Adolescent Daughters and Postwar American Culture*.

38 Ian Inglis, 'A Brief Life: Broken Hearts and Sudden Deaths,' *Popular Music and Society* 27:4 (2004), 486.

39 The circumstances surrounding the recording of this song are discussed in chapter 3.

40 Arlin, 'The"Shadow" Reappears,' part 1.

41 Terry Gross, 'Mary Weiss comes back for a *Dangerous Game*,' interview for *Fresh Air* on NPR.

42 Betrock, *Girl Groups: The Story of a Sound*, 102.

43 Iain Aitch, 'The Leader's Back,' *The Telegraph*, 14 Apr. 2007.

44 Stanley Cohen, *Folk Devils and Moral Panics: The Creation of the Mods and Rockers*.

45 Dave Laing, 'Twinkle Obituary,' *The Guardian* 27 May 2015; see also Richie Unterberger, 'Twinkle' (allmusic).

46 Laing, 'Twinkle Obituary'; see also Alan Clayson, *Death Discs: An Account of Fatality in Popular Song*, 49–50.

47 Dave McAleer, Andy Gregory & Matthew White, *The Virgin Book of British Hit Singles Vol. 2*, 420, 481.

48 Laing, 'Twinkle Obituary.'

49 Keith Altham, 'Nobody Objected to Shangri-Las in States,' *New Musical Express*, 29 Jan. 1965, 3.

50 Altham, 3.

51 Altham, 3.

52 Allen Evans, 'LPs by Allen Evans,' *New Musical Express*, 12 Mar. 1965, 13.

53 Monica Syrette, 'I Was a Teenage Shangri-La-holic,' *Bust*, Spring/Summer 1996, 66–7. My thanks to Monica for providing me with a copy of this article.

54 The Shangri-Las and Robert Goulet on *I've Got a Secret*, including a performance of "Leader of the Pack," 16 Nov. 1964 (YouTube).

55 See http://www.robertgoulet.com/man/bio/ (accessed 31 Dec. 2023).

56 See Lily Phillips's comments on the Eric von Zipper character featured in the Annette Funicello-Frankie Avalon Beach movies for a depiction of the biker as an absurd figure; Lily Phillips, 'Blue Jeans, Leather Jackets.'

57 "Leader of the Laundromat" (Pockriss/Vance), ROULETTE 4590,1964. *Billboard Hot 100*, 9 Jan. 1965; see also 'The Detergents are Cleaning Up the Music Business,' *Hit Parader*, May 1965, 12–13, 52. The four members of The Detergents were also from New York—three from Brooklyn, one from Staten Island.

58 See ASCAP entry for "Leader of the Laundromat." Richard Carlin states that Barry, Greenwich and Morton reached an out-of-court settlement after suing Vance and Pockriss but provides no evidence for this claim; see Carlin, *Godfather of the Music Business*, 136–7.

59 See BMI entry for "Eat It."

60 Sandra Peddie, 'Living the High Life,' *Newsday*, 3 Mar. 2020, 6.

61 Vicki Trent, *Pop Weekly*, 6 Feb. 1965, 15.

62 Gilbert, 3.

63 Fredric Wertham, *Seduction of the Innocent*, 148–71; Gilbert, 91–108.

64 See Ronald S. Green, *Innovation, Imitation, and Resisting Manipulation: The First Twenty Years of American Teenagers 1941–1961*, Unpublished PhD thesis, 28–32.

65 Quoted in Charles H. Brown, 'Self-Portrait: The Teen-Type Magazine,' *Annals of the American Academy of Political and Social Science* 338 (1961), 15; Gilbert, 202–3.

66 Schneider, 144–5.

67 Schneider, 144; see also Dick Hebdidge's discussion of subcultural 'communication' through 'working class' style and clothing in *Subculture: The Meaning of Style*, 100–106.

68 Phyllis Lee Levin, 'The Sound of Music?,' *New York Times*, 14 Mar. 1965, 72.

69 This is a very small sample—Inglis (477–88) discusses eleven examples released between 1959 and 1964; for a fuller account of this 'genre,' see Clayson, 47–60. "Tell Laura I Love Her" was written by Jeff Barry, who is credited, along with Morton, as co-writer of "Leader of the Pack."

70 The Cheers, "Black Denim Trousers and Motorcycle Boots," (Leiber/Stoller) b/w "Some Night in Alaska" (Levin), CAPITOL 3219, 1955.

71 Newman, 42.

72 The Cheers, "Black Denim Trousers," see Emerson, 227.

73 The Cheers, "Black Denim Trousers."

74 Emerson, 227; Lisa MacKinney, interview with Brooks Arthur, 18 Mar. 2008.

75 I thank Phil Milstein for pointing this out and providing me with copies of these tracks, especially Nervous Norvus's truly extraordinary "Transfusion" (Drake) b/w "Dig" (Drake), DOT 15470, 1956.

76 Derek Johnson, 'Fury's Latest was Worth Waiting For,' *New Musical Express*, 25 Dec. 1964, 4.

77 Aitch, 'The Leader's Back.'

78 Richard Goldstein, 'Pop Eye: The Soul Sound from Sheepshead Bay,' *Village Voice*, 23 June 1966, 8.

79 On the association of masculinity with technology, see Pigot, 47–49; for a more theoretical analysis of the 'man-machine interface' and the musicality of throttles, see Steven L. Thompson, 'The Arts of the Motorcycle: Biology, Culture and Aesthetics in Technological Choice,' *Technology and Culture* 41 (2000), 99–100, 107–9; John Alt, 'Popular Culture and Mass Consumption: The Motorcycle as Cultural Commodity,' *Journal of Popular Culture* 15:4 (1982), 133.

80 Hunter S. Thompson, *Hells Angels*, 96.

81 Jack Sargeant, 'Violence and Vinyl: Car Crashes in 1960s Pop,' in *Car Crash Culture*, ed. Mikita Brottman, 262–3.

82 *Scorpio Rising*, dir. Kenneth Anger, 1963. I thank Tony McMahon for insisting years ago that I see this film, and Bradley Eros for lending me his books on Kenneth Anger.

83 These ideas, which I wrote about at length (and published) in 2008, are used without acknowledgment by Ada Wolin in *Golden Hits of the Shangri-Las* (2019) 54–5; see Lisa MacKinney, '"Mmm, he's good-bad, but he's not evil . . .": The Shangri-Las, "Leader of the Pack," and the Cultural Context of the Motorcycle Rider,' *International Journal of Motorcycle Studies* 4:1 (Mar. 2008). For a detailed discussion of the homoerotic aspects of *Scorpio Rising* and their contexts, see Juan A. Suárez, *Bike Boys, Drag Queens and Superstars: Avant-Garde, Mass Culture, and Gay Identities in the 1960s Underground Cinema*.

84 Anna Powell, 'The Occult: A Torch for Lucifer,' in *Moonchild: The Films of Kenneth Anger*, ed. Jack Hunter, 74.

85 Suárez, 142; for an excellent discussion of this see also David E. James, *Rock 'n' film: Cinema's Dance with Popular Music*, 65–71.

86 Suárez, 167–8.

87 Carel Rowe, 'Myth and Symbolism: Blue Velvet,' in *Moonchild*, ed. Hunter, 21–2.

88 Rowe, 26.

89 See Gregory Markopolis, 'Scorpio Rising (First Impressions After a First Viewing, 10/29/63),' *Film Culture* 31 (Winter 1963–64), 5; for an extended discussion of Kenneth Anger's utilization of popular music, see Suárez, 114–18; for *Scorpio Rising* and popular culture more generally, Suárez, 141–180.

90 For a live studio performance, see the Shangri-Las, "Give Him a Great Big Kiss," *Shindig!*, 1965 (YouTube).

91 Quoted in Schneider, 142–3.

92 The link between the dark and brutal world of (bike) gangs and doo-wop style popular music is very strong in *Scorpio Rising*.

93 See Schneider, 140–1.

94 The Shangri-Las, "Give Him a Great Big Kiss" (Morton) b/w "Twist and Shout" (Russell/Medley), RED BIRD 018, Dec. 1964.

95 The Shangri-Las (as trio, with Ian Whitcomb), "Give Him a Great Big Kiss," *Shindig!*, 1965 (YouTube).

96 Schneider, 143.

97 The Shangri-Las, "Give Him a Great Big Kiss" (Morton) b/w "Twist and Shout" (Russell/Medley).

98 MacKinney, interview with George 'Shadow' Morton, 24 Apr. 2007.

99 MacKinney, interview with Morton.

100 MacKinney, interview with Morton; see also earlier discussion in chapter 2.

101 'A solo man': MacKinney, interview with Morton.

102 Greil Marcus, 'Girl Groups: How the Other Half Lived,' *Village Voice*.

103 Aitch, 'The Leader's Back.'

104 The Shangri-Las, "Out in the Streets" (Barry/Greenwich) b/w "The Boy" (Morton) RED BIRD 025, Apr. 1965. For credits on the record label, see Discogs entry. Greenwich and Barry are registered with BMI as writers, but there is also an ASCAP listing for the song, which credits Artie Butler, Jerry Leiber, and Morton as writers. I point this out because the origins of the anti-hero figure seem so closely connected with Morton.

105 Warwick, 193; see also Emerson, 228–9.

106 The Shangri-Las, "Out in the Streets" (Barry/Greenwich) b/w "The Boy" (Morton) RED BIRD 025, Apr. 1965.

107 The Shangri-Las, "Out in the Streets," *Shindig!*, 1965 (YouTube).

108 For another reading of pedestals, see Jacqueline Warwick, '"He Hit Me, and I was Glad": Violence, Masochism and Anger in Girl Group Music,' in *She's So Fine: Reflections on Whiteness, Femininity, Adolescence and Class in 1960s Music*, ed. Laurie Stras, 96–7.

109 *Masculin féminin*, dir. Jean-Luc Godard, 1966.

110 *Made in U.S.A.*, dir. Jean-Luc Godard, 1966; see Ryan Lattanzio, 'Watch: Marianne Faithfull Sings for Godard in "Made in U.S.A.,"' *Indie Wire*, 29 Dec. 2014 (online). In 1968 Godard would document the Rolling Stones rehearsing and recording "Sympathy for the Devil" in *One+One* (a.k.a. *Sympathy for the Devil*).

111 See Sixten Ringbom, *Icon to Narrative: The Rise of the Dramatic Close-Up in Fifteenth Century Devotional Painting* and Henk van Os, *The Art of Devotion in the Late Middle Ages in Europe 1300–1500*. For an overview of these developments, see Lisa MacKinney, *Recovering the Late Medieval Devotional World of Margery Kempe and her Book*, unpublished MA thesis, 59–82.

112 *Vivre sa vie* [*My Life to Live*], dir. Jean-Luc Godard, 1962; scene via YouTube.

113 Gabrielle Schwartz, 'All Shook Up,' *Apollo* Feb. 2019, 43.

114 Schwartz, 44; for the fire, see Rob Williams, 'Inside the Manchester Woolworths blaze—the fire that claimed ten lives—and changed Britain,' *Manchester Evening News*, 7 May 2019.

115 Schwartz, 44.

116 Schwartz, 44.

117 Richard Dorment, 'Turner Prize 2012, Tate Britain, review,' *Daily Telegraph*, London, UK, 2 Oct 2012, 27.

118 Dorment, 27.

119 Blake Williams, 'Indeed We Know: On the Video Art of Elizabeth Price,' *Cinema Scope* 70 (Spring 2017), 52–55.

120 The Shangri-Las, "I Can Never Go Home Anymore" (George Morton) b/w "Bull Dog" (Leiber/Stoller), RED BIRD 043, Nov. 1965.

121 Laura Oswald, 'Branding the American Family: A Strategic Study of the Culture, Composition, and Consumer Behaviour of Families in the New Millennium,' *Journal of Popular Culture* 37:2 (2003), 324.

122 The Shangri-Las, "Give Us Your Blessings" (Barry/Greenwich) b/w "Heaven Only Knows" (Barry/Greenwich) RED BIRD 030, May 1965.

123 William Shakespeare, *The Tragedy of King Lear*, Act III, Scene 1, lines 4–11. See also E. Catherine Dunn, 'The Storm in King Lear,' *Shakespeare Quarterly*, 3:4 (1952), 329–33; Josephine Waters Bennett, 'The Storm Within: The Madness of Lear,' *Shakespeare Quarterly*, 13:2 (1962), 137–55.

124 This is but one aspect of the storm's function: see George W. Williams, 'The Poetry of the Storm in King Lear,' *Shakespeare Quarterly*, 2:1 (1951), 57–71, esp. 58–61.

125 The Shangri-Las, "Give Us Your Blessings" (Barry/Greenwich) RED BIRD 030, 1965, (emphasis added).

126 The Shangri-Las, "Give Us Your Blessings" (Barry/Greenwich).

127 The Shangri-Las, "Leader of the Pack" (Barry/Greenwich/Morton) RED BIRD 014, 1964.

128 The Shangri-Las, "I Can Never Go Home Anymore" (George Morton), RED BIRD 043, 1965, (emphasis added).

129 The Shangri-Las, "I Can Never Go Home Anymore" (emphasis added).

130 Stephanie Coontz, *The Way We Never Were: American Families and the Nostalgia Trap*, 23–29; Elaine Tyler May, *Homeward Bound: American Families in the Cold War Era*, 19–20.

131 May, 11.

132 Ella Taylor, 'From the Nelsons to the Huxtables: Genre and Family Imagery in American Network Television,' *Qualitative Sociology* 12:1 (1989), 16–17; Coontz, 30–1.

133 Taylor, 17.

134 May, 10–29, 64–5.

135 Linna, *Mary Weiss of the Shangri-Las*, part 2.

136 Gross, 'Mary Weiss comes back for a *Dangerous Game*.'

137 Gross, 'Mary Weiss comes back for a Dangerous Game'; Linna, *Mary Weiss of the Shangri-Las*, part 7.

138 Kurt Loder, 'Where Are They Now? The Shangri-Las,' *Rolling Stone*, 12 Sept. 1985, 50; see also Emerson, 225–6.

139 'Suzi Quatro's Heroes of Rock 'n' Roll: Interview with Mary Weiss.'

140 Quoted in Emerson, 227.

141 'Suzi Quatro's Heroes of Rock 'n' Roll: Interview with Mary Weiss.'

142 Aitch, 'The Leader's Back.'

143 Arfin, 'The "Shadow" Reappears,' part 1; Dave the Rave, interview with the Goodies on 'Relics and Rarities,' WQMA Oldies Radio 1520AM, date unavailable. Copy supplied by Phil Milstein.

144 Arfin, 'The "Shadow" Reappears,' part 1.

145 Michael Martin, 'The Leader of the Pack is Back', *New York*, 25 Feb. 2007.

146 MacKinney, interview with Morton, 24 Apr. 2007.

147 MacKinney, interview with Morton, 24 Apr. 2007.

148 'From the Beat,' *KRLA Beat*, 25 Dec. 1965, 4.

CHAPTER SEVEN: *The Shangri-Las, Romanticism, and the Western Artistic Tradition*

1 Mitchell Cohen, 'Shangri-Las: A Teenage Melodrama,' *Let It Rock*, Dec. 1974 (online at Rock's Back Pages).

2 The Shangri-Las, 'Remember (Walkin' in the Sand) (Morton) b/w 'It's Easier to Cry' (Steinberg/Jackson/De Angelis) RED BIRD 08, 1964.

3 Ben Marcus, *From Polynesia with Love: The History of Surfing from Captain Cook to the Present* (online).

4 'Surf's Up!,' *Time* (82:6), Aug. 9, 1963, 49.

5 R.L. Rutsky, 'Surfing the Other: Ideology on the Beach,' *Film Quarterly* 52:4 (1999), 15–16. For the relationship of surf culture to the beat fascination with notions of primitive, exoticised, non-western cultures, see 19–21.

6 Joan Ormrod, '*Endless Summer* (1964): Consuming Waves and Surfing the Frontier,' *Film and History* 35:1 (2005), 40.

7 Carol Cooper, 'Surf Pop: The New Wave,' *Village Voice*, 17 Sept. 1996 (online, Rock's Back Pages).

8 Rutsky, 12.

9 Ormrod, 40.

10 Rutsky, 16.

11 George O. Carney, 'Cowabunga! Surfer Rock and the Five Themes of Geography,' *Popular Music and Society* 23:4 (1999), 4; see also Official Dick Dale Website (archived online).

12 Amanda Petrusich, 'Dick Dale, the Inventor of Surf Rock, Was a Lebanese-American Kid from Boston,' *New Yorker* 18 Mar. 2019; Official Dick Dale Website.

13 Official Dick Dale Website; Carney, 4.

14 The Official Dick Dale Website. I was lucky enough to witness Dale performing at the Central Club Hotel in Melbourne, Australia, in 1995. It was very, very loud.

15 Official Dick Dale Website.

16 'Catch this Giant Wave of Super-Selling Summer Surfing Sounds from Capitol,' *Billboard*, 11 July 1964, 7.

17 Gene Sculatti, 'Surfin' USA,' in *Let It Rock*, Aug. 1973 (Rock's Backpages).

18 'How Do We Get There?' *Teen*, Oct. 1964, 14.

19 The Mamas and the Papas, "California Dreamin'" b/w "Somebody Groovy" DUNHILL 4020, 1965.

20 The Shangri-Las, "Remember (Walkin' in the Sand)" (Morton) b/w "It's Easier to Cry" (Steinberg/Jackson/De Angelis) RED BIRD 08, 1964.

21 Arfin, 'The "Shadow" Reappears,' part 1; John Grecco, The Shangri-Las, *The Best of the Red Bird and Mercury Recordings*, Real Gone Music, RGM-1293, 2021 (liner notes).

22 I thank Professor Laurie Stras for pointing this out.

23 The Shangri-Las, "Remember (Walkin' in the Sand)" (Morton).

24 The Shangri-Las, "Remember (Walkin' in the Sand)" (Morton).

25 There are six ooohs and six aaaahs, a total of twelve.

26 The Shangri-Las, "Remember (Walkin' in the Sand)" (Morton).

27 See earlier discussion of related themes in chapter 6, 240–242. For an overview of emotional religiosity in the late Middle Ages, see Henk van Os, *The Art of Devotion in the Late Middle Ages in Europe 1300–1500*; for rosaries specifically, see MacKinney, 'Rosaries, Paternosters and Devotion to the Virgin in the Households of John Baret of Bury St. Edmunds,' *Parergon* 24:2 (2007), 93–114.

28 'That was my school, St. Thomas Aquinas. I got more education in the streets than I did from the sisters.' See Arlin, 'The "Shadow" Reappears,' part 1.

29 Jacqueline Warwick, *Girl Groups, Girl Culture*, 14–17.

30 William Chase Greene, 'The Sea in the Greek Poets,' *North American Review* 199:3 (1914), 427–443.

31 There is a long-standing debate over whether this relationship was sexual: see W.M. Clarke, 'Achilles and Patroclus in Love,' *Hermes* 106:3 (1978), 381–396.

32 Homer, *The Iliad*, ed. & trans. Robert Fagles, 588–9; see also Greene, 436.

33 Sophocles, *Philoctetes*, trans. Robert Torrance, ll. 676, 681–2, 687–90, in Oscar Mandel, *Philoctetes and the Fall of Troy: Plays, Documents, Iconography, Interpretations: Including Versions by Sophocles, André Gide, Oscar Mandel, and Heiner Müller*, 72–3; see also Greene, 436–7.

34 Margaret S. McCroskery, 'Tristan and the Dionysian Sea: Passion and the Iterative Sea Motif in the Legends of Tristan and Isolde,' *Midwest Quarterly* 13:4 (1972), 409–10.

35 Edwin Arlington Robinson, *Tristram*, 9. In *Tristram* there are two Isolts—the Isolt referred to in this section is not Irish Isolt, but Isolt of the white hands (daughter of Hoel of Brittany) who is also in love with Tristan. The Wagnerian version, to be discussed shortly, features only one Isolde.

36 McCroskery, 416.

37 Richard Wagner, *Tristan and Isolde*, trans. Stewart Robb, 17.

38 Wagner, *Tristan and Isolde*, 31.

39 "Give Us Your Blessings" (Barry/Greenwich) b/w "Heaven Only Knows" (Barry/Greenwich) RED BIRD 030, May 1965; see discussion in chapter 5.

40 McCroskery, 418–19.

41 "Past, Present and Future" (Morton/Leiber/Butler) b/w "Paradise" (Nilsson/Garfield/Botkin Jr/Spector), RED BIRD 10-068, June 1966. The second pressing of this single featured a different B-side, "Love You More than Yesterday" (Michaels/Gorman).

42 Grecco, *Out in the Streets*, part 3.

43 The Toys, "A Lover's Concerto" (Linzer/Randell) b/w "This Night" (Linzer/Randell), DYNOVOICE 209, 1965.

44 Serge Gainsbourg, "Initials B.B." (Gainsbourg), 1968.

45 Eric Carmen, "All By Myself" (Carmen/Rachmaninov) 1975; see 'Classical Influences in Popular Music,' (online) for a quite mindboggling list of examples.

46 Piano Sonata No. 14 in C-sharp Minor, Op. 27 No. 2. For the sake of ease, I will refer to this as the 'Moonlight' Sonata.

47 Ernest Kramer, 'Beethoven's Moonlight Sonata Glows Brightly After 200 Years,' *Clavier* 41:4 (Apr. 2002), 20; for biographical details and Rellstab's relationship with Beethoven, see Peter Clive, *Beethoven and His World: A Biographical Dictionary*, 283–4.

48 From Czerny's memoranda to Otto Jahn, reproduced by Alexander Wheelock Thayer in *Thayer's Life of Beethoven*, ed. Elliot Forbes, v.1, 297.

49 Quoted in Ludwig Van Beethoven, Anton Kuerti, and Heinrich Schenker, *Five Great Piano Sonatas*, ix.

50 The *Adagio sostenuto* movement upon which "Past, Present and Future" is based will be the main focus of this discussion.

51 Ludwig van Beethoven, *Piano sonata op. 27/2: Sonata quasi una Fantasia* (score), with 'Preface' by Peter Hauschild and 'Notes on Interpretation' by Boris Bloch, trans. Lionel Salter, 6; Lewis Lockwood, 'Re-shaping the Genre: Beethoven's Piano Sonatas from Op. 22 to Op. 28 (1799–1801),' *Israel Studies in Musicology* 6 (1996), 11.

52 Lockwood, 11.

53 For an overview of Romanticism and its expression in art, poetry and music, see Marvin Perry, *An Intellectual History of Modern Europe*, 173–185.

54 Perry, 179.

55 Lockwood, 2–3, 14–15.

56 J.A.P. Schulze's 'Sonate' was published in J.G. Sulzer, *Allgemeine Theorie der schönen Künste 2*, 688–89, which Glenn Stanley has described as 'an influential encyclopaedia of the arts.' See Glenn Stanley, 'Genre Aesthetics and Function: Beethoven's Piano Sonatas in Their Cultural Context,' *Beethoven Forum* 6:1 (1998), 3.

57 *Aesthetics and the Art of Musical Composition in the German Enlightenment: Selected Writings of Johann Georg Sulzer and Heinrich Christoph Koch*, ed. Nancy Kovaleff Baker and Thomas S. Christensen, 1995, 103–105, quoted in Stanley, 4 (italics mine).

58 See Alfred Einstein, *Music in the Romantic Era*, 20–25.

59 Kenneth Drake, *The Beethoven Sonatas and the Creative Experience*, 1.

60 However, see Max Unger and Willis Wager, 'From Beethoven's Workshop,' *The Musical Quarterly* 24:3 (July 1938), 328–9.

61 Stanley, 2–3; Marx, quoted in Stanley, 27.

62 Stanley, 27.

63 Stanley, 4 (italics mine).

64 Richie Unterberger has also noted this; 'Past, Present and Future,' (allmusic.com).

65 Clive, 141.

66 Translated and reproduced by Unger and Wager, 333–4.

67 *Thayer's Life of Beethoven*, ed. Forbes, v.1, 297; Kramer, 20; Myron Schwager, 'Some Observations on Beethoven as an Arranger,' *The Musical Quarterly* 60:1 (1974), 80–93.

68 Johann Gottfried Seume, 'Die Beterin' in *Sämmtliche Werke*, Vol. 7, 335–6. My sincere and grateful thanks to Dr. Leith Passmore for translating 'Die Beterin' into English for me.

69 For an overview, see van Os, and Lisa MacKinney, *Recovering the Late Medieval Devotional World of Margery Kempe and her Book*, chapters two and three.

70 Perry, 173–185.

71 The Shangri-Las, "Past, Present and Future" (Morton/Leiber/Butler).

72 The Shangri-Las, "Past, Present and Future" (Morton/Leiber/Butler).

73 Ruth Katz, 'The Egalitarian Waltz,' *Comparative Studies in Society and History* 15:3 (1973), 375; see also 373–5.

74 Warwick, 194.

75 Richard Goldstein, 'Pop Eye: The Soul Sound from Sheepshead Bay,' *Village Voice*, 23 June 1966, 30.

76 See above, 51–2; Ada Wolin, *Golden Hits of the Shangri-Las*, 71. Wolin's reading is based on an article by Devin McKinney which uses a 'painful' live version of "Past, Present and Future" by Alex Chilton from a 1970s bootleg as its starting point. His discussion of the Shangri-Las, like Wolin's, is riddled with inaccuracies. See Devin McKinney, 'Pop Irony: Past, Present and Future,' *The American Prospect: Ideas, Politics, Power*, 5 Jan. 2005.

77 Goldstein, 8.

78 'Three Shangri-Las: Grooving in Utopia,' *KRLA Beat*, 13 Aug. 1966, 7.

79 'Suzi Quatro's Heroes of Rock 'n' Roll: Interview with Mary Weiss.'

80 Drake, 3.

81 As reported by Deena Canalle, *Bomp List Archives* (online).

82 Ludwig van Beethoven, *Briefwechsel: Gesamtausgabe*, ed. Sieghard Brandenburg, 7 vols., no. 70. For a translation of the full text of the *Heiligenstadt Testament* see *Thayer's Life of Beethoven*, ed. Forbes, v.1, 304–306; this quotation is from 305, italics included in Thayer. For commentary, see Lewis Lockwood, *Beethoven: The Music and the Life*, 111–123.

83 Letter from Beethoven to Dr Franz Gerhard Wegeler, Nov. 16, 1801, reproduced in *Thayer's Life of Beethoven*, ed. Forbes, v. 1, 286.

84 Kramer, 20; Clive, 142.

85 See *Thayer's Life of Beethoven*, ed. Forbes, v. 1, 288–92; Eric Blom, *Beethoven's Pianoforte Sonatas Discussed*, 107–8. The danger in making too much of the dedication is that Beethoven seemed to not rate the sonata particularly highly. Also, he had originally dedicated another work, the Rondo in G Major, opus 51, No. 2, to Guicciardi, but withdrew the dedication, reassigned the Rondo to Princess Lichnowsky, and dedicated the 'Moonlight' to Guicciardi instead; see Blom, 108.

86 Clive, 142.

87 For text of the letter and two postscripts, see *Thayer's Life of Beethoven*, ed. Forbes, v.1, 533–4, and for a thorough discussion of the 'large and varied literature concerning this famous letter,' see Appendix F in vol. 2, 1088–1093; see also Ernest Newman, 'A Beethoven Hoax?,' *The Musical Times*, 52: 825 (Nov. 1, 1911), 714–717.

88 Blom, 107. It is now generally accepted that the letter and postscripts were written in 1812, and that Guicciardi was not the intended recipient.

89 Kramer, 20.

90 Clive, 143.

91 *Thayer's Life of Beethoven*, ed. Forbes, v. 1, 292.

92 *Piano sonata op. 27/2: Sonata quasi una Fantasia* (score), with 'Preface' by Peter Hauschild, 6. Thayer and Hauschild both contended that this visit took place in 1822, but this is disputed by Clive, 143, and Forbes (editor of *Thayer's Life of Beethoven*), 290–1, who argue that it took place in 1803, before the Gallenbergs left for Italy.

93 Clive, 143.

94 *Immortal Beloved*, dir. Bernard Rose, 1994.

95 Lockwood, *Beethoven: The Music and the Life*, 135.

96 'Si deve suonare tutto questo pezzo delicatissimamente e senza sordino.' See *Piano sonata op. 27/2: Sonata quasi una Fantasia* (score), with 'Preface' by Peter Hauschild, 7.

97 Andras Schiff, *Schiff on Beethoven, Part 4, Part 3: Piano Sonata in C-Sharp Minor, opus 27, No. 2* ('Moonlight') (online).

98 Stuart Isacoff, 'A Cultural Conversation with Andras Schiff: Lessons from Beethoven and Life,' *Wall Street Journal* (Eastern edition), Oct 31, 2007, D9.

99 Quoted in Stanley, 10.

100 Andras Schiff, *Schiff on Beethoven*.

101 Quoted by Patrick, *Sophisticated Boom Boom* (liner notes), 20–21.

CHAPTER EIGHT: *Four Last Songs*

1 Richard Strauss, *Four Last Songs*, 'September,' text by Herman Hesse, 1948, in Richard Stokes, *The Book of Lieder: The Original Texts of Over 1000 Songs*, 562–3.

2 Mitchell Cohen, 'Shangri-Las: A Teenage Melodrama,' in *Let It Rock*, Dec. 1974 (via Rock's Backpages).

3 The Shangri-Las, "Sweet Sounds of Summer" (Lawrence J. Martire) b/w "I'll Never Learn" (Sandy Hurvitz, [a.k.a. Essra Mohawk]), MERCURY 72645, Dec. 1966; "Take the Time" (Sal Trimarchi/Ritchie Cordell) b/w "Footsteps on the Roof" (Sal Trimachi/Ritchie Cordell), MERCURY 72670, Mar. 1967.

4 John Grecco, *Out in the Streets*, part 4.

5 Ada Wolin seems not aware of their existence at all, calling "Past, Present and Future" 'the Shangri-Las's [sic] last release'; see Ada Wolin, *Golden Hits of the Shangri-Las*, 70.

6 Alan Betrock, *Girl Groups: The Story of a Sound*, 109.

7 The Shangri-Las, "Sweet Sounds of Summer" (Lawrence J. Martire).

8 'Pop Spotlights,' *Billboard*, 24 Dec. 1966, 16.

9 Red Bird/Shangri-Las advertisement for "Give Him a Great Big Kiss" and "Maybe," *Billboard*, 19 Dec. 1964, 27.

10 John Grecco, The Shangri-Las, *The Best of the Red Bird and Mercury Recordings*, (liner notes); Mick Patrick, *Sophisticated Boom Boom* (liner notes), 22.

11 'Top Records of 1966,' *Billboard*, 24 Dec. 1966, 34.

12 For an overview of the development of psychedelic music in the mid-1960s, see Robert Palmer, 'Eight Miles High,' in *Rock & Roll: An Unruly History*, New York: Harmony, 1995, 157–73.

13 Russell Reising, 'Melting Clocks and the Hallways of Always: Time in Psychedelic Music,' *Popular Music and Society* 32:4 (2009), 525.

14 'Pop Spotlights: Top 60,' *Billboard*, 2 Apr. 1966, 18. Interestingly, Dylan's "Rainy Day Women No. 12 & 35" was the next single reviewed in the section for that week.

15 John Einarson, *Mr. Tambourine Man: The Life and Legacy of the Byrds' Gene Clark*, 82–7, esp. 83–4.

16 Quoted in Palmer, 166.

17 Richard Lingeman, 'Offerings at the Psychedelicatessen,' *New York Times*, 10 July 1966, 34.

18 Reising, 524.

19 Sheila Whiteley, *The Space Between the Notes: Rock and the Counter-Culture*, 3–4, quoted in Reising, 524.

20 See Palmer, 165–6; Einarson, 82–7.

21 Cam Cloud, *The Little Book of Acid*, Berkeley: Ronin, 1999, 11, quoted in Reising, 524.

22 See The Chambers Brothers, "Time Has Come Today" (YouTube); see also Donna Gaines, *A Misfit's Manifesto: the Spiritual Journey of a Rock & Roll Heart: a Memoir*, 127–8.

23 The Shangri-Las, "Sweet Sounds of Summer" (Lawrence J. Martire).

24 The Shangri-Las, "Sweet Sounds of Summer" (Lawrence J. Martire).

25 The Shangri-Las, "Sweet Sounds of Summer" (Lawrence J. Martire).

26 The Shangri-Las, "Sweet Sounds of Summer" (Lawrence J. Martire).

27 'Extend Probe of Bootleg Disk Ring to "Entertainment Field,"' *Billboard*, 12 Dec. 1960, 3, 14; 'Bogus-disk Plot Is Smashed Here,' *New York Times*, 9 Dec. 1960, 21; see also chapter 4 of this book. For Morris Levy, see Fredric Dannen, *Hit Men: Power Brokers and Fast Money Inside the Record Business*, 31–57; Richard Carlin, *Godfather of the Music Business: Morris Levy*.

28 'Kings County, N.Y., Grand Jury Indicts Six Charged in Disk Counterfeit Racket,' *Billboard*, 20 Mar. 1961, 2; '9 Accused Counterfeiters Plead Guilty in New York,' *Billboard*, 19 May 1962, 5.

29 'Transcripts of F.B.I. Bugging Disclose the Methods and Intrigues of the Mafia,' *New York Times*, 13 June 1969, 50; 'Extortionist Gets 30 Months,' *New York Times*, 25 Mar. 1972, 28.

30 Jim Bessman, 'N.J. Jury Issues Indictments in Cutout Probes,' *Billboard*, 4 Oct. 1986, 1, 91; Dannen, 38–9, 53–7. This incredibly complex case is dissected in gripping detail by William Knoedelseder in *Stiffed: A True Story of MCA, the Music Business, and the Mafia*.

31 Bessman, 91; Dannen, 53–6.

32 See BMI entry for Lawrence J. Martire.

33 See chapter 3, 139–141.

34 *The Left Banke Too* (allmusic.com).

35 See BMI listing for Joe Simmons. Interestingly, one of these songs, "I'll Believe It When I See It," was recorded by the Sierras and released on George Goldner's Gol-disc label. Promotional copies list Simmons as the sole writer; yet the official Gol-disc release has the name Grace Goldner (wife of George) added; photos of both versions are on the Discogs listing for "I'll Believe It When I See It." BMI lists Grace Goldner as co-writer.

36 Grecco, The Shangri-Las, *The Best of the Red Bird and Mercury Recordings* (liner notes).

37 See also Grecco, *The Best of the Red Bird and Mercury Recordings* (liner notes).

38 See Essra Mohawk Official Website; for an overview, see entry by Charles Donovan on allmusic.com; see also Alex Williams, 'Essra Mohawk, Self-Described Flower Child Singer-Songwriter, Dies at 75,' *New York Times*, 22 Dec. 2023.

39 Jamie Carter, "The Boy with the Way" (Hurvitz) b/w "Memory of Your Voice" (Hurvitz), LIBERTY 55815, 1965.

40 'Newcomer Pick,' *Cash Box*, 7 Aug. 1965, 16; 'Pop Spotlight,' *Billboard*, 7 Aug. 1965, 16.

41 Essra Mohawk Official Website.

42 The Shangri-Las, "I'll Never Learn," (Hurvitz).

43 The Shangri-Las, "I'll Never Learn," (Hurvitz).

44 A picture in *Billboard* (20 Aug. 1966, 3) shows Trimachi and Cordell signing 'an exclusive writing pact with the Robbins-Feist-Miller combine,' otherwise known as the Big 3. This was a massive publishing company. The implications this had for the Shangri-Las are not clear, but it demonstrates that Trimachi and Cordell were high-profile songwriters.

45 Carlin, 150; see also Tommy James with Martin Fitzpatrick, *Me, the Mob and the Music*, 91–2.

46 'Pop Spotlights,' *Billboard*, 25 Mar. 1967, 16.

47 Linna, *Mary Weiss of the Shangri-Las*, part 7. I have been unable to locate any other references to the Shangri-Las or Weiss performing shows for 'servicemen and women.'

48 Grecco, *Out in the Streets*, part 4.

49 Kenneth J. Bindas and Craig Houston, '"Takin' Care of Business": Rock Music, Vietnam and the Protest Myth,' *Historian* 52:1 (Nov. 1989), 1.

50 Bindas and Houston, 1–25; see also Lee Andresen, *Battle Notes: Music of the Vietnam War*, 104–137.

51 David E. James, 'The Vietnam War and American Music,' in John Carlos Rowe and Rick Berg [eds.], *The Vietnam War and American Culture*, 241.

52 Lee Ballinger, 'Deja Vu,' in *The First Rock & Roll Confidential Report*, ed. Dave Marsh, 210.

53 Andresen, 70.

54 B. Lee Cooper, 'Popular Songs, Military Conflicts, and Public Perceptions of the United States at War,' *Social Education* 56:3 (1992), 160.

55 Terry H. Anderson, 'American Popular Music and the War in Vietnam,' *Peace and Change* 11 (July 1986), 52–54; Bindas and Houston, 6–7; James, 'The Vietnam War and American Music,' 234–6.

56 Richie Unterberger, *Turn! Turn! Turn! The 60s Folk-Rock Revolution*, 167–8, 171.

57 For a 'live' studio version, with accompanying car wreckage and interpretive dance, see Barry McGuire, "Eve of Destruction," *Hullabaloo* 1965 (YouTube).

58 Unterberger, 169–70.

59 Quoted in Unterberger, 168.

60 Aaron Sternfield, 'Rock + Folk + Protest = An Erupting new Sound,' *Billboard*, 21 Aug. 1965, 1, 14.

61 Sternfield, 14 ('bomb' is given as 'vomb' in the original).

62 Unterberger, 168; for further discussion of the impact of "Eve of Destruction," see 167–173.

63 Ray Brack, 'Many Operators Shun 'Protest' Music,' *Billboard*, 23 Oct. 1965, 57.

64 See Unterberger, 169.

65 SSgt. Barry Sadler, "Ballad of the Green Berets" (Sadler) b/w "Letter from Vietnam," (Sadler), RCA 47-8739, 1966.

66 "Ballad of the Green Berets," RCA advertisement, *Billboard*, 22 Jan. 1966, 2.

67 For lengthy discussions of this recording, see Andresen, 132–6 and R. Serge Denisoff, 'Fighting Prophecy with Napalm: "The Ballad of the Green Berets," *Journal of American Culture* 13 (Spring 1990), 81–93; see also Kevin Hillstrom and Laurie

Collier Hillstrom, *The Vietnam Experience: A Concise Encyclopaedia of American Literature, Songs and Films*, 25–28.

68 Les Waffen and Peter Hesbacher, 'War Songs: Hit Recordings During the Vietnam Period,' *ARSC: Association for Recorded Sound Collections* 13 (1981), 6.

69 This may be the aforementioned Ed Sullivan appearance; unfortunately, the details of when this performance aired are not supplied with the clip. See Barry Sadler, "Ballad of the Green Berets," YouTube).

70 *Oxford Dictionary of Classical Art* ed. John Boardman, 224, 249.

71 *Oxford Dictionary of Classical Art*, 252–4.

72 SSgt. Barry Sadler, "Ballad of the Green Berets" (Sadler), italics added.

73 'Transcript of Johnson's Assessment in TV Interview of His First 100 Days in Office,' *New York Times*, 16 Mar. 1964, 18.

74 'Transcript of Johnson's Assessment . . . ,' 18.

75 'Transcript of Johnson's Assessment . . . ,' 18.

76 *Aggression from the North*, State Department White Paper on Vietnam, Feb. 27, 1965 (online).

77 "Long Live Our Love" (Jackson/Barnes) b/w "Sophisticated Boom Boom" (Morton) RED BIRD 048, Feb. 1966.

78 "Long Live Our Love" (Jackson/Barnes).

79 "Long Live Our Love" (Jackson/Barnes).

80 The Shangri-Las, "Long Live Our Love," *Hullabaloo*, 1966 (YouTube).

81 The Shirelles, "Soldier Boy" (Luther Dixon/Florence Greenberg), 1962.

82 B. Lee Cooper and Wayne S. Haney, *Rock Music in American Popular Culture III: More Rock 'n' Roll Resources*, 127.

83 *Songs of the Civil War*, comp. & ed. Irwin Silber, 175.

84 See Frank J. Cipolla, 'Patrick Sarsfield Gilmore,' *New Grove Dictionary of Music and Musicians*, ed. Sanley Sadie & John Tyrrell, 2nd ed., 871; Silber [ed.], 124–5, 174–5; John Anthony Scott, *The Ballad of America: The History of the United States in Song and Story*, 327.

85 Scott, 327. For a representative list of collections it appears on, see entry for "When Johnny Comes Marching Home" on allmusic.com.

86 William Emmett Studwell, *The National and Religious Song Reader: Patriotic, Traditional, and Sacred Songs from Around the World*, 23.

87 Andresen, 261–2.

88 Studwell, 23.

89 See Les Waffen and Peter Hesbacher's comments about the use of 'trumpet and fife and drum' in the 'traditionally patriotic' war song (6).

90 Grecco, *The Best of the Red Bird and Mercury Recordings* (liner notes).

91 *Billboard*, 'Hot 100,' 5 Mar. 1966, 18.

92 *KRLA Beat*, 9 July 1966.

93 John Michaels, 'Barry Sadler: You Don't Have to Shake Dandruff,' *KRLA Beat*, 9 July 1966, 1.

94 'Letters to the Editor,' *KRLA Beat*, 13 Aug. 1966, 4.

95 'Letters to the Editor,' *KRLA Beat*, 16 July 1966, 2; 'Letters to the Editor,' *KRLA Beat*, 23 July 1966, 2.

96 'Letters to the Editor,' *KRLA Beat*, 10 Sept. 1966, 4, 6; 'Letters to the Editor,' *KRLA Beat*, 24 Sept. 1966, 2, 4.

97 Aaron Sternfield, "The Vietnam Conflict Spawning Heavy Barrage of Disk Tunes,' *Billboard*, 4 June 1966, 1, 10 (italics mine).

98 Paul Lyons, *New Left, New Right, and the Legacy of the Sixties*, 73–4.

99 Quoted by Andresen, 129–30.

100 'Dirksen in Landslide—Cap. Presses Rolling,' *Billboard*, 17 Dec. 1966, 6.

101 The Shangri-Las, "Take the Time" (Trimarchi/Cordell) b/w "Footsteps on the Roof" (Trimachi/Cordell), MERCURY 72670, Mar. 1967.

102 The Shangri-Las, "Take the Time" (Trimarchi/Cordell).

103 The Shangri-Las, "Take the Time" (Trimarchi/Cordell).

104 Quoted in Christian G. Appy, *Working Class War: American Combat Soldiers and Vietnam*, 65.

105 Quoted in Appy, 65; on this theme, see James, 'The Vietnam War and American Music,' 245–6.

106 Gil McDougall, 'California: Gangs, Vietniks and Surfers,' *KRLA Beat*, 13 Aug. 1966, 10.

107 The Shangri-Las, "Take the Time" (Trimarchi/Cordell).

108 The Shangri-Las, "Take the Time" (Trimarchi/Cordell).

109 Linna, *Mary Weiss of the Shangri-Las*, part 6; see also http://www.classicbands. com/MonitRockInterview.html (accessed 2 Jan. 2024).

110 Miriam Linna noted the Lake resemblance during the interview: Linna, *Mary Weiss of the Shangri-Las*, part 6. Two of the photos under discussion are reproduced here.

111 Linna, *Mary Weiss of the Shangri-Las*, part 6. These photos are credited to *Journal Miss* magazine (1966); I have not been able to locate any copies of it.

112 'The Mad-Mod Look: Shangri-Las,' *Teen Datebook*, Oct. 1966, 28–29. I am tremendously grateful to Alex Moretti for providing me with a copy of these pages.

113 Ralph M. Newman, 'Only the Shadow Knows: An Interview by Ralph M. Newman,' *Time Barrier Express* 26 (Sept/Oct 1979), 40–46.

114 Warwick, *Girl Groups, Girl Culture*, 95.

115 Janis Ian, "Society's Child (Baby I've Been Thinking)," VERVE FORECAST KF5027, 1966.

116 George 'Shadow' Morton, quoted in Newman, 44.

117 Sarfraz Mansoor, '"I wanted to try cocaine, but Jimi was against it": Janis Ian on her tough, starlit life in music', *Guardian*, 26 Jan. 2022.

118 Mike Greenblatt, 'The Night Leonard Bernstein Introduced Janis Ian to America' (including YouTube link to TV footage), *Jersey Sound*, 3 January 2024.

119 Robert Shelton, 'Censors and the "New Reality,"' *New York Times*, 25 Sept. 1966, 535.

120 Lenny Kaye, 'You Can't Make Heroes Out Of Guys In Black Leather Jackets, They Told George 'Shadow' Morton. He Did . . . : Shadow Morton, Part 2,' *Melody Maker*, 9 Mar. 1974 (Rock's Backpages).

121 Shelton, 535.

122 Grecco, *Out in the Streets*, part 4.

123 The Vanilla Fudge, "You Keep Me Hanging On" (Holland/Dozier/Holland), ATCO 6495, 1968.

124 The Shangri-Las, "Footsteps on the Roof" (Trimachi/Cordell).

125 "Dressed in Black" (Gorman/Michaels/Morton), RED BIRD 053, 1966.

Sources

PRIMARY MATERIAL

Note: The majority of genealogical material referenced throughout has been accessed through the *Ancestry* website: https://www.ancestry.com/ (US version, subscription payment required). In many cases, scans of original records are accessible. Some of this material is also available through the *Family Search* website: https://www.familysearch. org/ which is a free genealogical service (registration required) operated by the Church of Jesus Christ of Latter-Day Saints. Individual references/endnotes in the main book text indicate record details as well as which website has been used so that original source material can be accessed if desired. It is not feasible to re-list each individually in this bibliography, or to include long web links.

Ancestry

Canada, Arriving Passengers Lists, 1865–1935.
Census, United States Federal data for years 1900, 1910, 1920, 1930, 1940, 1950 and *New York State Census* data for 1905, 1915, 1925.
Episcopal Diocese of New York Church Records, 1767–1970.
New York, New York, U.S., Birth Index, 1910–1965.
New York, New York, U.S., Index to Birth Certificates, 1866–1909.
New York, New York, U.S., Marriage License Indexes, 1907–2018.
New York City Marriage Records, 1829–1940 (New York City Municipal Archives, New York).
New York City Municipal Archives.
U.S., School Yearbooks, 1900–1999.
U.S., Social Security Applications and Claims Index, 1936–2007.
U.S., World War I Draft Registration Cards 1917–1918.
U.S., World War II Draft Cards Young Men, 1940–1947, New York (City).

Family Search

New York, New York City Municipal Deaths, 1795–1949.
U.S., Social Security Death Index.

Other Records and Historical Material

1966 Spring Spectacular (Seattle Center Coliseum) concert program, 30 Apr. 1966, https://www.facebook.com/permalink.php/?story_fbid=4093153807396604 &id=148014081910616 (accessed 31 Dec. 2024).

'Aggression from the North,' State Department White Paper on Vietnam, Feb. 27, 1965, https://www.digitalhistory.uh.edu/disp_textbook.cfm?smtID=3&psid=3640 (accessed 1 Jan. 2024).

Brooklyn, New York City, Telephone Directory, 1950, https://archive.org/details/brooklynnewyorkc1950newy/ (accessed 3 Oct. 2023).

Canadian Museum of Immigration at Pier 21, 'Railway Agreement, 1925,' https://pier21.ca/research/immigration-history/railway-agreement-1925 (accessed 6 Apr. 2021).

Canadian Museum of Immigration at Pier 21, 'Ship Arrival Database,' https://pier21.ca/research/immigration-records/ship-arrival-search (accessed 6 Apr. 2021).

Catalog of Copyright Entries, Washington, D.C.: Copyright Office, Library of Congress, multiple volumes and years. All volumes referred to are available online, and can be looked up individually using the details provided in the references/endnotes: https://onlinebooks.library.upenn.edu/cce/ (accessed 4 Apr. 2021).

Ganser, Mary Ann, 'Identification of Body,' uploaded to *Scott Michaels' Find a Death: The Forum,* https://findadeathforum.com/showthread.php?8219-Has-anyone-ever-heard-of-The-Shangri-La-s&highlight=ganser (accessed 12 Nov. 2021).

Jimmy Merchant and Herman Santiago, plaintiffs-appellees-cross-appellants, v. Morris Levy, Big Seven Music Corp. and Roulette Records, Inc., Defendants-appellants-cross-appellees, and Windswept Pacific Entertainment Co., intervenor-defendant-appellant-cross-appellee, 92 F.3d 51 (2d Cir. 1996), https://law.justia.com/cases/federal/appellate-courts/F3/92/51/517413/ (accessed 21 Sept. 2021).

Jini Dellaccio Photographs, approximately 1940–2013, University of Washington Libraries, Special Collections, https://archiveswest.orbiscascade.org/ark:80444/xv37075 (accessed 31 Dec. 2024).

NYC Marriage Index: https://www.nycmarriageindex.com/ (accessed 7 Jan. 2024).

New York City Phone Directory 1964–5: Queens.

Queens New York City Telephone Directory, Winter 1939–40, https://stevemorse.org/census/nycphonebook.html (accessed 30 Jan. 2022).

Shangri-Las 1964 English Tour Photos: http://www.gettyimages.com.au/detail/52629021, http://www.gettyimages.com.au/detail/52629017, http://www.gettyimages.com.au/detail/2669432 (accessed 3 Jan. 2024).

US Find A Grave Index, 1600–Current: https://www.findagrave.com/ (accessed 7 Jan. 2024).

Reports

Addisleigh Park: Report Prepared by Jane Cowan for the Historic Districts Council, Spring 2008, https://web.archive.org/web/20090320121916/http://www.hdc.org/Addisleigh_Park_Report.pdf (accessed 15 Sept. 2021).

Koval, M., *Opiate Use in New York City,* New York: New York State Narcotic Addiction Control Commission and New York City Narcotics Register, 1969.

'Long Island Headquarters of the New York Telephone Company,' *Landmarks Preservation Commission* Sept. 21, 2004, Designation List 356 LP- 2144, http://s-media.nyc.gov/agencies/lpc/lp/2144.pdf (accessed 30 Jan. 2022).

Occupational Outlook Handbook: Employment Information on Major Occupations for Use in Guidance prepared in cooperation with Veterans Administration Office of the Assistant Administrator For Vocational Rehabilitation And Education, Bulletin No. 998, Washington DC: United States Department of Labor, 1951.

Newspaper Articles

Note: In general, web links are provided for material that is free/open access. Most historical material from the *New York Times* requires paid subscription through an institution or library that has purchased access through *ProQuest Historical Newspapers. Rock's Backpages* is a paid subscription service that largely covers historical pop/rock music magazines, but does include some music-related material from newspapers, the *Village Voice*, for instance. The list below is in alphabetical order by author surname; if there is no byline, then by the first letter of the article title.

'4 More Persons Killed by Heroin Doses Here,' *New York Times*, 1 Mar. 1970, 65.

'4 Teenagers Die From Heroin Here,' *New York Times*, 17 Mar. 1970, 40.

'5 Heroin Deaths Recorded in Day; Koch Asks Increase in Federal Funds for Narcotics Programs Here,' *New York Times*, 8 Mar. 1970, 67.

Aitch, I., 'The Leader's Back,' *Telegraph*, 14 Apr. 2007, http://www.telegraph.co.uk/culture/3664489/The-Leaders-back.html (accessed 20 Aug. 2023).

Altman, L.K., 'Deaths Attributed to Narcotics, Mainly Heroin, Increase Here,' *New York Times*, 21 June 1970, 1.

Blumenthal, A., '40 Years Between Records: A Shangri-La Returns,' *New York Times*, 4 Mar. 2007, 25.

'Bogus-disk Plot Is Smashed Here,' *New York Times*, 9 Dec. 1960, 21.

Buder, L., '40 Policemen Guarding Jackson High,' *New York Times*, 1 Mar. 1969, 28.

Campbell, B., 'West Side Marchers Seek More Addict Facilities: Mothers Lead Youths to Roosevelt Hospital to Obtain 40 new Beds,' *New York Times*, 24 Mar. 1970, 30.

Chiu, D., 'Cambria Heights Singer Returns to Music,' *Queens Chronicle*, 4 Oct. 2007, https://www.qchron.com/qboro/stories/cambria-heights-singer-returns-to-music/article_f3ba3985-68cc-5f3e-84da-d2cad5e36543.html (accessed 16 Sept. 2021).

Conrad, Johanna, Death Notice, *New York Times*, 16 Sept. 1912, 13.

Conrad, Mary, Death Notice, *New York Tribune*, 20 Feb. 1920, 4.

'The Concerts and Tours,' (Rolling Stones), *Telegraph*, 1 Jan. 2001, http://www.telegraph.co.uk/news/1400294/The-concerts-and-tours.html (accessed 2 Jan. 2024).

Cooper, C., 'Surf Pop: The New Wave,' *Village Voice*, 17 Sept. 1996, http://www.rocksbackpages.com/Library/Article/surf-pop-the-new-wave (accessed 1 Sept. 2021).

Crowther, B., 'A Theater Closes: And an Era too as the Paramount Goes Dark,' *New York Times*, 23 Aug. 1964, XI.

DeMasters, K., 'Pop Music: There are Oldies, and there are New Oldies,' *New York Times*, 22 Aug. 1999.

'Dope Kills Singer Who "Broke Habit,"' *Washington Post, Times Herald*, 28 Feb. 1968, C11.

Dorment, R., 'Turner Prize 2012, Tate Britain, review,' *Daily Telegraph*, 2 Oct. 2012, 27.

Edwards, G., 'Mary Weiss, Who Sang "Leader of the Pack", Is Dead at 75,' *New York Times*, 22 Jan. 2024, https://www.nytimes.com/2024/01/22/arts/music/mary-weiss-dead.html (accessed 25 Feb. 2024).

Esterow, M., 'Summer Fetes Attracting Stars: Talent Converging on City in Version of the old Rush; Events at Randalls, Freedomland and Forest Hills Set,' *New York Times*, 29 June 1962, 13.

'Extortionist Gets 30 Months,' *New York Times*, 25 Mar. 1972, 28.

'Fair Calendar,' *New York Times*, 12 Oct. 1964, 59.

Fox, M., 'Shadow Morton, Songwriter and Producer, Dies at 71,' *New York Times*, 15 Feb. 2013.

'Frankie Lymon Dies in Apartment Here,' *New York Times*, 28 Feb. 1968, 50.

'Funeral Notices,' *Long Island Press*, 18 Mar. 1970, 47.

Genzlinger, N., 'David Dalton, Rock Writer Who Lived the Scene, Dies at 80,' *New York Times*, 15 July 2022.

Goldstein, R., 'Pop Eye: The Soul Sound from Sheepshead Bay,' *Village Voice*, 23 June 1966, 7–8, 30–1.

'Gospel Tent's "Screaming" Services Drive Neighbors to Court Protest,' *New York Times,* 11 Sept. 1951, 31.

Grimes, W., 'Billy Miller, Curator and Historian of Fringe Music, dies at 62, *New York Times,* 14 Nov. 2016.

Harrington, R., 'The Beatles' Helping "Hand"; She Triggered Beatlemania in 1963 But Prefers Her Role to Be Unsung,' *Washington Post,* 16 Jan 2004: C01.

Jacobson, A., 'Mary Weiss Is Trying to Get Back in the Rocker Pack,' *Los Angeles Times,* 6 Apr. 2007, https://web.archive.org/web/20151002193854/http://articles.latimes.com/2007/apr/06/entertainment/et-weiss6 (accessed 15 Sept. 2021).

Laing, D., 'Twinkle Obituary,' *Guardian* 27 May 2015, https://www.theguardian.com/music/2015/may/26/twinkle (accessed 31 Aug. 2021).

Levin, P.L., 'The Sound of Music?,' *New York Times,* 14 Mar. 1965, 72.

Lingeman, R., 'Offerings at the Psychedelicatessen,' *New York Times,* 10 July 1966, 6, 31–2, 34, 36, 38.

Mansoor, S., '"I wanted to try cocaine, but Jimi was against it": Janis Ian on her tough, starlit life in music', *Guardian,* 26 January, 2022, https://www.theguardian.com/music/2022/jan/25/janis-ian-jimi-hendrix (accessed 24 Mar. 2024).

Marcus, G., 'Girl Groups: How the Other Half Lived,' *Village Voice,* 8 Sept. 1975, https://www.villagevoice.com/girl-groups-how-the-other-half-lived/ (accessed 6 Jan. 2024).

'Mary Ann Ganser, Singer, Dies at 22,' *Long Island Press,* 18 Mar. 1970, 47.

Marzulli, J., 'Colombo underboss John (Sonny) Franzese betrayed by son, who'll testify against legendary mobster,' *New York Daily News,* 9 June 2010, https://www.nydailynews.com/news/crime/the-mob/colombo-underboss-john-sonny-franzese-betrayed-son-testify-legendary-mobster-article-1.179737 (accessed 1 Nov. 2021).

McCoy, A., 'Clark Race: Obituary,' *Pittsburgh Post-Gazette,* 28 July 1999, https://web.archive.org/web/20130301063809/http://old.post-gazette.com/regionstate/19990728race9.asp (accessed 1 Nov. 2021).

Peddie, S., 'Living the High Life,' *Newsday,* 3 Mar. 2020, 6.

Perez-Pena, R., 'Here's Who First Asked Rock's Big Question,' *New York Times,* 19 Nov. 1992, A1, B8.

'Queens Tops All Boroughs in Heroin User Increase,' *Long Island Press,* 18 Mar. 1970, 3.

'Rescue High in Air Brings Vail Award,' *New York Times,* 1 June 1940, 11.

Sander, E., 'The Journalists of Rock,' *Saturday Review,* 31 July 1971, 47, 49.

Schwartz, A., 'Obituary: Remembering Alan Betrock,' *Village Voice,* 7 Apr. 2001, https://www.rocksbackpages.com/Library/Article/remembering-alan-betrock/ (accessed 6 Feb. 2023).

Severo, R., '28 Users of Heroin Die Here in 10 Days,' *New York Times,* 25 June 1969, 33.

Severo, R., 'Narcotics Addicts Find Aid Is Scarce: Acute Shortage of Medical Facilities Plagues City,' *New York Times,* 26 Sept. 1969, 1.

Severo, R., 'The Scourge of Youth: Use of Heroin by Students Is Called Deadliest Fad Ever to Hit Campuses,' *New York Times,* 2 Feb. 1970, 24.

Shearer, L., 'The Beatles: How Long Will they Last?' *Long Island Press: Parade,* 2 Aug. 1964, 4–5.

Shelton, R., 'Censors and the "New Reality,"' *New York Times,* 25 Sept. 1966, 535.

Sherburne, M., 'Do You Remember Harbor Springs' Club Ponytail?', *Petoskey News-Review,* 11 Jan. 2014, https://www.petoskeynews.com/story/news/local/2014/01/11/do-you-remember-harbor-springs-club-ponytail/116836082/ (accessed 31 Dec. 2024).

Smith, G., 'Playing piano until the fingers get burnt: After 20 years in the music business, Billy Joel has a lot to teach about music. And a lot to learn about business,' *Independent,* 8 July 1993, https://web.archive.org/web/20160304140230/http://www.independent.co.uk/arts-entertainment/music/music-playing-piano-until-the-fingers-get-burnt-after-20-years-in-the-music-business-billy-joel-has-1483565.html (accessed 1 May 2024).

Takiff, J., 'How a small Philadelphia record company gave an Oscar contender its sound,' *Philadelphia Inquirer*, 20 Nov. 2018, https://www.inquirer.com/entertainment/green-book-music-jamie-records-20181119.html (accessed 8 Oct. 2021).

Talese, G., 'About the Fair: Blind Singers Sense the Excitement and Soak Up the Swirl of Sounds,' *New York Times*, 28 Apr. 1964, 31.

Talese, G., 'Beatles and Fans Meet Social Set, *New York Times*, 21 Sept. 1964, 44.

Thompson, H., 'Teen-agers Howl for the Animals,' *New York Times*, 5 Sept. 1964, 11.

'Transcripts of F.B.I. Bugging Disclose the Methods and Intrigues of the Mafia,' *New York Times*, 13 June 1969, 50.

'Transcript of Johnson's Assessment in TV Interview of His First 100 Days in Office,' *New York Times*, 16 Mar. 1964, 18.

Williams, A., 'Essra Mohawk, Self-Described Flower Child Singer-Songwriter, Dies at 75,' *New York Times*, 22 Dec. 2023.

Williams, A., 'Andy Paley, 73, Composer and Producer Whose Imprint Was All Over Pop Music,' *New York Times*, 3 Dec. 2024, B10.

Williams, R., 'Ellie Greenwich, 1940–2009,' *Guardian*, 27 Aug. 2009, http://www.guardian.co.uk/music/2009/aug/27/ellie-greenwich-obituary (accessed 24 Sept. 2021).

Williams, R, 'Inside the Manchester Woolworths blaze—the fire that claimed ten lives—and changed Britain,' *Manchester Evening News*, 7 May 2019, https://www.manchestereveningnews.co.uk/news/greater-manchester-news/inside-manchester-woolworths-blaze-fire-16214759 (accessed 9 Sept. 2021).

Magazine and Music Trade Paper Articles

In a major boon for popular music researchers, many historical issues of US trade papers *Billboard, Cash Box* and *Record World*, as well as other US and international magazines relating to music, broadcasting and television (including *New Musical Express* and *Melody Maker* in the UK) have been made available free online (after previously being accessible largely via microfilm in libraries and only in a very piecemeal/ad hoc manner). This incomplete but nevertheless extraordinary feat of DIY archiving by David Gleason has recently been honoured by the Library of American Broadcasters Foundation: see https://tvnewscheck.com/business/article/david-gleason-builds-a-digital-archive-worth-honoring/ (accessed 5 Jan. 2024). Articles (listed below) and other material (reviews, photos etc.) for which details are provided in endnotes from *Billboard, Cash Box, New Musical Express, Melody Maker, Pop Weekly* and others can located by issue (PDF) on Gleason's website and then scrolled through to find page number of cited reference: https://www.worldradiohistory.com/

Please note, however, that although it is extremely comprehensive, not every issue referred to is available via Gleason's site; some remain undigitised.

KRLA Beat issues from 1964 to1968 are available free online in PDF form at http://krlabeat.sakionline.net/ (accessed 5 Jan. 2024).

Rock's Backpages is a paid subscription service that largely covers historical pop/rock music magazines.

'2 Members of The Teenagers Awarded Royalties for "Fools",' *Billboard*, 28 Nov. 1992, 6, 96.

'9 Accused Counterfeiters Plead Guilty in New York,' *Billboard*, 19 May 1962, 5.

'*16*'s Fourth Annual Geegee Gold Star Awards,' *16 Magazine Spectacular*, Summer, 1965, 4–7.

Altham, K., 'Nobody Objected to Shangri-Las in States,' *New Musical Express*, 29 Jan. 1965, 3.

Barbee, B., 'Rocking Ronettes Rocket Toward Fame: Two Sisters and a First Cousin,' *Jet* 30:24 (Sept. 22, 1966), 60–1.

Bell, K., 'How the Go-Go's Found their Beat: An Oral History,' *Vogue*, 4 Aug. 2020, https://www.vogue.com/article/go-gos-40th-anniversary-beauty-and-the-beat-oral-history-belinda-carlisle (accessed 30 Jan. 2022).

Bessman, J., 'N.J. Jury Issues Indictments in Cutout Probes,' *Billboard*, 4 Oct. 1986, 1, 91.

'The Billboard Music Popularity Charts, Rhythm & Blues, Review Spotlight on . . . Records: The Teenagers-Frankie Lymon,' *Billboard*, 4 Feb. 1956, 58.

'Bios for Deejays: Shangri-las,' *Cash Box*, 12 Sept. 1964, 31.

Brack, R., 'Many Operators Shun "Protest" Music,' *Billboard*, 23 Oct. 1965, 57.

Bundy, J., 'R&B Disks Sock Pop Market; Major Firms Jump into Ring,' *Billboard*, 29 Jan. 1955, 56.

'Catch this Giant Wave of Super-Selling Summer Surfing Sounds from Capitol,' *Billboard*, 11 July 1964, 7.

Clarke, C.V., 'Redefining Beautiful: Black Cosmetic Companies and Industry Giants Vie for the Loyalty of Black Women,' *Black Enterprise*, June 1993, 243–252.

Cohen, M., 'Shangri-Las: A Teenage Melodrama,' in *Let It Rock*, Dec. 1974, http://www.rocksbackpages.com/Library/Article/shangri-las-a-teenage-melodrama- (accessed 1 Sept. 2021).

Dannen, F., 'The Godfather of Rock and Roll,' *Rolling Stone*, 17 Nov. 1988, 88–97, 164.

'The Detergents are Cleaning Up the Music Business,' *Hit Parader*, May 1965, 12–13, 52.

The De Villes, "Kiss Me Again and Again," 'Reviews of New R&B Records,' *Billboard*, 5 May 1958, 118.

'Dirksen in Landslide—Cap. Presses Rolling,' *Billboard*, 17 Dec. 1966, 6.

'Employment Section: Help Wanted,' *Billboard*, 15 Apr. 1967, 67.

Evans, A., 'LPs by Allen Evans,' *New Musical Express*, 12 Mar. 1965, 13.

'Extend Probe of Bootleg Disk Ring to "Entertainment Field,"' *Billboard*, 12 Dec. 1960, 3, 14.

Faggen, G., 'Vox Jox,' *Billboard*, 9 May 1964, 12.

Fannan, R., 'Da Doo Ron Ron,' *Rolling Stone*, 11 May 1968, pp.19–20.

Farber, J., 'Leader of the Pack Is Back: Girl-group Legend Comes Home,' http://www.publicbroadcasting.net/michigan/.artsmain/article/4/1083/1050095/Pop/Leader.of.the.Pack.Is.Back.Girl-group.Legend.Comes.Home/ (accessed 2 Nov. 2021).

Friedman, R.,'Ripp Off: Billy Joel's Early Career to Be Exploited on Screen by Sons of First Manager and Greedy Label Owner,' *Showbiz* 411, 10 Mar. 2022, https://www.showbiz411.com/2022/03/10/ripp-off-billy-joels-early-career-to-be-exploited-on-screen-by-son-of-first-manager (accessed 9 Jun. 2024).

'From the Beat,' *KRLA Beat*, 25 Dec. 1965, 4.

Gaines, D., 'Let's Talk About Sex,' *Rolling Stone* 773 (13 Nov. 1997), 91–94.

Goldberg, M., 'Lawsuit Over Lymon Song Settled,' *Rolling Stone*, 1 July 1993, 19.

'Goldner Buys Out 2 Labels,' *Billboard*, 16 Apr. 1966, 3.

'Goldner Sells Out to Levy; Stays in Field,' *Billboard*, 6 Apr. 1957, 16, 44.

Grevatt, R., 'Kama-Sutra Productions: Is Twenty-Three Too Young to Own a Record Company?,' *Hi Fi / Stereo Review* 15 (1965), 28, 32.

Green, R., 'Searchers talk about the Shangri-Las,' *New Musical Express*, 20 Nov. 1964, 13.

Hibbert, T., 'Billy Joel: We All Make Mistakes . . . ,' *Q*, Sept. 1987, http://www.rocksbackpages.com/Library/Article/billy-joel-we-all-make-mistakes (accessed 28 Oct. 2021).

Harris, J., 'Shangri-Las Make it Big,' *Music Business*, 31 Dec. 1964–9 Jan.1965, 10-11.

Hoskyns, B., 'Transistor Sisters: Alan Betrock's Girl Groups—The Story of a Sound' (book review), *New Musical Express*, 1982, https://www.rocksbackpages.com/Library/Article/transistor-sisters-alan-betrocks-igirl-groups---the-story-of-a-soundi/ (accessed 6 Feb. 2023).

Johnson, D., 'Fury's Latest was Worth Waiting For,' *New Musical Express*, 25 Dec. 1964, 4.

Kaye, L., 'Standing in the Shadow of Rock: Shadow Morton, Part 1,' *Melody Maker*, 2 Mar. 1974, http://www.rocksbackpages.com/article.html?ArticleID=2458 (accessed 22 Oct. 2021).

Kaye, L., 'You Can't Make Heroes Out of Guys in Black Leather Jackets, They Told George 'Shadow' Morton. He Did . . . : Shadow Morton, Part 2,' *Melody Maker*, 9 Mar. 1974, http://www.rocksbackpages.com/Library/Article/you-cant-make-heroes-out-of-guys-in-black-leather-jackets-they-told-george-shadow-morton-he-did (accessed 29 Jan. 2022).

'Kings County, N.Y., Grand Jury Indicts Six Charged in Disk Counterfeit Racket,' *Billboard*, 20 Mar. 1961, 2.

'Sadler Sounds Off,' *KRLA Beat*, 9 July 1966 (cover).

'Las to Merc,' *Cash Box*, 17 Dec. 1966, 51.

Lewis, M., 'Tweet The Beatles! How Walter Cronkite Sent The Beatles Viral . . . in 1963!,' *HuffPost*, 18 July 2009, https://www.huffpost.com/entry/tweet-the-beatles-how-wal_b_239202 (accessed 25 Jan. 2022).

Loder, K., 'Where Are They Now? The Shangri-Las,' *Rolling Stone*, 12 Sept. 1985, 50, 52.

'The Mad-Mod Look: Shangri-Las,' *Teen Datebook*, Oct. 1966, 28–29.

Marcus, G., 'How the Other Half Lives: The Best of Girl Group Rock,' *Let It Rock*, May 1974, http://www.rocksbackpages.com/article.html?ArticleID=668 (accessed 29 Jan. 2023).

Martin, M., 'The Leader of the Pack Is Back,' *New York*, 25 Feb. 2007, http://nymag.com/arts/popmusic/profiles/28500/ (accessed 23 July 2010).

McDougall, G., 'California: Gangs, Vietniks and Surfers,' *KRLA Beat*, 13 Aug. 1966, 10.

Michaels, J., 'Barry Sadler: You Don't Have to Shake Dandruff,' *KRLA Beat*, 9 July 1966, 1.

Millar, B., 'Frankie Lymon: Why Do Fools Fall in Love?' *Pye Records*, 1972, https://www.rocksbackpages.com/Library/Article/frankie-lymon-why-do-fools-fall-in-love/ (accessed 17 Sept. 2021).

'N.J. Jury Issues Indictments in Cutout Probes,' *Billboard*, 4 Oct. 1986, 1, 91.

'Official Entry Blank for Revlon's Big Natural Wonder SWINGSTAKES,' *KRLA Beat*, 12 May 1965, 3–4.

Oxley, B., 'How Do We Get There?' (Letters to the Editor), *Teen*, Oct. 1964, 14.

Peters, A., 'Comeback of a Child Star,' *Ebony*, Jan. 1967, 42–50.

Petrusich, A., 'Dick Dale, the Inventor of Surf Rock, Was a Lebanese-American Kid from Boston,' *New Yorker* 18 Mar. 2019, https://www.newyorker.com/culture/postscript/dick-dale-the-inventor-of-surf-rock-was-a-lebanese-american-kid-from-boston (accessed 1 Sept. 2021).

Quantick, D., 'Leaders of the Teen Beat: Remember (Walkin' in the Sand) with the Shangri-Las,' *New Musical Express*, 17 Sept. 1983, http://www.rocksbackpages.com/article.html?ArticleID=890 (accessed 1 Mar. 2023).

Rich K., 'Beaches S/T,' *Terminal Boredom: Record Reviews Spring 2010*, https://web.archive.org/web/20100606143052/http://www.terminal-boredom.com/reviews26.html (accessed 1 Mar. 2023).

Ripp, A.,'Kama Sutra: Past, Present and Future,' *Cash Box*, 16 Nov. 1968, B9.

'A Rock and Roll Double Header,' *Hit Parader*, Mar. 1965, 34–37, 52.

'The Ronettes: Rock 'n' roll girls trio teams up with the Beatles on a whirlwind, 14-city, U.S. entertainment tour,' *Ebony* 22:1 (Nov. 1966), 184–192.

Sculatti, G., 'Surfin' USA,' in *Let It Rock*, Aug. 1973, http://www.rocksbackpages.com/Library/Article/surfin-usa (accessed 1 Sept. 2021).

Shanfeld, E., 'Billy Joel Biopic "Piano Man" Greenlit by Michael Jai White's Jaigantic
    Studios,' *Variety*, 9 Mar. 2022, https://variety.com/2022/film/news/billy-joel-
    biopic-piano-man-jaigantic-1235199055/ (accessed 9 Jun. 2024).
'Shangri-Las Visit London Next Week,' *New Musical Express*, 16 Oct. 1964, 8–9.
Shaw, G., 'Charlie Feathers: The Minit-Stop,' *Phonograph Record*, July 1973, http://www.
    rocksbackpages.com/article.html?ArticleID=8075 (accessed 29 Jan. 2023).
Shaw, G., 'Leaders of The Pack: Teen Dreams and Tragedy in Girl Group Rock,'
    History of Rock, 1982, http://www.rocksbackpages.com/article.html?ArticleID=
    1983 (accessed 28 Dec. 2022).
Sinclair, T., 'School's Out!,' *Spin*, Sept. 2005, 90–96.
Sternfield, A., 'Rock + Folk + Protest = An Erupting new Sound,' *Billboard*, 21 Aug.
    1965, 1, 14.
Sternfield, A., 'The Vietnam Conflict Spawning Heavy Barrage of Disk Tunes,' *Billboard*,
    4 June 1966, 1, 10.
'The Supremes: Sweet-Sounding Detroiters Push To Top as New Rulers of "Rock",'
    Ebony 20:8 (June 1965), 80–88.
'Surf's Up!,' *Time* (82:6), Aug. 9, 1963, 49.
Syrette, M., 'I Was a Teenage Shangri-La-holic,' *Bust* Spring/Summer (1996), 66–7.
'Three Shangri-Las: Grooving in Utopia,' *KRLA Beat*, 13 Aug. 1966, 7.
'Tiny Hill Inked as Wax Star-Flacker of Disks and Dukes,' *Billboard*, 3 Nov. 1945, 14.
Trent, V., 'Should Death Discs Be Banned?,' *Pop Weekly*, 6 Feb. 1965, 15.
'Trimachi and Cordell sign "an exclusive writing pact with the Robbins-Feist-Miller
    combine,"' *Billboard*, 20 Aug. 1966, 3.
Trodglen, D., 'Who Says You Can Never Go Home Anymore? The Shangri-Las Once
    Did. But Mary Weiss Is Proving That Wrong with a Swell Return to Rock'
    in *Stomp and Stammer*, Nov. 2008, https://web.archive.org/web/
    20101201060214/http://stompandstammer.com/index.php (accessed 2 Nov.
    2021).
Wawzenek, B., 'Why Billy Joel Hated His First Album, *Cold Spring Harbour*,' *UCR*:
    Classic Rock & Culture, 1 Nov. 2016, https://ultimateclassicrock.com/billy-joel-cold-
    spring-harbor/ (accessed 6 June, 2024).
'West Coast Clamours for Dylan Tunes,' *Billboard*, 4 Sept. 1965, 12.

Books

Albertine, V., *Clothes Clothes Clothes, Music Music Music, Boys Boys Boys*, London: Faber
    & Faber, 2014.
Albertine, V., *To Throw Away Unopened*, London: Faber & Faber, 2018.
Baker, N.K., and Christensen, T., eds., *Aesthetics and the Art of Musical Composition in the
    German Enlightenment: Selected Writings of Johann Georg Sulzer and Heinrich Christoph
    Koch*, Cambridge: Cambridge University Press, 1995.
Beethoven, L.V., *Briefwechsel: Gesamtausgabe*, ed. Sieghard Brandenburg, 7 vols.,
    Munich: Henle, 1996–98.
Beethoven, L.V., Kuerti, A. and Schenker, H., *Five Great Piano Sonatas*, Mineola, N.Y.:
    Dover, 1999.
Beethoven, L.V., *Piano sonata op. 27/2: Sonata quasi una Fantasia* (score), with 'Preface'
    by P. Hauschild and 'Notes on Interpretation' by B. Bloch, trans. L. Salter, Vienna:
    Wiener Urtext Edition, 1994.
Bletter, R.H. and Queens Museum, *Remembering the Future: The New York World's Fair
    from 1939–1964* (exhibition catalogue), New York: Rizzoli, 1989.
Brownstein, C., *Hunger Makes Me a Modern Girl*, London: Virago, 2015.
Cosey Fanni Tutti, *Art Sex Music*, London: Faber & Faber, 2017.
Currie, C., with T. O'Neill, *Neon Angel: A Memoir of a Runaway*, New York: Harper
    Collins, 2010.

Duke, P., and Turan, K., *Call Me Anna: The Autobiography of Patty Duke*, New York: Bantam, 1987.

Flam, L. and Liebowitz, E.S., *But Will You Love Me Tomorrow: An Oral History of the '60s Girl Groups*, New York: Hachette, 2023.

Franzese, M., *Blood Covenant*, New Kensington PA: Whitaker House, 2003.

Goldstein, R., *Goldstein's Greatest Hits: A Book Mostly about Rock and Roll*, Englewood Cliffs: Prentice-Hall, 1970.

Gordon, K., *Girl in a Band*, London: Faber & Faber, 2015.

Grace, L.G., *Tranny: Confessions of Punk Rock's Most Infamous Anarchist Sellout*, New York: Hachette, 2017.

Homer, *The Iliad*, ed. & trans. Robert Fagles, New York: Penguin, 1990.

James, T., with Fitzpatrick, M., *Me, the Mob and the Music: One Helluva Ride with Tommy James and the Shondells*, New York: Scribner, 2010.

Kaufman, M., *Murray the K Tells it Like it Is, Baby*, New York, Chicago and San Francisco: Holt, Rinehart and Winston, 1966.

Leiber, J., Stoller, M., and Ritz, D., *Hound Dog: the Leiber & Stoller Autobiography*, New York: Simon & Schuster, 2009.

McAleer, D., Gregory, A., & White, M., *The Virgin Book of British Hit Singles* Vol. 2, London: Virgin, 2010.

O'Connor, S., *Rememberings*, Dublin: Penguin, 2021.

Petroski, H., *Paperboy: Confessions of a Future Engineer*, New York: Vintage, 2002.

Quatro, S., *Unzipped*, London: Hodder & Stoughton, 2007.

Robinson, E.A., *Tristram*, New York: Macmillan, 1927.

Schulze, J.A.P., 'Sonate,' in J.G. Sulzer, *Allgemeine Theorie der schönen Künste 2*, Leipzig: M.G. Weidmanns Erben und Reich, 1774, 688–89.

Seume, J.G., 'Die Beterin' in *Sämmtliche Werke*, Vol. 7, Leipzig: Johann Friedric Hartknoch, 1839, 335–6, unpublished translation by Dr Leith Passmore.

Shakespeare, W., *The Tragedy of King Lear*, ed. R.A. Foakes, London: Arden Shakespeare, 1997.

Smith, P., *Just Kids*, London: Bloomsbury, 2010.

Silber, I., comp. & ed., *Songs of the Civil War*, New York: Columbia University, 1960.

Sophocles, *Philoctetes*, trans. R. Torrance, in O. Mandel, *Philoctetes and the Fall of Troy: Plays, Documents, Iconography, Interpretations: including versions by Sophocles, Andre Gide, Oscar Mandel, and Heiner Müller*, Lincoln: University of Nebraska Press, 1981.

Spector, R., and Waldron, V., *Be My Baby: How I Survived Mascara, Miniskirts and Madness, or My Life as a Fabulous Ronette*, New York: Harmony, 1990.

Stein, S. with Murphy, G., *Siren Song: My Life in Music*, New York: St Martins, 2018.

Stokes, R., *The Book of Lieder: The Original Texts of Over 1000 Songs*, London: Faber, 2005.

Thompson, H.S., *Hells Angels*, Harmondsworth: Penguin, [1966] 1987.

Valentine, K., *All I Ever Wanted: A Rock 'n' Roll Memoir*, Austin TX: University of Texas Press, 2020.

Wagner, R., *Tristan and Isolde*, (libretto) trans. Stewart Robb, New York: Schirmer, 1965.

Wexler, J., and Ritz, D., *Rhythm and the Blues: A Life in American Music*, New York: Knopf, 1993.

Wilson, M., *Dreamgirl: My Life as a Supreme*, London: Arrow, 1986.

Interviews

Arfin, R., 'The "Shadow" Reappears—A Rare Talk with Producer George "Shadow" Morton,' *Goldmine*, Vol. 17, No. 14: Issue 286, 12 July 1991, reproduced at https://web.archive.org/web/20041109155000/https://www.limusichalloffame.org/lirock/shadow01.html (accessed 31 Aug. 2021).

Clarke, J., Mary Weiss interviewed by Jonathan Clarke on *Out of the Box*, Q1043FM, New York City, https://www.youtube.com/watch?v=8Chln5Ft1Ik (accessed 1 Nov. 2021).

Dave the Rave, interview with the Goodies on 'Relics and Rarities,' WQMA Oldies Radio 1520AM, date unavailable. Copy supplied by P. Milstein.

Greig, C., '*Spectropop* Presents Ellie Greenwich, interviewed by Charlotte Greig,' https://web.archive.org/web/20090831074628/http://www.spectropop.com/EllieGreenwich2/index.htm (accessed 30 Sept. 2021).

Gross, T., 'Mary Weiss comes back for a *Dangerous Game*,' interview for *Fresh Air* on NPR (National Public Radio), 6 Mar. 2007, http://www.npr.org/templates/story/story.php?storyId=7728783 (accessed 31 Aug. 2021).

'In What Ways Did Your Father Influence Your Life? : Mary Weiss,' *Growing Bolder*, 13 June 2008, https://web.archive.org/web/20080707200354/https://growingbolder.com/thoughtleaders/in-what-ways-did-your-father-156322.html (accessed 14 Sept. 2021).

Linna, M., *Mary Weiss of the Shangri-Las: Good-Bad, But Not Evil*, 2006, https://web.archive.org/web/20080820064234/http://www.nortonrecords.com/maryweiss/index.html (accessed 1 Apr. 2021). This lengthy interview with Mary Weiss was originally published on the Norton Records website in 2006. It has since been removed but can be accessed in full via this Web Archive link.

MacKinney, L., interview with George 'Shadow' Morton, 24 Apr. 2007.

MacKinney, L., interview with Brooks Arthur, 18 Mar. 2008.

MacKinney, L., interview with Rod McBrien, 10 Apr. 2008.

MacKinney, L., telephone conversation with Irene Brodsky, 27 Aug. 2009.

MacKinney, L., telephone conversation with David Dalton, 14 Dec. 2021.

Milstein, P., interview with Andy Paley, 20 Sept. 2001. Copy supplied by Milstein.

Milstein, P., interview with Rita Ganser, 14 Oct. 2001. Copy supplied by Milstein.

Milstein, P., interview with Robert Ganser, 14 Oct. 2001. Copy supplied by Milstein.

Newman, R. M., 'Only the Shadow Knows: An Interview by Ralph M. Newman,' *Time Barrier Express* 26 (Sept/Oct 1979), 40–46.

Quatro, S., 'Suzi Quatro's Heroes of Rock 'n' Roll: Interview with Mary Weiss,' BBC Radio 2, broadcast 24 Oct. 2007, https://www.bbc.co.uk/sounds/play/p00q6mb4 (accessed 4 Apr. 2021).

Schneider, M., *Night Talk* interview with Mary Weiss, 20 Apr. 2008, Part One, http://noolmusic.com/utube/night_talk_interview_with_mary_weiss_part_1_lead_singer.php (accessed 20 July 2010).

Schneider, M., *Night Talk* interview with Mary Weiss, 20 Apr. 2008, Part Two, http://noolmusic.com/utube/night_talk_interview_with_mary_weiss_part_2_lead_singer.php (accessed 20 July 2010).

Schneider, M., *Night Talk* interview with Mary Weiss, 20 Apr. 2008, Part Three, http://noolmusic.com/utube/night_talk_interview_with_mary_weiss_part_3_lead_singer.php (accessed 20 July 2010).

Recordings

The Shangri-Las

Note: The recordings by the Shangri-Las, listed chronologically below, are those released in the US while the group was active. With the exception of their first two pre-Red Bird releases and the live version of "Leader of the Pack" (audio links supplied below), most of these are available on *The Best of the Shangri-Las* (MERCURY/POLYGRAM) https://www.allmusic.com/album/the-best-of-the-shangri-las-mercury-mw0000184236/releases (accessed 1 Apr. 2021). Myrmidons of Melodrama (RPM RECORDS #136) is another noteworthy compilation from 1996 that includes more B-sides of singles, several album-only tracks and the group's Revlon endorsements for the Natural Wonder campaign.

For a complete Shangri-Las discography (not including reissues), see: https://web.
archive.org/web/20080723112419/http://www.nortonrecords.com/maryweiss/dis-
cog.html (accessed 1 Apr. 2021).

ALBUMS

The Shangri-Las, *The Shangri-Las* (also referred to as *Leader of the Pack*) RED BIRD
20-101, Feb. 1965. Liner notes by Faith Whitehill.

The Shangri-Las, *Shangri-Las 65!*, RED BIRD 20-104, Nov. 1965.

The Shangri-Las, *Golden Hits of the Shangri-Las*, MERCURY 61099, Dec. 1966.

The Shangri-Las, *The Best of the Red Bird and Mercury Recordings*, Real Gone Music,
RGM-1293, 2021. This is a beautifully presented double LP vinyl reissue, remastered
and with comprehensive liner notes by John Grecco.

SINGLES

The Shangri-Las, "Simon Says" (Michaels) b/w "Simon Speaks" (Mizrahi/Steinberg),
SMASH 1866, Dec. 1963. Audio of both sides: https://www.youtube.com/
watch?v=0wonxxGJK3s (accessed 1 Oct. 2023).

The Shangri-Las, "Wishing Well" (Monaco/Michaels) b/w "Hate to Say I Told You So"
(Jackson/Steinberg/Steinberg), SPOKANE 4006, Apr. 1964. Reissued on Scepter
Records in Jan. 1965 (SCEPTER 1291). Audio of "Wishing Well": https://www.
youtube.com/watch?v=ij5SaKYwC5M (accessed 1 Oct. 2023); audio of "Hate to Say
I Told You So": https://www.youtube.com/watch?v=GEgJK36YqeI (accessed 1 Oct.
2023).

The Shangri-Las, 'Remember (Walkin' in the Sand) (Morton) b/w 'It's Easier to Cry'
(Steinberg/Jackson/De Angelis) RED BIRD 08, Aug. 1964.

The Shangri-Las, "Leader of the Pack" (Barry/Greenwich/Morton) b/w "What Is
Love?" (Michaels/Morton) RED BIRD 014, Oct. 1964.

The Shangri-Las, "Leader of the Pack," recorded live (audio only) at the Brooklyn
Fox Theatre, (listed as) 1964 http://www.youtube.com/watch?v=8N_iTNdIcfs
(accessed 28 Dec. 2023).

The Shangri-Las, "Give Him a Great Big Kiss" (Morton) b/w "Twist and Shout"
(Russell/Medley), RED BIRD 018, Dec. 1964.

The Shangri-Las, "Maybe" (Goldner) b/w "Shout" (Isley/Isley/Isley) RED BIRD 019,
Dec. 1964.

The Shangri-Las, "Out in the Streets" (Barry/Greenwich) b/w "The Boy" (Morton)
RED BIRD 025, Apr. 1965.

The Shangri-Las, "Give Us Your Blessings" (Barry/Greenwich) b/w "Heaven Only
Knows" (Barry/Greenwich) RED BIRD 030, May 1965.

The Shangri-Las, "Right Now and Not Later" (Moseley/Bateman/Hollon) b/w "The
Train from Kansas City" (Barry/Greenwich) RED BIRD 036, Oct. 1965.

The Shangri-Las, "I Can Never Go Home Anymore" (George Morton) b/w "Bull Dog"
(Leiber/Stoller), RED BIRD 043, Nov. 1965.

The Shangri-Las, "Long Live Our Love" (Jackson/Barnes) b/w "Sophisticated Boom
Boom" (Morton) RED BIRD 048, Feb. 1966.

The Shangri-Las, "He Cried" (Daryll/Richards) b/w "Dressed in Black" (Michaels/
Gormann/Morton) RED BIRD 053, Apr. 1966.

The Shangri-Las, "Past, Present and Future" (Morton/Leiber/Butler) b/w "Paradise"
(Nilsson/Garfield/Botkin Jr/Spector), RED BIRD 068, June 1966.

The Shangri-Las, "Past, Present and Future" (Morton/Leiber/Butler) b/w "Love You
More than Yesterday"(Morton/Michaels/Gorman), RED BIRD 068, June 1966.

The Shangri-Las, "Sweet Sounds of Summer" (Martire) b/w "I'll Never Learn" (Sandy
[Hurvirtz]), MERCURY 72645, Dec. 1966.

The Shangri-Las, "Take the Time" (Trimarchi/Cordell) b/w "Footsteps on the Roof"
(Trimachi/Cordell), MERCURY 72670, Mar. 1967.

George 'Shadow' Morton (listed chronologically)

The Markeys featuring George Morton, "Hot Rod" (Morton/Monaco) b/w "Yakkaty Yak" (Jack Hammer), RCA 47-7256, 1958.

The Markeys featuring George Morton, "A Time To Love" (Morton/Monaco) b/w "Make a Record, Man" (Morton/Monaco/Monaco), RCA 47-7412, 1958.

The Lonely Ones, "My Wish" (Gianna/Monaco/Morton) b/w "I Want My Girl" (Morton/Monaco), SIR 270, 1959.

Morton, Georgie, "Some of These Days" (Shelton Brooks) b/w "My Mammy" (Donaldson-Lewis-Young) SWIRL 103, 1961.

George, Morton, "The Stretch" (Kelley [Morton]/Hilliard) b/w "Come on In" (Kelley [Morton]/Hilliard), AMY 858, 1962.

The Beattle-ettes, "Only Seventeen" (Billy Kelly/Joseph J. Monaco) b/w "Now We're Together" (Billy Kelly/Joseph J. Monaco) JUBILEE 5472 (1964). Audio of "Only Seventeen" with non-original visuals: http://www.youtube.com/watch?v=eJcz8tpxd70 (accessed 6 Oct. 2021).

Sophisticated Boom Boom: The Shadow Morton Story, Ace Records, CDTOP1369, 2013.

Other Recordings

Note: Many of these are long out-of-print and extremely rare. I have supplied links to online audio of the more obscure singles listed, where available.

The Beatlette's, "Dance Beatle Dance" b/w "We Were Meant to be Married" (JAMIE 1270), 1964. *Popsike* listing with photos and audio: https://www.popsike.com/Girl-Group-Rocker-45-Beatlettes-Dance-Beatle-Dance-Jamie-mp3-obscure/314367406943.html (accessed 27 Dec. 2023).

The Beatlettes, "Yes!!! You Can Hold My Hand Part One" b/w "Yes!!! You Can Hold My Hand Part Two," ASSAULT 1893, 1964. *45 Cat* listing with photo and audio: http://www.45cat.com/record/18931894 (accessed 27 Dec. 2023).

The Beetlettes, *Outside Carnegie Hall*, ASSAULT ASLP1001, 1964. *Popsike* listing with photos: https://www.popsike.com/Beatles-RelatedBeetlettes-Meet-The-Beetlettes-Assault-TX1895-RARE/153701617492.html

Belvin, Jesse, "Goodnight My Love" b/w "I Want You With Me Xmas," MODERN 1005, 1956. Belvin's first name is misspelled "Jessie" on the label.

Carmen, Eric, "All By Myself" (Carmen/Rachmaninov) 1975, audio https://www.youtube.com/watch?v=iN9CjAfo5n0 (accessed 1 Sept. 2021).

Carter, Jamie, "The Boy with the Way" (Hurvitz) b/w "Memory of Your Voice" (Hurvitz), LIBERTY 55815, 1965. Audio of "The Boy With the Way," http://www.youtube.com/watch?v=sB8vPrQijcc (accessed 1 Jan. 2024).

The Chantels, "He's Gone" (Smith/Goldner) b/w "The Plea" (Smith/Goldner), END E-1001, 1957. Link to images and audio: http://www.45cat.com/record/nc004289us (accessed 4 Apr. 2021).

The Cheers, "Black Denim Trousers and Motorcycle Boots," (Leiber/Stoller) b/w "Some Night in Alaska" (Levin), CAPITOL 3219, 1955. Audio of "Black Denim Trousers": https://www.youtube.com/watch?v=FtiEtPQUmAM (accessed 31 Dec. 2023).

The Detergents, "Leader of the Laundromat" (Pockriss/Vance) b/w "Ulcers," ROULETTE 4590, 1964. Audio of "Leader of the Laundromat": https://www.youtube.com/watch?v=Qi5yDBvYUcE (accessed 31 Dec. 2023).

The Dovells, "Bristol Stomp" b/w "Out in the Cold Again," CAMEO-PARKWAY 827, 1961. Audio and live performance of Bristol Stomp: https://www.youtube.com/watch?v=z9i6FzIFAvM (accessed 28 Dec. 2023).

The Dovells, "You Can't Sit Down" b/w "Stompin' Everywhere," PARKWAY 867, 1963. Audio of "You Can't Sit Down": https://www.youtube.com/watch?v=Wf0zgeW8oEE (accessed 2 Nov. 2021).

Gainsbourg, Serge, "Initials B.B." (Gainsbourg), 1968. Audio and television performance: http://www.youtube.com/watch?v=NuZklVrHspM (accessed 1 Jan. 2024).

The Goodies, "Dum Dum Ditty," (Boyce/Venet/Hart/Martire) b/w "Sophisticated Boom Boom" (Morton) BLUE CAT 117, June 1965.

King, Rev. M.L., *Great March to Freedom*, GORDY 906, 1963.

The Mamas and the Papas, "California Dreamin'" b/w "Somebody Groovy" DUNHILL 4020, 1965.

Music to Sell Teens By, Natural Wonder 'Swingstakes' promotional album: https://www.rootsvinylguide.com/ebay_items/dave-clark-five-shangri-las-music-to-sell-teens-by-rare-lp-10-poster-photos (accessed 2 Nov. 2021).

Nervous Norvus, "Transfusion" (Drake) b/w "Dig" (Drake), DOT 15470, 1956. Audio of "Transfusion": https://www.youtube.com/watch?v=HbhvZ2y1V80 (accessed 31 Aug. 2021).

Pleasure Seekers, "Never Thought You'd Leave Me" b/w "What a Way to Die," HIDEOUT 1006, 1965. Audio with extraordinary archival footage: https://www.youtube.com/watch?v=3thCM-t5hl8 (accessed 29 Dec. 2023).

SSgt. Barry Sadler, "Ballad of the Green Berets" (Sadler) b/w "Letter from Vietnam," (Sadler), RCA 47-8739, 1966.

The Shirelles, "Soldier Boy"(Luther Dixon/Florence Greenberg), b/w "Love Is a Swingin' Thing," SCEPTER 1228, 1962. Audio of "Soldier Boy": https://www.youtube.com/watch?v=3NNfF9LtAks (accessed 1 Jan. 2024).

The Teenagers featuring Frankie Lymon, "Why Do Fools Fall in Love" (Lymon/Goldner) b/w "My Girl" (Harrington-Saffer), GEE 1002, 1956.

The Toys, "A Lover's Concerto" (Linzer/Randell) b/w "This Night" (Linzer/Randell), DYNOVOICE 209, 1965. This live performance features several shots of a bust of Bach, presumably to acknowledge the actual composer: http://www.youtube.com/watch?v=im_OO6lN9iO (accessed 1 Sept. 2021).

The Tymes, "So Much in Love" (Jackson/Straigis) b/w "Roscoe James McClain," PARKWAY 871, 1963. Audio of "So Much in Love": https://www.youtube.com/watch?v=TRUQ1tg-VjM (accessed 2 Nov. 2021).

Live Footage and Video Material

The Shangri-Las

The Shangri-Las and Robert Goulet on *I've Got a Secret*, including "Leader of the Pack," 16 Nov. 1964, http://www.youtube.com/watch?v=U9WA5I2t26w (accessed 2 Apr. 2021).

The Shangri-Las, "Remember (Walkin' in the Sand), *Where the Action Is*, Episode 1.4, aired 1 July 1965: https://www.youtube.com/watch?v=AreUS8iUgm4 (accessed 28 Dec. 2023).

The Shangri-Las (as quartet), "Give Him a Great Big Kiss," *Shindig!*, 1965, http://www.youtube.com/watch?v=01YePzk29Mc (accessed 14 Sept. 2010).

The Shangri-Las (as trio, with Ian Whitcomb), "Give Him a Great Big Kiss," *Shindig!*, 1965 http://www.youtube.com/watch?v=cuNlEGbAKf0 (accessed 14 June 2007).

The Shangri-Las, "Give Him a Great Big Kiss," *Shivaree*, 1965, http://www.youtube.com/watch?v=gOdP_VvPKHU (accessed 22 Jan. 2023).

The Shangri-Las (as quartet), "Right Now and Not Later," *Shivaree*, 1965, http://www.youtube.com/watch?v=cM9orBt3ZWY&feature=related (accessed 3 Jan. 2024).

The Shangri-Las, "Out in the Streets," *Shindig!*, 1965, http://www.youtube.com/watch?v=ZK1-u0yHNSU (accessed 15 Sept. 2010).

The Shangri-Las, "Long Live Our Love," *Hullabaloo*, 1966, https://www.youtube.com/watch?v=tTgg94KUyB8 (accessed 1 Jan. 2024).

'The Shangri-Las on Entertainment tonight, 1989,' http://www.youtube.com/watch?v=JQB8mYd-ozo (accessed 30 Dec. 2023).

Other Video Footage

Aerosmith, "Remember (Walkin' in the Sand)," Live in Largo MD, 1980, http://www.youtube.com/watch?v=R-CKVgCndZk (accessed 22 Jan. 2023).

The Byrds, "Eight Miles High," 1966, https://www.youtube.com/watch?v=5HgHnp7tDes (accessed 1 Sept. 2021).

Cash, Johnny, "Personal Jesus," http://www.youtube.com/watch?v=jQcNiD0Z3MU (accessed 27 Oct. 2021).

Chambers Brothers, "Time Has Come Today," https://www.youtube.com/watch?v=AQSjV4DZ-Gg (accessed 2 Sept. 2021).

Everly Brothers, "All I Have to Do Is Dream" and "Cathy's Clown," Alma Cogan Show, 1961, https://www.youtube.com/watch?v=sL_zett_M7k (accessed 16 Sept. 2021).

Howard, R. S., "She Cried," live performance on *Studio 22*, ABC-TV Australia, Dec. 1999, http://www.youtube.com/watch?v=5nr5DyVLiW0 (accessed 22 Jan. 2023).

Ian, Janis, "Society's Child (Baby I've Been Thinking)," VERVE FORECAST KF5027, 1966; http://www.youtube.com/watch?v=yW_rYLoIR08 (accessed 2 Jan. 2023).

Lymon, F. and the Teenagers, "Why Do Fools Fall in Love," Frankie Laine Show, 1956, https://www.youtube.com/watch?v=xd23p_vUMYw (accessed 29 Jan. 2023).

McGuire, Barry, "Eve of Destruction," *Hullabaloo* 1965, http://www.youtube.com/watch?v=IwYNWYaS3bI (accessed 3 Sept. 2021).

Midler, B., "Leader of the Pack" (live concert version from *Divine Madness*, 1980) http://www.youtube.com/watch?v=xJEH9K04U5g (accessed 22 Jan. 2023).

New York Dolls, "Looking for a Kiss," Live at Max's Kansas City, New York City, 1973, https://www.youtube.com/watch?v=4tnMfiWx1YM (accessed 22 Jan. 2023).

Sadler, B., "Ballad of the Green Berets," https://www.youtube.com/watch?v=m5WJJVSE_BE (accessed 1 Jan. 2024).

Songmakers Collection (excerpt, Greg Shaw, Morton & Shangri-Las), http://www.youtube.com/watch?v=ANJGTyZ6v_A (accessed 4 Apr. 2021).

The Vanilla Fudge, "You Keep Me Hanging On," https://www.youtube.com/watch?v=NCwzCQcjC0M (accessed 2 Jan. 2024).

Vivre Sa Vie (My Life to Live), dir. Jean-Luc Godard, 1962; excerpt https://www.youtube.com/watch?v=DakhzmKPOdo (accessed 12 Sept. 2021).

Films

The 1964 World's Fair [videorecording], Chatsworth CA: Image Entertainment, 2000.

20 Feet From Stardom, dir. Morgan Neville, 2013.

Amy, dir. Asif Kapadia, 2015.

Fanny: The Right to Rock, dir. Bobbi Jo Hart, 2021.

Framing Britney Spears, dir. Samantha Stark, 2021.

The Go-Go's, dir. Alison Ellwood , 2020.

Her Aim is True, dir. Karen Whitehead, 2013.

Immortal Beloved, dir. Bernard Rose, 1994; see Internet Movie Database entry, http://www.imdb.com/title/tt0110116/ (accessed 28 Mar. 2009).

Janis: Little Girl Blue, dir. Amy Berg, 2015.

Made in U.S.A., dir. Jean-Luc Godard, 1966.

Mary J Blige's My Life, dir. Vanessa Roth, 2021.

Masculin féminin, dir. Jean-Luc Godard, 1966.

One + One (a.k.a. Sympathy for the Devil), dir. Jean-Luc Godard, 1968.

The Punk Singer: A Film About Kathleen Hanna, dir. Sini Anderson, 2013.

Reclaiming Amy, dir. Marina Parker, 2021.

Scorpio Rising, dir. Kenneth Anger, 1963.

Standing in the Shadows of Motown, dir. Paul Justman, http://www.
standingintheshadowsofmotown.com/ (accessed 30 Jan. 2023.
Suzi Q, dir. Liam Firmager, 2019.
Totally Go-Go's, Live at Palos Verdes High School, LA, Dec. 4, 1981, dir. M. Heggerty
and C.D. Taylor, 1981, https://www.youtube.com/watch?v=gdNvo4PIzIo (accessed
22 Jan. 2023.
Vivre Sa Vie (My Life to Live), dir. Jean-Luc Godard, 1962.
The Wild One, dir. Laslo Benedek, 1954.
What Happened, Miss Simone?, dir. Liz Garbus, 2015.

SECONDARY MATERIAL
Books and Journal Articles

Adorno, T.W., 'On the Fetish-Character in Music and the Regression of Listening,'
reproduced in S. Duncombe, *Cultural Resistance Reader*, London: Verso, 2002,
275–303.

Aichhorn, A., *Wayward Youth: A Psychoanalytic Study of Delinquent Children, Illustrated by
Actual Case Histories*, New York: Meridian, 1955.

Alt, J., 'Popular Culture and Mass Consumption: The Motorcycle as Cultural
Commodity,' *Journal of Popular Culture* 15:4 (1982), 129–141.

Anderson, T.H., 'American Popular Music and the War in Vietnam,' *Peace and Change* 11
(July 1986), 51–65.

Andresen, L., *Battle Notes: Music of the Vietnam War*, Superior, WI: Savage Press, 2000.

Appy, C.G., *Working Class War: American Combat Soldiers and Vietnam*, Chapel Hill:
University of North Carolina Press, 1993.

Aryel, R.M. and Wagner, M.M., 'Coroners and Medical Examiners' in M. M. Wagner,
A.W. Moore, R.M. Aryel, *Handbook of Biosurveillance*, Burlington, MA, Elsevier
Science & Technology, 2006, 179–181.

Baldwin, D.L., *Chicago's New Negroes: Modernity, the Great Migration, and Black Urban
Life*, Chapel Hill: University of North Carolina Press, 2007.

Ballinger, L., 'Déjà Vu,' in *The First Rock & Roll Confidential Report*, ed. D. Marsh, New
York: Pantheon, 1985, 210.

Bangs, L., *Blondie*, London: Omnibus, 1980.

Barson, M. and Heller, S., *Teenage Confidential: An Illustrated History of the American
Teen*, San Francisco: 1998.

Bashe, P.R, George-Warren, H., and Pareles, J., *The Rolling Stone Encyclopaedia of Rock &
Roll, Revised Edtion*, New York: Fireside/Simon & Schuster, 2001.

Bederman, G., *Manliness and Civilization: A Cultural History of Gender and Race in the
United States, 1880–1917*, Chicago: University of Chicago Press, 1995.

Benjaminson, P., *The Lost Supreme: The Life of Dreamgirl Florence Ballard*, Chicago:
Lawrence Hill, 2008.

Bennett, J.W., 'The Storm Within: the Madness of Lear,' *Shakespeare Quarterly*, 13:2
(1962), 137–55.

Betrock, A., *Girl Groups: The Story of a Sound*, London: Omnibus, 1982.

Bickerdike, J.O., *Being Britney: Pieces of a Modern Icon*, London: Nine Eight, 2021.

Bickerdike, J.O., *You Are Beautiful and You Are Alone: The Biography of Nico*, London:
Faber & Faber, 2021.

Bindas, K. J., and Houston, C., '"Takin' Care of Business": Rock Music, Vietnam and the
Protest Myth,' *Historian* 52:1 (Nov. 1989), 1–25.

Blom, E., *Beethoven's Pianoforte Sonatas Discussed*, London: J.M. Dent, 1938.

Boardman J., ed., *The Oxford Dictionary of Classical Art*, Oxford: Oxford University Press,
1993.

Bordowitz, H., *Dirty Little Secrets of the Record Business: Why So Much Music You Hear Sucks*, Chicago: Chicago Review Press, 2006.

Bradby, B., 'Do-Talk and Don't-Talk: The Division of the Subject in Girl-Group Music,' in Simon Frith and Andrew Goodwin [eds.], *On Record: Rock, Pop and the Written Word*, London: Routledge, 1990, 341–368.

Broven, J., *Record Makers and Breakers: Voices of the Independent Rock 'n' Roll Pioneers*, Urbana: University of Illinois Press, 2009.

Brown, C.H., 'Self-Portrait: The Teen-Type Magazine,' *Annals of the American Academy of Political and Social Science* 338 (1961), 13–21.

Bush, M.E.L., *Everyday Forms of Whiteness: Understanding Race in a 'Post-Racial' World*, Lanham, MD: Rowman & Littlefield, 2011.

Carlin, R., *Godfather of the Music Business: Morris Levy*, Jackson: University Press of Mississippi, 2016.

Carney, G. O., 'Cowabunga! Surfer Rock and the Five Themes of Geography,' *Popular Music and Society* 23:4 (1999), 3–29.

Carson, M., Lewis, T., and Shaw, S.M., *Girls Rock! Fifty Years of Women Making Music*, Lexington: University Press of Kentucky, 2004.

Chapple, S., and Garofalo, R., *Rock 'n' Roll Is Here to Pay: The History and Politics of the Music Industry*, Chicago: Nelson-Hall, 1977.

Cipolla, F.J., 'Patrick Sarsfield Gilmore,' *New Grove Dictionary of Music and Musicians*, ed. Stanley Sadie & John Tyrrell, 2nd ed., London: Grove, 2001, 871.

Clarke, W.M., 'Achilles and Patroclus in Love,' *Hermes* 106:3 (1978), 381–396.

Clayson, A., *Death Discs: An Account of Fatality in the Popular Song*, London: Sanctuary, [1992] 1997.

Clemente, J., *Girl Groups: Fabulous Females that Rocked the World*, Iola, WI: Krause, 2000.

Clive, P., *Beethoven and His World: A Biographical Dictionary*, Oxford: Oxford University Press, 2001.

Cloud, C., *The Little Book of Acid*, Berkeley, CA: Ronin, 1999.

Cloward, R.A., and Ohlin, L.E., *Delinquency and Opportunity: A Theory of Delinquent Gangs*, Glencoe, IL: Free Press, 1960.

Coates, N., 'Teenyboppers, Groupies and Other Grotesques: Girls and Women and Rock Culture in the 1960s and early 1970s,' *Journal of Popular Music Studies* 15:1 (2003), 65–94.

Cohen, A.K., *Delinquent Boys: The Culture of the Gang*, London: Routledge & Keegan Paul, 1956.

Cohen, M, 'Good-Bad, Not Evil': *The Golden Hits of the Shangri-Las,' Rock and Roll Globe*, 18 Apr. 2019, https://rockandrollglobe.com/pop/the-golden-hits-of-the-shangri-las/ (accessed 24 Jan. 2022).

Cohen, S., *Folk Devils and Moral Panics: The Creation of the Mods and Rockers*, London: MacGibbon and Kee, 1972.

Coontz, S., *The Way We Never Were: American Families and the Nostalgia Trap*, New York: Basic Books, 1992.

Cooper, B. L., 'Popular Songs, Military Conflicts, and Public Perceptions of the United States at War,' *Social Education* 56:3 (1992), 160–166.

Cooper, B.L., and Haney, W.S., *Rock Music in American Popular Culture III: More Rock 'n' Roll Resources*, New York: Haworth Press, 1999.

Copquin, C.G., and Jackson, K.T., *The Neighbourhoods of Queens*, New Haven: Yale University Press, 2007.

Cotter, B., and Young, B., *The 1964–1965 New York World's Fair*, Charleston, SC: Arcadia, 2004.

Coupe, L., *Beat Sound, Beat Vision: The Beat Spirit and Popular Song*, Manchester: Manchester University Press, 2007.

Cozzen, R. D., *Girl Bands of the '60s: Collector's Quick Reference*, Claremont, NC: Cozzen, 2017.

Cumberlidge, M.C, 'The Abuse of Barbiturates by Heroin Addicts,' *Canadian Medical Association Journal* 98 (June 1968), 1045–1049.

Curtis, J.M., *Rock Eras: Interpretations of Music and Society, 1954–1984*, Bowling Green, OH: Bowling Green State University Popular Press, 1987.

Cyrus, C.J., 'Selling an Image: Girl Groups of the 1960s,' *Popular Music* 22:2 (May 2003), 173–93.

Dale, R.T., & Dale, F.R., 'The Use of Methadone in a Representative Group of Heroin Addicts,' *International Journal of the Addictions* 8:2 (1973), 293–308.

Dannen, F., *Hit Men: Power Brokers and Fast Money Inside the Record Business*, New York: Crown, 1990.

Dawson, J., and Propes, S., *45 RPM: The History, Heroes & Villains of a Pop Music Revolution*, San Francisco: Backbeat Books, 2003.

Dean, J.P., 'Only Caucasian: A Study of Race Covenants,' *Journal of Land and Public Utility Economics*, 23:4 (1947), 428–432.

Denisoff, R. S., 'Fighting Prophecy with Napalm: "The Ballad of the Green Berets,"' *Journal of American Culture* 13 (Spring 1990), 81–93.

Detre, L.A., 'Canada's Campaign for Immigrants and the Images in *Canada West* Magazine,' *Great Plains Quarterly*, Spring 2004, 113–29.

Devlin, R., 'Female Juvenile Delinquency and the Problem of Sexual Authority in America 1945–1965,' *Delinquents and Debutantes: Twentieth-Century American Girls' Cultures*, ed. S. Inness, New York: New York University Press, 1998, pp. 83–106.

Devlin, R., *Relative Intimacy: Fathers, Adolescent Daughters and Postwar American Culture*, Chapel Hill: University of North Carolina Press, 2005.

Douglas, S. J., *Where the Girls Are: Growing Up Female With the Mass Media*, London: Penguin, 1994.

Douglas, S. J., *Listening In: Radio and the American Imagination*, Minneapolis: University of Minnesota Press, 2004.

Drake, K., *The Beethoven Sonatas and the Creative Experience*, Bloomingto, IN: Indiana University Press, 1994.

Dunn, E.C., 'The Storm in King Lear,' *Shakespeare Quarterly*, 3:4 (1952), 329–33.

Dyer, R., *White*, London: Routledge, 1997.

Ehrenreich, B., Hess, E., Jacobs, G., 'Beatlemania: Girls Just Want to Have Fun,' in *The Adoring Audience: Fan Culture and Popular Media*, ed. Lisa A. Lewis, London: Routledge, 1992, 84–106.

Einarson, J., *Mr. Tambourine Man: The Life and Legacy of the Byrds' Gene Clark*, San Francisco: Backbeat, 2005.

Einstein, A., *Music in the Romantic Era*, London: J.M. Dent, 1947.

Emerson, K., *Always Magic In the Air: The Bomp and Brilliance of the Brill Building Era*, New York: Viking Penguin, 2005.

Evans, M., *NYC Rock*, London: Sanctuary, 2003.

Feder, E.K., *Family Bonds: Genealogies of Race and Gender*, Oxford: Oxford University Press, 2007.

Filene, B., *Romancing the Folk: Public Memory and American Roots Music*, Chapel Hill: University of North Carolina Press, 2000.

Fishman, J.J., Conwell, D.P., Amsel, Z., 'New York City Narcotics Register: A Brief History,' *International Journal of the Addictions* 6:3 (1971), 561–569.

Frankenberg, R., 'Introduction: Local Whitenesses, Localizing Whiteness,' in *Displacing Whiteness: Essays in Social and Cultural Criticism*, ed. R. Frankenberg, Durham, NC: Duke University Press, 1997, 1–33.

Frankenberg, R., *Displacing Whiteness: Essays in Social and Cultural Criticism*, Durham, NC: Duke University Press, 1997.

Friedman, J.A., *Tell the Truth Until They Bleed: Coming Clean in the Dirty World of Blues and Rock 'n' Roll*, New York: Backbeat Books, 2008.

Frith, S. and Goodwin, A., eds., *On Record: Rock, Pop, and the Written Word*, London: Routledge, 1990.

Frost, O., 'The Housing Market in Queens,' *The Crisis*, 67:6 (June–July 1960), 349–354.

Gaines, D., 'Girl Groups: A Ballad of Co-dependency,' *Trouble Girls: The Rolling Stone Book of Women in Rock*, ed. Barbara O'Dair, New York: Random House, 1997, 102–115.

Gaines, D., *A Misfit's Manifesto: the Spiritual Journey of a Rock & Roll Heart: a Memoir*, New York: Villard, 2003.

Gavin, J., *Stormy Weather: the Life of Lena Horne*, New York: Atria Books, 2009.

Giallombardo, R., ed., *Juvenile Delinquency: A Book of Readings*, New York: Wiley, 1982.

Gilbert, J., *A Cycle of Outrage: America's Reaction to the Juvenile Delinquent In the 1950s*, New York: Oxford University Press, 1986.

Goldberg, D.T., '"Polluting the Body Politic": Racist Discourse and Urban Location,' in *Racism, the City and the State*, ed. M. Cross and M. Keith, London: Routledge, 1993, 45–60.

Gotham, K.F., *Race, Real Estate and Uneven Development: The Kansas City Experience 1900–2000*, Albany, NY: State University of New York Press, 2002.

Gracyk, T., *Rhythm and Noise: An Aesthetics of Rock*, Durham, NC: Duke University Press, 1996.

Grant, I., and Mohns, L., 'Chronic Cerebral Effects of Alcohol and Drug Abuse,' *International Journal of the Addictions*, 10:5 (1975), 883–920.

Grecco, J., *Out in the Streets: The Story of the Shangri-Las*, 2002, https://web.archive.org/web/20221125141145/http://www.redbirdent.com/slas1.htm (accessed 22 Jan. 2023).

Grecco, J., Milstein, P., *Spectropop Presents Lavender Girl: the Patty Michaels Story*, http://www.spectropop.com/PattyMichaels/index.htm (accessed 29 Dec. 2023).

Grecco, J., The Shangri-Las, *The Best of the Red Bird and Mercury Recordings*, Real Gone Music, RGM-1293, 2021 (liner notes).

Greene, W.C., 'The Sea in the Greek Poets,' *North American Review* 199:3 (1914), 427–443.

Greig, C., *Will You Still Love Me Tomorrow: Girl Groups From the 50s On*, London: Virago, 1989.

Gribin, A.J., and Schiff, M.M., *Doo-Wop: The Forgotten Third of Rock 'n' Roll*, Iola, WI: Krause, 1992.

Gribin, A.J., and Schiff, M.M., *The Complete Book of Doo-Wop*, Iola, WI: Krause, 2000.

Gripp, P., 'Party Lights: Utopic Desire and the Girl Group Sound,' in *Sexual Politics and Popular Culture*, ed. D.C. Raymond, Bowling Green, OH: Bowling Green State University Popular Press, 1990, 59–67.

Groia, P., *They All Sang on the Corner: A Second Look at New York City's Rhythm and Blues Vocal Groups*, West Hempstead, NY: Phillie Dee, 1983.

Gudmundsson, G., Lindberg, U., Michelsen, M., and Weisethaunet, H., 'Brit Crit: Turning Points in British Rock Criticism, 1960–1990,' in *Pop Music and the Press*, ed. S. Jones, Philadelphia: Temple University Press, 2002, 41–64.

Halley, J., Eshleman, A., and Vijaya, R.M., *Seeing White: An Introduction to White Privilege and Race*, Lanham, MD: Rowman & Littlefield, 2011.

Harris, S., 'Cosmetics,' *The Jim Crow Encyclopedia* ed. N. L. M. Brown, B. M. Stentiford, Westport, CT: Greenwood, 2008, 191–195.

Hebdidge, D., *Subculture: The Meaning of Style*, London: Methuen, 1979.

Hentoff, N., *At the Jazz Band Ball: Sixty Years on the Jazz Scene*, Berkeley: University of California Press, 2010.

Herman, A., Sloop, J.M., and Swiss, T., *Mapping the Beat: Popular Music and Contemporary Theory*, Oxford: Blackwell, 1997.

Hillstrom, K., and Hillstrom, L. C., *The Vietnam Experience: A Concise Encyclopaedia of American Literature, Songs and Films*, Westport, CT: Greenwood, 1998.

Hoffmann, F.W., and Ferstler, H., *Encyclopaedia of Recorded Sound*, 2 vols., New York: Routledge, 2005.

Holtzman, L., *Media Messages: What Film, Television, and Popular Music Teach Us About Race, Class, Gender, and Sexual Orientation*, Armonk, NY: M.E. Sharpe, 2000.

Hope, C., 'The Wonderment of the Bleak: Sculpting the Static,' *Art Monthly Australia* 225 (Nov. 2009), 45–47.

Horner, B. and Swiss, T., eds., *Key Terms in Popular Music and Culture*, Malden, MA: Blackwell, 1999.

Horner, C., Horner, P., and Shively, V., *The Musical Legacy of Richard Barrett Part One*, http://www.classicurbanharmony.net/Barrett%20Legacy%201%20copy%204.pdf (accessed 29 Aug. 2010).

Horner, C., Horner, P., and Shively, V., *The Musical Legacy of Richard Barrett Part Two: Richard Barrett and the Teenagers*, http://classicurbanharmony.net/wp-content/uploads/2016/02/Richard-Barretts-Musical-Legacy-Part-2-The-Teenagers.pdf (accessed 29 Dec. 2022).

Horner, C., and Horner, P., 'The Musical Legacy of Richard Barrett Part Three: Richard and the Heroines of Harmony,' http://classicurbanharmony.net/wp-content/uploads/2016/02/Richard-Barretts-Musical-Legacy-Part-3-The-Chantels-Clickettes-Fashions-Veneers.pdf (accessed 4 Apr. 2021).

Horner, C., Horner, P., and Shively, V., *The Musical Legacy of Richard Barrett Part Five: The Lewis Lymon and Jimmy Castor Stories*, http://classicurbanharmony.net/wp-content/uploads/2016/02/Richard-Barretts-Musical-Legacy-Part-5-Louis-Lymon-Teenchords-Jimmy-Castor-Juniors.pdf (accessed 29 Dec. 2022).

Inglis, I., 'Some Kind of Wonderful: The Creative Legacy of the Brill Building,' *American Music* 21:2 (2003), 214–235.

Inglis, I., 'A Brief Life: Broken Hearts and Sudden Deaths,' *Popular Music and Society* 27:4 (2004), 477–488.

Isacoff, S., 'A Cultural Conversation / With Andras Schiff: Lessons From Beethoven and Life,' *Wall Street Journal* (Eastern edition), Oct 31, 2007, D.9.

Jackson, J. A., *American Bandstand: Dick Clark and the Making of a Rock 'n' Roll Empire*, New York: Oxford University Press, 1997.

Jackson, K.T., 'Introduction,' in Copquin, C.G., and Jackson, K.T., *The Neighbourhoods of Queens*, New Haven: Yale University Press, 2007, xxi–xxviii.

James, D. E., 'The Vietnam War and American Music,' in *The Vietnam War and American Culture*, ed. J. C. Rowe and R. Berg, New York: Columbia University Press, 1992, 226–254.

James, D.E., *Rock 'n' Film: Cinema's Dance with Popular Music*, New York: Oxford University Press, 2016.

Johansen, C., *The Zombies: Hung Up on a Dream, A Biography 1962–1967*, London: S.A.F. Publishing, 2001.

John, M., 'Push and Pull Factors for Overseas Migrants from Austria-Hungary in the 19th and 20th Centuries,' in *Austrian Immigration to Canada: Selected Essays* ed. F. Szabo, Ottawa: Carleton University Press, 1996, 55–82.

Johnson-Grau, B., 'Sweet Nothings: Presentations of Women Musicians in Pop Journalism,' in *Pop Music and the Press*, ed. S. Jones, Philadelphia: Temple University Press, 2002, 202–218.

Jones S., ed., *Pop Music and the Press*, Philadelphia: Temple University Press, 2002.

Jones, S., and Featherly, K., 'Re-viewing Rock Writing: Narratives of Popular Music Criticism' in *Pop Music and the Press*, ed. S. Jones, Philadelphia: Temple University Press, 2002, 19–40.

Katz, R., 'The Egalitarian Waltz,' *Comparative Studies in Society and History* 15:3 (1973), 368–377.

Kaye, L., 'The Best of Acappella,' *The Age of Rock II*, ed. J. Eisen, New York: Vintage, 1970, 287–301.

Kelley, M., 'Cross Gender/Cross Culture,' *PAJ: A Journal of Performance and Art* 22:1 (Jan. 2000), 1–9.

Kelley, N. and Trebilcock, M., *The Making of The Mosaic: A History of Canadian Immigration Policy*, Toronto; Buffalo: University of Toronto Press, 1998.

Knoedelseder, W., *Stiffed: A True Story of MCA, the Music Business, and the Mafia*, New York: Harper Collins, 1993.

Kramer, E., 'Beethoven's Moonlight Sonata Glows Brightly After 200 Years,' *Clavier* 41:4 (Apr. 2002), 20–26.

Kroessler, J. A., 'Suburban Growth, Urban Style and Patterns of Growth in the Borough of Queens,' in *Long Island: The Suburban Experience*, ed. B.M. Kelly, Interlaken, NY: Heart of the Lakes, 1990, 25–35.

Kukushkin, V., *From Peasants to Labourers: Ukrainian and Belarusan Immigration from the Russian Empire to Canada*, Montreal: McGill-Queen's University Press, 2014.

Lieberman, J.E., and Lieberman, R.K., *City Limits: A Social History of Queens*, Dubuque, IA: Kendall/Hunt, 1983.

Lipsitz, G., *The Possessive Investment in Whiteness: How White People Profit From Identity Politics*, Philadelphia: Temple University Press, 2006.

Lockwood, L., 'Re-shaping the Genre: Beethoven's Piano Sonatas from Op. 22 to Op. 28 (1799–1801),' *Israel Studies in Musicology* 6 (1996), 1–16.

Lockwood, L., *Beethoven: The Music and the Life*, New York: Norton, 2003.

Lyons, P., *New Left, New Right, and the Legacy of the Sixties*, Philadelphia: Temple University Press, 1996.

McFarland, G. W., *Inside Greenwich Village: A New York City Neighborhood, 1898–1918*, Amherst: University of Massachusetts Press, 2001. https://scholarworks.umass.edu/umpress_books/3 (accessed 18 Apr. 2021).

MacKinney, L., 'Rosaries, Paternosters and Devotion to the Virgin in the Households of John Baret of Bury St. Edmunds,' *Parergon* 24:2 (2007), 93–114.

MacKinney, L., '"Mmmm, he's good-bad, but he's not evil . . .": The Shangri-Las, "Leader of the Pack," and the Cultural Context of the Motorcycle Rider,' *International Journal of Motorcycle Studies* 4:1 (Mar. 2008), https://web.archive.org/web/20180424011529/http://ijms.nova.edu/March2008/IJMS_Artcl.MacKinney.html (accessed 30 Aug. 2021).

MacKinney, L., 'The Book of Daughters and The Sonic aGender Guitar Project: Inclusivity as Guiding Principle' in *A Century of Composition by Women: Music Against the Odds* ed. L. Kouvaras, M. Grenfell and N. Williams, Basingstoke, UK: Palgrave Macmillan, 2022, 327–345.

McKinney, D., 'Pop Irony: Past, Present and Future,' *The American Prospect: Ideas, Politics, Power*, 5 Jan. 2005 https://prospect.org/article/pop-irony-past-present-future/ (accessed 12 Aug. 2022).

Marcus, G., 'The Girl Groups,' *The Rolling Stone Illustrated History of Rock and Roll*, ed. J. Miller, New York: Random House, [1976] 1980, 160–1.

Markopolis, G., 'Scorpio Rising (First Impressions After A First Viewing, 10/29/63),' *Film Culture* 31 (Winter 1963–4), 5–6.

Marcus, B., *From Polynesia with Love: The History of Surfing From Captain Cook to the Present*, http://www.surfingforlife.com/history.html (accessed 1 Sept. 2021).

May, E.T., *Homeward Bound: American Families in the Cold War Era*, New York: Basic Books, 1999.

McCroskery, M. S., 'Tristan and the Dionysian Sea: Passion and the Iterative Sea Motif in the Legends of Tristan and Isolde,' *Midwest Quarterly* 13:4 (1972), 409–422.

McLeod, K., 'Between a Rock and a Hard Place: Gender and Rock Criticism' in *Pop Music and the Press*, ed. S. Jones, Philadelphia: Temple University Press, 2002, 93–113.

Melnick, J., '"Story Untold": The Black Men and White Sounds of Doo-Wop,' in *Whiteness: A Critical Reader*, ed. M. Hill, New York and London: New York University Press, 1997, 134–150.

Meyer, S.G., *As Long as They Don't Move Next Door: Segregation and Racial Conflict in American Neighborhoods*, Lanham, MD: Rowman & Littlefield, 2000.

Mies, M., *Patriarchy and Accumulation on a World Scale: Women in the International Division of Labour*, London: Zed, 1986.

Miller, J., ed., *The Rolling Stone Illustrated History of Rock and Roll*, New York: Random House, [1976] 1980.

Miller, W.B., 'Lower Class Culture as a Generating Milieu of Gang Delinquency,' *Journal of Social Issues* 14:3 (1958), 5–19.

Milstein, P., *Spectropop Presents: Shangri-Las 77!* http://www.spectropop.com/Shangri-Las/ (accessed 4 Nov. 2021).

Mintz, S., *Huck's Raft: A History of American Childhood*, Cambridge, MA: Belknap Press of Harvard University Press, 2004.

Moorefield, V., *The Producer as Composer: Shaping the Sounds of Popular Music*, Cambridge, MA: MIT Press, 2005.

Morrow, B., and Maloof, R., *Doo Wop: the Music, the Times, the Era*, New York: Sterling, 2007.

Murray, S., *Suburban Citizens: Domesticity and Community Politics in Queens, New York, 1945–1960*, PhD Dissertation, New Haven: Yale University, 1994.

Neal, M.A., *What the Music Said: Black Popular Music and Black Public Culture*, New York: Routledge, 1999.

Needs, K., and Porter, D., *Trash! The Complete New York Dolls*, London: Plexus, 2006.

Newman, E., 'A Beethoven Hoax?,' *The Musical Times*, 52: 825 (Nov. 1, 1911), 714–717.

O'Dair, B., ed., *Trouble Girls: The Rolling Stone Book of Women in Rock*, New York: Random House, 1997.

Ormrod, J., '*Endless Summer* (1964): Consuming Waves and Surfing the Frontier,' *Film and History* 35:1 (2005), 39–51.

Os, H.W. van, *The Art of Devotion in the Late Middle Ages in Europe 1300–1500*, Princeton, NJ: Princeton University Press, 1994.

Oswald, L., 'Branding the American Family: A Strategic Study of the Culture, Composition, and Consumer Behaviour of Families in the New Millennium,' *Journal of Popular Culture* 37:2 (2003), 309–335.

Palladino, G., *Teenagers: An American History*, New York: Basic, 1996.

Palmer, R., *Baby that was Rock and Roll: The Legendary Leiber and Stoller*, New York: Harvest/HBJ, 1978.

Palmer, R., *Rock and Roll: An Unruly History*, New York: Harmony, 1995.

Patrick, M., *Girls with Guitars: All Girl Bands Axe Backed Babes and the Like . . .* , London: Ace Records CDCHD989, 2004 (liner notes).

Patrick, M., '*Spectropop* Presents Brooks Arthur: The Early Years,' 2006, http://www.spectropop.com/BrooksArthur/index.htm (accessed 6 Jan. 2024).

Patrick, M., *Sophisticated Boom Boom: The Shadow Morton Story*, Ace Records CDTOP1369, 2013 (liner notes).

Pavletich, A., *Sirens of Song: The Popular Female Vocalist in America*, New York: Da Capo, 1980.

Perry, M., *An Intellectual History of Modern Europe*, Boston: Houghton Mifflin, 1993.

Phillips, L., 'Blue Jeans, Black Leather Jackets, and a Sneer: The Iconography of the 1950s Biker and its Translation Abroad,' *International Journal of Motorcycle Studies* 1

(2005), https://web.archive.org/web/20180424010408/http://ijms.nova.edu/
March2005/IJMS_ArtclPhilips0305.html (accessed 31 Aug. 2021).

Picardie, J., and Wade, D., *Music Man: Ahmet Ertegun, Atlantic Records, and the Triumph of Rock 'n' Roll*, New York: Norton, 1990.

Picardie, J., and Wade, D., *Atlantic and the Godfathers of Rock and Roll*, Rev. edn.; London: Fourth Estate, 1993.

Pigot, J., 'Symbolic Identities: Masculinity and the Motorcycle,' *Artlink* 16:1 (1996), 47–9.

Potter, R.A., 'Race' in *Key Terms in Popular Music and Culture*, ed. B. Horner and T. Swiss, Malden, MA: Blackwell, 1999, 71–84.

Powell, A., 'The Occult: A Torch for Lucifer' in *Moonchild: The Films of Kenneth Anger*, ed. Jack Hunter, London: Creation, 2001, 47–104.

Pruter, R., *Chicago Soul*, Champaign: University of Illinois, 1991.

Randall, A.J., *Dusty! Queen of the Postmods*, New York: Oxford University Press, 2009.

Reising, R., 'Melting Clocks and the Hallways of Always: Time in Psychedelic Music,' *Popular Music and Society* 32:4 (2009), 523–547.

Rhodes, L., *Electric Ladyland: Women and Rock Culture*, Philadelphia: University of Pennsylvania Press, 2005.

Ribowsky, M., *He's A Rebel: Phil Spector, Rock and Roll's Legendary Producer*, Cambridge, MA: Da Capo, 2006.

Ringbom, S., *Icon to Narrative: The Rise of the Dramatic Close-Up in Fifteenth Century Devotional Painting*, Doornspijk, Netherlands: Davaco 1984.

Roediger, D.R., *The Wages of Whiteness: Race and the Making of the American Working Class*, London: Verso, 1991.

Rohlfing, M. E., 'Don't Say Nothin' Bad about My Baby: A Re-Evaluation of Women's Roles in the Brill Building Era of Early Rock 'n' Roll,' *Critical Studies in Mass Communication* 13:2 (1996), 95–114.

Rowe, C., 'Myth and Symbolism: Blue Velvet,' in *Moonchild: The Films of Kenneth Anger*, ed. Jack Hunter, London: Creation, 2001, 11–46.

Rutsky, R.L., 'Surfing the Other: Ideology on the Beach,' *Film Quarterly* 52:4 (1999), 12–23.

Salem, J.M., *The Late Great Johnny Ace and the Transition from R & B to Rock 'n' Roll*, Urbana: University of Illinois Press, 1999.

Savage, J., *Teenage: the Creation of Youth Culture*, New York: Viking, 2007.

Sargeant, J., 'Violence and Vinyl: Car Crashes in 1960s Pop,' in *Car Crash Culture*, ed. M. Brottman, New York: Palgrave, 2001, 259–266.

Scheurer, T.E., 'The Beatles, the Brill Building, and the Persistence of Tin Pan Alley in the Age of Rock,' *Popular Music and Society* 20:4 (1996), 89–102.

Schneider, E.C., *Vampires, Dragons and Egyptian Kings: Youth Gangs in Postwar New York*, Princeton, NJ: Princeton University Press, 1999.

Schuftan, C., *Hey! Nietzsche! Leave Them Kids Alone: the Romantic Movement, Rock & Roll, and the End of Civilisation as We Know it*, Sydney: ABC [Australian Broadcasting Commission], 2009.

Schwager, M., 'Some Observations on Beethoven as an Arranger,' *The Musical Quarterly* 60:1 (1974), 80–93.

Schwartz, G., 'All Shook Up,' *Apollo* Feb. 2019, 40–45.

Scott, J. A., *The Ballad of America: The History of the United States in Song and Story*, Carbondale & Edwardsville: Southern Illinois University Press, [1966] 1983.

Shepherd, J., Laing, D., Horn, D., Oliver, P., and Wicke, P., eds., *The Continuum Encyclopedia of Popular Music of the World Part One, Vol. 2: Performance and Production*, London: Continuum International Publishing Group, 2003.

Simmonds, J., *The Encyclopedia of Dead Rock Stars: Heroin, Handguns, and Ham Sandwiches*, Chicago: Chicago Review Press, 2008.

Skeggs, B., *Formations of Class and Gender: Becoming Respectable*, London: Sage, 1997.

Smith, B., *I Go To Extremes: the Billy Joel Story*, London: Robson, 2007.

Smith, J., and Fink, M., *Off the Record: An Oral History of Popular Music*, London: Sidgwick & Jackson, 1989.

Smith, J. C., 'Cosmetics,' *Encyclopedia of African American Popular Culture* ed. J. C. Smith, 4 vols., Santa Barbara CA: Greenwood, 2011, 373–6.

Solinger, R., *Wake Up Little Susie: Single Pregnancy and Race Before Roe v. Wade*, New York: Routledge, 1992.

Smith, S.E., *Dancing in the Street: Motown and the Cultural Politics of Detroit*, Cambridge: Harvard University Press, 1999.

Spizer, B., *The Beatles are coming! the Birth of Beatlemania in America*, New Orleans: 498 Productions, 2004.

Stanley, G., 'Genre Aesthetics and Function: Beethoven's Piano Sonatas in Their Cultural Context,' *Beethoven Forum* 6:1 (1998), 1–29.

Stern, R.A.M., and Massengale, J.M., *The Anglo American Suburb*, London: Architectural Design/St. Martin's Press, 1981.

Steward, S., and Garratt, S., *Signed Sealed and Delivered: True Life Stories of Women in Pop*, London: Pluto, 1984.

Stillwell, R.J., 'Vocal Decorum: Voice, Body, and Knowledge in the Prodigious Singer, Brenda Lee,' in *She's So Fine: Reflections on Whiteness, Femininity, Adolescence and Class in 1960s Music*, ed. L. Stras, Farnham, UK: Ashgate, 2010, 57–87.

Stos, W., 'Bouffants, Beehives, and Breaking Gender Norms: Rethinking "Girl Group" Music of the 1950s and 1960s' *Journal of Popular Music Studies*, 24:2, 2012, 117–154.

Stras, L., 'Introduction,' *She's So Fine: Reflections on Whiteness, Femininity, Adolescence and Class in 1960s Music*, ed. L. Stras, Farnham, UK: Ashgate, 2010, 1–29.

Stras, L., 'Voice of the Beehive: Vocal Technique at the Turn of the 1960s,' in *She's So Fine: Reflections on Whiteness, Femininity, Adolescence and Class in 1960s Music*, ed. L. Stras, Farnham, UK: Ashgate, 2010, 33–55.

Stras, L., ed., *She's So Fine: Reflections on Whiteness, Femininity, Adolescence and Class in 1960s Music*, Farnham, UK: Ashgate, 2010.

Stratton, J., 'Jews Dreaming of Acceptance: From the Brill Building to Suburbia with Love,' *Shofar* 27:2 (2009), 102–127.

Stratton, J., 'Jews Dreaming of Acceptance: From the Brill Building to Suburbia with Love,' in Jon Stratton, *Jews, Race and Popular Music*, London: Routledge, 2016, 37–58.

Studwell, W. E., *The National and Religious Song Reader: Patriotic, Traditional, and Sacred Songs from Around the World*, Binghamton, NY: Haworth, 1996.

Suárez, J.A., *Bike Boys, Drag Queens and Superstars: Avant-Garde, Mass Culture, and Gay Identities in the 1960s Underground Cinema*, Bloomington, IN: Indiana University Press, 1996.

Sugrue, T.J., *The Origins of the Urban Crisis: Race And Inequality in Postwar Detroit*, Princeton NJ: Princeton University Press, 1996.

Taylor, E., 'From the Nelsons to the Huxtables: Genre and Family Imagery in American Network Television,' *Qualitative Sociology* 12:1 (1989), 13–28.

Taylor, M., *The Original Marvelettes: Motown's Mystery Girl Group*, Jamaica, NY: Aloiv, 2004.

Thayer, A.W., *Thayer's Life of Beethoven*, ed. E. Forbes, 2 vols., Princeton, NJ: Princeton University Press, 1964.

Thompson, S.L., 'The Arts of the Motorcycle: Biology, Culture and Aesthetics in Technological Choice,' *Technology and Culture* 41 (2000), 99–115.

Thorn, T., *My Rock 'n' Roll Friend*, Edinburgh: Canongate, 2021.

Tobler, J., and Grundy, S., *The Record Producers*, London: British Broadcasting Corporation, 1982.

Trynka, P. *Iggy Pop: Open Up and Bleed*, London: Sphere, 2007.

Unger, M., and Wager, W., 'From Beethoven's Workshop,' *The Musical Quarterly* 24:3 (July 1938), 323–340.

Unterberger, R., *Turn! Turn! Turn! The 60s Folk-Rock Revolution*, San Francisco: Backbeat, 2002.

Waffen, L., and Hesbacher, P., 'War Songs: Hit Recordings During the Vietnam Period,' *ARSC: Association for Recorded Sound Collections* 13 (1981), 4–19.

Wagner, J.F., *A History of Migration from Germany to Canada, 1850–1939*, Vancouver: UBC Press, 2006.

Wald, E., *How The Beatles Destroyed Rock 'n' Roll: An Alternative History Of American Popular Music*, New York: Oxford University Press, 2009.

Wald, G., 'One of the Boys? Whiteness, Gender and Popular Music Studies,' in *Whiteness: A Critical Reader*, ed. M. Hill, New York: New York University Press, 1997, 151–167.

Walser, R., and McClary, S., 'Start Making Sense! Musicology Wrestles with Rock,' in *On Record: Rock, Pop, and the Written Word*, ed. S. Frith and A. Goodwin, London: Routledge, 1990, 277–92.

Ward, B., *Just My Soul Responding: Rhythm and Blues, Black Consciousness, and Race Relations*, Berkeley: University of California Press, 1998.

Warner, J., *American Singing Groups: A History From 1940s to Today*, Milwaukee: Hal Leonard, 2006.

Warwick, J., *Girl Groups, Girl Culture: Popular Music and Identity In The 1960s*, New York: Routledge, 2007.

Warwick, J., '"He Hit Me, and I was Glad": Violence, Masochism and Anger in Girl Group Music,' in *She's So Fine: Reflections on Whiteness, Femininity, Adolescence and Class in 1960s Music*, ed. L. Stras, Farnham, UK: Ashgate, 2010, 89–109.

Weise, A., '"The House I Live In": Race, Class and African American Suburban Dreams in the Postwar United States' in *The New Suburban History*, ed. K. M. Kruse and T.J. Sugrue, Chicago: University of Chicago Press, 2006, 99–119.

Welch, W.L., Burt, L.B.S., Read, O., *From Tinfoil to Stereo: The Acoustic Years of the Recording Industry, 1877–1929*, Gainesville: University of Florida Press, 1994.

Wertham, F., *Seduction of the Innocent*, New York: Rinehart, 1953.

Whiteley, S., *The Space Between the Notes: Rock and the Counter-Culture*, London: Routledge, 1992.

Whiteley, S., *Too Much Too Young Popular Music, Age And Gender*, London: Routledge, 2005.

Williams, B., 'Indeed We Know: On the Video Art of Elizabeth Price,' *Cinema Scope* 70 (Spring 2017), 52–55: https://cinema-scope.com/columns/filmart-indeed-we-know-on-the-video-art-of-elizabeth-price/ (accessed 10 Sept. 2021).

Williams, G.W., 'The Poetry of the Storm in King Lear,' *Shakespeare Quarterly*, 2:1 (1951), 57–71.

Williams, R., *Phil Spector: Out of his Head*, London: Omnibus, 2003.

Wolin, A., *Golden Hits of the Shangri-Las*, New York: Bloomsbury Academic 33⅓ Series, 2019.

Yang, W., Petkova, E., and Shaman, J., 'The 1918 influenza pandemic in New York City: age-specific timing, mortality, and transmission dynamics,' *Influenza and Other Respiratory Viruses* 8:2 (Mar. 2014), 177–188.

Theses

Green, R.S., *Innovation, Imitation, and Resisting Manipulation: The First Twenty Years of American Teenagers 1941–1961*, PhD thesis, University of Oklahoma, 1998.

Hetzel, W. M., *Romanticism in Sixties Rock: Literary Traditions in Anglo-American Folk and Rock Lyrics (1963–1977)*, PhD thesis, University of Maryland College Park, 2002.

Kroessler, J.A., *Building Queens: The Urbanization of New York's Largest Borough*, PhD thesis, City University of New York, 1991.

MacKinney, L., *Recovering the Late Medieval Devotional World of Margery Kempe and her Book*, MA thesis, Melbourne: La Trobe University, 2001, https://opal.latrobe.edu. au/articles/thesis/Recovering_the_late_medieval_devotional_world_of_Margery_ Kempe_and_her_book/24012819 (accessed 6 Sept. 2023).

MacKinney, L., *"Dressed in Black": The Shangri-Las and Their Recorded Legacy*, PhD thesis, The University of Western Australia, 2012, https://research-repository.uwa. edu.au/en/publications/dressed-in-black-the-shangri-las-and-their-recorded-legacy (accessed 6 Jan. 2024).

Roka, L.A., *Making Order Out of Chaos: Music Criticism in United States Newspapers in The 1960s*, PhD thesis, Ohio University, 2002.

Warwick, J., *I Got All My Sisters With Me: Girl Culture, Girl Identity and Girl Group Music*, PhD thesis (Musicology): UCLA, 2002.

Online Material
Websites

Note: for database-type websites where the entry can be easily looked up, the link to the website is provided below rather than multiple individual listings with long web links.

All Music: www.allmusic.com

American Society of Composers, Authors and Publishers (ASCAP): https://www.ascap. com/repertory#/

Broadcast Music Incorporated (BMI): https://repertoire.bmi.com/

Discogs (online platform for sale of physical recordings containing a multitude of useful release information): https://www.discogs.com/

Popsike (database of rare vinyl auction results, again with useful information on rare releases): https://www.popsike.com/

White Doo-Wop Collector (amateur site with hundreds of listings for white doo-wop groups, sometimes with rare photos): http://whitedoowopcollector.blogspot.com/

Other Secondary Material

45 Discography for ABC Paramount Records—9000 series, https://web.archive.org/ web/20130208030914/http://www.globaldogproductions.info/a/abc-a.html (accessed 1 Oct. 2023).

45 Discography for Baton/Sir Records, https://web.archive.org/web/20071214155544/ http://globaldogproductions.info/baton-sir.html (accessed 29 Sept. 2021).

45 Discography for Goldisc Records, https://web.archive.org/web/20150722154201/ http://www.globaldogproductions.info/g/goldisc.html (accessed 1 Oct. 2023).

45 Discography for Jamie Records, https://web.archive.org/web/20171012195408/ http://www.globaldogproductions.info/j/jamie.html (accessed 1 Oct. 2023).

45 Discography for Jubilee Records, https://web.archive.org/web/20200329223006/ http://www.globaldogproductions.info/j/jubilee.html (accessed 27 Dec. 2023).

45 Discography for Mala Records, https://web.archive.org/web/20180307120455/ http://www.globaldogproductions.info/m/mala.html (accessed 27 Dec. 2023).

Adams, C., 'In the record business, what do "b/w" and "c/w" mean?,' http://www. straightdope.com/columns/read/1352/in-the-record-business-what-do-b-w-and-c-w-mean (accessed 2 Apr. 2021).

Armstrong, S., '"Oh No!" How a 60s Girl Group Anthem Took Over TikTok,' *Udiscovermusic*, 21 July 2021, https://www.udiscovermusic.com/news/oh-no-tiktok-song/ (accessed 22 Jan. 2023).

Arthur, Brooks, *Official Website*, Photo Gallery, http://www.brooksarthur.com/ photogallery.html (accessed 2 Apr. 2021).

Bayley, Roberta, *Official Website*: http://www.robertabayley.com/ ; Shangri-Las Sire sessions and CBGB's show: https://www.gettyimages.com.au/search/2/image?family=creative&phrase=shangri-las+cbgb (accessed 5 Nov. 2021).

Beach Boys Tour and Sesssions, 1964, https://web.archive.org/web/20070522234040/http://www.btinternet.com/~bellagio/gigs64.html (accessed 28 Dec. 2023).

Buskin, R., 'Classic Tracks: The Ronettes 'Be My Baby,' *Sound on Sound* Apr. 2007, https://www.soundonsound.com/techniques/classic-tracks-ronettes-be-my-baby (accessed 2 Apr. 2021).

Byron Lee and the Dragonaires: *Official Website*: https://web.archive.org/web/20110708110604/http://www.byronleemusic.com/ska_era/skaera.html (accessed 1 Nov. 2021).

Canalle, D., *Bomp List Archives*, https://web.archive.org/web/20080416224407/http://bomplist.xnet2.com/0105/msg00205.html (accessed 1 Sept. 2021).

Capone-N-Noreaga, https://www.discogs.com/release/334684-Capone-N-Noreaga-The-Best-Of-Capone-N-Noreaga-Thugged-Da-F-Out (accessed 22 Jan. 2023).

Casiano, J., *The Shangri-Las '89 Reunion Concert*, https://web.archive.org/web/20050206072618/http://www.theshangri-las.com/89reunion.htm (accessed 5 Nov. 2021).

'Classical Influences in Popular Music,' https://web.archive.org/web/20070226221448/http://www.solopassion.com/node/971 (accessed 1 Sept. 2021).

Dale, Dick, *Official Website*: https://web.archive.org/web/19981202065643/http://www.dickdale.com/history.html (accessed 1 Sept. 2021).

Drug Abuse and Brain Damage (Encephalopathy), https://www.drugrehab.us/news/drug-abuse-brain-damage-encephalopathy/ (accessed 30 Dec. 2021).

Edwards, D., Eyries, P., and Callahan, M., 'The ABC-Paramount Story,' http://www.bsnpubs.com/abc/abcstory.html (accessed 22 Sept. 2021).

Edwards, D. and Callahan, M., 'End Records Discography,' https://web.archive.org/web/20051017143228/http://www.bsnpubs.com/roulette/end.html (accessed 20 Sept. 2021).

Edwards, D. and Callahan, M., 'The George Goldner Story,' https://web.archive.org/web/20051016040349/http://www.bsnpubs.com/roulette/goldner.html (accessed 20 Sept. 2021).

'First Master of Beatles Graduates,' http://news.bbc.co.uk/local/liverpool/hi/people_and_places/newsid_9376000/9376984.stm (accessed 1 Apr. 2021).

'Get Down with Iggy Pop's High School Band the Iguanas', *Dangerous Minds*, 22 Oct. 2019, https://dangerousminds.net/comments/get_down_with_iggy_pops_first_b (accessed 31 Dec. 2024).

Gonzales, E. and Betancourt, B., 'Zendaya Is in Talks to Star in a Ronnie Spector Biopic—Here's What to Know,' *Harper's Bazaar*, 14 Jan. 2022, https://www.harpersbazaar.com/culture/film-tv/a34222928/zendaya-ronnie-spector-biopic-news-cast-spoilers-date/ (accessed 23 Jan. 2022).

Goodies, *Official Website*: https://web.archive.org/web/20210301061131/https://www.thegoodiesgirlgroup.com/ (accessed 28 Dec. 2023).

Greenblatt, M., 'The Night Leonard Bernstein Introduced Janis Ian to America' (with YouTube link to TV footage), *Jersey Sound*, 3 January 2024, https://thejerseysound.com/history/the-night-leonard-bernstein-introduced-janis-ian-to-america (accessed 25 Mar. 2024).

Hasted, N., 'How Jack White and the White Stripes Breathed new Life into the Blues,' *Louder: Classic Rock*, https://www.loudersound.com/features/how-jack-white-and-the-white-stripes-breathed-new-life-into-the-blues (accessed 2 Nov. 2021.

Hemmingsen, P.A., 'Across Canada with the Dave Clark Five,' http://www.capitol6000.com/daveclark5.html (accessed 21 Oct. 2021).

International Association for the Study of Popular Music (IASPM), https://www.iaspm. net/ (accessed 25 Jan. 2023).

It's All the Streets You Crossed Not so Long Ago: 1964 World's Fair, http://streetsyoucrossed.blogspot.com/search/label/1964%20World%27s%20Fair (accessed 28 Dec. 2023).

Jubilee Records: http://www.bsnpubs.com/jubilee/jubjosie.html (accessed 6 Oct. 2021).

Lattanzio, R.,'Watch: Marianne Faithfull Sings for Godard in "Made in U.S.A.",' *Indie Wire*, 29 Dec. 2014, https://www.indiewire.com/2014/12/watch-marianne-faithfull-sings-for-godard-in-made-in-u-s-a-189549/ (accessed 12 Sept. 2021).

Leiber and Stoller, *Official Website*, http://www.leiberstoller.com/Discography.html (accessed 1 Apr. 2021).

Maurice Sendak Community School, P.S. 118 homepage: https://www. mauricesendakcommunityschool.org/ (accessed 28 Sept. 2021).

Mohawk, Essra, *Official Website*, https://web.archive.org/web/20110313100617/ http://www.essramohawk.com/index.php?option=com_ content&view=article&id=46&Itemid=53 (accessed 2 Sept. 2021)

Morton, G. 'Shadow,' Myspace Page: https://web.archive.org/web/ 20110202165710/https://myspace.com/shadowmorton (accessed 2 Oct. 2023).

Morton, George 'Shadow,' Wikipedia entry: http://en.wikipedia.org/wiki/Shadow_ Morton (accessed 2 Oct. 2023).

'Music Response: An Overview of the Answer Record,' https://rateyourmusic.com/list/ monocle/music_response__an_overview_of_the_answer_record/1/ (accessed 22 Oct. 2021).

Neurological Disorders Caused by Substance Abuse, https://sunrisehouse.com/addiction-demographics/neurological-disorders/#3 (accessed 30 Dec. 2021).

New York World's Fair website: http://www.nywf64.com/ (accessed 1 Nov. 2021).

Nobleman, Marc Tyler, 'Bill Finger's medical examiner report and death certificate,' https://www.noblemania.com/2012/07/bill-fingers-medical-examiner-report.html (accessed 28 Dec. 2021).

Paley, Andy, official website: https://www.andypaley.com/about-andy/ & https://www. andypaley.com/experience/ (accessed 5 Nov. 2021).

The Persianettes Discography, http://www.soulfulkindamusic.net/persianettes.htm (accessed 8 Oct. 2021).

The Rolling Stones' Opening Acts: A Partial List, http://www.timeisonourside.com/guests. html (accessed 1 Nov. 2021).

Sacred Heart Roman Catholic Church, Cambria Heights, https://www.sacredheartny. com/ (accessed 4 Nov. 2021).

Schiff, A., *Schiff on Beethoven, Part 4, Part 3: Piano Sonata in C-sharp minor, Opus 27, No. 2 ('Moonlight'),'* http://www.guardian.co.uk/music/musicblog/2006/nov/23/ schiffonbeethovenpart4 (accessed 1 Sept. 2021).

Scott Michaels' Find a Death: The Forum, https://findadeathforum.com/showthread. php?8219-Has-anyone-ever-heard-of-The-Shangri-La-s&highlight=ganser (accessed 10 Nov. 2021).

Sire Records discography, http://www.bsnpubs.com/warner/distributed/sire.html (accessed 5 Nov. 2021).

Somerstein, L., 'The Corner,' *LFS: The Storyteller*, http://leezardonlife.blogspot. com/2008/12/corner.html (accessed 15 Sept. 2021).

Somerstein, Lee, 'Far From (Seventh) Heaven,' *LeeZard on Life—Commentary; Humor; Politics; Life; People*, http://leezardonlife.blogspot.com/2009/02/far-from-seventh-heaven.html (accessed 15 Sept. 2021).

St Joseph's Villa: Mission & History, https://www.neverstopbelieving.org/about-us/ our-story/mission-history/ (accessed 26 Dec. 2023).

The St Joseph's Villa Story, https://www.youtube.com/watch?v=JnLrs_gpnq4 (accessed 11 Oct. 2022).

Storch, J., From a Naked Window,' http://fantasy0807.blogspot.com/2008/09/jeremy-storch-from-naked-window-us.html (accessed 22 July 2010).

Storch, J., Official Website: https://web.archive.org/web/20070713092046/http://www.jeremystorch.org/bio.html (accessed 4 Nov. 2021).

Stuffed Animal, 'Mambo Gee Gee: The Story of George Goldner and Tico Records, Part One' http://www.spectropop.com/tico/TICOpart1.htm (accessed 17 Sept. 2021).

Stuffed Animal, 'Mambo Gee Gee: The Story of George Goldner and Tico Records, Part Two,' http://www.spectropop.com/tico/TICOpart2.htm (accessed 17 Sept. 2021).

'Timmy Carr,' *Sir Shambling's Deep Soul Heaven,* http://www.sirshambling.com/artists_2012/C/timothy_carr/index.php (accessed 8 Oct. 2021).

'Vera Carey of the Persianettes,' http://www.drivingwheel.co.uk/vera.htm (accessed 27 Dec. 2023).

Where to Find Medical Records for Closed Hospitals in New York State, https://www.health.ny.gov/facilities/hospital/docs/medical_records_from_closed_hospitals.pdf (accessed 12 Dec. 2021).

Index

ABOUT THE AUTHOR

Lisa MacKinney is a historian and musician from Melbourne, Australia. She has a Masters degree in medieval history, and *Dressed in Black: The Shangri-Las and Their Recorded Legacy* started life as her PhD thesis (University of Western Australia, 2012); it has been considerably expanded and updated for publication in book form. MacKinney has contributed numerous articles to academic journals, books, and music magazines, including *Uncut* and *Limelight*. She plays guitar and organ, and has performed extensively in Australia and internationally, both solo (as Mystic Eyes) and with bands including Super Luminum, Taipan Tiger Girls, and Hospital Pass.

www.ingramcontent.com/pod-product-compliance
Lightning Source LLC
Chambersburg PA
CBHW020917140626
46545CB00015B/86